The Experience of Work in Early Modern England

This book applies the innovative work-task approach to the history of work, which captures the contribution of all workers and types of work to the early modern economy. Drawing on tens of thousands of court depositions, the authors analyse the individual tasks that made up everyday work for women and men, shedding new light on the gender division of labour, and the ways in which time, space, age, and marital status shaped sixteenth- and seventeenth-century working life. Combining qualitative and quantitative analysis, the book deepens our understanding of the preindustrial economy and calls for us to rethink not only who did what but also the implications of these findings for major debates about structural change, the nature and extent of paid work, and what has been lost as well as gained over the past three centuries of economic development. This title is also available as open access on Cambridge Core.

Jane Whittle is Professor of Economic and Social History at the University of Exeter, and her publications include *The Development of Agrarian Capitalism* and *Consumption and Gender in the Early Seventeenth-Century Household.*

Mark Hailwood is Senior Lecturer in Early Modern History at the University of Bristol and author of *Alehouses and Good Fellowship in Early Modern England*, as well as a number of articles on everyday life in the period.

Hannah Robb is a Postdoctoral Research Associate at Birkbeck, University of London, and has published in leading journals on micro-credit and debt litigation.

Taylor Aucoin is a British Academy Postdoctoral Research Fellow at the University of Edinburgh and has published on topics ranging from Carnival, pancakes, and football to labour laws and magic.

The Experience of Work in Early Modern England

Jane Whittle

University of Exeter

Mark Hailwood

University of Bristol

Hannah Robb

Birkbeck, University of London

Taylor Aucoin

University of Edinburgh

CAMBRIDGE
UNIVERSITY PRESS

CAMBRIDGE
UNIVERSITY PRESS

Shaftesbury Road, Cambridge CB2 8EA, United Kingdom

One Liberty Plaza, 20th Floor, New York, NY 10006, USA

477 Williamstown Road, Port Melbourne, VIC 3207, Australia

314–321, 3rd Floor, Plot 3, Splendor Forum, Jasola District Centre, New Delhi – 110025, India

103 Penang Road, #05-06/07, Visioncrest Commercial, Singapore 238467

Cambridge University Press is part of Cambridge University Press & Assessment, a department of the University of Cambridge.

We share the University's mission to contribute to society through the pursuit of education, learning and research at the highest international levels of excellence.

www.cambridge.org
Information on this title: www.cambridge.org/9781316519943

DOI: 10.1017/9781009019743

First published 2025
Cover image: *Labors of the Months.* Image copyright The Metropolitan Museum of Art / Art Resource / Scala, Florence.

A catalogue record for this publication is available from the British Library

A Cataloging-in-Publication data record for this book is available from the Library of Congress

ISBN 978-1-316-51994-3 Hardback

Contents

Figures

The data in all figures should be assumed to be unfiltered (by information status) and unadjusted (by the female multiplier) unless otherwise stated in the figure 'notes'.

Tables

The data in all tables should be assumed to be unfiltered (by information status) and unadjusted (by the female multiplier) unless otherwise stated in the table 'notes'.

Preface

This book is the result of a decade of work, and the lists of specific tasks and of individual actors involved in its making are both extensive. The foundations were laid by a Leverhulme Trust-funded project on 'Women's Work in Rural England, 1500–1700: A New Methodological Approach' between 2015 and 2019. During this project Jane, as Principal Investigator, and Mark, as a Postdoctoral Researcher, developed the 'work-task methodology', and with the invaluable help of Mark Merry at the Institute of Historical Research, designed the work-task database. During this period Mark (Hailwood) collected and entered the material from the south-west of England, as well as entering coroners' data kindly supplied by Steven Gunn and Tomasz Gromelski from their Economic and Social Research Council (ESRC)-funded project on 'Everyday Life and Fatal Hazard in Sixteenth-Century England'. Charmian Mansell also worked on the project in 2017–18 and undertook some important developmental work on the database. This initial project was then followed up with a European Research Council grant to research 'Forms of Labour: Gender, Freedom, and Experience of Work in the Preindustrial Economy', with Jane as Principal Investigator and Mark as Co-Investigator, one strand of which provided the resources to expand the work-task dataset. Hannah and Taylor were hired as Postdoctoral Researchers, and between 2019 and 2022 they collected and entered new data from the north and east of England, with Hannah concentrating on church court records and Taylor on quarter sessions material. In this phase Ian Wellaway at the University of Exeter provided valuable help in improving the design of the database, and the broader Forms of Labour project team – Vivienne Bates, James Fisher, Li Jiang, and Grace Owen – all supplied helpful advice and support through regular project meetings. After the completion of the data collection in late 2022, Jane, Mark, Hannah, and Taylor worked together analysing the data and writing this book. All parts of the book have received input from all four authors, and it very much represents a collective endeavour. Each chapter was made the primary responsibility of at least one author, who undertook the main bulk of drafting and analysis, and readers might find it helpful to know who those were for the purposes of directing queries or seeking out follow-up conversations: Introduction – Jane; Chapter 1 – Mark; Chapter 2 – Mark; Chapter 3 – Jane, with Section 3.3 by Mark; Chapter 4 – Taylor, with Section 4.4 by Mark; Chapter 5 – Jane (housework) and Hannah (carework); Chapter 6 – Jane; Chapter 7 – Taylor; Chapter 8 – Hannah; Conclusion – Jane.

Throughout this book gender is treated as a binary distinction between females and males. This is for ease of analysis and adopts the common understanding of gender in early modern England. It is not intended to imply that this is the only way that gender difference exists or can be understood.

Developing and applying a new methodological approach relies on a considerable amount of advice and feedback from experts in the field who understand the issues and the sources, and we have benefited enormously from the critical engagement and generous encouragement of our fellow historians. A special mention must go to Maria Ågren, Jonas Lindström, Karin Hassan Jansson, and the entire Gender and Work team at Uppsala University, whose collaboration has been central to the development of our methods and analysis. We would also like to thank everyone who has participated in an advisory role on either of our two projects, which includes Amy Burnett, Nandini Chatterjee, Nick Collins, Elise Dermineur, Amy Erickson, Henry French, Maria Fusaro, Laura Gowing, Steven Gunn, Charmian Mansell, Craig Muldrew, Sheilagh Ogilvie, Alexandra Shepard, John Styles, Brodie Waddell, Garthine Walker, and Nicola Whyte. The conference and seminar audiences that have offered insightful comments and suggestions on various aspects of our approach or results are too numerous to specify, but we are no less grateful for each opportunity we have had to discuss this work.

This book is dedicated to our families: Alex, Esther, Andrew, Laura, Arthur, Ralph, Bea, Louise, and Cora.

Note on the text

Dates given are modern, with the year beginning on 1 January. Currency is given in pounds (£), shillings (s), and pence (d). A pound consisted of 20 shillings, and a shilling contained 12 pence. The spelling in extracts taken from depositions has been modernised. Percentages are rounded to whole numbers except when directly citing from tables, which are rounded to one decimal place.

Abbreviations

BI	–	Borthwick Institute [accessed via www.dhi.ac.uk/causepapers/index.jsp]
CALS	–	Cheshire Archives and Local Studies
CRD	–	Coroners' Reports Database
CUL	–	Cambridge University Library
DHC	–	Devon Heritage Centre
DUIC	–	Durham University IIF Collections [accessed via http://iiif.durham.ac.uk/jalava/#index]
HALS	–	Hertfordshire Archives and Local Studies
HRO	–	Hampshire Record Office
LaA	–	Lancashire Archives
LiA	–	Lincolnshire Archives
NAS	–	Northamptonshire Archives Service
NRO	–	Norfolk Record Office
NYCRO	–	North Yorkshire County Record Office
SHC	–	Somerset Heritage Centre
TNA	–	The National Archives
WSHC	–	Wiltshire and Swindon History Centre
WYAS	–	West Yorkshire Archive Service (Wakefield)

Introduction

Upon 'a certain market day happening in the spring time' in 1604, Henry Burrell, a 50-year-old miller from Farleigh Hungerford in Somerset, overtook 'Joan Hedges going home from market at the towns end of Bath near the almshouse there, with a basket upon her arm'. He 'took her basket from her being on horseback and she on foot, to shift her of her carriage, and passing along together' he began to discuss a marriage proposal his friend, Robert Bartlett, wished him to negotiate with Joan. Bartlett was 'a widow man and wanting a wife to help gain his living with him'. Henry told Joan of the money that Robert might settle on her, doubling any dowry she received from her father. But Joan would have none of it, and as Henry recalled, she declared, 'I will not have him if he (meaning the said Bartlett) were worth £200' for she had given her 'word and promise to Richard Reade' to marry him and she would 'be as good as my word while I live'. At this, Henry said, 'God speed you well' and they went their separate ways.

This is just one exchange recorded as part of an inquiry into the marriage between Richard Reade and Joan Hedges of South Stoke near Bath in the Bath and Wells church court that year. As well as Henry Burrell, three other men gave evidence. Thomas Hudd, a husbandman from South Stoke, aged 63, deposed that 'Richard Reade and Joan Hedges have so usually and commonly kept company together both by day and night, early and late, as well in going to Bath market as coming home and at the house of William Hedges' (Joan's father) that the whole parish assumed they were already man and wife. Robert Lane, a 26-year-old tailor from nearby Wellow, recounted that 'Richard Read hath confessed unto [him] that he and … Joan Hedges were man and wife and that she hath lain in his arms most part of the night together in the hall of her father's house'. Robert Lane said he knew that Richard and Joan were 'commonly accounted man and wife' by the inhabitants of South Stoke because he 'being a tailor by his occupation, hath diverse times wrought in the same parish at many men's houses where he gathered the same so reported and said'. William Smyth, a 30-year-old yeoman from South

Stoke, recalled a conversation held with Joan Hedges 'about a year since' when he was in a field neighbouring that belonging to William Hedges, 'where the said Joan was milking', about the exact nature of the marriage agreement between Richard and herself. Henry Burrell also conducted a conversation with Joan, who was going 'out into her father's ground being fast by the house, to milking', when he first broached the idea of a marriage to Robert Bartlett.[1]

Depositions in the church and criminal courts have long been used to investigate crimes and disputes but are also rich in other more contextual evidence about life in early modern England.[2] This book uses depositions to investigate the nature of work. The marriage case between Richard Reade and Joan Hedges records the occupations of the four male witnesses, but while we collected such evidence it is not the focus of this book. Instead, the analysis rests on the work activities recorded in depositions: evidence of particular people carrying out specific work tasks. In this case, these include Robert Lane, a country tailor, working at his craft in other men's houses; Joan Hedges milking her father's cows; and Joan, Richard, and Henry going to and from market in nearby Bath. Collected *en masse*, work tasks from depositions allow a new history of work in early modern England to be created from the bottom up, based on a multitude of everyday work activities.

The book is titled *The Experience of Work* because it investigates what it was like to work in sixteenth- and seventeenth-century England as well as what work people did. Work was a central experience in everyone's life, then as now. Yet too often the history of work is studied at one remove, via ideas like the work ethic, or by studying wages, or most often via the consequences of work – the raw materials, food, manufactured goods, and services that were produced within the economy. When the worker is portrayed, and they are often surprisingly absent from economic history, he is usually an adult man.[3] This book takes a different approach that is inclusive, holistic, and people-centred. The evidence used records women and men, people of all ages, and people of all levels of wealth from beggars to the gentry. It records almost all commonly practised types of work, including unpaid work within the home and work in small farms and workshops. It is an approach which emphasises the agency of ordinary people by demonstrating how their actions collectively created the economy.

[1] SHC, D/D/Cd/36, *Reade v. Hedges*.
[2] On marriage disputes, see O'Hara, *Courtship and Constraint*.
[3] The classic example is Thompson, *Making of the English Working Class*.

The work-task approach adopted in this book has not been applied to England before. It provides new findings that demonstrate the importance of women's work; integrates housework, carework, petty commerce, and travel into our view of the economy; and quantifies the location of workspaces for the first time. It suggests corrections to existing views about by-employment; married women's work; and time-use across the day, week, and year. This introduction surveys the existing approaches to work that our research findings address. It provides essential background and context for the chapters that follow. Section 0.1 looks at how the early modern economy and change within it have been conceptualised. Most histories of the early modern economy focus on change, explaining the route and speed of England's transformation from the medieval economy based on small peasant farms in around 1500, to the leading global industrial nation by 1800. Depicting and measuring change over time is not a central aim of this study. Instead, the work-task approach offers new insights into how the early modern economy functioned, but in doing so it offers corrections to other approaches that measure change over time.

Another particular focus of existing research has been paid work, the topic of Section 0.2. A surprisingly high proportion of the English population worked for wages at an early date, and labourers, servants, and building craftsmen have been studied via wage accounts that record their terms of employment and pay. However, reliance on accounts – which survive only for wealthy employers – and on paid work more generally, creates a lopsided view of early modern work. The work-task approach illuminates these gaps and rebalances our understanding of early modern work. Unpaid work, either income-generating or for the sustenance and care of the family, took place within the household economy, the focus of Section 0.3. The household was the basic unit of production in early modern society. While the importance of the household and the 'family economy' has long been recognised, historians have struggled to look within the 'black box' of the family and understand who did what.[4] The opening up of this black box is one of the major contributions of the chapters that follow, demonstrating, for instance, the type of work undertaken by married women, children, and servants. Section 0.4 turns to the inspiration behind the work-task approach: the inclusive definition of work provided by economist Margaret Reid; time-use studies as an effective way to illuminate poorly documented types of work, particularly women's work but also work in peasant households; and previous studies

[4] de Vries, *Industrious Revolution*, p. 8.

that have used incidental and contextual evidence from legal records and other sources to explore the history of work.[5] The chapter finishes with an overview of the book as a whole.

0.1 The Early Modern Economy and Economic Change

From the writings of Adam Smith and Karl Marx onwards, the early modern economy has been characterised as one of transition, teleologically envisaged as a period of intensified commercialisation linking the feudal economy of the medieval period to industrialisation in the late eighteenth century. Historians also highlight processes of urbanisation, specialisation, and proletarianisation, as well as increased productivity and work intensity. Recent studies have drawn these processes together under the umbrella of structural change with a particular focus on England's occupational structure. They show that between the sixteenth century and early eighteenth century the number of men with primary sector occupations – mostly agriculture – fell from around 65 per cent to 43–51 per cent, while those with secondary sector or manufacturing occupations rose from 16–28 per cent to 31–42 per cent.[6] This indicates a trend of 'industrialisation before industrialisation'.[7] It was accompanied by increased urbanisation, with the proportion of the population living in large towns growing from 6 per cent in 1520 to 17 per cent in 1700, while the rural non-agricultural population grew from 19 per cent to 28 per cent by E. A. Wrigley's estimates.[8] The increased specialisation of the English economy was mapped by Ann Kussmaul. She argued that the seasonality of marriage was influenced by economic activity: in communities where arable farming was important couples tended to marry in the autumn after harvest, in pastoral communities marriages were more often in the spring, and in industrial communities there was no clear seasonality. The mapping of marriage seasonality shows that England went from having no clear regional specialisation in the sixteenth century, to a distinct division between the arable east and midlands, and the industrial and pastoral north and west, by the early eighteenth century.[9]

Structural change of this type implies increased productivity. Between 1500 and 1700, England experienced no significant technological

[5] Reid, *Economics of Household Production*.

[6] Broadberry, Campbell, and van Leeuwen, 'When did Britain industrialise?'; Shaw-Taylor and Wrigley, 'Occupational structure'; Keibek, 'Male occupational structure'; Wallis, Colson, and Chilosi, 'Structural change'.

[7] Kreidt, Medick, and Schlumbohm, *Industrialization before Industrialization*.

[8] Wrigley, *People, Cities, and Wealth*, p. 170.

[9] Kussmaul, *General View*.

transformations and remained largely self-sufficient in food. An increased non-agricultural population making a living from industry and services therefore demonstrates that agricultural labour became more productive, providing food for a larger non-agricultural population. In a survey of the outputs of the major sectors of the economy, Broadberry et al. estimate that British GDP per head kept pace with population growth from 1500 to 1650, and then grew by 90 per cent between the 1650s and 1770s.[10] They argue this was not only the consequence of structural change but also 'an industrious revolution as workers increased the numbers of days worked in order to maintain household incomes'.[11]

Arguments about changing patterns of time-use in work stretch back to E. P. Thompson's statement that the rise of industrial capitalism and the factory replaced the traditionally lax work patterns of the early modern period with the order, regularity, and strictness of modern clock-time.[12] More recently, Jan de Vries argued that after 1650 workers, including women and children, became more 'industrious'. They increased worktime to earn extra income to purchase new consumer goods, while also finding work in the industries that produced those goods.[13] Direct evidence of workers increasing the number of days worked each year is weak. Hans-Joachim Voth collected evidence of time-use from depositions, using a method close to that deployed in this book. He found that the observance of 'St Monday', a practice by which craftsmen took Monday off as well as Sunday, declined over the eighteenth century, alongside the number of official holidays.[14] Yet, Voth's evidence is not clear-cut. In so far as St Monday ever existed, it was restricted to male craftsmen in London and so would have had a limited effect on the population as a whole.[15] Another approach is suggested by Jane Humphries and Jacob Weisdorf. They compare the annual wage rates earned by male servants with men's daily wage rates and assume workers paid by the day would only work the number of days necessary to equal a servant's annual wage. This shows that the annual number of days worked by casual workers increased steadily and markedly during the seventeenth century from around 150 to 250.[16] However, if this was the case, it remains unclear whether such workers were decreasing their

[10] Broadberry et al., *British Economic Growth*, p. 404.
[11] Ibid., p. 405. They also cite a third reason: the European Marriage Pattern suppressing fertility and thus population growth.
[12] Thompson, 'Time, work-discipline'. [13] de Vries, *Industrious Revolution*.
[14] Voth, *Time and Work*, pp. 268–9; Broadberry et al., *British Economic Growth*, pp. 263–5.
[15] Hailwood, 'Time and work'. See also Section 4.3.
[16] Humphries and Weisdorf, 'Unreal wages?' (esp. p. 2880).

leisure time or swapping unpaid work with their own resources for paid labour.

The process of proletarianisation, by which workers become more dependent on earning wages rather than independent forms of income generation using their own property in small farms, craft production, and petty commerce, has been poorly integrated into this discussion. For agriculture, evidence is found in the ratio between male farmers and agricultural wage labourers. In the late sixteenth and early seventeenth centuries male farmers outnumbered male labourers, but by the early eighteenth century, labourers outnumbered farmers by almost three to one.[17] This illustrates the transition from a farming economy dependent on small family farms to one in which most rural-agricultural households lacked land and relied on wage labour. Men worked as agricultural labourers, but women and children also found work in spinning. Craig Muldrew estimates that the number of women earning income from spinning more than doubled between 1590 and 1700, adding weight to de Vries' suggestion that women also increasingly sought waged employment.[18]

The question of how far the dynamics of economic change applied to women's work as well as men's is an important one. Estimates of structural change have relied on evidence of men's occupations because equivalent information for women does not exist. Judith Bennett famously commented that women's work remained unchangingly 'low-status, low-paid, and low-skilled' across these centuries.[19] However, other historians and economists have discussed fluctuations in women's employment over time. Claudia Goldin suggested women's labour force participation during industrialisation followed a U-shaped curve because women's employment first falls as work moves away from the home and farm but later increases again as observed in Western economies in the late twentieth century.[20] Earlier changes have also been noted. In the century after the Black Death, from c.1350 to c.1450, sharp population decline seems to have allowed women to enter a wider range of occupations and find more paid work.[21] As already noted, the 'industrious revolution' from c.1650 to c.1750 caused by the expansion of textiles and clothing production may have provided increased employment for women.[22] Yet for women to periodically enter the workforce in this way,

[17] Shaw-Taylor, 'Rise of agrarian capitalism'; Whittle, *Development of Agrarian Capitalism*, p. 236. See also Kussmaul, *Servants in Husbandry*, p. 17.

[18] Muldrew, '"Th'ancient distaff"'.

[19] Bennett, *History Matters*, p. 62.

[20] Goldin, 'U-shaped female labor force function'.

[21] Goldberg, *Women, Work, and Life Cycle*; Penn, 'Female wage-earners'; McIntosh, *Working Women*; de Moor and van Zanden, 'Girl power'.

[22] de Vries, *Industrious Revolution*; Muldrew, '"Th'ancient distaff"'.

they must also have left it in the intervening periods. There is some evidence for this. For instance, in the late fifteenth and sixteenth centuries, guild regulations increasingly sought to exclude women from craft occupations, including those which women had previously dominated such as weaving and tailoring.[23] In the late eighteenth century the mechanisation of spinning deprived women of a significant area of employment.[24] These observations imply that women formed a 'reserve army of labour': entering the workforce when labour is in short supply only to be pushed out again when not needed. But this begs the question of what women did when they were 'not needed', particularly as their supposed exclusion from the labour force occurred precisely when real wages were low, and women's income was vital for labouring households. Increasingly sophisticated attempts to calculate family income including women's contribution still struggle to document the variety of women's work and how this changed over time.[25]

Theories of economic change during the early modern period are based on historical data which is incomplete, and which can be interpreted in a variety of ways. Information about women's work is often lacking, and the meaning of occupations and patterns of time-use require more investigation. The work-task approach offers new evidence relating to all these facets of work, providing a new way of thinking about the early modern economy. It shows that the idea of an occupation is more complicated than many theories have allowed, that paid work, although pervasive, was more varied than has been assumed, and that women's work had more importance across all areas of the economy than existing estimates suggest.

0.2 Types of Waged Work

Since the nineteenth-century research of J. E. Thorold Rogers, wages have been a central theme in histories of economic change.[26] Rogers' data was later used to construct wage series stretching from the thirteenth to nineteenth centuries in order to measure the wage levels and living standards of building workers and agricultural labourers.[27] More recently,

[23] Clark, *Working Life of Women*, pp. 102–3; Goldberg, *Women, Work, and Life Cycle*, p. 34; Bennett, *History Matters*, pp. 95–101; Ogilvie, *European Guilds*, p. 232–305.

[24] Schneider, 'Technological unemployment'.

[25] Muldrew, *Food, Energy*, pp. 208–59; Horrell, Humphries, and Weisdorf, 'Family standards of living' and 'Beyond the male breadwinner'.

[26] Rogers, *History of Agriculture and Prices*.

[27] Phelps Brown and Hopkins, 'Seven centuries'; Allen, 'Great divergence'; Clark, 'Long march'; Allen and Weisdorf, 'Was there an "industrious revolution"'.

additional data has allowed new series relating to female labourers and servants and male labourers and servants to be added to the list.[28] Such series cover impressive sweeps of time, but it is important to understand their weaknesses as well as their potential.[29] Wage series do not reveal the number of people who worked for wages, or how dependent on wages as a source of income such people were. When used to calculate standards of living, wages are compared with the cost of a 'basket of consumables' consisting of food and other necessities. This raises further issues about how diet changed over time and varied by region, as well as how dependent on purchases of food different groups were.[30]

Christopher Dyer suggests that between 32 and 59 per cent of the adult population were wage earners by the 1520s, with levels varying by county.[31] This proportion certainly increased in the period up to 1700, as discussed in the previous section. However, estimating the exact proportion of wage workers is fraught with uncertainty. Dyer's figures are derived from tax returns, and thus relate mainly to adult men, not the whole population. The highest proportions were found in Norfolk, where the figures relate to male servants and smallholders as well as wage labourers.[32] It is unclear how wage dependent these people were. Labourers and servants both worked for wages but did so in ways that entailed very different relationships to the wider economy. Servants were typically employed for longer periods of time – several months to a year – and lived with their employer. Around 80 per cent of their wage was received in kind, as food and lodgings.[33] Thus, although they earned a wage, they were not dependent on purchasing daily necessities in the market. Women were more likely to work as servants than as labourers. It is important therefore to know the proportion of servants to labourers in the economy. Servants outnumbered labourers throughout the early modern period. The Gloucestershire Muster List for 1608 suggests a ratio of 1.9 male servants to each labourer, while Arthur Young's farm tours of the 1760s give a ratio amongst all farm workers, male and female, of 1.5 servants to each labourer.[34] For their part, labourers tended to live in their own households but often supplemented income from wages with that from other activities of work such as keeping their

28 Humphries and Weisdorf, 'Wages of women' and 'Unreal wages?'.
29 Hatcher and Stephenson (eds.), *Seven Centuries of Unreal Wages*.
30 Allen, *British Industrial Revolution*, pp. 25–56; Muldrew, *Food, Energy*, pp. 29–116.
31 Dyer, *Age of Transition?*, p. 120.
32 Whittle, *Development of Agrarian Capitalism*, pp. 227–37.
33 Whittle, 'Servants in rural England', pp. 94–7; Humphries and Weisdorf, 'Wages of women', pp. 413–5; Whittle, 'Different pattern', pp. 68–75.
34 Muldrew, *Food, Energy*, pp. 221–3; Kussmaul, *Servants in Husbandry*, pp. 16–18.

own livestock. Thus, the place of wages in labourers' household economies also needs to be considered.

Alan Everitt's study of farm labourers in the period 1500 to 1640 depicts them as small farmers who combined earning wages with working their own land and raising livestock.[35] Keith Snell's view of the later period from 1660 to 1834 is much harsher, highlighting labourers' vulnerability to seasonal unemployment, the negative consequences of enclosure, and dependence on poor relief to supplement wages.[36] This contrast partly reflects change over time, but it is also a product of research methods. Everitt used evidence from probate inventories, assuming that men below a certain level of wealth were at least partly wage dependent.[37] Inventories, which record moveable goods owned at the time of death, document multiple sources of income via evidence of livestock, crops, raw materials, and tools but say nothing about quantity or regularity of waged work. Everitt failed to consider women's work at all. Snell's research leaned heavily on evidence from settlement examinations, documents drawn up either when people requested poor relief, or if they were seen as likely to require assistance in the future: a source that focuses on the poor and mobile. Settlement examinations offer potted histories of people's previous employment, with an emphasis on service rather than more casual labour. Neither of these approaches offers a clear view of the lives of early modern wage labourers.

Craig Muldrew presents a more balanced picture, looking carefully at labourers' diet and living costs, and reconstructing household income generated by men, women, and children from casual agricultural labour, spinning, and ownership of land and livestock. This suggests that labouring families struggled to make ends meet in the late sixteenth and early seventeenth centuries but were better off in earlier and later periods.[38] Muldrew, like Everitt, relies on probate inventories to document multiple sources of income. Useful as they are, inventories fail to capture the quantity of wage income or days worked for wages and are biased towards the better off. Limited evidence from wage accounts suggests more men were working an increasing number of days for wages each year in the seventeenth century.[39]

Everitt imagined labourers as men, yet women also worked for wages. The extent to which they found such work in agriculture remains uncertain. Michael Roberts described the gender division of labour at harvest time in which men harvested hay, barley, and oats with scythes, and

35 Everitt, 'Farm labourers'. 36 Snell, *Annals*. 37 Everitt, 'Farm labourers', p. 413.

38 Muldrew, *Food, Energy*, p. 257.

39 Whittle and Jiang, 'Gender, wages, and agricultural labour'.

mixed groups of men and women made hay, harvested wheat and rye with sickles, and raked, stacked, and transported the crops.[40] The high labour demands of harvest time made it the peak in the rural wage-earning year. Snell argued that the increased use of the scythe to harvest wheat, the main bread crop, in the eighteenth century led to a decrease in the waged work available for women.[41] A. Hassell Smith showed that in one estate in north Norfolk, women were employed for more days of casual agricultural labour than men in the late sixteenth century, although Pamela Sharpe's study of Essex contradicts this, suggesting women's involvement in agricultural wage labour was already low by that date.[42] Recent research by Jane Whittle and Li Jiang shows that women's agricultural wage work was high in the sixteenth century, making up around 39 per cent of the days worked on large gentry farms, but declined significantly across the seventeenth century, earlier than the period suggested by Snell.[43] More evidence of day labouring in early modern England is needed, to demonstrate the range of tasks men with the occupation of 'labourer' undertook, and the extent of women's casual waged work.

Service, as a form of labour, was distinctive to medieval and early modern Western Europe.[44] The requirement of living in the employer's household meant it was largely young unmarried people who were employed as servants, typically between the ages of 14 and 24. Another important characteristic of service is that almost as many women were employed as men.[45] Service was instrumental in allowing women to delay marriage until their mid-20s, and thus was one of the causal influences behind the European Marriage Pattern, characterised by relatively late marriage for women and the establishment of independent households on marriage.[46] It was a neglected element of early modern wage labour until Kussmaul's study of servants in husbandry, published in 1981. Kussmaul argued that the popularity of service as a form of employment in England declined from a post-Black Death high point still evident in the mid-sixteenth century to a low point in the mid-seventeenth century before rising again to a new peak in 1750 and declining thereafter.[47] The existence of a mid-seventeenth-century dip

[40] Roberts, 'Sickles and scythes'. [41] Snell, *Annals*, p. 49–51.

[42] Smith, 'Labourers [Part I]', p. 29; Sharpe, 'Female labour market', p. 171 and *Adapting to Capitalism*, pp.73–80.

[43] Whittle and Jiang, 'Gender, wages, and agricultural labour'.

[44] Whittle (ed.), *Servants*.

[45] Whittle, 'Housewives and servants', p. 55; Kussmaul, *Servants in Husbandry*, p. 4.

[46] de Moor and van Zanden, 'Girl power'.

[47] Kussmaul, *Servants in Husbandry*, esp. p. 98: measured by tracking Michaelmas marriages.

in service has been disputed, and although her book addresses early modern England, its richest data is from 1680 onwards rather than for the earlier part of the period.[48] The contrast between Kussmaul's study, which is concerned primarily with male agricultural service, and studies of female service in London also unwittingly gives the impression of a stark gender division between men's work in farm service, and women's in urban domestic service.[49] Charmian Mansell's study of female servants in rural England corrects that misconception. She uses an approach similar to that in this book to demonstrate the widespread employment of female servants and the variety of their work tasks including significant quantities of agriculture.[50]

Apprenticeship shared important characteristics with service: young people predominated, and apprentices lived with their employer receiving food and lodgings. However, while the work of servants was general and flexible, apprenticeship contained a more explicit element of training and led into a specialist occupation in craft or retail. As a consequence, a premium was usually paid to enter apprenticeship, and apprentices did not usually receive a cash wage.[51] While servants were both female and male, girls were only rarely apprenticed to specialist occupations.[52] In England, craft apprenticeships and service existed alongside pauper or parish apprenticeships. Orphans and the children of the labouring poor were forcibly placed in parish apprenticeships under the remit of the poor laws from 1600 onwards. Parish apprenticeships were typically in husbandry or housewifery rather than specialist occupations and were unpaid. Young people could be placed in these arrangements when as young as eight years old and were expected to stay with their employer until aged 21 or 24, or until marriage, although many absconded from these arrangements.[53] Discussions of apprenticeship have focused on apprenticeship agreements and contracts; the work-task approach provides evidence of the work apprentices carried out.

The existence of institutions such as parish apprenticeships is a reminder that work for others was not always freely contracted or paid. From 1349 onwards waged work was regulated in England by a series of labour laws. These laws made unemployment illegal, set maximum wage

48 Woodward, 'Early modern servants'; Whittle, 'Different pattern'.
49 Gowing, *Domestic Dangers*; Meldrum, *Domestic Service*.
50 Mansell, *Female Servants*, esp. pp. 183–217.
51 Dunlop and Denman, *English Apprenticeship*; Davies, *Enforcement of English Apprenticeship*; Lane, *Apprenticeship in England*; Wallis, 'Apprenticeship in England'.
52 Although see Snell, *Annals*, pp. 270–319; Gowing, *Ingenious Trade*.
53 Hindle, *On the Parish?*, pp. 191–223; Fisher, 'Bound to the Soil (Part I)' and 'Bound to the Soil (Part II)'.

rates, and controlled entrance into many crafts. The laws showed a strong preference for service rather than casual wage labouring, placing unemployed or partially employed people in service where in theory they could be overseen by a responsible householder.[54] Service was the preferred form of control because once they had entered a contract, servants had little say in what type of work they did or the hours they worked each week; employers were expected to regulate all aspects of their behaviour. Although Humphries and Weisdorf assume servants worked five days a week, there is no evidence of servants having two days off per week; half a day on Sunday seems more likely.[55] Because servants lived in such close proximity to their employers, relationships between servants and employers varied, from strong, semi-familial bonds to extreme abuse. The work-task approach offers new evidence about the work of servants and apprentices, focusing on the types of work they did, and how that differed from the work of householders and labourers.

Skilled workers were also sometimes paid in wages. Some craftsmen, such as shoemakers, made a living from making goods and selling them, but others, such as building workers, were necessarily paid time or task wages. The position of building craftsmen as both skilled workers and wage earners brought them under the scrutiny of labour legislation, suggesting that elite employers found the independence of building workers hard to deal with. A 1495 statute attempted to regulate building workers' exact working hours in summer and winter including meal breaks, while the 1563 Statute of Artificers banned them from leaving work unfinished.[56] The availability of accounts recording wages paid to building workers in institutional archives from cathedrals to Oxbridge colleges and country houses has made them an attractive subject for historians. The first wage series by E. T. Phelps Brown and Sheila Hopkins focused on the wages of building workers.[57] Donald Woodward studied the work practices of northern building craftsmen across the early modern period, while Malcolm Airs examined those who built country houses.[58] Judy Stephenson's research on London building workers from 1660 to 1785 has criticised the careless interpretation of wages for building work that underpins many wage series. She echoes Woodward in pointing out that building craftsmen and their teams are not representative of other forms of wage labour because of the ways they

54 Whittle, 'Attitudes to wage labour'.
55 Humphries and Weisdorf, 'Wages of women', pp. 412–3 and 'Unreal wages?', pp. 2876–8. Servants weekly work patterns are discussed in Section 4.3.
56 Whittle, 'Attitudes to wage labour', pp. 45–6.
57 Phelps Brown and Hopkins, 'Seven centuries'.
58 Woodward, *Men at Work*; Airs, *Tudor and Jacobean Country House.*

organised and charged for work.[59] The work-task data adds further glimpses of these men's working practices, such as the distances they travelled from home to work and the range of tasks they engaged in.

Medical professionals are rarely considered as wage workers, but nonetheless physicians and midwives provided healthcare in return for monetary payment. Ian Mortimer used probate accounts to reconstruct and quantify the medical care provided to the dying and demonstrated a dramatic increase in paid medical care across the seventeenth century. He found medical expertise provided by men and nursing by women.[60] Other than nurses and midwives, women are assumed to have provided 'household medicine' for family members as part of their unpaid carework, with elite households offering the most detailed evidence.[61] The work-task approach presents a rather different picture. We find healthcare to be dominated by women, but typically carried out for people outside the household, implying – and sometimes specifying – that it was paid work. This raises the possibility that a significant sector of the economy has hitherto gone largely undocumented: grassroots paid healthcare provided by women. The employment of male physicians may have increased, but women dominated paid as well as unpaid healthcare.

Studies of waged work provide some of the most detailed and carefully contextualised research on work in early modern England. Yet even here there are gaps: there is more information about what people were paid than what they were actually employed to do. Further, it is important to know how paid work fitted with other ways of making a living in the households of wage workers and in the economy as a whole. This book provides more detail about the work labourers, servants, apprentices, building workers, and healthcare providers actually did. Our approach does not always allow us to identify which work was paid, but work undertaken for people outside the household can be identified and indicates the forms of work more likely to be paid. However, much of work in the early modern economy was not paid, and the strength of the work-task approach is its ability to recover all types of work, paid and unpaid.

0.3 Working in a Household Economy

Conceptions of the economy within economic history are dominated by the Smithian model, which separates processes of production, trade, and

59 Stephenson, *Contracts and Pay.*
60 Mortimer, 'Rural medical marketplace' and *Dying and the Doctors.*
61 Thomas, 'Early modern midwifery'; Nagy, *Popular Medicine*; Leong, 'Making medicines'; Stobart, *Household Medicine.*

consumption. Yet from the writings of Xenophon in Ancient Greece to Gregory King's social tables in the late seventeenth century, the economy was understood as centred on the household.[62] In this model, the ideal household provided as many of its own needs as possible, producing food, fuel, textiles for clothing, and building materials.[63] When the economy is conceived in this way, there is little need to separate production from consumption, or income-generating work from work to sustain the family unit. The model was aspirational: very few, if any, households in early modern England achieved full self-sufficiency. Nonetheless, it is important to take the values it conveyed seriously. Although it assigned different work roles to women and men, women's work was seen as crucial to the economy rather than peripheral. Unpaid housework and carework were essential to sustaining the household in the long run. The ethos of thrift meant that work that saved expenditure was just as valued as that which brought in income. As studies of modern peasant societies show, varied work activities were valued as offering the household increased economic security and independence.[64] This section surveys approaches to early modern work that are rooted in the household economy. These include studies of women's work, but also the literature on by-employment.

The concept of the family or household economy was used by early feminist historians such as Alice Clark, and Louise Tilly and Joan Scott, to write women back into the economy.[65] They pointed out that most work was located in the home, and that wives and children worked alongside husbands in the activities that generated income, in contrast to the male breadwinner model in which only the man does income-generating work. Yet this approach tends to portray women's work as assisting, supporting, or helping that of men, inadvertently suggesting women's work was secondary and obscuring women's independent work activities. Early modern documents encourage this view, given the frequency with which they record male occupations while women are described as servant, spinster, wife, or widow.[66] The laws of coverture also obscured married women's activities by giving ownership rights to goods and property to the husband alone. The 'two-supporter model' put forward by the Swedish gender and work project corrects this by

62 Discussed in Whittle, 'Gender and consumption', pp. 200–4; Xenophon, *Oeconomicus*; on Gregory King see Harte, 'Economics of clothing'.

63 Tusser, *Five Hundred Points*; Estienne, *Maison Rustique*; Markham, *English Husbandman* and *English Housewife*.

64 Thorner et al. (eds.), *A. V. Chayanov*; Ellis, *Peasant Economics*.

65 Clark, *Working Life*; Tilly and Scott, *Women, Work, and Family*.

66 Shepard, *Accounting for Oneself*, p. 14.

emphasising the extent to which the married couple jointly took charge of the household economy and worked to maintain its prosperity, rather than the man alone.[67] When an early modern man such as Robert Bartlett wanted 'a wife to help gain his living with him', as mentioned at the start of the chapter, he recognised the importance of a wife in increasing household prosperity rather than making the home comfortable. Recent research has highlighted the extent to which married women ran their own businesses and had work specialisms that were separate from their husband's occupation.[68] For instance, a farmer might be married to a woman who ran an alehouse, or a blacksmith to a woman who dealt in second-hand iron. Rather than marriage impeding women's ability to work in the wider economy, increasing evidence suggests that the marital household provided the support and resources that enabled women to engage in a wider range of economic opportunities.[69] Households headed by unmarried women and widows were less wealthy partly because women's work was less well paid than men's work, but also because they were headed by one person rather than two.[70]

The gender division of labour describes the interlocking patterns of women's and men's work. The distinctions can be weak, as Ågren found in early modern Sweden where marital status was more significant than gender in defining work roles.[71] Or it can be strong as is evident in craft production, both as revealed by Ogilvie's research on early modern Germany and our own previous findings for south-west England.[72] Ogilvie summarises the explanations offered for the gender division of labour in medieval and early modern Europe as technological, cultural, or institutional.[73] Technological explanations emphasise the tools and equipment used to carry out work activities. Cultural explanations stress the interplay between work and wider social attitudes, such as patriarchal assumptions about male superiority, or household formation systems such as the European Marriage Pattern. Institutional explanations look to the organisations that structure the economy via rules or laws, such as the state, guilds, manors, and parishes. Only a small number of studies have examined the gender division of labour in early modern England in any detail, mostly importantly research by Michael Roberts and Amanda

67 Ling et al., 'Marriage and work'.
68 Erickson, 'Married women's occupations'; Whittle, 'Enterprising widows'; Shepard, *Accounting for Oneself*, pp. 149–80.
69 Ling et al., 'Marriage and work'.
70 Whittle, 'Enterprising widows'; Moring and Wall, *Widows*; Froide, *Never Married*.
71 Ågren, 'Conclusion', p. 211.
72 Ogilvie, *Bitter Living*, pp. 321–2; Whittle and Hailwood, 'Gender division'.
73 Ogilvie, *Bitter Living*, pp. 7–15.

Flather.[74] Flather used an approach very similar to that used in this book, although unquantified, to show how men's and women's work patterns varied across the year. Sometimes men and women worked together, as at harvest time, but in other seasons women worked at home while men laboured in the fields. Age and marital status affected work patterns as well as gender, as has been noted for early modern Sweden.[75] The work-task approach allows work patterns to be quantified and explored not only by gender but also by age and seasonality. This sheds further light on the reasons behind gender differences, suggesting causes differed in different parts of the economy.[76]

The groundbreaking histories of women's work by Alice Clark and Ivy Pinchbeck in the early twentieth century, and the pioneers who studied work in the second phase of women's history, such as Bridget Hill, Merry Weisner-Hanks, Pamela Sharpe, Sara Mendelson and Patricia Crawford, and Majorie McIntosh have provided a thorough knowledge of the wide range of work undertaken by early modern women.[77] However, typically they give examples rather than quantified data that the economic historians discussed in Section 0.1 can integrate into their models of economic change. Instead, economic historians such as de Vries and Broadberry et al. have made guesses or projected nineteenth-century data back onto the early modern period. This book aims to bridge these two approaches by providing quantified evidence of women's work.

Women's contributions to housework and carework are in particular need of further research. This work is assumed to take up a large proportion of women's time but has rarely been considered worthwhile to investigate, in part because it is rarely acknowledged as part of the economy. Pervasive cultural assumptions see women's responsibility for care of the home and family as an unchanging historical fact. The Nobel Prize-winning economist Gary Becker voiced these assumptions when he stated, wrongly, that married women 'traditionally have devoted most of their time to childbearing and other domestic activities', while married men 'have hunted, soldiered, farmed, and engaged in other "market" activities'.[78] Similarly, when Broadberry et al. considered women's

[74] Roberts, 'Sickles and scythes', '"Words they are women"', and '"To bridle the falsehood"'; Flather, *Gender and Space*, 'Space, place, and gender', and 'Women, work, and land'.

[75] Ågren (ed.), *Making a Living.*

[76] Whittle and Hailwood, 'Gender division'.

[77] Clark, *Working Life*; Pinchbeck, *Women Workers*; Hill, *Women, Work, and Sexual Politics*; Sharpe, *Adapting to Capitalism*; Mendelson and Crawford, *Women in Early Modern England*; McIntosh, *Working Women*. See Macleod, Shepard, and Ågren (eds.), *Whole Economy*, for a recent summary of research on gender and work.

[78] Becker, *Treatise on the Family*, p. 30.

labour force participation between the fourteenth and nineteenth centuries, they estimated women spent only 30 per cent of their worktime on income-generating activities because of the time taken by unpaid housework and carework.[79] For the medieval period, Hatcher argued that women's hours of paid work were constricted by 'the need to care for their families and to work in the house', while Flather suggests that cooking took up many hours of the day in early modern England.[80] Housework and carework are explicitly included within the economy in this book. The tasks required, their place in women's and men's work repertoires, and their relationship to paid work and time-use are all investigated. The evidence demonstrates that although women undertook much of this work, it was not as time-consuming, disconnected from the market, or static as has been assumed.

Women's responsibility for most housework and carework leads to other misconceptions about the location and social context of women's work, which is assumed to take place in the home and in private. Given the near-total absence of specialist workplaces, it is clear that the domestic house was the main centre of early modern work, but the actual location of work has remained a matter of conjecture and anecdote. Early modern writers such as Gervase Markham located women's work inside and men's outside, but we know women frequently worked in the fields and sold goods at market.[81] Even when people worked inside, the early modern house was not a place of privacy. Studies of English vernacular architecture emphasise the physical and social openness of the house – often without glazed windows until the late sixteenth or early seventeenth century. Middling householders shared their houses with servants. Poorer houses were flimsy and offered limited space meaning work activities spilled outside. There was a culture of openness and neighbourly intervention that regarded privacy with suspicion.[82] As Ågren and Joachim Eibach state, the early modern house 'should not be conceptualised as a "container" ... but rather as an open, permeable structure'.[83] The evidence presented in this study emphasises the lack of privacy within the home, and that work within it was not limited to housework and carework.

By-employment, defined as having more than one occupation, is implicit in early modern conceptions of the household economy.

[79] Broadberry et al., *British Economic Growth*, p. 348.

[80] Hatcher, 'Women's work reconsidered', p. 194; Flather, 'Space, place, and gender', p. 348.

[81] Markham, *English Housewife*.

[82] Johnson, *Housing Culture* and *English Houses*; Crowley, *Invention of Comfort*; Orlin, *Locating Privacy*; Hamling and Richardson, *Day at Home*.

[83] Ågren, 'Introduction', p. 7, citing Eibach, 'Das offene haus'.

Members of a household undertook multiple activities to generate income and care for the farm and family. Joan Thirsk's pioneering work using evidence from probate inventories demonstrated the prevalence of by-employment in early modern England, particularly cloth production combined with livestock farming in the households of pastoral regions.[84] The theory of protoindustrialisation built on insights such as these to explore the dynamics of widespread expansion of rural industry, particularly cloth and clothing production, before factory-based industrialisation after 1750.[85] These ideas were in turn integrated into Jan de Vries' idea of the industrious revolution, a period of household-based industrialisation that took place in the century before factories appeared.[86] Mark Overton et al. returned to probate inventories to show that the combination of weaving and farming suggested by Thirsk was only one of many permutations of by-employment in rural England. They also note that household by-employment was not necessarily caused by the male household head having two occupations but by the activities of multiple household members – women and men, householders and servants, adults and children – engaging in different activities.[87] Sebastiaan Keibek and Leigh Shaw-Taylor critique this approach. Probate inventories, they note, have a bias towards by-employed households. Inventories record moveable goods owned at death, and because by-employed households necessarily contained more equipment and products, they were more likely to fall above the £5 threshold of goods that required inventories to be made. When women's activities are discounted, they argue that in the poorer households individual – rather than household – by-employment for male labourers and weavers was rare.[88] This supports the approach to measuring structural economic change using male occupations by suggesting it was common for men to have a single occupation.

The work-task approach sheds light on many of these issues. It allows the range of work activities undertaken by people with certain occupations to be explored and shows that by-employment was common for men of all levels of wealth and thus should be taken seriously as a feature of the economy. More radically than that, however, it encourages a dissection of the idea of an occupation. Many occupations required work in more than one sector: for instance, a baker not only made bread but sold it; farmers not only produced crops and livestock but transported them to market and

84 Thirsk, 'Industries in the countryside'.

85 Kreidt, Medick, and Schlumbohm, *Industrialization before Industrialization*; Clarkson, *Proto-Industrialisation.*

86 de Vries, *Industrious Revolution.*

87 Overton et al., *Production and Consumption*, esp. p. 65–6.

88 Keibek and Shaw-Taylor, 'Early modern rural by-employments'.

sold them there. The occupational labels so commonly adopted or given to male householders in early modern documents were identifiers used to supplement surnames in distinguishing between individuals. They indicated what was most distinctive about a man's skills and work but did not encompass all their work activities, let alone all those that took place in their household. The household context is essential for an understanding of work in early modern England. Household economies combined women's and men's work and could encompass multiple activities and occupations. Houses were places of work and employment. Early modern thought drew little distinction between income generation and other activities essential to the household's long-term survival.

0.4 A Work-Task Approach

The previous sections have offered a survey of existing knowledge about work in the early modern economy, and the areas where we need to know much more. Recent studies have shown that a focus on work activities, rather than wages, occupations, or inventories, has the potential to achieve this. These studies, often described collectively as 'verb-oriented' approaches as they focus on evidence of work actually being done, are the subject of this section. A crucial feature of these studies, and this book, is not just how we study work but how we define it. Historians of work either implicitly or explicitly adopt a definition of work used in modern economics: labour force participation. Measures of labour force participation exclude unpaid housework and carework undertaken for family members. Feminist theorists also adopt a similar definition by distinguishing between production, or productive, income-generating work, and social reproduction. Social reproduction, the care of the home and family, is seen as a distinct form of work that takes place outside the economy.[89] This book rejects these distinctions and adopts a definition of work that includes unpaid housework and carework, as well as other unpaid work. It does so for two reasons. First, it is not only difficult but often impossible to distinguish between income-generating work and work aimed at directly supporting the household in preindustrial societies. Such households engaged in subsistence production activities, and as discussed in the previous section, drew no distinction between work to support the family (care and housework) and work to support the household as a productive unit. Additionally, because so many early modern households contained paid employees in the form of servants, the

[89] For a more extended discussion, see Whittle, 'Critique of approaches'.

distinction between work for the family and the productive household was blurred. Second, the exclusion of unpaid housework and carework from conceptions of work devalues women's involvement in the economy. Women did most of such work, and housework and carework were absolutely essential for the functioning of the economy, so there is no logical reason for their exclusion from our definition of work.[90]

Instead, we adopt the definition of work provided by the economist Margaret Reid in her 1934 book *Economics of Household Production*. Reid explored the economic value of unpaid work in the home in early twentieth-century America. She argued that not only paid and income-generating work but also any unpaid work that could be replaced with paid work or purchased goods should be defined as work and part of the economy, a principle known as the 'third party criterion'.[91] This means, for instance, that caring for your child rather than sending the child to daycare, or cooking a meal at home rather than going to a restaurant, should be defined as work. After campaigning by feminist economists, Reid's definition was adopted by the UN as its definition of work in the guidelines used by countries around the world to calculate GDP, although the UN still excludes unpaid housework and carework from actual GDP measures as 'a compromise'.[92] Reid's definition has proved relatively straightforward to apply to the early modern economy.

Reid also observed that the best way to collect data about all types of work, including unpaid work, was the time-use study. Already in the early twentieth century, time-use studies had been used to calculate the economic value of unpaid work.[93] They became widespread from the mid-twentieth century onwards as a tool for collecting work data in the Global South as well as Western industrial nations, proving to be well-suited to recording work activities in peasant households.[94] In 1995 the Beijing Declaration for advancing women's rights reasserted that the most effective way of acknowledging the full range of women's (and men's) work, paid and unpaid, across the globe was the time-use study. It is only by measuring and accounting for the full range of work in this way that women's economic contribution can be properly assessed.[95]

[90] Waring, *Counting for Nothing*.

[91] Reid, *Economics of Household Production*, p. 11; Yi, 'Margaret G. Reid'.

[92] UN, *System of National Accounts* (1993), pp. 5–6, 148–51; UN, *System of National Accounts* (2008), pp. 461–7, 542.

[93] Reid, *Economics of Household Production*, pp. 160–9.

[94] UNDP, *Human Development Report* (1995); Esquivel et al., 'Explorations: time-use surveys'.

[95] UN, *Report on the Fourth World Conference on Women* (1995), pp. 87–8. Antonopoulos and Hirway (eds.), *Unpaid Work*.

Of course, it is not possible to retrospectively conduct a time-use study in a historical society to the same standard as a carefully planned present-day survey. However, the work-task approach allows similar data to be collected for past societies. The technique of collecting incidental and contextual descriptions of work activities from court depositions or witness statements has similarities to a random-hour recall method of gathering time-use data, which asks participants to recall what they were doing at randomly chosen moments and reconstructs broader time-use patterns from that information.[96] The main differences are that we cannot control for the day or time that is reported, nor can we select our informants, although analysis in Chapter 1 demonstrates that the method accesses a balanced cross-section of early modern social groups. Women are under-represented, but the data can be adjusted to compensate for this. Collecting evidence from court records means that certain circumstances may be over- and underrepresented, but the use of a range of courts and types of cases mitigates this. No historical data can exactly replicate a modern time-use study, but the work-task approach can get surprisingly close and generate data about many aspects of the early modern economy that have previously been hidden or imperfectly understood.

This book analyses the work tasks recorded in witness statements quantitatively and qualitatively to reconstruct the world of work in early modern England. A number of historians independently developed this type of approach for a range of purposes, time periods, and locations. Social historians such as Laura Gowing, Bernard Capp, and Amanda Flather have demonstrated the rich detail available about work, alongside other topics, in the church court depositions of early modern England.[97] Barbara Hanawalt pioneered the quantitative analysis of activities recorded in coroners' records to examine activities within medieval peasant households.[98] Hans-Joachim Voth used the records of criminal courts to measure the changing timing of the working day and year from 1750 to 1830.[99] Peter Earle used witnesses' descriptions of how they made a living from the preambles found in London court records to look at women's work in the capital from 1665 to 1725.[100] Alexandra Shepard scaled that approach up into a national study of how the women and men of early modern England understood the relationship between wealth, work, and reputation.[101]

96 Voth, *Time and Work*, pp. 18–23. On time-use survey methods, see Gershuny and Sullivan, *What We Really Do*, pp. 5–11; Antonopoulos and Hirway (eds.), *Unpaid Work*, pp. 9–14, 314–21.

97 Gowing, *Domestic Dangers*; Capp, *When Gossips Meet*; Flather, *Gender and Space*.

98 Hanawalt, *Ties That Bound*.

99 Voth, *Time and Work*.

100 Earle, 'Female labour market'.

101 Shepard, *Accounting for Oneself*.

The main inspiration for the current study, however, comes from two studies of gender and work in early modern continental Europe by Sheilagh Ogilvie on south-west Germany and by Maria Ågren and her team on early modern Sweden.[102] Both use a range of court records to quantify work activities and measure the gender division of labour. Ogilvie has explained her method as transforming qualitative into quantitative data, while the Swedish team describe their approach as the 'verb-oriented method'.[103] Our approach incorporates these innovations but adapts them in various ways. Ogilvie combined evidence of work activities with a demographic study to provide a more detailed analysis of a smaller geographical area. We collected more evidence of work over a wider geographical area, but as a consequence are not able to support it with demographic information, other than the national data provided by Wrigley and Schofield.[104] We were more restrictive in the evidence of work we recorded than either Ogilvie or the Swedish team, who for instance collected evidence about property transfers, and general statements about working or being in service. We collected evidence only of specific people doing particular tasks, hence the description of our distinctive method as the work-task approach. This was possible due to the richness of English court depositions and simplifies the analysis by collecting evidence about time-specific work tasks rather than more general ways of making a living. The English records also provide plentiful evidence about the location and timing of work that allow additional dimensions to be explored. We introduce various methodological innovations, such as adjusting figures to compensate for the under-recording of women, recording the 'information status' of work tasks, and work 'for another' in lieu of paid work, as explained in Chapters 1 and 2. Making adjustments allows women's contribution to the economy to be more accurately represented. Recording 'information status' and work 'for another' provides additional information that allows work to be contextualised according to its relationship to the legal case from which it was taken, and in terms of the social relations embodied in the work task.

[102] Ogilvie, *Bitter Living*; Ågren, (ed.), *Making a Living*. Also important were two Exeter University PhDs: Charmian Mansell developed aspects of the work-task methodology for her PhD, now enhanced and published as *Female Servants*; and Nick Collins further developed the work-task approach to include other forms of time-use in his PhD on 'Time-use and gender'.

[103] Carus and Ogilvie, 'Turning qualitative into quantitative evidence'; Fiebranz et al., 'Making verbs count'.

[104] Wrigley and Schofield, *Population History*.

0.5 Book Outline

This introduction has suggested some of the ways that the following chapters can contribute to existing debates about the nature of work in early modern England and offer a richer understanding of the economic and social experience of work. Chapter 1 sets out the methodology of the work-task approach in more detail before providing an overview of the findings. The remaining chapters fall into two parts. Chapters 2 to 4 look at the broad contours of work, while Chapters 5 to 8 examine particular types of work in more depth. The gender of workers is considered throughout.

Chapter 2 focuses on types of workers. It examines how work varied by age and marital status, showing that while men's work remained fairly stable across the lifecycle, women's work varied significantly. Evidence of working 'for another', outside the family household, is analysed in relation to debates about paid work. Evidence of occupations and status indicators are compared with work tasks to address the debates about by-employment and explore the work of labourers and servants. Although women typically lacked such descriptors, some analysis of how wives' activities varied according to their husband's occupations is possible.

Chapter 3 turns to the location of work, examining the spatial dimensions of work on various scales. It begins by looking at regional differences and the contrasts between rural and urban work. The former were remarkably muted, but rural–urban differences are clear. Travel and types of transport are considered as an important element of work largely neglected in existing studies. The final part of the chapter examines workspaces, quantifying inside and outside work and considering the dimension of privacy.

Chapter 4 explores time-use and work intensity. The seasonality of work across the year shows that not only agriculture but other types of work had distinct seasonal patterns. Evidence of the working year, working week, and hours of the day provides new data on much-debated issues and highlights the experiences of women and servants, as well as male householders. This suggests that early modern work patterns were remarkably stable and structured, rather than erratic or lax.

Chapter 5 begins a tour of the variety of work in early modern England by examining the neglected topics of housework and carework. To correct misconceptions, it focuses on the location of these tasks, who performed them, and whether they were paid. This demonstrates that much of this work took place outside the home; housework was most commonly undertaken by young unmarried women rather than married women; and that carework was more often skilled healthcare than childcare, was undertaken predominantly by women, and was typically paid work.

Chapter 6 focuses on agriculture and food processing. Analysis demonstrates that women undertook a little more than a third of agricultural work tasks, doing more work in animal husbandry than arable agriculture but participating widely in both. The work-task approach also allows less well-documented activities such as work on common land to be analysed for the first time. The gender division of labour in agriculture is shown to have been flexible.

Chapter 7 turns to work in crafts and construction, an area of the economy that displayed much sharper distinctions between men's and women's work. It explores the role of apprenticeship in creating these gendered patterns before looking at one male-dominated work area, building and construction, and two in which women were often employed, textile and clothing production. Despite the absence of guilds in the great majority of localities providing evidence, the requirement of apprenticeship in many craft occupations effectively excluded women from those areas of work. Yet women's skilled work in some areas of textile and clothing production, alongside the contributions of non-craftsmen in construction, suggests that specialisation through apprenticeship was just as much about status and prestige, as it was about skill acquisition.

Chapter 8 considers commerce and money management, the second largest category of work in the work-task database. This provides a detailed view of petty commerce, the typically small transactions that took place every day across the country, with women and men almost equally involved. Markets remained the most common locations of commerce, but transactions took place everywhere, including the home, the street, and, occasionally, the specialist retail shop. Evidence of administering debts and pawning goods demonstrates the significant role played by married women in these activities.

The work-task approach allows the everyday work activities of women and men in early modern England to be illuminated in unprecedented detail. Knowledge of these activities serves to revise many widely held assumptions about the early modern economy and the roles of women and men within it.

1 Uncovering the World of Work

In October of 1559 Margaret Grills, a 28-year-old widow, was 'spinning in a certain entrance of Richard Irish at Berry Pomeroy' in south Devon. From her vantage point in this doorway, presumably chosen to maximise the autumnal light available to her as she set about her work, Margaret was able to see into Irish's barn, where she observed his wife Elizabeth and one Joan Myller 'winding [winnowing] of corn'. These two women discussed a rumour that the local gentleman had fathered a child on one of their neighbours, a claim that the implicated neighbour, when she heard of it, deemed defamatory; she subsequently sued Elizabeth Irish for defamation in the church courts. Margaret Grills was called as a witness to the words being spoken, and in the course of her testimony provided the details cited above.[1]

This kind of evidence represents rich raw material for the work-task approach to the history of work, with deponents providing accounts of everyday work activities being undertaken at the time that a defamation, crime, or other legally significant incident took place. From this case alone, it is possible to record an example of spinning, and two instances of women winnowing, as well as contextual information such as the gender and marital status of the actors involved, and the dates and locations of work. By consulting tens of thousands of such depositions, a detailed picture of everyday working life can be constructed. That, in essence, is what this book does. But uncovering broader patterns of work through the collection and analysis of individual work tasks is not as straightforward as it might sound, and it requires a range of careful decisions to be made about precisely what material to consult, and what activities and information to record – or not record – that all have an impact on the picture that emerges. For readers to fully comprehend the results presented in this book, it is important that they are acquainted with those decisions and the particularities of the approach adopted here.

[1] DHC, Chanter 855, 438r–39v.

Whilst the Introduction set out the rationale and underlying principles behind our research methodology, this chapter explains in more detail how these were applied in practice. The first section discusses the types of source material used and the main challenges associated with using them. The chapter then moves on to a detailed account of our methodology for identifying and recording work tasks. This is followed by an overview of the sample of sources used, before a long section discussing the overall results of the study.

1.1 Sources

There is a wide range of sources that verb-oriented methods can and have been applied to, with account books, diaries, petitions, and legal records of various types – from prosecutions for sabbath breaking to disputes over common rights – all containing verb phrases that tell us about the ways individuals made a living.[2] The focus in this study is on records, like the example above, that contain detailed testimony given by individuals in the process of being examined in legal cases. This type of material has several advantages over other records, especially for the pursuit of the work-task variant of the verb-oriented method used here. These testimonies have a narrative element, which means they tend to be fuller and more detailed in the tasks they describe than many other types of record, and often contain richer and more precise contextual information about who was doing tasks, and where and when, than sources such as wage payments in account books. This contextual information plays a major role in the subsequent analysis. They also provide reports of work tasks that the deponent was either a participant in or a direct witness of, rather than a more abstract account of work recorded at a distance from the activities themselves: this makes it possible to establish with greater certainty who undertook specific tasks.

Whilst diaries might meet some of these criteria, legal testimony has the advantage of being far more socially inclusive and plentiful than diary material. The English legal system in the early modern period was not equally accessible to everyone, but participation in the machinery of the courts was remarkably widespread across the social scale. There were fees involved in bringing a case to the courts. Pursuing a defamation case like the one above could result in plaintiff's costs of several pounds, or more than one hundred days' wages for a labourer.[3] When in 1675, John

[2] The Swedish Gender and Work project use a range of these sources, see Ågren (ed.), *Making a Living*; Ogilvie, *Bitter Living*, used records of sabbath breaking.

[3] See Ingram, *Church Courts*, pp. 56–7.

Table 1.1 *Social/occupational status of male deponents in the dataset*

	No of individuals	%
Gentry and professions	109	5.4
Artisans and tradesmen[a]	696	34.3
Yeomen	178	8.8
Husbandmen and agricultural trades	572	28.2
Labourers	219	10.8
Servants and apprentices	204	10.1
Miscellaneous	49	2.4
Total	2027	100.0

[a] Tradesmen = commercial and transport trades.

Cotterell of Salisbury called Mary Bannister 'whore', he taunted her that 'she had not money to begin her suite' against him for defamation.[4] Contemporaries clearly knew that justice was more affordable to some than others. Still, Mary Bannister did manage to bring a suit against Cotterell, and the financial restraints on plaintiffs did not apply in the same way to witnesses: their costs were usually paid by the party that produced them. In the criminal courts such as the quarter sessions, men and women of any social status could be asked to give testimony if they were suspected of or witness to a crime. Whilst the testimony of the poor and of women was seen as less trustworthy than that of middling sort men, being present when an incident took place was the most important factor in determining who was called to give testimony in the courts used in this study.[5] Table 1.1 shows that where it is possible to identify the social profile of male deponents whose testimony is drawn upon in this study – including plaintiffs, defendants, and other witnesses – it is broad based.[6] As female deponents were rarely accorded social or occupational descriptors, the same analysis is not possible for female witnesses, and although the gender profile of witnessing is not balanced, a point returned to below, women do make up a significant proportion of deponents at 27 per cent; they were not excluded from giving testimony.

[4] WSHC, D1/42/61, 99v.

[5] For more on the relationship between gender, wealth, and witnessing, see Shepard, 'Worthless witnesses?'.

[6] These proportions are similar to those found in Alexandra Shepard's study of deponents giving statements of worth in church court records: see Shepard, *Accounting for Oneself*, p. 20. As discussed in Section 2.4 they reflect a similar social structure – at least when we group statuses into primary, secondary, and tertiary sectors – as larger scale attempts to reconstruct the occupational and social structure for this period.

The legal testimony used for this book is drawn from three sources: quarter sessions courts, church courts, and coroners' reports into accidental deaths. All of these have produced an abundance of surviving vignette-style material with a good geographical and chronological spread. The quarter sessions were county-level courts, held four times a year, which oversaw administrative matters such as alehouse licensing and labour legislation, as well as serving as a criminal court. They dealt with less serious offences, or 'misdemeanours', such as thefts and non-lethal acts of violence, although they did at times also try more serious crimes such as murder, which should technically have been referred to higher courts such as the Assizes. The testimony that survives from these courts takes the form of 'examinations': statements that victims, suspects, or witnesses gave before local magistrates as the latter investigated a crime, which were later presented as evidence when the sessions met. They are the magistrate's summary of what the witness said, rather than their verbatim account, but they regularly contain information about everyday activities both related to and incidental to the offence being investigated.[7]

Church courts had an eclectic jurisdiction, dealing with matters as diverse as disciplining clerical offences, arbitrating in disputes over church seating plans, and providing a forum for the settling of local defamation disputes. Officially these were divided into two main strands of business: office cases, brought by the Church against offenders, and instance cases, which were inter-party disputes between members of the community. It was the latter that tended to produce extensive testimonies, as parties called on witnesses to support their claims in disputes over tithe collection, testamentary administration, matrimonial contracts, and defamatory words. These witnesses travelled to the diocesan capital (such as Exeter for the Exeter Diocese) to give testimony to a court official at the cathedral or in a nearby building, though not usually in open court. They responded to a series of questions drawn up by the lawyers – or proctors – of the parties in the case, and their answers were likely taken down in note form before being written up by court officials and signed off by the deponent. Again, they are not verbatim statements, but like quarter sessions examinations those court officials who committed them to paper often included a good deal of quotidian detail that lends itself to the work-task method of analysis.[8]

[7] For more on quarter sessions records, see Court Depositions [website]; French, 'Legal and judicial sources'; Herrup, *Common Peace.* Statements by plaintiffs were sometimes called 'informations' rather than 'examinations', but the latter is used in this book as a short-hand to cover all types of statements given before the quarter sessions.

[8] For more on church court records, see Court Depositions [website]; Gowing, *Domestic Dangers*, ch. 2.

Between them the quarter sessions and church courts provide the overwhelming majority of the testimony drawn upon, but this material is supplemented with a third body of evidence of a different character: coroners' reports.[9] The main point of difference is that these are not depositions given by individuals; rather, they are reports written up by a coroner undertaking an investigation of an accidental death. They do, however, have much in common with the other material, in that they take the form of narrative vignettes of the everyday activities an individual was engaged in at the time of their death, reconstructed by the coroner in consultation with a jury of local men who were tasked with gathering evidence of precisely what had happened from local witnesses. And, of course, accidental deaths could befall anyone, so these reports represent another socially inclusive archive of detailed descriptions of everyday work tasks reported by witnesses.[10]

Finding legal testimonies that describe everyday work tasks in the above sources is not a problem, but that is not the same as saying these sources are not problematic. Historians have long been aware that testimony produced in early modern courts cannot simply be taken at face value; that it was crafted to persuade the judge or jury of a particular version of events rather than representing a disinterested account of 'what really happened'.[11] Still, the stories that deponents told have continued to have an enduring appeal to historians as an access point into the lives of ordinary people in particular, which are not easily recovered through other types of source material, and they continue to be used by researchers, albeit rarely without a prefatory acknowledgement that they are not straightforward accounts of the truth. But a recent body of scholarship has called social historians to account for this approach to depositional sources, in which their mediated element is recognised but then largely set aside; something that scholars 'acknowledge and then ignore'.[12] Frances Dolan, Heather Falvey, and Hillary Taylor have all shown in different ways that a fuller interrogation of the generic conventions, legal processes, and socio-economic structures that shaped the act of giving testimony casts serious doubt on claims that depositions represent expressions of the 'voice' or sentiments of ordinary people.[13]

9 Material from coroners' reports covering the period 1500 to 1600 was generously shared with the project, in transcribed form, by Steven Gunn and Tomasz Gromelski, from their Economic and Social Research Council project 'Everyday Life and Fatal Hazard in Sixteenth Century England'.

10 For more on coroners' reports, see Hanawalt, *Ties that Bound*; Smith, 'Medieval coroners' rolls'.

11 These issues are most famously discussed in Davis, *Fiction in the Archives*.

12 Dolan, *True Relations*, p. 113.

13 Ibid.; Falvey, 'Relating early modern depositions'; Taylor, 'The price of the poor's words'.

This provides a timely reminder to historians to be careful and critical when working with depositional material. For the purposes of this book, some of the issues with these sources are more pertinent than others. They are not used here to try to recover the 'authentic voice' or 'interiority' of a deponent. What they are mined for are accurate accounts of everyday activities. Can we trust that depositions provide this, given that they are in effect stories designed to persuade judges and juries? Part of our approach is to focus on incidental information, rather than the main events of a case; what people were doing at the time of, or in the build-up to, witnessing a crime or an incident. This is less likely to have been wilfully constructed than their accounts of the events at the heart of the case that were being contested by different parties. However, even this information is not always entirely innocent: witnesses – and proctors – may have reached for seemingly incidental details such as 'sitting in a doorway' or 'going to market' as handy narrative devices that gave shape and credence to an account that was in practice more complex or controversial. Witnesses were less likely to report themselves engaging in idleness or activities that were not respectable or legal. Scholars have picked up on the widespread tendency for witnesses to report seeing illicit activities through keyholes or windows, arguing that this was not simply incidental detail but a conventional motif that put the witness at a physical remove from transgressive behaviour whilst being specified in canon law as an acceptable form of proof.[14] Moral and legal discourses combined to help shape the way stories of witnessing-through-holes-in-the-wall were constructed. It is not enough, therefore, to simply ask what the details in a deposition are; we also need to think carefully about why they are there.

Accepting that some seemingly incidental details were included because they contributed to good legal storytelling does not mean that this material is incompatible with the aims of this book. Reflecting on the function of such details in testimonies suggests that they have value whether they were strictly true or not. As Dolan puts it, 'the convention of mentioning the hole through which one witnessed what was happening next door can only function to authorize speech if litigants, defendants, and officers of the court all know that such holes do indeed exist'.[15] In other words, the details provided need to be *plausible* if they are to add legitimacy to a witness' version of events. This plausibility is what makes these accounts valuable, rather than their truthfulness. We aim to recover conventional everyday behaviour: if the stories told needed to sound like conventional everyday working behaviour to persuade judges and juries,

[14] Dolan, *True Relations*, pp. 145–53. [15] Ibid., p. 148.

then they offer valuable evidence, even if some individual instances may not have been true.

This view of depositions as plausible accounts also provides a way around trying to judge between competing narratives of activity given by witnesses and allows the inclusion of more than just incidental details from cases. Alibis provided by individuals accused of a crime, such as a deponent claiming that a sheep they are accused of stealing was in fact bought at market, are not disinterested statements of activity. However, they are plausible vignettes of everyday activity designed to persuade a court and are therefore useful. Rather than trying to determine the truth in these cases, any account that appears to give a plausible version of an everyday work task is useful for reconstructing patterns of work. Particularly important for this book is that a key element of making an account of everyday work activities plausible would have been the gender division of labour described; it would have had to be plausible that a man or woman would have undertaken the task they were reported as doing. It is likely that even untrustworthy testimony is generally reliable with regard to the gender division of labour it reported.

The plausibility principle can be illustrated more clearly by examining some examples that reveal the dynamics behind the construction of false testimony. In June of 1630 Lewis Symons, a labourer of East Brent in Somerset, was examined by a magistrate in a quarter sessions case. Symons told his examiner that he had been offered money by one Richard Rood to 'say and swear when he should be required … that a little before the death of Widow Andridge … he together with one John Bacon [another labourer] … were thrashing in the said Widow's barn' and at that time heard the said Widow say to her servant that she had left all of her estate barring 40s to the said Rood. Symons refused the offer, and neither he nor Bacon had ever undertaken any threshing for Widow Andridge: it was a ruse on Rood's part, and that was the cause of a case being brought against him. The case demonstrates the prospect of false accounts of work tasks appearing in the archives. In this specific instance we would not have recorded them as no witness in the case claimed it to be a true account. But it is safe to assume that Rood thought this account – that two labouring men might undertake this work activity, threshing, for a third party, the widow, in a barn – was plausible enough that it would stand up to scrutiny in a testamentary case if he had persuaded the men to swear to it.[16] If they had taken the bribe, we would have recorded it as a work task.

[16] SHC, Q/SR/62, 37.

Defendants were certainly conscious of the need to be plausible. When the butcher John Syms was accused of stealing sheep in Ditcheat, Somerset, in 1638, he admitted under examination that he had initially lied to the local constable when questioned on where he had obtained six lambs in his possession. He had told the constable that he 'bought the said lambs of one Bennett of Glastonbury' because 'he was afraid that if he should have told him that he had them so far off he should have been suspected to have stolen them'. Syms had, or so he claimed, bought the lambs unusually far from home, and thought the truth would therefore sound more suspicious than a lie. He rendered his account so it would be truer to everyday work experiences, even though this technically falsified it.[17] These contextual details could be challenged in court if they were deemed dubious by other parties in a case. In a defamation case heard in the Winchester diocesan church courts in 1585, the fuller Edward Potter claimed to have overheard the exchange of defamatory words whilst 'sitting in his shop at work and seeing and looking upon the said parties' in their neighbouring garden. But other witnesses were prepared to depose that it was 'not possible' for Potter to have seen the exchange if he had been working in his shop, given the angles involved and the position of his window. If an account did have a whiff of implausibility about it, it could undermine the testimony.[18]

If the reliability of legal testimony can to a certain extent be overcome by a focus on plausibility rather than truth, there are still other issues with the source material that need to be considered. The most important of these is that different courts, and different types of cases, each have inherent biases towards recording certain forms of work and not others. Most obviously, many quarter sessions examinations arise from contexts in which crimes took place, and therefore tasks undertaken in especially 'criminogenic' contexts, such as in alehouses or at night, may be over-represented relative to their actual occurrence. It is not only criminal records that present such issues. The most common type of case in the church courts was tithe disputes, and as these usually focused on disagreements about the quantity of tithe corn due, this material provides a particularly high concentration of observations of related harvest work tasks. The result is that church court records capture twice the proportion of agricultural work compared to the quarter sessions material. Coroners' reports are much more likely to include accounts of dangerous activities, such as cutting down trees, driving carts, or fetching water, than they are of low-risk tasks that were less likely to result in accidental

[17] SHC, Q/SR/77, 52. [18] HRO, 21M63/C3/9, 257–8, 278–82.

deaths. There can also be regional quirks to the records. A particular concern with paternity cases in the Cheshire quarter sessions, for instance, can make the midwifery that was often occurring whilst a mother-in-labour was being examined about the identity of a baby's father appear more prevalent in that county than elsewhere. Sheep theft cases were very common in the south-west of England; associated activities such as skinning and butchering the stolen sheep are therefore more likely to occur in the records of this region (although this probably reflects the local economy more than a high number of midwives delivering babies did in Cheshire). Another concern is that activities that took place in more public contexts, where they were more likely to be witnessed, may be reported more often than tasks done alone, or in more private spaces. In short, the nature of work that emerges from the depositions is shaped in a number of ways by the court, case, and context from which those depositions emerge. The danger is that the pattern of work uncovered significantly overrepresents certain tasks relative to their actual occurrence in everyday life.

It is not possible to overcome these concerns entirely, and even modern time-use studies are not able to capture work patterns with infallible accuracy, despite using custom-designed survey material. It is possible, however, to take measures that tackle the most egregious forms of overrepresentation and help to ensure that the data collected have a meaningful relationship with actual patterns of work. Crucial is the fact that our results are drawn from a range of courts, and within those courts a range of different case types. An approach that relied entirely on criminal cases would find it difficult to avoid work activities that took place in criminogenic contexts being overrepresented. But, as discussed in Section 1.3, just over half of the work tasks recorded for this study are drawn from the quarter sessions; the rest come from other courts that do not have the same inherent biases. Within the church courts material comes primarily from four types of cases: defamation, tithe, matrimonial, and testamentary. Each have their own inherent biases, but they are very different. For instance, whilst tithe cases are likely to involve examples of harvest work in the fields, testamentary cases are more likely to include care for a dying person in a private chamber. The relationship between different types of courts, cases, and types of work is shown in more detail in Appendix A. The full range of cases drawn upon is shown in Table 1.4, but it is a varied combination that together provides access to work done in a wide variety of contexts. The data captures work undertaken in both public and private spaces. It captures work done in social contexts, but also undertaken alone: an accidental death could happen to an individual working alone, for instance, and a defendant in a theft case might provide an alibi of working by themself. Roughly half of the tasks in the dataset were tasks witnesses reported themselves doing, and the other half were activities reported by someone else. This means not all tasks took place when people were being observed by others. It also mitigates concerns that witnesses may have avoided reporting themselves doing activities that were not seen as respectable: witnesses of the activities of others, who were often opponents in a legal case, would not have been constrained to the same extent. This also applies to tasks that were not technically legal, such as undertaking craft work without an apprenticeship or providing certain forms of healthcare without a license.

Drawing on a range of cases that originate in a range of contexts provides multiple perspectives on the world of work, rather than one view heavily distorted by the characteristics of a particular genre of testimony. That said, it is not as simple as the inherent biases of different types of cases 'balancing' each other out, and issues still remain. Other mechanisms have been used where certain activities were being significantly overrepresented in certain types of cases: a series of exclusions and filters that will be explained in more detail in the next section. Certain activities have been excluded from the data because including them would have overwhelmed the material collected. Theft is the most obvious example, but the same applies to the work of clergymen and local officials, and a fuller list of examples is discussed below. There are other types of work that are underrepresented in the material. Childcare, for instance, was often undertaken simultaneously with other tasks and therefore not always mentioned by witnesses as the primary task they were involved in when an incident occurred. Spinning is another. Witnesses, and especially female witnesses, often described themselves as sitting in doorways 'at their work'. It is highly likely many of these women were spinning, as in the example that opened this section, but the term 'work' is not sufficiently specific for inclusion in the dataset. It is much more difficult to devise mechanisms that deal with this underrepresentation of certain tasks than it is to tackle forms of overrepresented activity. As a result, the patterns of work presented and discussed in this book cannot be said to fully capture every aspect of the experience of work in early modern England.[19]

In summary, the material at the heart of this study presents a number of challenges when it comes to recovering the world of work. Nonetheless, the work-task approach still provides the most effective methodology

[19] This issue is returned to in the book's Conclusion.

for capturing the most common forms of work activity in this period that is currently available to historians, and its careful application can produce results that provide a close approximation of real patterns of work. The next section provides a detailed account of the guidelines that were used in the collection and recording of our data.

1.2 Methodology

1.2.1 Criteria for Recording Work Activities

In important ways the work-task approach used in this book differs from the pioneering works of Ogilvie and Ågren et al. that first developed the verb-oriented method. For instance, whilst Ågren's Gender and Work project looks for verb phrases that indicate the use of time with the goal of making a living, we adopt a relatively narrow focus on descriptions of specific individuals engaged in specific tasks.[20] Examples such as 'running a farm', or 'working in service', which the Gender and Work project would include, are excluded here. These examples obscure as much as they reveal. An individual described as 'running a farm' may rely on others to carry out agricultural tasks – to manage the farm accounts, to take its goods to market, and to sell them. It reveals relatively little about who does what tasks on that farm. Likewise with 'working in service': this could cover a range of activities from agricultural labour to housework and selling goods at market that represent very different types of work. By focusing this study on evidence of specific individuals actively engaged in specific tasks, a clearer sense emerges of who is actually doing what at the everyday level, recording individuals caught in the (work) act. We describe this as the work-task approach, and as a variant of the broader verb-oriented method.

To apply this approach, quarter sessions examinations, church court depositions, and coroners' reports were searched for work tasks that met the criteria of (a) a specific individual (b) professing to have done or observed doing (c) a specified work task:

(a) a specific individual

As a minimum requirement for an individual to be recorded their gender needed to be known, given the importance of examining the gender division of labour. Any other information (name, age, marital status, etc.) was recorded when supplied, but was not essential. It was also necessary to be confident that the

[20] Ågren (ed.), *Making a Living*, p. 13.

individual had engaged in the work task themselves, rather than engaging someone else to do it for them. For instance, a farmer in a tithe dispute might refer to 'growing oats on his land', but that would not be sufficient evidence that he himself either sowed or harvested the oats: he could possibly have paid others to do all of these tasks, and therefore statements such as this were not included.

(b) professing to have done or observed doing
As discussed above, the crucial point is that we were not looking for definitive proof that an individual undertook a task, only that there was a *plausible* account of them doing so. For example, in 1598 one Thomasine Weather, of Uplowman in Devon, was accused of having stolen a sheep, but claimed that she could not have done so because at the time of the crime she had been elsewhere. She deposed that:

> upon Thursday was fortnight about five of the clock in the afternoon, she went forth from her mother's house to fetch a burden of wood, who went for the same to one Henry Burnard's ground called the Butte Moore about a quarter of a mile off, and then returned home again about six of the clock in the same night, and after that stayed in her mother's house all night.[21]

True or not – and it seems from other witness statements in the case that it may not have been, as they all had different versions of precisely when she had gone out and come back, and what sort of wood she had gathered – this would nonetheless be recorded as a plausible account of a work activity: fetching wood.

(c) a specified work task
Following Margaret Reid's third-party criterion, any activity that could be substituted with purchased goods or services qualified as a work task. Such tasks needed to be specific, such as spinning, mowing, or collecting water, rather than a more general description such as 'service' or 'labouring' that could encompass any range of tasks. Another illustrative example highlights how this applied in practice. When Alice Kingston, of Exeter, Devon, deposed in a church court tithe case in 1634, she said that she:

> did live with Mr Street late of St Edmund's parish three years and half or thereabout ended now about a year since, and in that time the said Mr Streete did keep three milk kine [cows] which commonly all the summer time did pasture upon the grounds of [Mr] Joanes in every the said years … and saith that this deponent hath divers times in the said years milked the said kine in the grounds called the shillowes.[22]

Here Alice Kingston would be recorded as a specified individual, professing to have done a specific work task, milking cows. Nothing else would be recorded. Mr Street may have helped to secure a living by 'keeping three milk cows', but there is not enough evidence here to say what tasks, if any, he was involved in as a result. He may simply have owned them, and paid others, such as Alice Kingston, to do the specifics of 'keeping' them. Mr Jones may have taken cows in to pasture

[21] DHC, QS/4/Box 5, Epiphany, 62. [22] DHC, Chanter 866, *March v. Joanes*.

on his land as a way of making a living but again, the deposition is not sufficiently explicit what specific tasks this involved him in for any task by Mr Jones to be recorded.

1.2.2 *Exclusions and 'Information Status'*

Whilst some verb phrases are excluded for not being specific enough, other types of activity have been excluded due to concerns that they would otherwise be drastically overrepresented in the database. The most significant of these exclusions is criminal activity, not because it was not often a form of work, but because it would have been the largest category of work tasks in the dataset given its prominence in the quarter sessions in particular. For similar reasons we also excluded the performance of any form of office-holding, including the official duties of constables and the clergy, because of the regularity with which these appeared in the legal records. For instance, constables searching for stolen goods, or clergymen performing divine service, are frequently referenced in theft and clerical misconduct cases, respectively. Any activities that constituted part of the legal process itself were also excluded due to their intrinsic overrepresentation in the legal sources: this includes activities such as the drawing up of wills in testamentary cases and any duties undertaken by an executor in the process of administering a will; any fetching of witnesses to wills or marriage contracts or any other contract or payment central to the case, or fetching of people to discuss the central features of a case with them, or fetching of suitors in matrimonial cases; the writing, witnessing, discussion of bonds, contracts, and debts when these are central to the case itself.

Other activities were excluded on the grounds of being intrinsic to certain types of commonly occurring cases. For instance, the preparation of tithe corn for collection, and its collection, was excluded as this would have been significantly overrepresented by the large number of tithe cases in the church court records. Similarly, the delivery, exchange, or purchase of gifts in matrimonial cases are excluded. The principle here was to try and avoid the overrepresentation of tasks that were not routine or typical work activities, such as making a will; searching a house for stolen goods; buying wedding gifts; burying a corpse; collecting tithe payments; giving a sermon; and ministers or officials carrying out duties. That is not to say that unusual or rare work tasks were not recorded, or that we do not see these tasks as work. Instead, excluding these relatively unusual activities that appear prominently in the records was important to producing a set of results that captured something closer to the common experience of everyday working life.[23]

[23] A full list of what was included/excluded can be supplied by the authors on request.

Certain types of tasks that were recorded are still likely to be overrepresented. For example, buying and selling frequently appears in theft cases as these activities are given as plausible alternatives to accusations of theft. Yet these were included because, unlike the examples above, the buying and selling of goods undoubtedly were routine and typical work activities, and the material provides valuable contextual detail about everyday forms of commerce. To deal with this type of task, another mechanism was adopted that helps control for the overrepresentation of certain activities without excluding them entirely: each work task recorded was assigned an 'information status'.[24] Where the work was mentioned simply in passing and had nothing to do with the central matter of the case, for instance if a deponent was weeding in a field when they overheard defamatory words exchanged by two passers-by, the task was recorded as 'incidental' information. Where a work activity was at the centre of a case, and its occurrence itself was either in dispute or closely connected to a criminal activity that was the subject of a case, such tasks were recorded as 'integral' information. Common examples include accounts of having bought goods that an individual had been accused of stealing, and individuals conducting legitimate work tasks with stolen goods, such as boiling stolen mutton. Such activities were recorded in the deposition because of their significance in the case, and they are therefore much more likely to be overrepresented in that type of case than entirely 'incidental' tasks.

A third status of 'related' information was also used for instances that fell somewhere between the first two. A common example of this comes from tithe cases, such as the one discussed above of milking cows, where an activity was not the central matter of the case or under dispute itself but did have some bearing on the case. If an individual gave evidence that they knew how much tithe corn their master should pay because they had helped to reap their master's corn that summer, it was the value of tithe due that was under dispute, not the activity of reaping the corn itself. Such tasks are not the central matter in tithe cases, but their recording is not completely incidental; they are likely to be heavily represented in that type of case but not to the extent that integral activities are. This classification allows analysis to filter out, where necessary, work tasks that still appear to be overrepresented by certain types of court cases even after the above exclusions have been applied.

[24] In theory we could have done this for activities we excluded, such as crime and office-holder duties, but it would have been so time-consuming to record every instance of those in the database that our overall sample of other types of work would have been considerably smaller.

It is also important to highlight the approach taken to 'verbs of command', those instances when an individual orders or asks another individual to do something, not least because the approach here differs from other projects that have used the verb-oriented method. For instance, in 1598 Edmund Bishop of Culmstock, Devon, deposed that Matthew Foxe 'willed him' to deliver a heffer to Tiverton.[25] In this study the delivery of the heffer would have been recorded as a work task, but 'will another to deliver heffer' on the part of Matthew Foxe would not have been. This is because there is not enough detail here about what this 'willing' involved above and beyond a speech-act, which does not easily fit within the third-party criterion. This applies where all we have is the verb of command attached to the individual doing the ordering. However, in instances where ordering/asking takes place and there is contextual detail about someone expending time and energy going somewhere to arrange something, this has been included as a work task. In other words, for it to be a work task a verb of command has to be accompanied by another verb that denotes evidence of time-use above and beyond a speech-act. This also helps to clarify that the commander has personally engaged in the task, whereas a command without this could in theory have been communicated by sending another to pass on the instruction. This approach allows the recording of some instances of this type of managerial work, without the requirement to record every, very frequently recorded and often quite abstract, verb of command as a work task.

1.2.3 *Information Recorded in the Work-Task Database*

When an activity met the above criteria, as much detail as possible was recorded about the case, the individuals involved, and the context in which the activity took place. First, a variety of archival information and references were recorded, including the type of case and the county it took place in. Then information was recorded about the actors and witnesses involved in a task. Where it was provided, and almost all the following categories were unevenly recorded across the sources, their name, gender, marital status, parish of residence, and age were noted. Their relationship to the task was recorded (whether they were the actor who performed the task, a witness of it, or both) and any occupational or status descriptors accorded to them, something that allows us to compare occupational titles with the work tasks an individual actually engaged in.

[25] DHC, QS/4/Box 5, Epiphany, 68.

With regard to the task itself, a transcription was recorded in the database of the relevant passage of the deposition describing the task. This was converted into a standardised task, usually in the verb-noun format such as 'milk cow' or 'plough field', which was entered and then assigned to an overarching work category, such as agriculture and land, or commerce, and a subcategory within that. As much information as possible was recorded about the date and time at which it took place, as well as the parish and any more specific information about the task's location. All tasks in the dataset were then categorised as taking place either in the actor's 'own household' or 'outside the household', or as 'unknown' where this was not clear. 'Own household' represented the person performing the task's house of residence, so a servant working in a master's household would have been recorded as 'own household'. 'Own household' included outbuildings, yards, and gardens, not just work inside of a house itself. 'Outside the household' included work done on, or inside, the premises of someone else, and is not therefore strictly a measure of working 'outside', though all of these tasks took individuals away from their own home and grounds. The task was assigned an 'information status', as explained above, and we recorded whether the task was done 'for another' and if so the nature of that relationship including if it was paid work, or part of service, if this was specified. We also recorded information about rates of pay, or the values of goods in a commercial exchange. Taken together this information allows for analysis of the ways in which both women's and men's work was structured by age, seasonality, location, time, employment relations, and so forth, as well as by gender.

1.3 Sample

The material that the above methodology was applied to was drawn from three regions of England: the south-west, the north, and the east. These were chosen to represent a range of landscapes, agricultural economies, and industries. For each region a sample was taken of quarter sessions material, church court depositions, and coroners' records, focused on a selection of counties from that region. Not all types of records survived for every county studied, so the proportion of tasks recorded from each type of court is not balanced geographically, as Table 1.2 demonstrates. For quarter sessions and church courts, roughly one-year-in-ten was sampled. This meant that one year's worth of sessions per decade, or one deposition book per decade, for periods where the records survived, was consulted, though in practice this was often adapted depending on the extent of detail in, and survival and chronological coverage of, each collection. For coroners' records all surviving reports for that county from

Table 1.2 *Overview of the sample*

	Population in 1600	Task total	People per task	Quarter sessions tasks	Quarter sessions dates	Church court tasks	Church court dates	Coroners' reports tasks	Coroners' reports dates
South-West									
Cornwall	100,064	35	2859	7	1610–1680	27	1557–1597	1	1516
Devon	261,534	1449	180	870	1594–1700	560	1555–1692	19	1515–1598
Hampshire	105,384	578	182	0	n/a	529	1532–1632	49	1509–1599
Somerset	170,910	169	101	1223	1600–1699	395	1532–1694	76	1512–1600
Wiltshire	116,475	750	155	346	1602–1693	317	1550–1678	87	1504–1598
South-West Total	754,367	4506	167	2446		1828		232	
East									
Cambridgeshire	73,318	376	195	141	1632–1664[a]	123	1555–1598	112	1523–1600
Hertfordshire	58,766	433	136	169	1589–1695	183	1549–1612	81	1501–1599
Lincolnshire	175,173	489	358	373	1618–1699	0	n/a	114	1509–1599
Norfolk	173,113	1195	145	700	1591–1687	328	1555–1700	169	1521–1599
Northamptonshire	93,113	241	386	123	1658–1699	0	n/a	118	1509–1599
East Total	573,483	2734	210	1506		634		594	
North									
Cheshire	74,738	557	134	471	1581–1692	86	1551–1695	0	n/a
Durham	77,355	151	512	0	n/a	151	1555–1662	0	n/a
Lancashire	183,692	541	340	521	1606–1697	20	1558–1694[b]	0	n/a
Yorkshire	369,781	1161	319	510	1660–1700[c]	391	1553–1694	260	1508–1600
North Total	705,566	2410	293	1502		648		260	

Notes: These numbers are based on the county the case came to court in. Some tasks took place in a different county, but the numbers of these are very small. Dates are based on earliest and latest tasks recorded from each county, and therefore covered by the data, and not necessarily the earliest and latest depositions consulted. Where a task took place much earlier than the year of the earliest deposition from a county; for example, when a task from 20 years ago was remembered, they have been excluded from the date range to avoid confusion over the years covered by those courts. Populations from Wrigley, *Early English Censuses*.

[a] Cambridgeshire quarter sessions from Isle of Ely jurisdiction only.

[b] Lancashire church court tasks were recorded in the Chester diocesan records.

[c] Yorkshire quarter sessions from North Riding and West Riding jurisdictions only.

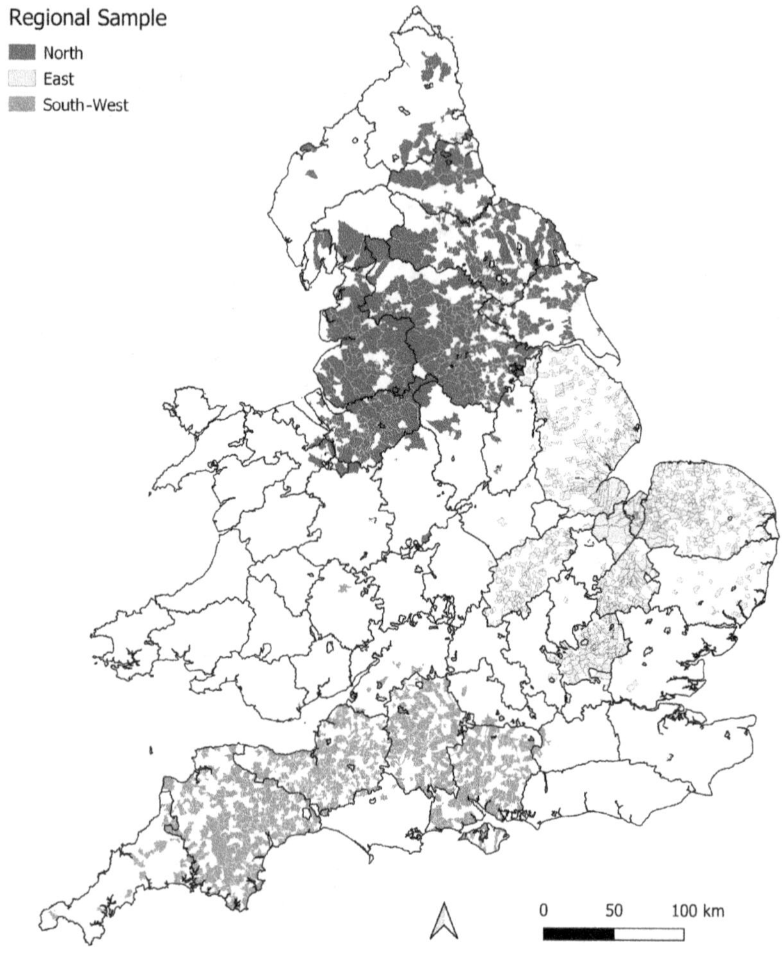

Figure 1.1 Geographical distribution of tasks in the dataset.
Notes: Highlighted parishes are those from which the work-task dataset records at least one task.

the period 1500 to 1600 were consulted.[26] Approximately 40,000 depositions were read in total, which yielded a dataset of 9,650 work tasks.

The geographical spread of work tasks recorded is also displayed in Figure 1.1, which indicates each parish from which at least one work task was recorded. The activities come from 1,918 different parishes,

[26] This was the scope of the material provided by the 'Everyday Life and Fatal Hazard in Sixteenth-Century England' project.

Table 1.3 *Tasks by court, region, and time period*

	Tasks	%	% by F
Court			
Quarter sessions examinations	5,454	56.5	29.4
Church court depositions	3,110	32.2	27.8
Coroners' reports	1,086	11.3	19.8
Total	9,650	100.0	27.8
Region			
South-West	4,506	46.7	29.1
North	2,410	25.0	29.3
East	2,734	28.3	24.5
Total	9,650	100.0	27.8
Period			
1500–1549	457	4.7	15.5
1550–1599	2,455	25.4	23.9
1600–1649	3,261	33.8	31.0
1650–1700	3,477	36.0	29.3
Total	9,650	99.9	27.8

meaning roughly 20 per cent of all English parishes are represented in the database. The vast majority of these were rural parishes or modest market towns, though a small percentage of tasks, at 8 per cent, occurred in large towns or cities, which roughly reflects the percentage of the population of these counties that would have lived in larger urban areas, as is discussed further in Section 3.2. Specifically, urban courts, such as borough courts, were consciously avoided for sampling precisely because we wanted the sample to be representative of the actual rural and urban division of work in this way, which using specifically urban material would have undermined.

Table 1.3 shows how the tasks are distributed across court type, region, and period, as well as the proportion of tasks undertaken by women in each part of the sample. Just over half of the sample is drawn from quarter sessions examinations, about one-third from the church courts, and just over one-tenth from coroners' reports. This largely has to do with 'hit rates' – the percentage of depositions from a given collection that contain a work task. These vary considerably across court types, as well as from collection to collection, and even sample year to sample year, but in general they are much higher in the quarter sessions where as many as 70 per cent of examinations contain recordable work tasks. In the church courts the number is more often between 10 and 15 per cent of depositions. In other words, it is much more labour intensive to find work activities in the church courts than in the quarter sessions. Hit rates were also higher for the south-west collections than for the north

Table 1.4 *Tasks by case type*

	Tasks	%	% by F
Theft	3,906	40.5	26.5
Tithe	1,117	11.6	10.8
Accidental death	1,086	11.3	19.8
Miscellaneous[a]	713	7.4	24.3
Defamation	688	7.1	41.6
Unclear	593	6.1	26.1
Testamentary	478	5.0	35.1
Paternity	288	3.0	71.9
Matrimonial	252	2.6	43.3
Physical assault	234	2.4	30.8
Rape/sexual assault	79	0.8	70.9
Adultery	74	0.8	59.5
Witchcraft	68	0.7	38.2
Murder	41	0.4	31.7
Church seating	33	0.3	18.2
Total	9,650	100.0	27.8

[a] This includes cases where multiple offences were being examined, for example, a string of complaints against one individual, as well as a range of other single offences ranging from unlicensed ale-selling to clergy misconduct to sabbath breaking.

and east, and the surviving material was also more abundant and detailed, hence why it comprises the largest regional sample. The paucity of activities for the first half of the sixteenth century is a consequence of the fact that only coroners' reports provide full coverage for this period. Church court material survives in good quantities from the mid-sixteenth century onwards and quarter sessions material from the beginning of the seventeenth century onwards. The coroners' reports used only cover the sixteenth century.[27] It is also important to note, as Table 1.2 shows, that the proportion of each type of court material used for each region varied, again due to hit rates and survival. This is important to bear in mind when comparing the findings for each region.

Table 1.4 shows the types of cases across all the courts that have yielded the most work activities. Theft cases from the quarter sessions produced just over 40 per cent of all tasks in the database, by far the largest proportion from any case type. This undoubtedly has a significant effect on the data and is discussed further in the results section below.

[27] This is because the coroners' data we used came from Steve Gunn's project, which focused on the sixteenth century, but it is also the case that coroners' reports become less detailed for the seventeenth century.

Beyond theft cases work tasks were collected from a varied mix of case types and therefore contexts. Table 1.4 also demonstrates the types of cases in which women's work activities are most likely to be recorded. The relationship between certain categories of work and types of cases is shown in Appendix A.

Overall, these tables show that the data is not evenly spread between cases, courts, regions or over time, and these imbalances need to be kept in mind in the analysis of patterns of work that follows. That said, they also show that the dataset has a good range across the country, the period, and types of cases, allowing multiple avenues of enquiry.

1.4 Results

1.4.1 Categories of Work

To aid analysis, the 9,650 work tasks are sorted into nine main categories and 62 subcategories. Decisions about categorisation can have a significant impact on the overall shape of the results. An activity such as milking, for example, could be placed in either the category of agriculture and land or that of food processing. It involves working closely with animals and might therefore be seen as a form of animal husbandry, a branch of agriculture; but it is also closely related to dairying, which sits within the broader category of food processing. As milking was almost exclusively a female activity, placing milking within the category of agriculture, as we chose to, is more likely to challenge existing perceptions of women's work, increasing the proportion of women's work in agriculture, whereas placing it in food processing would have reinforced them by placing milking alongside activities such as dairying and brewing which early modern advice books conventionally allotted to women. Threshing provides a similar example: an almost exclusively male activity, it is normally placed within agriculture. However, as it prepares grain for consumption it can equally be considered a form of food processing, which is how we categorised it.

Given the complexity of categorisation, especially when converting qualitative sources into quantitative data, we were initially reluctant to impose fixed categories onto the tasks in the dataset, favouring instead a flexible approach driven by different principles for different parts of the analysis.[28] At times in this book the tasks have been reworked into different categories where there was a good case for doing so, and this is made

[28] Carus and Ogilvie, 'Turning qualitative into quantitative evidence'.

explicit when it occurs. In general, however, it was deemed more practical to develop a set of fixed categories to make the results coherent and intelligible. The resulting categories are intended to be meaningful and useful to historians, reflecting existing sub-fields in the history of work such as agriculture, commerce, and housework. At the same time, we have also sought to consciously challenge some of the assumptions that underlie these categories, especially with regard to gender stereotypes, as the examples of milking and threshing demonstrate. Food processing has been consciously separated from housework, with which it is frequently confused, because goods produced were often intended for sale, despite being seen as forms of women's housewifery.[29] That said, we also include activities within the broader housework category that could be commercialised, such as laundry and food and drink provision. It is important therefore for readers to look carefully at our list of subcategories to see what goes where.[30]

Each task recorded was placed in a single category and subcategory for ease of analysis, although this could be a complex decision in many cases. Work activities that involved movement were particularly challenging. For example, an individual 'carting barley' could simply be taking it from the fields to a barn, which would logically fall in the category of agriculture. But if they were moving it over a longer distance, say to a market, this might be more appropriately categorised as transport. Contextual information in the case was used to determine the precise character of such tasks, but where the context was unclear a set of guidelines was followed to ensure that the same type of task was consistently recorded in the same subcategory and category. Chapters 5 to 8 interrogate the meanings of categories by examining the constituent tasks within them. Here we look at an overview of the results when arranged into the nine broad categories.

1.4.2 The Gender Division of Labour

Table 1.5 sorts the 9,650 work tasks recorded into the nine main categories and shows the gender division of labour in each category. What is immediately striking is that women undertook between 16.8 per cent and 69.9 per cent of tasks in every category. Whilst the gender division of labour was uneven across these categories, there was no main area of the

29 Whittle, 'Critique of approaches'.

30 A full list of subcategories and categories can be seen in Appendix B. A more detailed guide of what tasks were placed in each subcategory is available from the authors on request.

Table 1.5 *Gender division of labour by category, unadjusted*

	F tasks	M tasks	Total tasks	% by F
Agriculture and land	473	2,162	2,635	18.0
Carework	368	196	564	65.2
Commerce	556	1,559	2,115	26.3
Crafts and construction	206	736	942	21.9
Food processing	131	476	607	21.6
Housework	523	225	748	69.9
Management	172	473	645	26.7
Transport	208	1029	1237	16.8
Other	49	108	157	31.2
Total	2,686	6,964	9,650	27.8

economy from which women's work was absent. Arguably the most significant figure in Table 1.5 is that only 27.8 per cent of all the tasks recorded were performed by women. This clearly undermines any claim that these results have a meaningful correlation with actual patterns of work, unless we were to accept that women did considerably less work than men and had more leisure time. Given that the work-task methodology records unpaid as well as paid work, and work performed both inside and outside of the home, important forms of women's work are not systematically excluded in the way that an exclusive focus on paid work would do. Modern time-use studies of non-industrialised nations that use the third-party criterion of work adopted here produce results in which women do slightly more than half of all work recorded.[31] It would be reasonable to expect to find a similar pattern in pre-industrial England.

The main reason women's work is under-recorded is the gender imbalance in witnesses of work tasks. The tasks in the database were reported by 3,893 different witnesses, with the average witness–both male and female–reporting 2.2 work tasks each.[32] But 73 per cent of those witnesses were male. As roughly half of tasks, at 53 per cent, were self-reported – that is, undertaken by the witness themselves – having a higher proportion of male than female witnesses produces a gender imbalance in the self-reported activities in the database. But the problem

31 Whittle and Hailwood, 'Gender division'. The same is also true of industrialised nations, but the figure is slightly higher for non-industrial nations.

32 Coroners' reports have not been included in this analysis of witnesses, as we just have the coroners' overall account rather than information disaggregated by witness. Witness here means the witness of a work activity, so it includes plaintiffs, defendants, as well as witnesses who were not a main party in the case.

goes deeper than that. Taking only those activities where a witness was reporting someone else doing the work task, very different patterns of reporting for male and female witnesses are evident. When male witnesses reported the work of others, 75 per cent of the activities they reported were done by men, and just 25 per cent done by women. When female witnesses reported the work of others, 50 per cent of activities reported were done by men and 50 per cent were done by women. In other words, female witnesses reported an even amount of men's and women's work, but male witnesses reported far more men's work than women's work.

One possible explanation could be that everyday working life was to a certain extent segregated by gender, so men were less likely to encounter women at work in the course of their day.[33] But that does not sit well with the fact that women witnessed plenty of men at work during their everyday activities. Another explanation is that male witnesses had a tendency to overlook women's work, or at least to underreport it, in their testimony. In January of 1611 Peter Joseph of Crediton, Devon, was spotted wearing a fashionable new falling band collar. His neighbours had a similar item stolen from them and asked Joseph how he had acquired it. He told them he had bought it from Christian Slee, the wife of a Crediton cordwainer. When Slee was herself subsequently examined, she partially confirmed his story: the falling band had been purchased from her, but she had 'sold the same to the foresaid Peter Joseph's wife for 12d', not directly to Peter Joseph.[34] Wilfully or not, Joseph had obscured the work of his wife in his own testimony, claiming a work task undertaken by a member of his household as his own. In a 1680s testamentary dispute from the Devon village of East Anstey two witnesses were asked to describe the role that John Wood's wife had played in managing their household. John Avery, a gentleman, told the court that 'Mrs Wood was very little entrusted with the management of her said husband's concerns save in the necessary management of the household affairs incumbent on woman to manage', but he provided no further details. Mary Thorne, wife to a yeoman, concurred that Mrs Woods 'was not entrusted nor did concern herself with the management of her said husband's estate or outdoor affairs only with the necessary affairs of housekeeping incumbent of a wife to look after', but went on to add 'as the taking care to provide meat and other necessaries for the family and the making of butter and cheese and such like'.[35] As in many other cases,

[33] Flather, *Gender and Space*, ch.3, explores this question, as do Sections 3.4 and 4.2.
[34] DHC, QS/4/Box 16, Easter, Exam of Christian Slee.
[35] DHC, Chanter 8299, 22v–28v.

Table 1.6 *Gender division of labour by category, female multiplier applied*

	F tasks	M tasks	Total tasks	% by F	F tasks adj.	% by F adj.
Agriculture and land	473	2,162	2,635	18.0	1,225	36.2
Carework	368	196	564	65.2	953	82.9
Commerce	556	1,559	2,115	26.3	1,440	48.0
Crafts and construction	206	736	942	21.9	534	42.0
Food processing	131	476	607	21.6	339	41.6
Housework	523	225	748	69.9	1,355	85.8
Management	172	473	645	26.7	445	48.5
Transport	208	1,029	1,237	16.8	539	34.4
Other	49	108	157	31.2	127	54.0
	2,686	6,964	9,650	27.8	6,957	50.0

Notes: adj. = adjusted (x2.59).

here the female witness was more forthcoming with a detailed description of women's work than a male counterpart who described women's work in a general, unspecific manner.

Thus, there are clearly gendered patterns to the information provided by witnesses. Even if there were an equal number of male and female witnesses in the sample, and it would be possible to apply a multiplier to the data to create this effect, there would still be a much higher number of male than female activities in the dataset due to men's tendency to overwhelmingly report the work of other men, in a way that women did not do for other women.[36] Instead, it is possible to apply a different form of multiplier. Making the conservative assumption that at least 50 per cent of all work was undertaken by women, a multiplier can be applied that increases the total number of female work tasks to be the same as men's. That multiplier, 2.59, can then be applied to the totals for each category. This creates an overall gender division of labour of 50:50. This adjustment relies on the simple assumption that if we were to continue collecting data using the same proportions of each source type, but only of work tasks done by women, until we had an equal number of male and female tasks, those extra tasks would be distributed across the categories in the same proportion as the current sample. The results of applying this multiplier can be seen in Table 1.6.

[36] This type of multiplier is explored in Whittle and Hailwood, 'Gender division', pp. 12–3.

This represents a more realistic picture of the actual gender division of labour across the different sectors of the early modern English rural economy. The figures show that women undertook at least a third of the work activities undertaken in each category. They dominated care-work and housework, as might be expected, but they were not confined to such work. Women did almost half of the recorded commercial work, food processing, crafts and construction work, and management activities, whilst also playing a significant role in agriculture and transport. Precisely what work men and women undertook within each of these broader categories form the subject of much of the rest of this book, and Appendix B presents the data broken down into our subcategories, including both our raw data and an 'adjusted' percentage of activities undertaken by women in each subcategory for which the multiplier has been applied. These subcategories reveal a more pronounced gender division of labour in relation to certain types of activity than the main categories capture. However, only six out of 62 subcategories are gender exclusive (hedging, mill maintenance, woodwork, tobacco processing – all gendered male; dairying; miscellaneous housework – gendered female), and only a further 13 are highly gendered, with more than 90 per cent of activities done by one gender. Over two-thirds of the subcategories have a relatively mixed-gender division of labour.

1.4.3 Work Repertoires

In addition to revealing the gender division of labour in relation to different types of work, the dataset can also be used to analyse the distribution of work activities between different categories: what we call work repertoires.[37] The relative size of each category is shown in Table 1.7. It shows that agriculture and land, and commerce, were the two largest categories of work tasks, followed by transport.

An important question is the extent to which these relative category sizes relate to the proportion of time expended on each type of work. Work repertoires cannot claim to be fully representative of worktime budgets, in part because certain forms of work have not been recorded, as discussed above. That said, the work tasks that have been consciously excluded are generally those that were not especially widespread or common, but might appear so from these sources, and would therefore not have accounted for a significant amount of time-use across the economy as a whole, such as the work of the clergy, or the annual

[37] The term 'work repertoires' is taken from the Gender and Work project: Ågren (ed.), *Making a Living.*

Table 1.7 *Distribution of tasks across categories*

	Tasks	% of total tasks
Agriculture and land	2,635	27.3
Carework	564	5.8
Commerce	2,115	21.9
Crafts and construction	942	9.8
Food processing	607	6.3
Housework	748	7.8
Management	645	6.7
Transport	1,237	12.8
Other	157	1.6
Total	9,650	100.0

collection of tithe corn. It is unlikely their exclusion significantly distorts the average work repertoire recorded here. It is the case that certain tasks may be under-recorded in the material, but this is true to some extent for all time-use surveys, none of which capture a perfect picture of working life.

In many respects, as discussed in the Introduction, the approach adopted in this study closely approximates the random-hour recall approach to modern time-use surveys, which ask participants to recall what they were doing at randomly chosen moments and reconstructs broader time-use patterns from that information. One advantage of this approach is that it is not necessary to know the duration of a specific work task undertaken, information which is typically lacking in our sources, as tasks that took up a greater proportion of people's time would be more likely to be counted by such checks than tasks that were not so time-consuming. Similarly, those tasks that were more common are captured more often than those that were performed infrequently. It is not possible to control our sample as precisely as a modern time-use study, but we have shown that participants are broadly socially representative, and the results can be adjusted to account for imbalances in gender, as discussed above. Whilst each type of source material used has its own impact on the shape of the results, this can to a certain extent be mitigated by applying the 'information status' filters discussed above, and the database as a whole can be seen as three aggregated time-use surveys, each from a different court, that used in conjunction provide a more rounded picture of overall patterns of time-use. The results presented here are undoubtedly less precise than modern time-use surveys, but they approximate them to a high degree, and certainly much more closely than any other historical methodology. The work repertoires presented in this book may

Table 1.8 *Information status by category*

	Integral tasks	%	Related tasks	%	Incidental tasks	%
Agriculture and land	314	11.8	1,687	35.7	634	28.0
Carework	27	1.0	396	8.4	141	6.2
Commerce	1,104	41.6	607	12.8	404	17.8
Crafts and construction	180	6.8	458	9.7	304	13.4
Food processing	313	11.8	177	3.7	117	5.2
Housework	142	5.3	359	7.6	247	10.9
Management	200	7.5	312	6.6	133	5.9
Transport	328	12.3	666	14.1	243	10.7
Other	49	1.8	63	1.3	45	2.0
Total	2,657	99.9	4,725	99.9	2,268	100.1

not, then, be exact budgets of working time-use, but they should nonetheless be seen as having a strong correlation with actual patterns of worktime distribution.

These work repertoires are especially valuable when comparing the proportions of different categories of tasks done by different groups of actors, such as women and men. However, to render these as meaningful approximations of time-use budgets for men and women, it is important to consider whether certain categories of work are being significantly overrepresented in the sources. Relevant here is our system of assigning an 'information status' to each task recorded, with 'integral' used to identify activities that were most likely to be overrepresented by certain types of cases. Table 1.8 looks at the distribution of different 'information status' tasks across our main categories.

The most notable result here is that commercial activities were far more prevalent in integral material than in either related or incidental testimony. This is straightforward to account for: many of those integral commerce activities are instances of buying and selling that were offered as alibis when an individual was accused of theft. Theft cases were also the most common form of case type by a considerable margin and thus provide many such work tasks. Using the information status filter shows that theft cases are indeed having a distorting effect on the data, leading to the overrepresentation of commercial activities. It is preferable therefore to filter out all integral tasks to create a less distorted picture of the relative sizes of the different categories in the average work repertoire. Whilst related tasks are also to some extent shaped by the case they are recorded in, the pattern of work from related tasks is broadly similar to that from purely incidental observations of work activities, so there is not

Table 1.9 *Male and female repertoires compared, integral excluded*

	F tasks	F repertoire (%)	M tasks	M repertoire (%)	Percentage difference in repertoires
Agriculture and land	411	20.2	1,910	38.5	18.3
Carework	357	17.6	180	3.6	−13.9
Commerce	272	13.4	739	14.9	1.5
Crafts and construction	157	7.7	605	12.2	4.5
Food processing	80	3.9	214	4.3	0.4
Housework	464	22.8	142	2.9	−20.0
Management	98	4.8	347	7.0	2.2
Transport	156	7.7	753	15.2	7.5
Other	36	1.8	72	1.5	−0.3
	2,031	99.9	4,962	100.1	0.2

Notes: Integral excluded.

a strong case for filtering them out. Table 1.9 shows the male and female work repertoires with the integral activities removed, and displaying the main differences between the gendered repertoires.

Men's work is heavily dominated by agriculture, at 38.5 per cent. For both women and men commerce is a significant category. For men transport, and crafts and construction made up a similar proportion of activities. The combined categories of carework and housework account for 40.4 per cent of women's work: a significant proportion, but notably less than half of all their work tasks. What we might think of as more traditional forms of women's work did not therefore take up sufficient time to prevent them from working in other areas of the economy, as their repertoire clearly shows. In subsequent chapters we compare the work 'repertoires' of different groups of workers beyond comparisons between all men and all women, and consider the influence of age, marital status, region, occupation, and a range of other factors on the experience of working life.

Filtering the data by information status and applying a female multiplier are both valuable adjustments, but they are not applied universally in the analysis throughout this book. For instance, excluding integral tasks does not have a significant impact on the gender division of labour within categories, and integral tasks are less of an issue when looking at patterns within categories rather than comparing across them. For some forms of analysis, the gender division of labour is not itself under investigation, and it has not therefore been necessary to apply the multiplier to female tasks. All subsequent tables and figures explicitly state when they have excluded integral tasks, and when they have applied a female multiplier.

1.4.4 *Change over Time*

There are a number of major debates about the extent of changes in patterns and intensity of work across the early modern period. The work-task methodology is more effective at providing a detailed picture of working life in the sixteenth and seventeenth centuries as a whole, which can then be compared with studies of earlier and later periods, than it is at capturing change within our period of study. This is because the different source bases are not evenly distributed across the period. Due to survival rates and changes in the details recorded, we have drawn on different proportions of coroners' reports, church court records, and quarter sessions material for different periods within the two hundred years covered. If the tasks are divided into two roughly equal-sized samples, one covering 1500 to 1630, one 1631 to 1700, the first would draw on 45 per cent church courts, 34 per cent quarter sessions, and 22 per cent coroners' reports; the latter on 81 per cent quarter sessions, 19 per cent church courts, and no coroners' reports. Given that each type of court produces a distinctive repertoire of work tasks, as shown in Table 1.10, any differences between the earlier and later halves of the dataset would reflect the composition of the sample as much as any real changes in the experiences of work.

It is not possible to apply multipliers to balance the proportions of material used from each court in each of the two periods because the dataset contains no coroners' data for the seventeenth century, and very little quarter sessions data for the sixteenth. An alternative is to explore change over time using only the incidental tasks in the dataset, as these are less influenced by the type of court material used and therefore less susceptible to changes in the underlying composition of the sources used. This has the disadvantage of removing all of the coroners' data, which was all marked as related, but does at least allow some analysis of change over time within the quarter sessions and church court material. Table 1.11 uses this method to compare typical work repertoires for two different periods, using 1630 as the mid-point with roughly equal numbers of tasks recorded on either side of this date. What is notable here is how muted changes in work repertoires appear to be, overall and for both men and women. Only the proportion of agricultural work undertaken by men, which increases by 6.9 per cent in the latter sample, represents a change of more than 4 per cent across all other categories. Tentative as this may be, it does suggest that the proportion of different

Table 1.10 *Work repertoires by court*

	Quarter sessions tasks	QS repertoire (%)	Church courts tasks	CC repertoire (%)	Coroners' reports tasks	CR repertoire (%)
Agriculture and land	970	17.8	1,192	38.3	473	43.5
Carework	325	6.0	224	7.2	15	1.4
Commerce	1,569	28.8	540	17.4	6	0.5
Crafts and construction	466	8.5	333	10.7	143	13.2
Food processing	457	8.4	106	3.4	44	4.1
Housework	423	7.8	191	6.1	134	12.3
Management	417	7.6	224	7.2	4	0.4
Transport	720	13.2	264	8.5	253	23.3
Other	107	2.0	36	1.2	14	1.3
Total	5,454	100.1	3,110	100.0	1,086	100.0

Notes: Integral included.

Table 1.11 *Changes in repertoires over time*

	1500–1630 repertoire (%)	1631–1700 repertoire (%)	1500–1630 F repertoire (%)	1631–1700 F repertoire (%)	1500–1630 M repertoire (%)	1631–1700 M repertoire (%)
Agriculture and land	26.6	29.6	23.7	20.7	28.3	35.2
Carework	6.5	5.9	9.4	11.8	4.7	2.2
Commerce	18.5	17.0	16.2	18.2	19.9	16.2
Crafts and construction	14.3	12.4	11.0	9.9	16.2	14.0
Food processing	5.2	5.2	5.0	2.5	5.2	6.9
Housework	11.3	10.4	23.5	22.4	4.1	2.8
Management	5.5	6.3	2.9	5.2	7.1	7.0
Transport	10.3	11.2	6.8	7.4	12.4	13.6
Other	1.9	2.1	1.5	2.0	2.1	2.2
Total	100.1	100.1	100.0	100.1	100.0	100.1
Total tasks	1,220	1,048	456	406	764	642

Notes: Incidental tasks only.

categories of work undertaken within the early modern English rural economy did not change dramatically across our period. This contradicts recent research on occupational structure, a point we return to in the book's conclusion.[38]

1.5 Conclusion

This chapter has set out the methodology and source material of this study, laying the foundation for the following chapters and offering a model that we hope other researchers will follow. Like all primary source materials, the legal testimony used in this project must be handled with care and requires careful reflection. It is never possible to 'fix' all of the complexities of historical sources, but we have developed a methodology that allows this complex qualitative material to be converted into meaningful quantitative data about patterns of work in early modern England, shedding light on aspects of the economy that have previously been largely hidden to historical research. The headline results are striking, especially with regard to the extent to which women worked across all the main areas of the economy. But the richness of the data, and especially the contextual information relating to each work task, means that the experience of work in early modern England can be explored at a much finer-grained level than the broad overall results presented here. Proof of the efficacy of the methodology lies in the chapters that follow.

[38] See also Whittle, 'Putting women back in'; Aucoin et al., 'Structural change'.

2 Working People

In October of 1620, the family of Thomas Conant–a husbandman of Moretonhampstead on the edge of Dartmoor, Devon–fell under suspicion of stealing sheep from their neighbour John Hutchins.[1] Curiously, Thomas himself was not examined by the magistrate, or if he was his testimony does not survive, but other members of his household were. His wife Joan was asked to explain the presence of two ewe sheep that the local constable had found in her husband's barn with their legs bound by a piece of cord. Joan denied any knowledge of the sheep-napping, but she explained of the '60 weight of wool' also found in their house by the constable that 'she bought the same of certain men of Chagford [4 miles away] whose names she knoweth not'. Her daughter Thomasine was examined next, and the magistrate asked her if a basket of mutton found in the barn was her mother's: she replied that it could not be, as 'their basket was sent to the house of John Howe of St Thomas [a suburb of Exeter 12 miles away] unto a sister of this examinant about three weeks before Michaelmas last to fetch home this examinants clothes', and that the said basket 'was either left there or lost by the way'. The magistrate then examined John Conant, a son of Thomas and Joan who had 'served Giles Kingwell of Crediton [a cloth town 12 miles away] … by the space of five years until Lammas last and then he came home unto his father's house'. He too denied all knowledge of any sheep stealing but did confess that 'he was on the said Hutchins' ground on Saturday last and did drive a mare into the said ground'.

His brother Benjamin was the next examinant to face the magistrate and in a more fulsome response than his siblings described a plethora of work tasks. Where had his sister been on the Saturday that the sheep went missing? She was at home in bed sick all day 'until it was almost night, at which time his sister rose to bake three loaves of bread'. What about his brother? 'John went forth in the evening into their own ground

[1] DHC, QS/4/Box 24, Epiphany, 8.

to set or till springles [traps] to catch woodcocks.' What did he know about the basket? He himself had 'carried the basket unto the aforesaid Howe's house to fetch peas from the said house, but there were none, and therefore left the basket there'. The constable had also found a basket of wet wool when searching the Conant house and barn, but here too Benjamin Conant could explain: 'it was wool he gathered up about the house, and washed the same himself to make him clothes'. And whilst he also denied any involvement with the sheep theft, he did confess that the family owned a length of cord, for 'his brother Richard brought with him from sea about ten days last past a certain bunch of cord, which this examinant sayeth his mother did use to hang clothes to dry from'.

It is not possible to know if the Conants took the sheep, or whether the various work tasks they attested to were cover stories or accurate accounts of their everyday work tasks. But if we accept that the stories the family told to the magistrate were plausible accounts of everyday work activity, and therefore reflect the realities of everyday life in this society, we can draw from the case a number of insights that are crucial to understanding the experience of work in early modern England. For a start, it provides a reminder that household economies in rural England were remarkably versatile and diverse: there is evidence here of engagement in commerce, baking, hunting, washing and gathering wool, horse husbandry, fetching peas, laundry, and making clothes. One son had worked in service, and another at sea, and both were still contributing to the family economy; one daughter lived at home and baked bread, and another lived in Exeter, possibly in service, and appears to have either washed or mended clothes for her sister. What is more, none of these activities were undertaken by the male head of household, Thomas Conant, who was not examined and was not mentioned doing any work tasks in the depositions. Yet he is the only worker in the case who is given an occupational descriptor: husbandman. This reinforces the importance of looking beyond occupational titles when seeking to uncover a fuller picture of who did what in the preindustrial economy. Instead, we need to recognise a diverse cast of workers that centres married women, children and young people, servants, and others, as much as male heads of household with occupational titles.

As the case of the Conants highlights, both the work tasks undertaken and the types of people doing them were wide ranging in our period. This chapter aims to go beyond this important but rather general point to establish in more detail clear patterns of what types of people tended to engage in what types of tasks. To do so, it draws on the biographical details that witnesses provided when reporting work tasks.

2.1 Biographical Preambles

'The Information of Joan Frend the wife of William Frend of Brixham labourer taken before me Ambrose Bellott Esquire … the 4th day of February 1619.'[2]

Witness testimony in the early modern English courts was typically introduced by a preamble of this sort, providing details of when and by whom the deposition was taken, alongside biographical information about the deponent. These personal details, especially marital and occupational statuses, and ages when given, are of immense value to the work-task approach to the history of work, allowing the connections between certain types of work and the types of people who performed them to be identified. From her deposition we know that Joan Frend roasted some pilchards for a man who called at her alehouse, before going to a neighbour's house to buy faggots of wood (during which time the man stole away with a shirt of her husband). Not only is there evidence here of women's work tasks, these can also be classified as performed by a married woman, and by the wife of a labourer. Recording such information across the dataset allows for comparisons of the types of tasks done by women and men of different marital and occupational statuses, as well as examining the relationship between the work done by women and the occupation of their husband. It is also possible to compare the tasks performed by different age groups: although not given in this example from the quarter sessions, where age was rarely given, it was regularly included in church court depositions. In fact, none of this biographical information was consistently provided. As well as variations between courts, there were also variations over time and geography, with some clerks making a habit of recording certain things and not others. Most significantly, there were key gendered differences in what was recorded: occupational status was very rarely recorded for women; marital status was very rarely recorded for men. Nonetheless, we have been able to gather enough information about age, marital status, and occupation, to analyse the impact of all three on the experience of work.

It is important to do so, for historians of gender have long emphasised that exploring differences between women and men is insufficient for understanding the range of experiences of either. As Alexandra Shepard has argued, we need an understanding of gender 'not solely premised on … dynamics between the sexes but which also takes into account the relations between different categories of men and of women'.[3] As her

[2] DHC, QS/4/Box 24, Easter 1620, 4–5.

[3] Shepard, *Meanings of Manhood*, p. 251.

study of masculinity in early modern England demonstrated, patriarchal values privileged certain men over and above others, with middle-aged householders benefitting more than young men and poorer men. These differences were related to marital status, which was also of fundamental importance to shaping women's life experiences. In her work on single women in early modern England, Amy Froide argued that marital status was 'just as crucial' as gender to understanding the operation of patriarchy, and the Gender and Work project has recently described marriage as of 'immense importance' to working life in early modern Sweden.[4] To understand the experience of work in early modern England, attention should be paid to these intersecting hierarchies that worked with gender to shape the lives of women and men.

Using biographical preambles to explore these hierarchies is not without its pitfalls. The accuracy of the ages provided by deponents must be questioned, as ages ending in nought are consistently overrepresented in reported age listings in the period. People reached for a convenient round number rather than absolute precision.[5] But as a rough guide to the relationship between age and work, they are still useful. The main limitation of marital status information is that it was not provided for men in preambles. In some instances, it is possible to identify married men if the testimony itself mentions a wife, but it is uncommon to find even these incidental references to the state of bachelor- or widowerhood, so it is not possible to compare the work done by men of differing marital statuses. Women's marital status was commonly recorded across our sources in the form of 'wife of', 'widow', and for never-married women of any age, 'spinster' (though variants, such as 'singlewoman', were occasionally used instead). Whilst wife and widow are relatively straightforward designations, spinster does present some challenges of interpretation, because it also has occupational connotations of working as a spinner that complicate treating it simply as a marital status. Amy Erickson and Amy Froide have suggested that the use of spinster as an occupational descriptor was a medieval inheritance that had largely given way to its use as a marital status by the early modern period, but with the caveat that it did persist in some regions such as the north-west, even into the nineteenth century.[6] Here it is treated as a marital status, in line with its most common usage, except for instances where it appears alongside other contradictory evidence of marital status, in either a preamble or

[4] Froide, *Never Married*, p. 7; Ågren (ed.), *Making a Living*, p. 154.
[5] Thomas, 'Numeracy', p. 126.
[6] Froide, *Never Married*, p. 159; Erickson, 'Marital status'.

incidentally in a deposition, that suggests it was being deployed as an occupational status.[7]

If the terms used to denote marital status contain elements of ambiguity, the same is even more true of occupational descriptors. They were commonly recorded for men, but precisely what they record is far from straightforward.[8] Many were hybrid designations of social and occupational status, such as yeoman or husbandman, whose precise relation to wealth could vary regionally and chronologically, and were rather vague as a guide to the specific work that individual might do. The same is true of terms like servant or labourer, which tell us more about employment relations than types of work. If some terms are unhelpfully imprecise, others convey a false sense of specialisation, with a title such as carpenter or shoemaker potentially failing to reflect 'the piecemeal quality of many people's existence', which often drew on varied sources of income.[9] The descriptors that deponents laid claim to were just that: claims. They were built upon the realities of working life, but they were also intimately tied to individual and social identity formation, which renders them capricious guides to the working lives of their claimants.[10] There was, for instance, a tendency for individuals in more subordinate positions to 'claim up'; servants often claimed a title such as husbandman in their preamble, only for further questioning to reveal their junior status, and a similar pattern can be found in the depositions of artisan apprentices, and labourers.[11] Older men often still claimed a specialist occupational title, such as blacksmith, despite having ceased to make their living that way.[12] In court cases where these tensions emerge, we are often left with multiple occupational descriptors for a single individual: described, for instance, as a husbandman in their preamble but in the course of their own deposition as 'a day labourer'. These multiples not only complicate the logistics of categorisation and analysis; they provide a valuable reminder that certain occupational groups, such as servants and labourers, are likely to be underrepresented in our data. For every case where

[7] Such instances were rare. In most cases where spinster appeared alongside another descriptor, it did so alongside servant, reinforcing the notion that it was a marital status appearing alongside an occupational status. There are only three examples in the database where we have explicit evidence of spinster not denoting marital status – in each case a married woman is described as a spinster, one from Devon, one from Norfolk, one from Lincolnshire.

[8] For a helpful discussion of several of the problems with occupational and social descriptors provided to the courts, see Shepard, *Accounting for Oneself*, pp. 232–6.

[9] Ibid., p. 261.

[10] Hailwood and Waddell, 'Work and identity'.

[11] Shepard, *Accounting for Oneself*, p. 236. This trend is more evident in church courts than quarter sessions, as the former involved closer scrutiny of witnesses' status claims.

[12] Ibid., p. 261.

we can see a servant 'claiming up', there are likely to be many more where this claim was successfully enshrined in the legal record as fact. For this reason, when categorising all those who were identified as both a husbandman and a servant were grouped as the latter, to help balance out this effect, and on the basis that most of these individuals were in all likelihood servants in husbandry. Those identified as both husbandman and labourer have been classified differently, as multiples, because the precise relationship between these two claims is harder to establish, as is explored below.

Historians have become increasingly aware of the issues surrounding occupational descriptors and their complex relationship with the working lives of the individuals associated with them. But they are not meaningless, and the fact that they were so widely used by contemporaries makes it imperative to develop a fuller appreciation of their meaning. The work-task approach can play a key role here. By comparing occupational descriptors with the tasks done by the people claiming them, we can deepen our understanding of what these designations signified.

2.2 Working 'For Another'

As well as seeking to establish the work tasks undertaken by different groups of people in early modern England, this chapter investigates the terms on which such work was undertaken. Interpretations of differences between key groups of working people – such as between husbandmen and labourers, or between married and unmarried women – have often hinged on the degree to which they were either required or able to undertake work that generated an income. Were husbandmen distinguished from labourers by their freedom from wage dependency and the need to sell their labour?[13] Did married women have greater or fewer opportunities to generate income for their household than unmarried women?[14]

The work-task data does not record the exact terms under which all tasks were performed. Only 5 per cent of all tasks in the database include explicit references to individuals being paid for their labour or doing work that was formally contracted, a number that increases to 12 per cent when tasks explicitly undertaken as part of service are included. If most of the material is imprecise about the terms of employment under which

[13] Shepard argues they were converging in their degree of wage dependency across the seventeenth century, *Accounting for Oneself*, p. 264.

[14] See Ågren (ed.), *Making a Living*, p. 88, for the argument that marriage 'facilitated rather than prevented women's work and income earning'.

work was done, it is not silent on the issue. What we have been able to record are frequent references to work undertaken 'for another' outside of the worker's household unit. For instance, in 1631 John Smith of Bathwick, Somerset, deposed in a tithe case that he 'at the request of the said William Fisher was the man which weighed his wool which were shorn from his sheep'.[15] One year later in the parish of Camerton in the same county, haymaking was done by Edward Bigg, who 'came to the close and with his wife made the same up into bigger cocks for and in the name of Robert Eaton of Wellow'.[16] In thousands of other instances deponents reported similar examples of work done 'for' others, or which they had been 'willed' or 'requested' to do by other individuals, or offered other details, such as 'reaping the corn of Widow Love', that made it clear this was work done for an individual outside of their own household and not as direct subsistence work.

The language used by deponents to describe working for others was generally ambiguous about the precise employment relations involved. It is likely that in many cases such work was paid. In others it may have formed part of a reciprocal exchange of labour or goods. In some cases, it may have been an act of charity or kindness. But it is not possible to know the proportions of each. In many instances deponents made no reference to any form of employment relationship, simply reporting a task like 'milking a cow' with no further information, but that does not mean that such work was not undertaken 'for another', for pay or otherwise. Likewise, if an individual is recorded as making goods such as clothing or ale that may well have been sold, or a tailor is detailed repairing a pair of trousers, this could not be recorded as evidence of work done 'for another' unless the deponent explicitly stated they were making such goods or performing such services for a specific person outside of their household. Given the blurred lines between production for the household and production for the market, assumptions cannot be made about whether tasks such as these were income generating or not. As a result, it is likely that many more tasks were performed 'for another' than the proportion that have been explicitly identified. At the same time, it was rarely possible to be certain that any tasks were strictly subsistence only with no income-generating potential, and this was not therefore deployed as a category in our analysis.

The category of work undertaken 'for another' on unspecified terms can therefore only be taken as a very rough proxy of work that might have been income generating. But set alongside tasks that are known to have

[15] SHC, D/D/Cd/75, *Lewes v. Fisher*. [16] SHC, D/D/Cd/75, *Hodson v. Love*.

Table 2.1 *Work tasks performed 'for another'*

'For another' type	F tasks	%	M tasks	%	Total tasks	%
Explicitly paid	72	2.7	425	6.1	497	5.2
Service	256	9.5	452	6.5	708	7.3
Unspecified terms	647	24.1	1,544	22.2	2,191	22.7
No evidence	1,711	63.7	4,543	65.2	6,254	64.8
Total	2,686	100.0	6,964	100.0	9,650	100.0

been explicitly paid, and work done as part of service, it provides another measure for thinking about work undertaken for others outside the household unit. In particular, it can be illuminating to compare the extent and variety of 'for another' work carried out by different groups of workers along lines of age, marital status, and occupation. To lay the foundation for such comparisons, Table 2.1 provides an overview of this data for the whole dataset. It shows the number and proportion of tasks in three 'for another' categories – explicitly paid, service, and unspecified terms – alongside the number and proportion of tasks for which there was no evidence of work being undertaken for an individual outside of the household. Taken together, the three 'for another' categories account for over one-third of all work tasks in the dataset, suggesting a relatively high proportion of work tasks that were conducted were potentially undertaken for payment of some sort. Significantly, although there is some difference in the distribution across the three categories for men's and women's 'for another' work, there is very little difference in the overall percentage of this work done by men, at 34.8 per cent, and by women, at 36.3 per cent, in our data. Nor do these patterns change over time: the overall percentage of 'for another' work for the period before 1630 is 36 per cent, and for the period after 1630 it is 35 per cent. If income-generating work was increasingly prevalent in this period, it is not reflected in this analysis.

The prevalence of 'for another' work across different areas of the economy is presented in Table 2.2, where the three 'for another' categories have been combined. For agriculture and land, or crafts and construction, the results are not especially surprising; these were types of work that were often done for others, but also often done as forms of work within the household unit as well. The most eye-catching figures here relate to carework, which was overwhelmingly 'for another' for both men and women. Carework, alongside housework, is the category of work most commonly characterised as unpaid 'domestic' work, existing outside of the market and the economy as they are conventionally

Table 2.2 *Work tasks performed 'for another' by work category*

	F tasks 'for another'	% of F tasks 'for another'	M tasks 'for another'	% of M tasks 'for another'	Total tasks 'for another'	% of total tasks 'for another'
Agriculture and land	189	40.0	1,012	46.8	1,201	45.6
Carework	279	75.8	162	82.7	441	78.2
Commerce	37	6.7	84	5.4	121	5.7
Crafts and construction	79	38.3	425	57.7	504	53.5
Food processing	42	32.1	147	30.9	189	31.1
Housework	251	48.0	76	33.8	327	43.7
Management	17	9.9	67	14.2	84	13.0
Transport	74	35.6	400	38.9	474	38.3
Other	7	14.3	48	44.4	55	35.0
Total	975	36.3	2,421	34.8	3,396	35.2

conceived by economists. Our data calls for a major reappraisal of this assumption: care for the sick, the dying, newborns, and children was routinely something that individuals who were not part of that household were called on to perform, and it is likely they were often paid to do so. Some of this work was undertaken by servants, but this alone does not explain the high levels of 'for another' work undertaken in the category of carework. It is an issue returned to in Chapter 5, but it is worth noting here that carework and indeed housework were commonly performed 'for another'.

This chapter now turns to the main categories of analysis that biographical preambles permit us to explore when combined with the work-task data. First, it analyses the ways in which repertoires of work tasks and patterns of 'for another' work changed across the lifecycle and were affected by marital status. Second, it explores the relationship between occupations and work tasks across two sections: one comparing the relative sectoral distributions of each, engaging with the PST (primary, secondary, tertiary) classification system, and one exploring at length the relationship between different occupational groups and their work repertoires.

2.3 Age and Marital Status

In 1653, John Saunders of Ottery St Mary, in East Devon, gave to his daughter Anne, who lived with him, a goose and a gander, for 'the

Table 2.3 *Work tasks per age group*

Age group	Tasks	% of all tasks
0–14	119	6.2
15–24	360	18.7
25–34	498	25.8
35–44	383	19.9
45–54	293	15.2
55–64	219	11.4
65+	56	2.9
Total	1,928	100.1

keeping and increase of the said geese'.[17] Anne was just three or four years old at the time but was already being asked to enter the world of work and take responsibility for the care of a pair of geese. Anne was not the only child of this age put to work. In July of 1629 the four-year-old Thomas Britten of Upton Noble, Somerset, was sent by his mother as a 'messenger' to fetch her sister-in-law to come to their house to buy a parcel of yarn.[18] If Elizabeth Twise of Northenden, Cheshire, started so young, her working life would have begun in the reign of Queen Elizabeth and still been going strong well into that of Charles II: at the age of '80 and upwards' she was delivering babies as a midwife in 1674.[19] Work shaped the lives of early modern women and men from some of their earliest years to their last. When Elizabeth Upham died in Crowcombe, Somerset, in 1620, her neighbour John Welshowe confirmed that 'the said Elizabeth was near 80 years old before her death and did spin and card hard until shortly before her death'.[20]

These examples represent some of the youngest and oldest workers recorded in the database, but as Table 2.3 shows, the work-task data's main strength is that it captures a good spread across all the ages in between. Ages are not always provided, but we are able to identify the age of the actor for precisely 20 per cent of all work tasks, just under 2,000 tasks, with similar proportions for women and men, and an average age of 36 for both.[21]

[17] DHC, Chanter 880, 98v–101r. [18] SHC, Q/SR/62, 99.
[19] CALS, EDC/5/1674, 3. [20] SHC, D/D/Cd/55, *Upham v. Stronge*.
[21] Age data was routinely provided in the church court records, but only sporadically elsewhere, and 81 per cent of the tasks in this analysis are taken from the church courts. This shapes the results, as each type of court has a distinct task profile (see Appendix A) but does not preclude meaningful comparisons between different age groups found within the church court material. Integral tasks have been included in the analysis in this section to ensure a large enough sample. This does serve to inflate the number of commerce tasks, but it does so across age and marital status groups, and does not have a significant impact on comparisons between them.

The smallest number of tasks recorded were those undertaken by the very old and the very young. That is a reflection of demographic structure in the case of the very old: they were a small proportion of people. Wrigley and Schofield estimated that the proportion of the population over 60 in the seventeenth century was between 8 and 9 per cent; the number of tasks in the data performed by people aged 60 and over is 9 per cent. The youngest age group is undoubtedly underrepresented: Wrigley and Schofield estimated they made up between 31 and 34 per cent of the population, but they performed just 6 per cent of tasks in our data. This may well reflect their reduced economic contribution relative to other groups but is also a consequence of young children being far less likely to appear as witnesses before the courts and to detail their own work tasks.[22] Our 15 to 24 category is in line with the demographic data that puts it at 17–18 per cent of the population, but our 'middle age' groupings are overrepresented. Wrigley and Schofield estimate 25 to 59-year-olds as 40–43 per cent of the population, whereas they account for two-thirds of all of our work tasks.[23] To some extent this reflects their high levels of economic activity compared to the very young and the old, but they were also more likely to depose than young adults who carried less status.

Whilst the category of children's work is a relatively small one, it is worth exploring the material that is available, given how difficult this subject is to study. One clear pattern is that the work of both young boys and young girls was much more heavily concentrated in a small number of categories than the work repertoires of adults. For boys under the age of 15, the point at which they are likely to have entered service, agricultural work dominated, and within that animal husbandry in particular. Boys fed oxen, herded sheep, and drove geese and pigs. They were also employed to do a range of fetching and carrying jobs. In addition to taking messages, they collected firewood, drew water from wells, and might in their early teens be entrusted with driving carts, especially within the farm. They were also commonly charged with guarding crops against birds, which included climbing trees to destroy the nests of crows and magpies. The work of young girls was concentrated within the category of housework. They made beds, washed food and tableware, and above all collected water, a task which would often have taken them outside of the household, and was a physically demanding one, so it is

[22] Our youngest deponent was a nine-year-old boy who was examined after being accused of theft. There are multiple witnesses for each age from 11 upwards, so this seems to have been a de facto qualifying age for deposing.

[23] Wrigley and Schofield, *Population History*, pp. 528–9.

Table 2.4 *Women's lifecycle repertoires*

	0–24 age group		25–44 age group		45+ age group	
	Tasks	Repertoire (%)	Tasks	Repertoire (%)	Tasks	Repertoire (%)
Agriculture and land	34	24.6	39	20.2	31	20.5
Carework	11	8.0	41	21.2	57	37.7
Commerce	8	5.8	25	13.0	9	6.0
Crafts and construction	16	11.6	25	13.0	8	5.3
Food processing	2	1.4	3	1.6	1	0.7
Housework	54	39.1	28	14.5	27	17.9
Management	1	0.7	10	5.2	8	5.3
Transport	9	6.5	15	7.8	8	5.3
Other	3	2.2	7	3.6	2	1.3
Total	138	99.9	193	100.1	151	100.0

perhaps surprising to see this subcategory dominating the work of young girls. They also engaged in some agricultural tasks: keeping geese, milking cows, and weeding fields. Amanda Flather has suggested that 'little girls and boys parted company very early' in their working lives, with their work concentrated in different spaces.[24] Whilst there may have been opportunities for encounters between them at the local well or river when collecting water, this conclusion generally holds true. In fact, with over 50 per cent of boys' work concentrated in agriculture, and closer to 60 per cent of girls' work in housework, the differences between male and female work repertoires were more pronounced for children than they were for adults. As Flather puts it, 'gender boundaries could be blurred by age'; they generally started out as quite rigid for the youngest of workers.[25]

Table 2.4 shows the average work repertoires for women at different stages of the lifecycle, demonstrating that women's work became more diverse as they reached adulthood. The age groupings used here are broader than those used in Table 2.3 to ensure that a reasonable number of tasks can be attributed to each, but they are also intended to capture key phases of the lifecycle: 0 to 24 was a period of childhood followed for most by a period of service before marriage; 25 to 44 would have represented the main period of childbearing and raising young children for most women; and 45 and over a stage of life where the duty of care for young children would have eased as those children grew more independent.

[24] Flather, 'Space, place, and gender', p. 350. [25] Ibid.

Table 2.5 *Women's lifecycle repertoires: top subcategories*

Age group	Largest subcategories (no. of tasks)
0–24	Collecting water (21)
	Animal husbandry (11)
	Textile production (11)
	Food and drink provision (11)
25–44	Fieldwork (23)
	Textile production (17)
	Healthcare (14)
	Childcare (14)
45+	Midwifery (27)
	Healthcare (25)
	Fieldwork (13)
	Animal husbandry (10)

Notes: Commercial activities do not make the top four for any of these age groups; this is because they were rarely recorded in the church court material on which this analysis is largely based, not because it was not an important form of women's work.

Agricultural activities formed a significant part of women's work repertoires throughout the lifecycle, but beyond that the balance of tasks women undertook shifted considerably as they aged. The most striking pattern here is the significant rise in carework across the life course, which became prominent in the main child-raising phase of life but continued, and indeed increased, in importance in later life. The proportion of housework trended in the opposite direction; it was the largest category of work for children and for service-age women but formed a less substantial component of the work repertoires of those 25 and above. These changes are further illuminated by looking at the main subcategories of work at different stages of the lifecycle, as in Table 2.5.

For younger women the category of housework that loomed large in their repertoires was itself dominated by the collecting of water for household duties, and the provision of food and drink, which included both preparing and serving food. Their agricultural work was focused on animal husbandry. For women in 'middle age' the character of agricultural work shifted, with fieldwork becoming more prominent, suggesting that the opportunity to undertake seasonal summer work was an important one for married mothers.[26] As we might expect, childcare became an important part of the work repertoire at this life-stage, but the upsurge in carework was also due to a rise in the provision of healthcare. This was a

[26] This is explored in more detail in Chapter 6, Table 6.3.

Table 2.6 *Men's lifecycle repertoires*

	0–24 age group		25–44 age group		45+ age group	
	Tasks	Repertoire (%)	Tasks	Repertoire (%)	Tasks	Repertoire (%)
Agriculture and land	169	49.6	333	48.4	166	39.8
Carework	14	4.1	28	4.1	19	4.6
Commerce	17	5.0	102	14.8	59	14.1
Crafts and construction	34	10.0	92	13.4	69	16.5
Food processing	17	5.0	11	1.6	20	4.8
Housework	20	5.9	11	1.6	5	1.2
Management	6	1.8	46	6.7	29	7.0
Transport	60	17.6	60	8.7	43	10.3
Other	4	1.2	5	0.7	7	1.7
Total	341	100.2	688	100.0	417	100.0

subcategory that remained important for older women, alongside that of midwifery, both forms of work that required the experience and skill that came with age.[27] Older women's agricultural activity represented a blend of animal husbandry and fieldwork, bringing together tasks that had dominated at different stages of the lifecycle. The care of animals, to some extent, took a back seat in mid-life when childcare made greater demands, though wives still did a higher proportion of all animal husbandry than either servants or widows because there were more of them.[28] Textile production, and especially spinning, featured in women's work repertoires across their lives. Although it was a smaller subcategory for older women (7 tasks), it was still a notable one, and the database includes examples of women between the ages of 58 and 80 scouring, spinning, and carding wool.

Age was an important factor in shaping the work tasks that women undertook in early modern England. The same is less true for men. Table 2.6 demonstrates that agriculture remained the largest category of men's work throughout their lifecycle. Involvement in commerce and management was more common for men over the age of 25, whereas more time-consuming and menial transportation work played a larger part in the working lives of younger men.

27 For a similar pattern of carework being related to age, see Ågren (ed.), *Making a Living*, p. 138.

28 See Chapter 6, Table 6.3.

Table 2.7 *Work performed 'for another' by age group*

Age group	F tasks 'for another'	% of F tasks 'for another'	M tasks 'for another'	% of M tasks 'for another'
0–14	15	34.1	23	30.7
15–24	58	61.7	169	63.5
25–44	99	51.3	389	56.5
45–54	48	67.6	148	66.7
55–64	38	61.3	93	59.2
65+	8	44.4	16	42.1

Notes: These percentages are high compared to those for the database as a whole in Table 2.1. That is because we have more 'for another' work recorded for those people for whom we also have an age provided, because both types of information were reported more frequently in the church courts than in the quarter sessions.

At the level of subcategories, continuity across the lifecycle outweighs change. Fieldwork dominated for all ages of men, with animal husbandry and farm transport figuring in the top four subcategories for each group too. Younger men were more likely to be involved in transport work, and especially that which involved driving carts, whereas the two older groups of men were instead more likely to be involved in building work, which included thatching, masonry, and assessing buildings for repairs. As with women's work, there was a shift across the lifecycle towards work that required more authority (management), experience (commerce), or skill (buildings), and away from certain forms of more menial physical work (carting), but these changes were muted, with agricultural activity constantly outnumbering other types of tasks for all men. Age did influence the types of tasks men undertook but in ways that were less pronounced than for women.

Did patterns of work 'for another' change across the lifecycle? As Table 2.7 shows, the rates of such work were lower for children than for all other age groups, as their work was more likely to be performed at the request of another member of the household unit, especially parents. The percentages are nonetheless high, with around a third of children's work done 'for another', but that is in large part accounted for by a number of 'service' activities in the database performed by children under 14. Beyond that we can identify a pattern, for both women and men, of a greater prevalence of working 'for another' during the main ages of service, and again after the main phase of childrearing had passed, than during the 'middle' phase of life, though this still was an important period of performing work for people outside of the household. Those in the oldest age group performed less work 'for another', perhaps because they were less able to.

These patterns can be interrogated further by considering the main categories of 'for another' work undertaken by women and men. The main source of 'for another' work for women changed across the life cycle, from housework when young/service age (0–24), to agriculture in middle age (25–44), to carework when older (45+). For women in middle age, the overwhelming majority of agricultural tasks performed were undertaken 'for another', at 85 per cent, again suggesting that for women in this age bracket working in agriculture, especially in seasonal fieldwork, served as an important source of income.[29] Moreover, the figures warn against assuming that women in this age group had reduced opportunities to undertake income-generating work because of the burden of carework that fell on them in these years. Instead, much of the carework they performed, especially healthcare, was done 'for another'. It may be that many married women in this grouping were able to monetise skills they developed providing care for their own families to bring in additional income by offering care services to others. They continued to perform this work 'for another' in later life too. Turning to men's work 'for another', such changes are less pronounced: agriculture was the main source of such work for men of all ages. Age and experience had less of an impact on what men did 'for another'. It may have influenced what they were paid or on what terms, but the work-task data does not reveal this information.

Was marital status 'as crucial as gender' in shaping the experience of work in early modern England? There is a close correlation between marital status and different lifecycle stages, but not all unmarried people were young, and not all widows and widowers were old people, and vice versa, so it is important to analyse the relationship between work and marital status separately from age. It is not possible to do this for the men in our database. Marital status can only be identified for around 10 per cent of men, and for over 90 per cent of these that status is married, as it has been deduced from reference to a wife in their deposition. For tasks performed by women, on the other hand, marital status is noted in two-thirds of instances, providing a healthy sample of just under 1,800 tasks for analysis. Of those, 21 per cent were performed by never-married women, 64 per cent by married women, and 15 per cent by widows. This underrepresents the work of never-married women, who accounted for somewhere between 30 and 35 per cent of the adult female population in this period, and overrepresents that of married women, who accounted for closer to 50 per cent, whilst being roughly in proportion

[29] Whittle and Jiang, 'Gender, wages, and agricultural labour'.

Table 2.8 *Women's repertoires by marital status*

	Never-married tasks	Never-married repertoire (%)	Married tasks	Married repertoire (%)	Widowed tasks	Widowed repertoire (%)
Agriculture and land	85	22.8	175	15.3	36	13.3
Carework	30	8.0	145	12.7	62	23.0
Commerce	66	17.7	275	24.1	68	25.2
Crafts and construction	29	7.8	87	7.6	20	7.4
Food processing	14	3.8	62	5.4	17	6.3
Housework	88	23.6	209	18.3	29	10.7
Management	14	3.8	98	8.6	15	5.6
Transport	43	11.5	79	6.9	17	6.3
Other	4	1.1	11	1.0	6	2.2
Total	373	100.1	1141	99.9	270	100.0

for widows.[30] Nonetheless, it does allow meaningful comparisons of the work repertoires of women of each marital status, as shown in Table 2.8.

This data shows a clearer distinction between the proportions of agricultural work undertaken by different groups of women than in the age group analysis, implying that it was marriage rather than age per se that reduced the proportion of agricultural work women undertook. Other patterns here accord more closely with the age data, with a clear rise in the proportion of carework aligning with changes in marital status in ways that mirror lifecycle developments. Women who were either married or widowed were more heavily involved in commercial and management activities, and dedicated less of their working lives to housework and transport tasks, than single women. Much of this is in line with the findings for early modern Sweden, where Ågren et al. have emphasised the importance of marriage for creating hierarchies between women's experiences of work.[31] In England, never-married women were more likely to engage in menial, arduous, and time-consuming tasks than other women: they washed sheep, checked on cattle, took clothes to be mended, took corn to the mill, took linen to be washed, cleaned rooms, collected water, served drinks, washed clothes, and milked cows; very

[30] See Froide, *Never Married*, pp. 2–3. Similarly to the discussions about age above – a higher proportion of never-married women fell in the 15–24 age group that was less likely to be called to give testimony, and hence self-reporting of their tasks is lower.

[31] Ågren (ed.), *Making a Living*, p. 88.

often as servants in subordinate roles to married women. Married women might also perform any of these tasks, but they did so less frequently, and they also took on work that required more skill or authority: they sheared sheep; they butchered sheep; they purchased, sold, and pawned goods; they delivered and nursed babies; made clothes; settled debts and lent money; brewed ale and beer; and treated the sick and dying. They were also more likely to direct the work of others, both artisans and their servants, such as arranging for keys to be made, or pies to be baked.

The tasks performed by widows were closer to those done by married women than they were to those by never-married women, supporting the argument of Ågren et al. that it is the distinction between never-married and ever-married women that mattered most. If the work tasks of widows appear similar to those of married women, the picture of their work repertoires presented here does differ in interesting ways from that obtained by other approaches to widows' work. Work on probate inventories highlights caring for livestock, food processing, textile production, and money lending as key work categories for enterprising widows.[32] The database does include examples of widows droving sheep and treating sick colts, brewing beer and winnowing barley, spinning yarn and carrying wool, and lending money and making and receiving payments, but none of these represent major categories of widows' work. Instead, the depositional material captures aspects of widows' work that would have been less likely to leave a material trace in the probate record: their buying and selling of goods and their extensive involvement in midwifery. This material adds a valuable dimension to our understanding of how widows were able to run households, with commerce and carework very prominent in their work repertoires.

The conclusion that never-married women were more likely to do work that was lower-skilled, more menial, and lacking in authority relative to the work of ever-married women is not surprising, given that most of these single women were young and working in service. This is a reasonable assumption, but it is important to recognise that not all unmarried women would have fallen into this category. Amy Froide's work has been particularly important for exploring the working lives of those women who remained single into adulthood, especially in urban contexts.[33] The database contains 373 tasks performed by never-married women, but we can only identify 32 of these as being undertaken by never-married women over the age of 25, half of which were performed

[32] Whittle, 'Enterprising widows', p. 288. [33] Froide, *Never Married*.

Table 2.9 *Women's work performed 'for another' by marital status*

	Never-married tasks 'for another'	% of never-married tasks 'for another	Married tasks 'for another'	% of married tasks 'for another'	Widowed tasks 'for another'	% of widowed tasks 'for another'
Agriculture and land	36	42.4	51	29.1	14	38.9
Carework	21	70.0	105	72.4	48	77.4
Commerce	10	15.2	8	2.9	3	4.4
Crafts and construction	19	65.5	17	19.5	7	35.0
Food processing	4	28.6	9	14.5	4	23.5
Housework	56	63.6	68	32.5	19	65.5
Management	4	28.6	7	7.1	1	6.7
Transport	18	41.9	18	22.8	8	47.1
Other	0	0.0	4	36.4	0	0.0
Total	168	45.0	287	25.2	104	38.5

by women in their late 20s, many of whom were still working in service. Of the 16 done by never-married women aged 30 or over, five were also explicitly done as part of work in service, a useful reminder that not all servants were young.[34] One of the remaining examples is Catherine Edwards, a 35-year-old spinster living in Crediton, Devon, in 1674, 'being employed there for some few weeks as nursekeeper to Zachary Smith's wife then in childbed'.[35] Another was Elizabeth Luenden, 30 years of age and working in Gosport, Hampshire, in 1590, 'attending in her sickness' one Elizabeth Spenser whom she had used to work alongside as a fellow servant.[36] These examples suggest that never-married women who had left service might, like middle-aged and older women who had married, have been able to undertake carework for pay. But both instances come from relatively large towns, and may well be indicators, alongside the lack of other examples of the work of older never-married women in rural contexts, that options were sufficiently limited to push older single women to move into urban environments to find work.

Never-married women were, as Table 2.9 suggests, more likely to be engaged in work 'for another' than their ever-married counterparts: 45.0

[34] Mansell, 'Variety of women's experiences'.
[35] DHC, Chanter 875, 209r–14r.
[36] HRO, 21M65/C3/10, *Spenser v. Dee.*

per cent of their work tasks were undertaken for someone outside of their household or as a servant. There are clearer differences here between married women, for whom the figure was just 25.2 per cent, and widows, for whom it was 38.5 per cent. If they performed similar work repertoires, widows were more likely to do these tasks 'for another'. This has interesting implications for how married women's work is characterised. Whilst the Gender and Work project has argued that 'marriage facilitated rather than prevented women's work and income-earning', in the English context married women were less likely to undertake work for people outside of their household, reducing one form of income-generating work. It is important to bear in mind the limitations of our 'for another' category here though, as it does not reliably capture all forms of income generation, such as producing and selling goods on the market, so we cannot conclude that married women generated less income through their work than women outside of marriage.[37] These differences in work 'for another' could therefore be interpreted positively, as evidence married women were more fully engaged in income-generating work within the household, or negatively as a consequence of coverture.

For women, marital status was a key factor in shaping the experience of work in early modern England, in ways that were closely related to age and the lifecycle. For the young and the unmarried work was lower status and lower skilled, and often performed 'for another'. Marriage and 'middle age' brought women more authority, and tended to involve more skilled work activities, alongside a partial retreat from working for others. Older age or widowhood did not entail a significant shift in the repertoire of tasks done, but the terms on which they were performed changed once again, with a return to doing more work for others, although much of this was now carework that utilised skills and experience obtained in mid-life. The data reveals little about the impact of marital status on men's working lives, but if it too follows similar patterns to the lifecycle analysis then it was far more muted than for women's. There may have been similar changes in the amount of work done 'for another' according to marital status, but the repertoires of work that men performed across their lives were relatively stable.

2.4 Occupations, Tasks, and Sectors

Occupational descriptors have played a fundamental role in the history of work. Their use by contemporaries across a range of legal and administrative

[37] Ågren (ed.), *Making a Living*, p. 88.

Table 2.10 *Social/occupational status of male actors in the dataset*

	No.	%
Gentry	52	1.9
Professions	82	3.0
Yeomen	140	5.1
Commercial trades	75	2.8
Artisans	820	30.2
Husbandmen	536	19.7
Agricultural trades	76	2.8
Transport trades	43	1.6
Labourers	432	15.9
Servants	320	11.8
Apprentices	26	1.0
Multiple	46	1.7
Miscellaneous	71	2.6
Total	2,719	100.0

Notes: Most of these categories are self-explanatory and directly reflect the descriptors given, but others are composites of less common occupations. Professions include clerical, medical, legal, and educational titles; commercial trades include merchants, shopkeepers, victuallers, and other retailers; agricultural trades include shepherd, fisherman, gardener, shearman, ploughman, and other specified occupations directly involved in agricultural work; transport trades include carriers, carters, sailors, drovers, ostlers, and other occupations directly involved in transport; multiple includes instances where two descriptors were given for an individual from two different categories, and to which the rules specified in Section 2.1 were applied. The totals in this table are higher than those in Table 1.1, which only includes men who deposed before the courts, whereas this incorporates all men who were witnessed performing tasks.

records, as well as in cultural mediums such as plays and cheap print, make them the most ubiquitous indicators of the work that was undertaken by people in the past. Their abundance in the historical record has made them particularly valuable to quantitative approaches to historical work patterns, most notably serving as the focal point in recent discussions of structural economic change in early modern England.[38] As discussed above, however, there are questions about the reliability of occupational descriptors as guides to the work individuals actually did, and therefore about the value of quantifying them to measure economic change. The work-task approach provides a way to bridge these two perspectives, allowing the relationship between occupational descriptors and the work done by their claimants to be investigated, whilst still attempting meaningful quantification of patterns of work across society.

[38] See Section 0.1 of the Introduction.

One limitation of occupational descriptors that is difficult to overcome is that they were rarely provided for women. There are two exceptions: servants and midwives. Of the just under 2,000 female actors (those who performed work tasks) recorded in the database there are occupational descriptors for just 341, or 17 per cent. Of those, 62 per cent were servants and 28 per cent were midwives. The remaining 10 per cent included baker, seamstress, alehouse-keeper, chandler, peddler, bookseller, cook, hosier, housekeeper, and stockinger. As a consequence, the data relating to female occupations is very uneven and heavily concentrated on just two occupations, and so not especially useful for assessing differences in women's work. Nonetheless, some analysis is attempted later in this chapter, but in the first instance the focus is on male occupations, which provide richer data: 56 per cent of male actors have an occupational or social descriptor, just over 2,700 individuals. These have been grouped into occupational categories in Table 2.10.

As was the case with male deponents discussed in Chapter 1 this is a fairly representative cross-section of the male population of early modern England. The possible exception is the underrepresentation of labourers. It has already been noted above that this may be due to a reluctance on the part of labouring men to claim such a descriptor if they could instead pass as a husbandman before the courts, but it may also be due to regional variations and the composition of our sample. Almost half of these actors are drawn from our south-west sample, where only 7 per cent of men with descriptors were styled as labourer. In the northern sample this figure was 20 per cent, and in the Eastern sample 28 per cent, which is in keeping with what historians know about regional patterns of proletarianisation.[39] It is the dominance of the south-west material in our dataset, where dependence on wage labour was less common, that makes the percentage of labourers appear relatively low overall.

Another way to interrogate how representative the male workers in the work-task dataset are is to compare the occupational profile with that of the large sample of probate data assembled by Sebastiaan Keibek for his PhD as part of The Cambridge Group for The History of Population and Social Structure's (CamPop) occupational structure project.[40] Central to the approach of CamPop and others investigating structural change in the early modern economy is the grouping of occupational descriptors into the primary, secondary, and tertiary sectors to establish the proportion

[39] Shaw-Taylor, 'Rise of agrarian capitalism'.
[40] Keibek, 'Male occupational structure'; CamPop, Occupational Structure [website].

Table 2.11 *Male actors' occupations by sector*

	No. of occupations	% of occupations	Keibek's data, 1631 (%)
Primary	1,515	55.8	59.0
Secondary	893	32.9	32.4
Tertiary	305	11.2	8.7
Total	2,713	99.9	100.1

Notes: This excludes six male actors whose occupations were unclassifiable, hence the different total to Table 2.10. Keibek's data is from 'Male occupational structure' p. 152. His figures for 1621 and 1641 have been averaged to provide an estimate for 1631.

of men working in these different key areas of the economy.[41] The same can be done with our data to provide a comparison. Occupations were assigned to sectors using CamPop's PST look-up table.[42] Assigning servants and labourers to sectors is more complicated as their allocation to a sector depends on what type of work they were employed to do. This is a problem Keibek dealt with in his PhD. To produce comparable results, we divided servants and labourers between sectors using the same proportions as Keibek. The servants of upper-status individuals are split 40:60 between farm servants (primary) and domestic servants (tertiary), with all other servants considered to be farm servants (primary); 10 per cent of labourers have been placed in the secondary sector, with the rest in the primary sector.[43] The results of this classification are shown in Table 2.11.

As a point of comparison, Keibek's sectoral distribution has been taken for the year 1631, which represents an approximate median for our dataset with roughly equal numbers of tasks from before and after this date. The results are reassuringly similar, with the secondary sector very closely aligned, and a slightly larger tertiary sector in our data compared to Keibek's, but the overall proportions do not differ substantially. They

[41] Broadberry, Campbell, and van Leeuwen, 'When did Britain industrialise?'; Shaw-Taylor and Wrigley, 'Occupational structure'; Keibek, 'Male occupational structure'; Wallis, Colson, and Chilosi, 'Structural change'.

[42] CamPop, PST Coding Scheme [website].

[43] Keibek, 'Male occupational structure': For the discussion of how to distribute servants, see pp. 54–5; for the proportion of labourers in each sector, see the table on p. 70, which is based on figures for a later period but which Keibek argues would have been similar to allocations for earlier periods. It is not always possible for us to identify the status of a servant's master, but we have estimated about 15 per cent of our servants worked for the gentry/other upper status individuals on the basis of the 102 examples, where we have recorded the status of the master. Individuals in the Multiple category with two descriptors belonging in two different sectors have been counted as 0.5 of a person in each sector. A small number of the Miscellaneous descriptors were not classifiable.

Table 2.12 *Sectoral distribution of tasks*

	Tasks	%	F tasks adj.	%	M tasks	%
Primary	3,077	31.5	1,041	21.3	2,036	41.6
Secondary	1,239	12.7	546	11.2	693	14.2
Tertiary	5,461	55.9	3,300	67.5	2161	44.2
Total	9,778	100.1	4,888	100.0	4,890	100.0

Notes: Integral excluded; adj. = adjusted (x2.45). The multiplier here differs from the standard x2.59 multiplier, as it is intended to create an equal number of male and female tasks remaining *after* integral tasks have been excluded from this analysis.

are also similar to the proportions obtained by Keibek applying a PST analysis to the 1608 Gloucestershire Muster Roll, which results in a primary sector of between 54 and 58 per cent, a secondary sector of 35–37 per cent, and a tertiary sector of 6–8 per cent.[44] The proportion of men in the work-task dataset with occupations in each sector, based on occupational title, is therefore very similar to measures of the occupational structure of the economy at this time deduced from completely different sources. But what does the sectoral distribution look like if the tasks performed are classified rather than occupational titles?

To classify tasks each of the 62 subcategories of work tasks were assigned to a sector, using the PST look-up table for occupational titles associated with work in that subcategory.[45] At this stage it also makes sense to apply one of the tools discussed in the methodology chapter and filter the data by information status. Removing those tasks classed as integral, the tasks which we know to be most heavily shaped and likely overrepresented by certain types of court cases, provides a more accurate picture of the actual distribution of tasks across these subcategories in the economy. To produce the overall total of tasks a multiplier has been applied to the totals for women's work tasks so that half of all work tasks were undertaken by women. The results are shown in Table 2.12.

This presents a very different perspective on the sectoral distribution of work in the early modern English economy from an analysis based on

[44] Ibid., p. 55.

[45] In most instances the subcategories were assigned to the same sector as the larger category that they sit within; that is, subcategories within agriculture and land were placed in primary, those within crafts and construction, and food processing, in secondary, and those within carework, commerce, housework, management, and transport, in tertiary. Those within Other were excluded from this analysis. The exceptions were mining and quarrying, a subcategory which sits within our crafts and construction category but was classified here as primary; and threshing and winnowing which sits within food processing but again was classified here as primary.

Table 2.13 *Sectoral distribution of tasks performed 'for another'*

	Tasks 'for another'	%	F tasks 'for another' adj.	%	M tasks 'for another'	%
Primary	1,479	34.7	453	20.8	1026	49.2
Secondary	656	15.4	230	10.6	426	20.4
Tertiary	2,124	49.9	1,492	68.6	632	30.3
Total	4,259	100.0	2,175	100.0	2,084	99.9

Notes: Integral excluded; adj. = adjusted (x2.45).

occupational descriptors, with a dramatically larger tertiary sector comprised of high numbers of tasks performed in commerce and transport for both genders, and in carework and housework for women. In certain respects, this striking contrast is not difficult to explain: women's tasks were more heavily concentrated in the tertiary sector, so introducing women's work into the overall totals inflates that sector compared to the results based solely on male occupational descriptors presented in Table 2.11. But it is also clear that men's occupations significantly underrepresent their work in the tertiary sector in comparison to work tasks. It is also likely that the work-task data captures more unpaid work than occupations do. Overall, work tasks offer a more complete view of the economy incorporating forms of work, such as women's work and unpaid work, that have been overlooked in conventional approaches to economics and economic history. For comparison, we can analyse the sectoral distribution of tasks that were performed 'for another' and were therefore more likely to have been income-generating work, as shown in Table 2.13.

This attempt to align our data more closely with forms of income-generating work does little to change the distribution of women's work across sectors. This is an important finding in itself, highlighting that women's tertiary work cannot simply be dismissed as 'unpaid'. It does however serve to reduce the proportion of men's tasks in the tertiary sector, mainly by removing most of the commercial tasks, especially buying and selling, which were seldom recorded as done 'for another'. The sector nevertheless remains roughly three times the size indicated by occupational descriptors, largely due to the importance of various transport activities such as carting, carrying goods, and droving.[46] Another

[46] Although the transportation of goods or animals within a property were placed in the primary sector.

Table 2.14 *Sectoral distribution of 'for another' tasks excluding carework and housework*

	Tasks 'for another' exc. carework and housework	%	F tasks 'for another' exc. carework and housework adj.	%	M tasks' for another' exc. carework and housework	%
Primary	1,479	52.7	453	48.6	1,026	54.8
Secondary	656	23.4	230	24.7	426	22.8
Tertiary	670	23.9	250	26.8	420	22.4
Total	2,805	100.0	933	100.1	1,872	100.0

Notes: Integral excluded; adj. = adjusted (x2.45).

adjustment that can be made is to remove the categories of carework and housework altogether. Studies of occupational structure largely exclude these types of work, assuming they are unpaid work for the maintenance of the worker's own family, which falls outside the definition of labour force participation used in economics.[47] We reject this characterisation of carework and housework, which often were paid in this period and certainly fall within the third-party criterion definition used in this book, but for the purposes of a closer comparison between the datasets it can be filtered out of the work-task data, as in Table 2.14.

The impact on the sectoral distribution of women's work is dramatic, as these are very large categories within women's work repertoires, and this in turn has an impact on the overall figures. With these additional adjustments, the primary sector for men, based on tasks, is now in proportion to the primary sector based on occupational titles alone. However, the tertiary sector remains considerably larger, and the secondary sector smaller, than we would expect from occupational data. This analysis shows that the work-task approach requires a revision of our understanding of the importance of the tertiary sector in this period, not only because it was prominent in women's work but also a crucial part of men's work. Moreover, a key reason why the secondary sector appears relatively small in the sectoral distribution from tasks is that many of the tasks performed by men with secondary sector occupational descriptors were actually tertiary tasks. It is to the relationship between descriptors and tasks that the following section now turns.

47 Shaw-Taylor, Sudgen, and You, 'Preliminary estimate', p. 1.

2.5 Occupations, Repertoires, and By-Employment

A valuable recent contribution to debates about the utility of occupational and social descriptors has been research that uses qualitative material to investigate what individuals with certain descriptors actually did in their working lives. This can be approached at the level of individual examples, or in some cases at scale when larger datasets are available.[48] Research by the Gender and Work project, and by Alexandra Shepard, has shown that the relationship between occupations and ways of making a living was not straightforward, with descriptors often concealing the piecemeal character of working life. In these examples the focus has been on comparing descriptors with the full range of different ways of making a living or maintaining oneself and family that were deployed by men and women. Here, we add to this work by focusing on the relationship between descriptors and the specific tasks that people undertook.

Individual examples are suggestive here. The 21-year-old William Ricketts was a resident of East Knoyle, Wiltshire, in the year 1600. When giving a deposition in a local tithe dispute, he told the clerk that he was 'a carpenter and doth that way wholly employ himself'. And yet, elsewhere in his statement, he recounted how 'at harvest last' he had been employed by a Mr Goldsborowe to 'make up into hay' a piece of ground, the which hay he 'dried and made up into cocks' before setting out the appropriate amount for tithe collection.[49] Carpentry clearly was not his whole employment. On a Saturday morning in September of 1618, Owen Perfitt of West Cranmore, Somerset, 'came into the field to fetch home some wheat', where he likewise noted some had been illicitly taken. Perfitt gave his occupational title as 'smith'.[50] In May of 1686, Thomas Mercer, a Lancashire bricklayer, drove his sheep to and from the West Derby brecks.[51] Such examples of mismatches between titles and tasks are not difficult to find, but to what extent, if any, are they illustrative of wider patterns in the relationship between the two? What proportion of an individual's work involved tasks unrelated to their principal occupational descriptor? One way to examine this is to construct the work repertoires for all men within specific occupational groupings, as shown in Table 2.15.[52]

[48] See Paul, 'Accounting for men's work'; Ågren (ed.), *Making a Living*, pp. 34–6; and Shepard, *Accounting for Oneself*, Table 7.4. This question has also been approached by using probate inventories, but the relationship between the occupation given and the work that individual undertook is much harder to establish with certainty: Overton et al., *Production and Consumption*, pp. 65–86.

[49] WSHC, D1/42/18, 1b–4b. [50] SHC, Q/SR/31, 8.

[51] LaA, QSB/1/1686, Michaelmas, Info of Thomas Mercer.

[52] Integral tasks have been left in for the analysis in this section to create a larger sample for each occupation, but their impact on the results, where significant, is noted in what follows. The main implication is that commercial activities are overrepresented, but this is true across all occupations, and therefore does not have a major impact on comparisons between them.

Table 2.15 *Male repertoires by social/occupational status*

	Average male repertoire (%)	Gentry repertoire (%)	Professions repertoire (%)	Yeomen repertoire (%)	Artisan repertoire (%)	Husbandmen repertoire (%)	Labourer repertoire (%)	Servant repertoire (%)
Agriculture and land	31.0	25.0	14.5	35.8	13.1	46.9	36.5	42.2
Carework	2.8	9.7	40.2	5.1	1.6	2.1	2.5	2.2
Commerce	22.4	18.1	13.7	29.8	28.8	18.9	14.2	7.2
Crafts and construction	10.6	1.4	0.9	5.1	27.4	5.4	9.6	7.6
Food processing	6.8	2.8	0.0	1.9	8.3	6.4	9.3	10.1
Housework	3.2	5.6	3.4	1.4	1.8	1.7	2.0	5.2
Management	6.8	22.2	16.2	10.2	6.7	4.7	4.7	5.2
Transport	14.8	9.7	5.1	8.8	11.3	13.1	20.0	18.9
Other	1.6	5.6	6.0	1.9	1.0	0.7	1.0	1.3
Total	100.0	100.1	100.0	100.0	100.0	99.9	99.8	99.9
Total tasks	6,964	72	117	215	1,267	829	591	445

The results for specific groups are discussed at various points throughout this section, but one clear overall pattern is the relative diversity of work repertoires for all types of occupation; for no occupational group is there one category that accounts for more than half of their work tasks. That said, there are clearly meaningful degrees of specialisation. The work of the professions, most of which are medical professionals such as physicians and apothecaries, has carework as by far the largest category at 40.2 per cent. The work of husbandmen is dominated, as would be expected, by agricultural tasks, which account for 46.9 per cent of their repertoire. Interestingly, the work of artisans is not as heavily concentrated in the category of crafts and construction, which accounts for only just over a quarter of their work tasks. Here the importance of tertiary tasks to those with secondary sector occupational titles is evident; commerce is in fact the largest category of activity for artisans, and transport also accounts for more than 10 per cent. Those working in the secondary sector spent a considerable proportion of their working lives buying and selling materials and goods, and fetching and carrying them between suppliers, employers, and customers. The tiler John Laurence of York, for instance, bought bricks, stone, and lime in 1594, while the plumber John Spurrel carried lead on horseback from Overstrand to Southrepps in Norfolk in September 1672.[53]

This is further illustrated by looking at the subcategories of work performed by some specific artisans. For butchers, 21 per cent of tasks recorded fall in the subcategory of butchery, but a further 28 per cent come from the buy subcategory, and 20 per cent from the sell subcategory, making commerce by far the largest of their work categories.[54] This might be expected from more retail-oriented occupations such as butcher or baker, but commerce and transport are also well represented in the task profiles of manufacturing-oriented occupations. The proportion of commerce for shoemakers is 28 per cent, whereas the clothes and shoes subcategory, which includes shoemaking itself, accounts for 19 per cent.[55] Interestingly, fieldwork represents a larger subcategory than shoemaking, at 21 per cent. Recently, Keibek and Shaw-Taylor have challenged the prevalence of by-employment in early modern England, particularly questioning the extent to which secondary sector workers

[53] BI, CP.G.2792, *Churchwardens of York v. William Barton and Edward Eardley*; NRO, C/S3/50, Exam of John Spurrell.

[54] As explained in Section 1.4, commercial tasks are the most likely to be overrepresented in our data, but even removing the integral data here still leaves the commerce category representing 40 per cent of the tasks of butchers, and butchery itself just 12 per cent.

[55] Removing the integral here results in 16 per cent commerce and 20 per cent clothes and shoes.

Table 2.16 *Work repertoires of certain artisans*

	Weaver tasks (no.)	Tailor tasks (no.)	Shoemaker tasks (no.)	Carpenter tasks (no.)
Agriculture and land	23 (18%)	23 (20%)	14 (25%)	15 (14%)
Carework	2	6	0	2
Commerce	29 (22%)	12 (10%)	16 (28%)	14 (13%)
Crafts and construction	29 (22%)	43 (37%)	11 (19%)	57 (53%)
Food processing	9	1	0	5
Housework	3	2	3	3
Management	10	12	7	7
Transport	23	11	7	5
Other	3[a]	5[b]	0	0
Total tasks	131	115	57	108
Tasks related to craft[c]	49 (37%)	57 (50%)	22 (39%)	66 (61%)

[a] All 'begging'
[b] 4 of 5 'begging'
[c] This includes tasks from all categories that might be considered related to that occupation: for instances, a weaver buying or selling yarn, or transporting cloth.

were also engaged in agricultural work which would belong in the primary sector.[56] For artisans as a whole, 13.1 per cent of all tasks recorded fall within the agriculture category, a not insignificant proportion of their work profile. This total conceals some telling differences between artisanal groups, however. Table 2.16 shows the overall work repertoires of four artisanal occupations frequently recorded as undertaking agricultural tasks. An additional row at the bottom of the table tallies all tasks possibly related to that occupation; so for weavers, this includes buying and transporting yarn, for instance, in addition to weaving.

This analysis shows a spectrum of by-employment ordered along socio-economic lines. Traditionally low-income manufacturers, such as weavers, tailors, and shoemakers, were more likely to participate in agricultural work than the average artisan. Moreover, the poorer the primary occupation, the more likely individuals were to pursue work outside of and unrelated to it; weavers and shoemakers devoted less time to their primary occupations than did carpenters, who had access to

[56] See Keibek and Shaw-Taylor, 'Early modern rural by-employments'. See also Wallis, Colson, and Chilosi, 'Structural change', who dismiss by-employment as a significant factor.

better-paid construction work. Keibek and Shaw-Taylor have argued that by-employment was more common among relatively wealthy individuals, since the probate inventories of lower-income workers show little material sign of multiple occupations. From this they extrapolate that impoverished workers were more likely to rely on a single occupation, which mutes the overall effect of by-employment on measurements of sectoral distribution using occupational data, as discussed in Section 2.4. Yet our results indicate the opposite; poorer workers in the secondary sector, like weavers, shoemakers, and tailors, were more likely to seek work where they could find it. Much of this work might have been done 'for another' – 33 per cent of tasks performed by all artisans were recorded as such – and therefore often using others' equipment or resources, materials which would not show up in the actor's probate inventory.

If 'out of sector' work was only undertaken by artisans occasionally and seasonally, during the harvest, it may not have made a significant impact to the overall distribution of their work activity across different sectors of the economy.[57] Certainly, our analysis of seasonality in Section 4.2 shows that craftsmen and tradesmen performed 50 per cent of their agricultural tasks during the harvest quarter. Yet, importantly, this distribution of labour was no more seasonal than that of husbandmen and yeomen, who did 47 per cent of their agricultural work in the same season. The share of artisans' repertoires devoted to agriculture remained between 11 and 15 per cent during the other three quarters of the year, suggesting that such by-employment in agriculture was not merely a seasonal phenomenon. If husbandmen and yeomen were by-employed in craftwork to the same extent that artisans were in agriculture, then the overall effect on the economy and sectoral distribution would be limited.[58] But as Table 2.15 shows, only 5.4 and 5.1 per cent of tasks undertaken by husbandmen and yeomen respectively fell within the crafts and construction category, as opposed to the 13.1 per cent of artisans' tasks that were agricultural. This suggests that there was a significant degree of agricultural by-employment among artisans, and particularly among their poorest (and also most numerous) contingent. This helps to account for the sectoral distribution of tasks, with a much smaller secondary sector than one based on occupational descriptors, as discussed

[57] Keibek and Shaw-Taylor, 'Early modern rural by-employments', p. 257

[58] This would also rely on the proportions of each in the population as a whole being similar. Table 1.1, based on all male deponents in the database, shows that yeomen, husbandmen, and agricultural trades combined accounted for 37.0 per cent and artisans 34.3 per cent. Table 2.10, which is based only on male actors in the dataset, shows yeomen, husbandmen, and agricultural trades as 27.6 per cent and artisans as 30.2 per cent. In both tables, the proportions are therefore similar.

Table 2.17 *Proportion of types of work performed by male occupational groups*

	Agricultural tasks		Crafts and food tasks		Commerce and management tasks		Transport tasks	
	no.	%	no.	%	no.	%	no.	%
Gentry and professions	35	2.8	4	0.5	64	5.7	13	2.3
Artisans	166	13.4	452	54.4	450	40.3	143	25.4
Yeomen, husbandmen, agricultural trades	523	42.2	123	14.8	317	28.4	150	26.6
Labourers	216	17.4	112	13.5	112	10.0	118	21.0
Servants and apprentices	203	16.4	83	10.0	68	6.1	88	15.6
Tertiary (commercial and transport trades)	17	1.4	21	2.5	81	7.2	30	5.3
Other (miscellaneous and multiple)	78	6.3	36	4.3	26	2.3	21	3.7
Total	1,238	99.9	831	100.0	1,118	100.0	563	99.9

in Section 2.4. Those with secondary sector occupations undertook a significant number of tasks in both the primary and tertiary sectors.

Another way to think about sectoral distribution and the extent of specialisation is to investigate the proportion of work falling into certain categories that was performed by different occupational groups. In Table 2.17 the main occupational categories and work categories have both been grouped along broadly sectoral lines. It demonstrates that those with explicitly agricultural occupational descriptors performed 42.2 per cent of male agricultural work, with over half of agricultural tasks being undertaken by other occupational groups, including servants and labourers, some of whom would have specialised in agricultural work. Work tasks in secondary sector categories, those focused on crafts and food processing, were primarily performed by men with artisanal titles, at 54.4 per cent. The picture is very different for tertiary categories of work, where less than 10 per cent of male tasks were performed by individuals with a specific tertiary occupation. Instead, both agricultural workers and especially artisans undertook significant proportions of the work performed in the tertiary sector. If substantial proportions of primary and secondary sector men's work were performed by specialists in those sectors, the same was not true of tertiary sector work. This offers further explanation as to why tertiary work is underrepresented by occupational data for this period, even when focusing on men's work alone.

Indeed, as the analysis here has shown, the relationship between occupational titles, work repertoires, and the sectoral distribution of work was far from straightforward.

If cross-referencing occupational titles and tasks performed can inform debates about the overall shape of the early modern English economy, it can also help historians to investigate the work undertaken by those with more opaque descriptors, which were particularly prevalent in the early modern period. From 'gentleman' and 'yeoman' to 'servant' and 'labourer', preambles often accorded people titles that said more about status or employment relations than the type of work an individual actually did. This is certainly true in the case of those women who were described as 'wife', a term that historians have argued might be seen as a form of occupational descriptor as well as a marital status, but which reveals little about the specifics of the work involved.[59] Section 2.3 investigated the work repertoires of married women, but we can also use our data to examine the proportion of tasks undertaken by different groups of wives. In some instances, preambles recorded the occupational descriptor of a woman's husband, and these can be used to reconstruct repertoires for the wives of husbandmen, artisans, and labourers.[60] This is not to suggest that a husband's occupational title can be readily extended to his wife; rather, it allows the extent of any correlation between the work of husbands and wives to be examined. This has been a subject of debate, especially in relation to the wives of artisans, where some historians have argued that the work done by artisans and their wives was very different, and others have suggested it was more complementary, with different but related tasks performed side by side.[61] It could of course vary from case to case. Amy Erickson suggested that in eighteenth-century London, it was more common for couples in the middling ranks to work in the same trade but unusual at lower socio-economic levels; even in the middling ranks, however, no more than half of such couples worked together or in related occupations.[62]

As Table 2.18 shows, wives of husbandmen did not consistently work side by side with their husbands in agriculture. Instead, they had a varied work repertoire, where commerce was the largest category, and much of the rest of their work was evenly distributed across the categories of agriculture, carework, housework, and transport. The only

59 Shepard, *Accounting for Oneself*, pp. 257–60.
60 The numbers are too small to attempt this for other occupational groups.
61 Flather, 'Space, place, and gender'; Whittle, 'Enterprising widows'.
62 Erickson, 'Married women's occupations'.

Table 2.18 *Work repertoires of wives of certain occupations*

	Average female repertoire (%)	Wife of husbandman repertoire (%)	Wife of artisan repertoire (%)	Wife of labourer repertoire (%)
Agriculture and land	17.6	14.6	9.5	12.0
Carework	13.7	13.6	6.3	14.7
Commerce	20.7	29.1	27.8	33.3
Crafts and construction	7.7	9.7	12.0	12.0
Food processing	4.9	3.9	5.7	1.3
Housework	19.5	10.7	18.4	14.7
Management	6.4	3.9	12.0	4.0
Transport	7.7	14.6	8.2	8.0
Other	1.8	0.0	0.0	0.0
Total	100.0	100.1	99.9	100.0
Total tasks	2,686	103	158	75

two subcategories for the wives of husbandmen that accounted for more than 10 per cent of their activities were buy, at 21 per cent, and carry goods, at 12 per cent, suggesting that rural wives took on considerable responsibility for the commercial activities of farming households, and that their work was particularly diverse. The work of wives of labourers appears to be similarly diverse, with commerce again dominating, but craft and construction taking a more prominent role. It is hard to say much about patterns at the subcategory level here, due to the small sample, but the differences between the wives of husbandmen and of labourers were limited.

Wives of artisans performed less work in agriculture than wives of husbandmen, and more work in crafts and construction, as might be expected. They also played a key role in the commercial activities of their household, with both buying and selling appearing in their top three subcategories, alongside textile production. Management activities also formed a significant proportion of their work repertoires. This could imply that the wives of artisans often did have a close working relationship with their husbands, helping to manage a household business, selling goods it produced, and dealing with associated payments and finances, although it could also be evidence that they were running enterprises of their own that required these tasks. This can be examined further by analysing whether the tasks recorded for the wives of artisans in any way matched the occupation of their husband. Here this is defined as belonging in the same subcategory as their husband's occupation, or fetching, selling, or buying goods related to their husband's occupation. This shows a match in only 23 per cent of cases. Closer examination shows that these were mostly instances of the wives of textilemakers, and that they carried out the same textile and clothing work which women were associated with more broadly, such as spinning, and thus were not especially distinctive to wives whose husband worked in that trade. As such, we cannot assume they were directly collaborating with their husbands when doing such tasks. Other examples of 'matches' were the wives of butchers or bakers selling meat and bread, showing that there was potential for commercial partnership between wives and their artisan husbands. For instance, at a Monday market in July 1631, the blacksmith William Foster and his wife Christian together 'were standing to sell their commodities', including nails, at a stall in Spilsby, Lincolnshire.[63] A close working relationship between married couples may have been more prominent in some trades than others, but the work-task data suggests it was not widespread. In the remaining 77 per cent of tasks undertaken by artisan's wives, there was no clear correlation between the task undertaken and the husband's occupation.

A man's occupational title cannot be taken to show what work his wife undertook. In some cases, the descriptors accorded to men did not provide much indication of the tasks their own working life revolved around either. Gentleman and yeoman are both titles that say as much about social status as they do about work, but by reconstructing the work repertoires of each, it is possible to explore the types of tasks they were likely to perform. As Table 2.15 showed, the work of the gentry was more heavily concentrated in managerial work than it was for any other occupational group, and involvement in secondary sector work was extremely rare. Yeomen performed more agricultural tasks than their social superiors, but their working lives also involved high proportions of management and commercial activities, and fewer transport and food processing tasks than husbandmen and labourers: they were less likely to get their hands and boots dirty. Historians have found it particularly difficult to reconstruct the working lives of labourers, as wage accounts record only their paid work and probate inventories are biased towards wealthier labourers.[64] As shown in Table 2.15, their repertoire suggests that the work of labourers was relatively diverse. Agriculture was the largest category, at 36.5 per cent, but this was not as high a proportion as it was for husbandmen. Transport was much higher for labourers, at 20.0 per cent, than for any other occupation, suggesting that the low-skill,

[63] LiA, LQS/A/1/4/1631, 108, 123.

[64] See Section 0.2 of the Introduction.

Table 2.19 *Largest subcategories (25+ tasks) for labourers, husbandmen, and male servants*

Labourers	Tasks	Husbandmen	Tasks	Servants (M)	Tasks
Fieldwork	57	Fieldwork	152	Animal husbandry	86
Animal husbandry	49	Animal husbandry	104	Fieldwork	48
Buy	47	Buy	80	Farm transport	29
Carting	36	Farm transport	69	Carting	28
Farm transport	34	Sell	55	Carry goods	26
Carry goods	33	Carry goods	46		
Sell	29	Wood husbandry	28		
Threshing	28	Butchery	26		

time-consuming work of moving goods in this society often fell upon the shoulders of this group. This is confirmed by Table 2.19, which shows the top subcategories of the labourer's repertoire. It also shows that labourers were heavily involved in buying goods, which may well reflect their dependence on the market because they lacked their own resources to grow or manufacture the products needed to run a household.

The profile of labourers' work can usefully be compared to that done by husbandmen, two groups that historians have argued were growing increasingly convergent in the seventeenth century, with many of the latter effectively living a similar existence to labourers despite claiming a higher status title.[65] At the level of both categories and subcategories, labourers and husbandmen performed a similar set of tasks: agriculture, commerce, and transport were the top three categories for both. However, the work of husbandmen was much more heavily concentrated in the first of these categories. Indeed, as Table 2.19 shows, whilst both groups had the same top three subcategories, for husbandmen the gap between their top two categories and their other main subcategories was significantly wider than it was for labourers. Where the husbandman's working life was dominated by agricultural activity, the labourer was required to be more of a generalist to make ends meet.[66]

[65] See Shepard, *Accounting for Oneself*, pp. 264, 273.

[66] We also have 25 tasks that were performed by individuals with the multiple descriptors of husbandman and labourer – the former usually provided in the preamble, the latter in response to questioning about how they made a living. Of these 16 were fieldwork tasks, which puts these individuals closer to the specialist husbandman than the generalist labourer. These individuals look more like husbandmen who worked as day labourers in the harvest season for additional income, rather than men who depended on wages throughout the year.

Table 2.20 *Work repertoires for servants*

	Average F repertoire (%)	F servant repertoire (%)	M servant repertoire (%)
Agriculture and land	17.6	21.6	42.2
Carework	13.7	8.9	2.2
Commerce	20.7	8.2	7.2
Crafts and construction	7.7	6.9	7.6
Food processing	4.9	5.5	10.1
Housework	19.5	37.5	5.2
Management	6.4	2.7	5.2
Transport	7.7	7.6	18.9
Other	1.8	1.0	1.3
Total	100.0	99.9	99.9
Total tasks	2,686	291	445

Servants are another group for whom it is difficult to recover the precise nature of their work, and a repertoire analysis can be applied here too for both male and female servants, as shown in Table 2.20. For male servants, agriculture emerges as the largest category at 42.2 per cent. Crafts and construction account for only 7.6 per cent, and housework and carework combined just 7.2 per cent, which suggests that most male servants were servants in husbandry rather than domestic servants or assistants to craftsmen. Food processing accounts for 10.1 per cent of tasks, but a quarter of these were threshing, which for PST purposes would be seen as a primary sector activity. Like labourers, male servants engaged in a significant number of transport tasks, again suggesting that this type of work was the lot of the lowest status workers.[67] Their subordinate position within households resulted in them engaging in far fewer commercial transactions than husbandmen or labourers. Within the category of agriculture male servants concentrated in particular on animal husbandry. Feeding and checking on livestock, and moving them around the farm, were routine tasks often delegated to male servants.

Female servants are one of the few female occupational groups for which a repertoire can be reconstructed, as we have 291 tasks performed by women described as servants.[68] By comparing Table 2.20 with Tables 2.4 and 2.8, it is evident that the work of female servants was similar to that of young and never-married women; this is expected,

[67] See also Section 3.3 on this point.

[68] See Mansell, *Female Servants*, ch. 6. for a similar analysis that uses a different set of categories.

given the considerable overlap between these three characteristics. Female servants did a higher proportion of their tasks in agriculture compared to the average female repertoire, and also less commerce, carework, and management than other women. Their largest category of work by some distance was housework. Table 2.20 also shows that male and female servants had quite distinctive work profiles, in large part due to the considerable discrepancy in the amount of housework undertaken. And whilst agriculture was a top two category for both, the types of agriculture each engaged in differed. Male servants' top two subcategories were animal husbandry and fieldwork; milking was the largest agricultural subcategory for female servants, whose top three subcategories overall were food and drink provision (35 tasks), milking (24), and laundry (21). Undoubtedly, the work of female and male servants overlapped, especially during the harvest, but overall they concentrated their time on quite different tasks. These findings for female servants also present an interesting contrast to some of the existing literature, which has used sources such as wage assessments where dairying is the most commonly mentioned form of work, and farm books like Robert Loder's and Henry Best's, which list brewing, baking, and malting alongside washing and milking as key tasks for female servants.[69] Of these, only washing and milking appear in our top 10 subcategories for this occupational group. It may be the case that these more specialist work activities such as dairying, brewing, baking, and malting were undertaken by fewer households than more general tasks like milking, washing, and food preparation, and that our methodology is capturing the more common tasks, those that servants would have performed in almost every household in which they were employed.[70]

One of the things that marked servants out from other categories of worker was the extent to which they performed tasks 'for another'. For male servants the proportion was 76.4 per cent of all their tasks, and for female servants 80 per cent. This indicates the extent to which service involved giving almost all your working time to your employer. The average for all male tasks in the dataset was 35 per cent and for all female tasks 36 per cent. As Table 2.21 shows, most male occupations fell within a range of roughly 10 per cent either side of the average, suggesting that the proportion of 'for another' work undertaken did vary by occupation in this period but not dramatically for those not in service. The other exception was the professions, at 55.6 per cent, where many of our examples relate to the provision of healthcare for people outside of

[69] Whittle, 'Housewives and servants', p. 62.

[70] On these more specialist activities as more commercialised, see Ibid.

Table 2.21 *Proportion of work tasks 'for another' by occupation (male)*

Occupation	Tasks 'for another'	% of tasks done 'for another'
Gentry	20	27.8
Professions	65	55.6
Yeomen	51	23.7
Commercial trades	33	30.8
Artisans	417	32.9
Husbandmen	300	36.2
Agricultural trades	57	44.5
Transport trades	29	46.8
Labourers	202	34.2
Servants	340	76.4
Apprentices	32	78.0
Multiple	51	68.0
Miscellaneous	51	56.0
Overall	1,648	40.8

the household, and in general professionals specialised in providing services to others. The surprise here is that the work undertaken by labourers was not more commonly done 'for another' outside of their own household than was the case for other men. Whilst our 'for another' category is only loosely correlated to all income-generating work, this does suggest that the labourers in our sample were not wholly absorbed in working for wages and still engaged in a considerable amount of subsistence-oriented work. In this respect, they again look to have been a poor relation of, rather than a different species to, the average husbandman.[71]

2.6 Conclusion

This chapter has demonstrated the more detailed approach to work enabled by work-task data. Exploration of work by age group shows how women's work varied significantly over the lifecycle in a way that men's work did not. This finding is reinforced by variations in women's work according to marital status. Most significantly, young, unmarried

[71] There is little evidence that these proportions changed much over time either. Prior to 1630 the figure for husbandmen was 38 per cent, and after 1630 it was 35 per cent. There is no evidence here of a dramatic increase in dependence on paid work for husbandmen across our sample, though our data is not best designed for capturing change over time. For labourers the percentage of 'for another' work rose slightly from 34 per cent to 35 per cent.

women did the highest proportion of housework, while responsibility for carework increased with age, and reached its highest proportion among widows. Married women's work repertoires were characterised by high proportions of commerce and management, suggesting the responsibilities and opportunities that came with being joint head of household.

Evidence of men's occupational descriptors shows that the distribution of occupations of men carrying out work in the work-task dataset differed little from that of occupations calculated by Keibek from probate documents. However, when work tasks are arranged to show sectoral distribution, the pattern is very different from that shown by male occupations. The tertiary sector was much larger, and the primary and secondary sectors smaller. This was not only because much of women's work falls into the tertiary sector, but because occupations under-record men's tertiary sector work. Both primary and secondary sector occupations required large quantities of work transporting and marketing goods.

Work tasks allow us to look inside occupations and see how they were constituted of different tasks. This shows the prevalence of by-employment, with men with all types of occupations engaging in agriculture. By-employment was particularly important for less wealthy artisans, who worked at a range of activities to make ends meet. It also allows the graded differences in agriculture-related work undertaken by men of different levels of wealth and status, from gentlemen and yeomen, through to husbandmen, labourers, and servants, to be viewed with clarity. Wealthier agriculturalists did more management and commerce; wage workers did more transport and threshing; those in the middle did more tasks closely related to agriculture. Differences in women's agricultural work are also evident, with young women and female servants doing a higher proportion of agricultural work, particularly milking, while married women had a significant place in the harvest workforce.

Work 'for another' provides another important dimension with which to analyse early modern work tasks and reveals some surprises. Carework was the most likely category of work to be undertaken either for pay or for people outside the household. Housework was almost as often 'for another' as agricultural work. The lives of servants were dominated by work 'for another', but other occupations combined 'for another' work with varied forms of production and subsistence work. These themes form the foundation on which the analysis in the following chapters is based.

3 Places of Work

In 1626 Stephen Morvell, a chapman from Colne in Lancashire, travelled to Preston fair to purchase linen. Having bought a large quantity, he returned to the inn where he was lodging to measure it and noticed that he had lost his purse. Margaret Slater, the wife of an alehouse-keeper from Ribchester, from whom he had purchased linen earlier that day, was present in the same room. Stephen's purse contained three particularly distinctive foreign coins, known as 'cardecus', and later the news that these coins were circulating in Ribchester led Stephen to suspect Margaret had stolen his purse.[1] Margaret's neighbours testified that she had spent an unusually large amount of money at the fair, and by her own admission 'she paid for flax 12s, for a jerkin-cloth 2s, for exchange of a pewter flagon 18d, for 2 geese 18d and lent 12d to Henry Dewhurst'. She explained that she had brought some of her spending money from home, 'and sold yarn for the rest'. However, this did not account for the foreign coins. Christopher Norcrosse recalled that Margaret's husband, John, had come into Thomas Ireland's alehouse in Ribchester with a cardecus, which he had exchanged for 13.5d. Another cardecus was received by George Rawcliffe of Ribchester for butcher's meat sold to Margaret.[2]

As well as recording information about work tasks, depositions are rich in evidence about spatial locations. From the case of Stephen Morvell's lost purse, we learn that Morvell travelled 27 miles to Preston from the Pennine town of Colne to attend the fair. The journey was far enough that he needed to lodge at an inn overnight. As a chapman, it is likely his trip was to purchase cloth that he could then retail closer to home. Margaret Slater travelled 10 miles from Ribchester to Preston, a return journey that could be accomplished in a day, to sell yarn and cloth and buy flax and other goods. Thus, fairs drew people in from the wider

[1] 'Cardecus' was the English name for *quart d'écu*, a French silver coin worth a quarter of the écu, or 15 sous tournois; the coin circulated between the late sixteenth and the eighteenth centuries: OED online.

[2] LaA, QSB/1/17, 25–6.

region, and commerce caused people to travel from town to town, and from smaller settlements such as Ribchester to larger towns such as Preston. Although no one in the case is described spinning or weaving, the prominence of flax, yarn, and linen cloth in this case is distinctive to Lancashire, an important region for English linen production.[3] The case also offers glimpses of interior spaces where work was carried out: the public room in the inn where Stephen Morvell measured his cloth, and the alehouses of Ribchester which not only sold beer but allowed coins to be exchanged along with gossip. This chapter looks at all these themes, exploring regional differences, contrasts between rural and urban work, transport and travel, inside and outside workspaces, and privacy.

Spatial location is an essential element of the experience of work. Although not always explicitly acknowledged, location is also essential to how historians view work and economic change in early modern England. Industrialisation and urbanisation from the late eighteenth century onwards involved the creation of specialist workspaces which separated work and home. These included not only factories but banks, offices, hospitals, workhouses, and non-residential retail shops. The growth of towns and industry, and the relative decline in agricultural work, reduced the proportion of work taking place outside. Specialisation in industry and agriculture reduced the extent of by-employment. New modes of transport revolutionised the business of moving goods and people. But what did the economy look like, in spatial terms, before these changes took place? Both urbanisation and regional specialisation caused work to be gradually relocated even before the upheavals of the eighteenth and nineteenth centuries, but the extent and impact of these changes has been difficult to measure. We know that people from rural settlements must have travelled to market towns to engage in commerce, but the extent and means of this movement has rarely caught historians' attention. Transport is more often studied as a technology or network, rather than as work and time-use.

The work-task data offers insight into all these issues and the findings are not always what we might expect. It is commonplace to state that people worked at home in preindustrial economies, but very few historians have explored, let alone measured, the actual location of work in the period before 1700. This chapter does just that. Gender historians have paid more attention to workspaces, responding to the assertation of an inside/outside division between women's and men's work that was frequently reiterated in early modern didactic literature. Amanda Flather's

[3] Lowe, *Lancashire Textile Industry*.

detailed study of Essex court depositions has shown that while women did work inside more than men, the locations of women's and men's work also overlapped a great deal.[4] Here, we use our wider sample to quantify gendered work patterns. The chapter begins by exploring regional contrasts: the work-task data shows remarkably few differences at the level of general categories although some regional differences in farming regimes, diet, and specialist industries are evident. The contrasting patterns of work between large towns, market towns, and villages are more clearcut, as shown in Section 3.2. Section 3.3 turns to the topic of transport, examining the distances travelled and methods of movement. This is a reminder of the often time-consuming and difficult task of moving things, people, and information around the early modern landscape. The final two sections address the spatial dimension of workplaces, first examining the division between inside and outside tasks and the house as a place of work, before in the final section considering the lack of privacy experienced in all locations.

3.1 Regions

When Dorothy Tottle sat by a window making bone lace in a house at Luppitt near Honiton in east Devon in 1614, or Robert Arcle drew 'coals at the coal pit in East Brandon' in County Durham in 1633, or Thomas Browne grew and sold 'six acres of turnips in a close called maypole close in Horning' in Norfolk in 1693, they were all undertaking regionally distinctive forms of work related to local specialisms.[5] The work-task data was collected from three regions chosen to represent England's contrasting economies: the north, the south-west, and eastern England. Figure 1.1 and Table 1.2 in Chapter 1 show the counties from which evidence was collected. Ann Kussmaul's *General View of the Rural Economy* provides an overview of England's early modern economic regions. She used the seasonality of marriage to map parishes that were dominated by arable agriculture, with October marriages after the harvest; pastoral agriculture, with April, May, or June marriages after spring lambing and calving; and industrial parishes, with no strong seasonality. Her data shows that by the early eighteenth century, the south-west was dominated by a mixture of pastoral and industrial parishes, the east by

[4] Flather, 'Space, place, and gender'.

[5] DHC, Chanter 867, *Follett v. Stone and Tottle*; Yallop, 'Honiton lace industry'; DUIC, DDR: Consistory court depositions (loose), *Fletcher v. Newton*; Hatcher, *British Coal Industry*, p. 83; NRO, DN/DEP/53/58A, *Stone v. Hall*; Overton, *Agricultural Revolution*, p. 95.

arable parishes, and the north by industrial parishes.[6] However, Kussmaul also demonstrated that there was significant change over time. Her maps for the late sixteenth century show far fewer contrasts, with arable parishes spread across the whole of England.[7] Historians have also suggested that the gender division of labour varied regionally, again using evidence from the eighteenth century and later. For instance, Snell argued that women found more agricultural work in south-west England than in the east, while studies of the late eighteenth and nineteenth centuries show that women found more agricultural work in northern England.[8]

The work-task data shows a notable lack of regional differences for 1500 to 1700 in both the gender division of labour and work repertoires more generally. Table 3.1 demonstrates that the proportion of agricultural work done by women varied by less than one percentage point between the three regions, ranging between 35.6 per cent in the east, and 36.5 per cent in the south-west. The proportion of secondary sector work done by women in the crafts and construction and food processing categories was also quite stable regionally, although somewhat higher in the south-west than elsewhere. The biggest differences appear where least expected, in commerce, housework, and transport, as discussed in more detail below.

The large categories of work used in Table 3.1 hide some important differences in specific tasks. For instance, winnowing, the process of separating threshed grain from the chaff, was done by women in western England and men in the east. There are 29 examples of winnowing in the database. In Devon, Cornwall, and Cheshire, all winnowing was carried out by women; in Somerset, Wiltshire, Hampshire, and Lancashire some men were recorded but women outnumbered them; while in Norfolk, Lincolnshire, and Yorkshire only men undertook this task. Sheep shearing was another activity in which women's participation was regionally specific. Of the 75 examples of sheep shearing recorded, 11 were done by women. Of these, 9 came from Devon and 2 from Somerset. Interestingly, medieval manorial accounts suggest that this form of women's work had once been much more widespread.[9]

The overall uniformity of the gender division of labour stemmed, at least in part, from the uniformity of work tasks more generally between regions as shown in Table 3.2. This reveals that the proportion of

[6] Kussmaul, *General View*, Figure 1.1. [7] Kussmaul, *General View*, Figure 1.4.
[8] Snell, *Annals*, p. 49; Verdon, *Rural Women Workers*; Burnette, 'Wages and employment', pp. 678–9, 685.
[9] Rogers, *History of Agriculture and Prices*, Vol. 1, p. 280.

Table 3.1 *Gender division of labour by region*

	S. West		North		East		S. West	North	East
	F tasks adj.	M tasks	F tasks adj.	M tasks	F tasks adj.	M tasks	% by F adj.	% by F adj.	% by F adj.
Agriculture and land	586	1,018	275	482	365	659	36.5	36.3	35.6
Carework	290	72	369	64	297	60	80.1	85.2	83.2
Commerce	886	867	236	357	294	335	50.5	39.8	46.7
Crafts and construction	271	341	133	204	127	193	44.3	39.4	39.6
Food processing	183	230	60	92	96	156	44.3	39.6	38.0
Housework	551	88	251	60	596	76	86.2	80.7	88.7
Management	178	161	142	146	124	166	52.5	49.3	42.7
Transport	239	381	181	262	108	386	38.6	40.8	21.9
Other	12	38	58	36	62	34	24.0	61.7	64.6
Total	3,196	3,196	1,704	1,703	2,067	2,065	50.0	50.0	50.0

Notes: adj. = adjusted. Female work tasks are adjusted using a different multiplier for each region to preserve a 50:50 overall division of tasks within each region: S. West (x2.44), North (x2.41), East (x3.09).

Table 3.2 *Work repertoires by region*

	Total tasks	All tasks repertoire (%)	S. West repertoire (%)	North repertoire (%)	East repertoire (%)
Agriculture and land	2,631	27.3	27.9	24.7	28.4
Carework	564	5.8	4.2	9.0	5.7
Commerce	2115	21.9	27.3	18.9	15.7
Crafts and construction	945	9.8	10.0	10.7	8.6
Food processing	609	6.3	6.8	4.9	6.8
Housework	747	7.7	7.0	6.8	9.8
Management	645	6.7	5.2	8.5	7.5
Transport	1,237	12.8	10.6	14.0	15.4
Other	157	1.6	1.0	2.5	2.0
Total	–	99.9	100.0	100.0	99.9
Total tasks	9,650	9,650	4,506	2,410	2,734

agricultural tasks was slightly lower in the north, and the proportion of crafts and construction slightly lower in the east, but the differences are minimal. As with the gender division of labour, larger differences are evident in categories that would not be expected to vary significantly, such as commerce, transport, and carework. Table 3.2 shows raw data, and some of these variations can be explained by the make-up of the samples.[10] A high proportion of work tasks in the eastern region were taken from coroners' reports: 22 per cent compared to 11 per cent in the north and 5 per cent in the south-west. Coroners' reports record a high number of transport tasks, because they led to accidents, particularly while driving carts. The percentage of transport tasks recorded in the coroners' reports was almost identical in the east and the south-west, at 22.6 per cent and 22.4 per cent, respectively. This indicates that the difference between the regions is largely due to the larger proportion of tasks from coroners' reports in the eastern region. A similar issue occurs with carework. Paternity cases brought to the quarter sessions, in which unmarried women were questioned about the identity of their baby's father while giving birth, recorded many carework tasks relating to midwifery and childcare. In the east and south-west such cases contributed 10 per cent of carework tasks recorded, while in the north the percentage was 44 per cent. Most of the northern cases came from a single county, Cheshire, which provided two-thirds of the carework tasks from northern paternity cases, inflating the proportion of carework tasks in the north as a whole, as discussed in Section 1.1.

[10] See Table 1.2.

Table 3.3 *Regional differences in agricultural work tasks*

Region	S. West		East		North		All	
	Tasks	%	Tasks	%	Tasks	%	Tasks	%
Arable	560	35.8	291	30.2	215	30.1	1,065	32.9
Pastoral	367	23.5	245	25.4	254	35.5	868	26.8
Other agriculture and food processing	636	40.7	428	44.4	246	34.4	1,307	40.3
All agriculture and food processing	1,563	100.0	964	100.0	715	100.0	3,240	100.0
Sheep	175	59.3	84	36.7	93	40.3	352	46.6
Cattle	54	18.3	46	20.1	57	24.7	157	20.8
Horses	38	12.9	61	26.6	52	22.5	151	20.0
Poultry	9	3.1	16	7.0	15	6.5	40	5.3
Other animal husbandry	19	6.4	22	9.6	14	6.1	55	7.3
All animal husbandry	295	100.0	229	100.0	231	100.0	755	100.0

Notes: Arable includes fieldwork, gathering food (mostly gleaning), and threshing and winnowing; pastoral includes animal husbandry, milking, and dairying.

To identify significant regional differences it is necessary to look within the larger categories of work, such as agriculture. There is an extensive literature on regional specialisation within early modern English agriculture, developing out of Joan Thirsk's intricate maps based on evidence from probate inventories.[11] The work-task methodology provides a more muted picture of regional difference in agriculture, as shown in Table 3.3. More agricultural work tasks were involved in livestock husbandry in the north, compared to the south-west or east: in both the south-west and east arable work tasks outnumbered pastoral ones, but the balance was switched round in the north where pastoral work tasks were more common. There were also differences within each type of agriculture. In the south-west and east there were more work tasks mentioning wheat than oats, to a ratio of 2.5:1 in the south-west, and 2:1 in the east. In contrast, in the north there were more work tasks relating to oats, giving a wheat-to-oats ratio of 0.9:1. This is expected, given the difficulties of cultivating wheat in much of northern England and the dominance of oats in the northern diet.[12]

[11] Thirsk, *Agricultural Regions*; Overton, *Agricultural Revolution*, pp. 46–62.
[12] Muldrew, *Food, Energy*, pp. 60–2.

Less expected were the regional contrasts in the ratio of mutton to geese mentioned in work tasks, an indicator of both farming systems and diet. The term 'mutton' allows work relating to sheep flesh to be distinguished from the keeping of live sheep. No such precise distinction is possible with geese, although the majority of geese-related work tasks concern preparation for eating. The database contained 160 work tasks mentioning mutton, mostly relating to butchering, commerce, and food processing, in contrast to 188 that mentioned geese. In the north and east geese were prevalent: for every work task mentioning mutton, there were 4.8 mentioning geese in the north and 3.2 in the east. In the south-west the balance was reversed with 2.8 work tasks mentioning mutton for every one that mentioned geese. These differences highlight regional variations in animal husbandry that are not immediately obvious from Table 3.3, as geese were relatively easy to keep and so did not create large quantities of agricultural work, though they do appear in food processing and preparation tasks. Differences in keeping larger animals are more evident in Table 3.3. Sheep farming was most prevalent in the south-west, while in the north there was more of a balance between sheep, cattle, and horses. In the east, horse-related tasks were particularly common, likely because of their predominance as plough beasts in that region.[13]

As noted at the start of the section, specialisms are evident in the places we would expect. Women making bone lace in the first half of the seventeenth century are found not only at Luppitt but at Trull outside Taunton and Kingsdon near Yeovil in Somerset, and at Amersham in Buckinghamshire.[14] The production of linen yarn and cloth is found in Lancashire, Cheshire, and the North Riding of Yorkshire, with another pocket of activity in Cambridgeshire. Hemp was cultivated most frequently in Cambridgeshire and Norfolk.[15] Work activities in fulling mills, used in the production of heavy woollen broadcloth, occur most frequently in Devon and the West Riding of Yorkshire. Tin mining was found at Calstock parish in Cornwall where a man was 'working in a certain tinworks called Drakewalls' in 1560, and at Ashburton on the edge of Dartmoor in Devon, where another man was 'working in tin workings digging with a tin hook' in 1571.[16] Coalmining is found in County Durham and across the West Riding of Yorkshire where it is documented by coroners' reports at Whitkirk and Barwick in Elmet near

[13] Overton, *Agricultural Revolution*, p. 126. [14] Spenceley, 'Origins'.
[15] On linen and hemp, see Evans, *East Anglian Linen Industry*; Lowe, *Lancashire Textile Industry*, ch. 4.
[16] DHC, Chanter 855, *Thomasine Bligh v. John Prowte*; TNA, KB/9/631a/119. On tin-mining in Cornwall and Devon, see Hatcher, *Rural Economy*. Drakewalls is a village in Calstock parish where the landscape is still scarred by tin-mining.

Leeds, at Bradford, at Sandal Magna outside Wakefield, and at Darfield and Wath upon Dearne in southern Yorkshire.[17]

However, regionally distinctive forms of production had a limited effect on overall work patterns because they took place alongside tasks that were commonplace to every community. An example is provided by Manchester. Early modern Manchester was a centre of the cloth industry, and an early producer of cotton cloth in the seventeenth century. There are 40 work tasks from Manchester in the database. Six come from a single case in 1627 involving a 5 lb sack of cotton wool taken from the warehouse of Henry Wrigley, a Salford chapman, and then pawned with the wife of a Manchester alehouse-keeper.[18] The only other case relating directly to the cloth industry describes Robert Brooke 'being as a workman and weaving' in the 'dwellinghouse' of Edward Dawson in 1666.[19] In contrast, the most common Manchester work tasks were agricultural, a reminder that this was still a rural area.[20] Manchester's status as a market town is evident from six tasks relating to buying and selling, and a further six relating to the transport of goods. There were three management tasks, all relating to borrowing goods and arranging delivery. The remaining six tasks were housework and carework. Thus, Manchester's distinctive manufacturing profile is drowned out by a plethora of work tasks commonly found in other places.

The lack of regional differences, particularly in agriculture and secondary sector activities, is an important finding. When Kussmaul observed marked regional differences in the seasonality of marriage in the early eighteenth century, she suggested this was the consequence of increased regional specialisation. The work-task data shows less difference between regions. It is particularly striking that south-west England seems to have been as arable as eastern England: a pattern also shown by Kussmaul's map for the late sixteenth century. The same map shows more industrial parishes, or parishes with little seasonality in marriage patterns, in the north of England, and particularly the north-west.[21] Figure 3.1 explores regional differences in the seasonality of work tasks, and reveals a similar pattern. The north had less seasonality with multiple peaks and work evenly spread across the summer months, indicative of a

[17] Hatcher, *British Coal Industry*, esp. Map 5.5.
[18] LaA, QSB/1/27, 78. In the 1640s Henry Wrigley had goods worth £5143 stored at London, see Willan, 'Manchester clothiers', p. 180.
[19] LaA, QSB/1/1666, April, Info of Grace Chadwick and Elizabeth Rainsley.
[20] There were eight agricultural tasks and four food processing tasks, including winnowing oats and making oatmeal.
[21] Kussmaul, *General View*, p. 12.

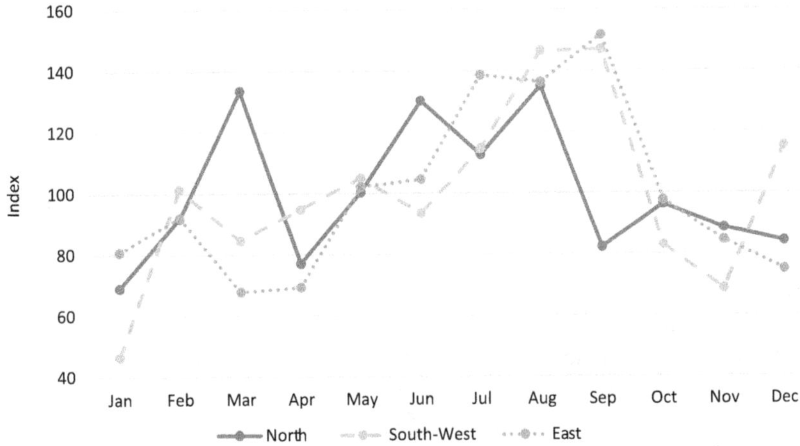

Figure 3.1 Regional seasonality: distribution of monthly tasks compared.
Notes: 100 = monthly average; Integral excluded. The monthly task totals have been subject to a series of weightings and other adjustments explained in Section 4.1 and Appendices C and D. F adjusted = the female multiplier differs from the standard multiplier as it is designed to give an equal number of male and female tasks for each region with monthly data attached, and therefore varies by region: south-west (x2.30), east (x2.81), north (x2.03).

pastoral/industrial economy.[22] In contrast, the east and south-west show an arable-farming pattern with clear peaks of work in the harvest months of August and September.

Overall, the work-task data shows few marked regional differences. Regional economic differences were more muted in the sixteenth and seventeenth centuries than they became in the eighteenth and nineteenth centuries, as shown by Kussmaul.[23] There were important differences in local and regional economies, especially in agriculture, as historians such as Thirsk have demonstrated.[24] However, these differences did not necessarily lead to contrasting patterns of work. The plethora of commonplace tasks drowns out those that were regionally distinctive, as the example of Manchester shows. Some important regional differences do emerge from the work-task approach: the south-west had more sheep farming, the seasonality of work suggests the north was more pastoral and

[22] The March peak is largely caused by the Cheshire carework tasks associated with paternity cases.
[23] Kussmaul, *General View*. [24] Thirsk, *Agricultural Regions*.

industrial, and specialist industries were dotted across the country. Nonetheless, the importance of shared patterns of work is most evident, a feature of the early modern economy that is often overlooked.

3.2 Town and Country

Towns differed from other settlements not only by their size as centres of population but by their distinctive economic activities and patterns of work, particularly by the presence of weekly markets and the higher proportion of non-agricultural occupations.[25] This section explores the different patterns of work in large towns, market towns, and rural parishes of villages or scattered settlements. Large towns are defined as having populations of 3,000 or more in 1522 or 5,000 or more in 1700.[26] No specifically urban records were consulted to gather evidence of work tasks, but those collected approximately reflect the distribution of population between towns and smaller settlements. Of these, 8 per cent came from large provincial towns, slightly more than Wrigley's estimates of their proportional population, which rose from 3 per cent in c.1520 to 6 per cent in 1700.[27] Market towns were identified using the lists compiled by Everitt for 1500 to 1640.[28] Glennie and Whyte estimate that if these smaller towns are included, 30–33 per cent of England's population was urban in the period from 1540 to 1700.[29] In the work-task database market towns contributed 32 per cent of work tasks. Defined in this way, urban work tasks are slightly overrepresented, making up just under 40 per cent of the total sample.[30]

Table 3.4 explores rural-urban differences in two ways. First, it looks at work tasks according to where the work took place, and, secondly, according to where the worker lived. The clearest differences in work patterns between towns and countryside are found in the categories of agriculture, commerce, and crafts and construction. More agriculture took place in the rural parishes, as would be expected. Nonetheless, it is also clear that agriculture took place in urban parishes.[31] For instance,

25 Dyer, 'Small market towns', p. 427.

26 These are the 31 largest provincial towns in England in each period: see Slack, 'Great and good towns', p. 352.

27 Wrigley, *People, Cities, and Wealth*, p. 162. Wrigley's proportion is of towns of 5,000 or more, excluding London; we include some smaller towns with populations of 3,000–5,000 in the earlier period.

28 Everitt, 'Marketing of agricultural produce', pp. 468–75.

29 Glennie and Whyte, 'Towns in an agrarian economy', p. 169.

30 9,358 out of 9,650 tasks could be located in specific communities. Tasks without specific locations are not included in this analysis.

31 Glennie and Whyte, 'Towns in an agrarian economy', p. 173.

Table 3.4 *Rural and urban work repertoires by task location and worker residence*

	By location of task				By residence of worker			
	All locations repertoire (%)	Large towns repertoire (%)	Market towns repertoire (%)	Rural repertoire (%)	All residence repertoire (%)	Large towns repertoire (%)	Market towns repertoire (%)	Rural repertoire (%)
Agriculture and land	27.4	12.8	17.2	34.7	27.4	15.3	19.8	31.2
Carework	5.9	6.8	6.0	5.7	5.9	7.6	7.0	5.6
Commerce	21.6	31.2	32.4	14.8	21.6	21.8	26.6	20.6
Crafts and construction	9.8	12.0	9.7	9.6	9.8	16.0	11.7	8.4
Food processing	6.2	2.6	4.9	7.3	6.2	3.4	6.0	7.1
Housework	7.8	7.8	6.8	8.4	7.8	7.9	7.2	7.3
Management	6.8	10.4	7.8	5.7	6.8	11.2	7.8	6.6
Transport	12.8	14.7	13.4	12.3	12.8	13.9	12.1	11.8
Other	1.6	1.8	2.0	1.4	1.6	2.9	1.9	1.3
Total	99.9	100.1	100.2	99.9	99.9	100.0	100.1	99.9
Total tasks	9,358	734	2,954	5,670	7,850	555	2,311	4,984

Notes: See text for definition of large towns and market towns. 'Rural' contains work tasks in all other parishes. Totals differ because not all tasks can be located by parish, and not all workers have place of residence recorded.

there were more agricultural tasks than tasks involving crafts and construction in market towns, as we saw in the case of Manchester discussed above. On the other hand, large towns and market towns were more than twice as likely to be locations of commerce than rural parishes. Interestingly, however, if we look at where the people engaging in commerce lived, there was relatively little difference between settlement types. This is because many people conducting commerce in towns travelled in from surrounding villages, as in the case of Margaret Slater from Ribchester doing business in Preston, discussed at the beginning of this chapter. The opposite effect was evident for crafts and construction. By location of task, market towns differed little from rural parishes in the proportion of crafts and construction activities, yet looking at the residence of workers shows that people engaged in crafts and construction were twice as likely to be resident in large towns as rural parishes, and somewhat more likely to live in market towns too. As discussed in Section 7.2, building craftsmen and tailors often travelled out from their urban places of residence to undertake work in the surrounding areas.

Exeter provides an example of the range of work observed in large towns. With a population of around 8,000 in the 1520s, growing to 14,000 in 1700, Exeter was among the largest cities in England.[32] It was smaller than London, Norwich, and Bristol but had a similar population to other regional centres such as York and Salisbury in 1500, and Newcastle and York in 1700.[33] A total of 103 work tasks were collected from Exeter, of which 43 related to commerce, 15 to crafts, and 14 to transport. Commonplace tasks such as agriculture and housework could take on a particular local complexion. For instance, in 1633 Alice Hingston deposed that while she was a servant resident in St Edmunds parish in Exeter she milked the three cows belonging to her employer 'all the summer time' while they grazed in the urban commons by the river Exe; 'sometimes they did pasture below the bridge in the ground called the Shillows, and sometimes in the Bonay, and sometimes in other ground adjoining there called the shooting marsh'.[34] These locations correspond to Shilhays, Bonhay, and the Shooting Marsh, all of which survive as modern street names close to the historic Exe Bridge in modern Exeter. Similarly, Agnes Morell alias Wheaten testified that she did laundry, rinsing clothes in 'the tail of the mills situate near Exe Bridge' in 1619, drawing attention both to the mills that clustered in the area near the bridge, and the types of location used for urban laundry work.[35]

[32] MacCaffrey, *Exeter 1540–1640*; Stephens, *Seventeenth Century Exeter*.
[33] See Wrigley, *People, Cities, and Wealth*, p. 160. All other towns were smaller.
[34] DHC, Chanter 866, *March v. Joanes*. [35] DHC, Chanter 867, *Wills v. Miller*.

While many of the commercial transactions recorded for Exeter, such as buying and selling foodstuffs like meat, cheese, and bread, were found in large and small towns across the country, others were more distinctive. Three different cases mention visiting goldsmiths to have items valued, to sell gold and silver, and make purchases. The only other place in the work-task database where a goldsmith was recorded was King's Lynn, another port city. Also distinctive to Exeter was the sale of fresh sea fish within the city. When a dispute arose among the fish-sellers with stalls 'a little above the Guildhall' in Exeter High Street in 1674, two of the sellers who gave evidence came not from Exeter but from Teignmouth on the coast, one described as an 'agricola' or farmer, and another as the wife of a sailor.[36] They were among the many people working in Exeter who did not live in the city but came there to buy and sell goods at the markets, fairs, and shops. People also came seeking work. Peternell Bowden, a servant, ran away from her employer in Bishopsteignton and headed for Exeter where she was apprehended at the city's Westgate in 1610. Similarly, Christopher Tooker, accused of stealing a shirt in Topsham, also made his way to Exeter looking for work in 1620.[37]

Women outnumbered men in early modern towns. Souden found a sex ratio of 83 men for every 100 women in large towns, compared to 90 in small towns, and 100 in villages in the late seventeenth century.[38] This difference was reflected in the work tasks collected. In the raw unadjusted data 28 per cent of work tasks were carried out by women overall, but the proportion was 26 per cent in rural settlements, 30 per cent in market towns, and 35 per cent in large towns. This pattern is also found in the residence of workers. Women were 26 per cent of workers living in villages, 32 per cent in market towns, and 36 per cent in larger towns. Souden suggested the high numbers of women in towns resulted from their employment as urban domestic servants, while male servants were employed in the countryside in agriculture.[39] Table 3.5 compares the work repertoires of women who lived in rural settlements with those who lived in towns. There is no suggestion that urban women did more housework; in fact, housework was more common in the countryside. Instead, urban women did less agriculture and food processing, and more commerce and management, as well as slightly more of all other types of work. Souden also found that women who migrated to towns

[36] DHC, Chanter 875, *Office v. Grant*.
[37] DHC, QS/4/Box 16, Michaelmas, 9–12; QS/4/Box 24, Epiphany, 7.
[38] Souden, 'Migrants and the population structure', p. 150. His large towns were Bristol, Norwich, Ipswich, Gloucester, Bury St Edmunds, Leicester, Lichfield, and Southampton.
[39] Ibid, p. 152.

Table 3.5 *Women's rural and urban work repertoires compared, by residence of worker*

	F rural repertoire (%)	F urban repertoire (%)
Agriculture and land	21.2	11.4
Carework	14.1	15.5
Commerce	18.7	23.9
Crafts and construction	7.7	9.2
Food processing	5.5	3.4
Housework	18.8	16.9
Management	5.9	8.7
Transport	7.0	8.9
Other	1.2	2.1
Total	100.0	100.0
Total tasks	1,293	890

Notes: Integral excluded; large towns and market towns combined as urban settlements.

were more likely to be unmarried.[40] The work-task data provided no evidence that unmarried women predominated amongst women working in towns: the proportion of female work tasks undertaken by never-married women was marginally higher in the countryside at 22 per cent, and lowest in large towns at 19 per cent.[41]

Patterns of work differed between towns and the countryside. Unsurprisingly, the higher proportion of agriculture characterised rural settlements while higher proportions of crafts and commerce characterised towns. Women's work was more evident in towns, indicating they made up a higher proportion of urban populations, as other studies have found. Distinguishing between where work tasks were performed, and where workers lived shows that although towns were sites of commerce, many of those engaged in that commerce lived in the countryside. Conversely, while those engaged in crafts and construction were more likely to live in towns, a significant proportion of their work was conducted in the countryside.

3.3 Transport and Travel

In June of 1652, Katherine Singard was walking the 8 miles home from Cranage Mill to Great Budworth, Cheshire, carrying some meal on her

[40] Ibid, p. 138.

[41] Just over a third of women were of unknown marital status and are excluded from these figures.

head. Understandably, she stopped off at an alehouse in Cranage to 'beg some small drink' for refreshment.[42] If moving stuff was thirsty work, it was also absolutely central to the experience of working life in early modern England. Histories of transport have concentrated on technologies, speed, and cost, while studies of people's movement have focused on permanent migration, vagrancy, and the culture of travel.[43] The most comprehensive study is offered by Mark Brayshay, who explores ordinary and elite users of highways through a range of sources.[44] Our approach is different: it contextualises transport and travel as an essential element of people's working lives.

Moving goods, animals, and occasionally people from A to B was far more time-consuming in the preindustrial past than in recent centuries. Horses and carts played some part in the process, but in the majority of cases these journeys were undertaken on foot. At a good pace Katherine Singard's trip to the mill would have taken two hours each way; with a load of meal on her head, it likely took longer than that. The overall proportion of working hours taken up by moving things is not fully captured by our transport category, even though it is the third-largest category of work tasks in the database, accounting for 13 per cent of all tasks. The ubiquity of movement activity means that many tasks placed in other categories had an element of transportation attached to them: carrying thatch up a ladder to thatch a roof was treated as a buildings task (crafts and construction); coming home from the woods with a bundle of firewood was classified as collecting fuel (agriculture and land); taking crops from a field to a nearby barn as farm transport, and moving animals *within* a farm as animal husbandry, to name but a few. Many other activities that were recorded, such as going to reckon a debt, or to check on a flock of sheep, also involved travel but not necessarily the transportation of anything but the self, and these were not classed as transport tasks either.[45]

In other words, tasks involving an element of moving things were both extremely numerous and one of the most difficult things to neatly classify. This section analyses a sub-section of such tasks, whilst recognising that we cannot easily provide a comprehensive picture of all transport

[42] CALS, QJF/80/2, 63.

[43] Willan, *Inland Trade*; Cooper, 'Speed and efficiency'; Wrigley, 'Urban growth'; Erickson and Schmidt, 'Migration'; Whyte, *Migration and Society*; Beier, *Masterless Men*; McRae, *Literature and Domestic Travel*; Fumerton, *Unsettled.*

[44] Brayshay, *Land Travel*, esp. ch. 4.

[45] Travel without a clear purpose, or for leisure, was not recorded as a work task, and nor was simply traveling to a place of work, as it was not clear this was something a third party could undertake instead.

Table 3.6 *Intra-parish tasks vs inter-parish tasks, by gender*

	Tasks	%	F tasks	%	M tasks	%	% by F adj.
Intra-parish	480	47.4	128	59.0	352	44.2	48.5
Inter-parish	533	52.6	89	41.0	444	55.8	34.2
Total	1,013	100.0	217	100.0	796	100.0	41.4

Notes: adj. = adjusted (x2.59). Totals reflect tasks where intra or inter-parish data is known.

activity. As a general rule of thumb, the tasks that were classified as transport activities were those where moving something was the main purpose of the task, rather than a subsidiary part of it and where the distance involved took the actor beyond their immediate environs: 97 per cent of all tasks included in the analysis below took the actor 'outside the household', where their own household was defined as including barns, outbuildings, and gardens.[46] To preserve this focus, the analysis here does not include all tasks that were placed in the large transport category. The subcategory of loading, which involved moving goods but onto carts or horses rather than over distances, was excluded, as were some of the tasks from the horses subcategory, where they related to the care of horses rather than their movement. In addition to the remaining transport subcategories – boats, carry goods, carting, droving, messages, and passengers – the analysis also incorporates the commerce subcategory of go to market. Whilst the transportation of goods bought or to sell was not always explicit in such cases, it is reasonable to assume it was commonly part of a trip to market, and such cases do provide interesting insights into everyday movement activities. This produces a total of 1,212 transportation tasks which form the basis of the analysis here.[47]

One way to examine these tasks is to compare the number that took place within a single parish (intra-parish) with those that involved crossing at least one parish boundary (inter-parish). As Table 3.6 shows, there is a fairly even split between movement tasks that took place within a single parish, such as in 1598 when John Bech of Redbourn, Hertfordshire, went to collect some chaff that he had previously bought from a neighbour, and those that took actors into a different parish, as when Alice Yeomans went in 1618 from her home in Frome, Somerset, to Wells, 14 miles away, to deliver to a clothier a bundle of yarn she had spun.[48]

[46] This 'outside the household' category is explained more fully in Section 1.2.3.
[47] Integral tasks are included in the analysis in this section as they do not have a clear distorting effect on the pattern of transport tasks.
[48] HALS, ASA8/5, 9–10; SHC, Q/SR/33, 122–3.

Table 3.7 *Intra-parish and inter-parish repertoires*

	Intra-parish F repertoire (%)	Inter-parish F repertoire (%)	Intra-parish M repertoire (%)	Inter-parish M repertoire (%)
Boats	0.8	0.0	6.0	4.5
Carry goods	79.7	41.6	55.7	27.3
Carting	2.3	0.0	10.5	14.2
Droving	3.1	5.6	9.7	19.6
Go to market	2.3	40.4	2.8	16.7
Horses	2.3	4.5	6.3	10.4
Messages	9.4	5.6	7.1	4.1
Passengers	0.0	2.2	2.0	3.4
Total	99.9	99.9	100.1	100.2
Total tasks	128	89	352	444

There were some gender differences apparent here, with a higher percentage of women's transport tasks taking place intra-parish, whereas men's activities were more likely to take them inter-parish, but these should not be overstated: both women and men undertook a significant proportion of both types of journeys. Where gender differences are more pronounced is in the types of transport tasks that took actors across a parish boundary, as shown in Table 3.7. Subcategories were defined partly by the form of transport – boats, carts, horses – and partly by what was being transported – goods, messages, passengers, livestock. Travel on foot was rarely specified, but it can be assumed that the majority of carrying goods and carrying messages involved foot travel as other modes of transport were rarely mentioned, and the same is true for going to market. Given the size of these categories, foot travel made up the majority of transport.

For both women and men, intra-parish activities were dominated by the subcategory of carry goods. This encompassed a wide variety of tasks – taking grain to and from mills, collecting purchased crops or other goods, fetching wool, or returning yarn – as well as others such as taking shoes to a shoemaker to be mended, taking linen to be washed, or fetching pans lent to neighbours. This kind of small-scale haulage was not always confined to short journeys though, and carry goods was also the largest category in the repertoire of inter-parish tasks for both women and men alike. It did, however, represent a smaller percentage of the total repertoire of inter-parish tasks for both. For women, inter-parish activity was overwhelmingly, and more or less equally, comprised of just two subcategories: carrying goods and going to market. For men, their

Table 3.8 *Inter-parish task distances (one way)*

Miles	All tasks	%	F tasks	%	M tasks	%
1 to 8	291	64.0	53	71.6	238	62.5
9 to 20	112	24.6	18	24.3	94	24.7
21+	52	11.4	3	4.1	49	12.9
Total	455	100.0	74	100.0	381	100.0
Mean distance (miles)[a]	10.0		7.0		10.6	
Mode (miles)	2		2		2	
Median (miles)	5		6		6	

[a] This average excludes the two longest journeys undertaken, 190 miles (by three male actors together) and 170 miles (by two male actors together) as these were exceptional but had a disproportionate impact on the average. If included the overall average would be 11.9, and for men 12.8. The next highest distance was 111 miles.

repertoire was more diverse, with these two subcategories part of a mixed portfolio alongside carting, droving, and transport involving horses. If men and women crossed parish boundaries with similar frequency, the transport tasks they were undertaking when they did so were often quite different.[49]

The comparison between men's and women's experiences of transport work can be extended by looking at the distances involved in these inter-parish tasks. For 85 per cent of inter-parish tasks, it is possible to calculate the rough distance between the start and end parishes involved.[50] Table 3.8 sorts these into three categories, which are informed by the timescales involved: the first, 1 to 8 miles, represents a journey that done at a purposeful average walking speed of 4 miles per hour would take up to 2 hours to complete. All distances are for one-way trips, so to complete a task would likely have involved a return trip, and thus taken up to 4 hours of the day. Such journeys were time-consuming, but could comfortably be completed within a working day, only taking up part of it. The average distance travelled to a market, 7.4 miles, sits just within this category.[51] This is remarkably similar to the 6.7 miles that the medieval lawyer, Bracton, suggested was a reasonable day's journey to market.[52] The

[49] This is partly a reflection of the overall gender division of labour within these transport subcategories: see Appendix B.

[50] For the other 15 per cent, it is clear the task involved inter-parish travel, but the start or end point was not specified.

[51] For women the average for 'go to market' is 6.1 miles, for men 9.3 miles.

[52] Cited in Unwin, 'Rural marketing', p. 244; Brayshay, *Land Travel*, p. 128. Bracton suggested a round trip of 20 miles, in which one-third each was travel to market, walking about town while at the market, and travel home.

second category, 9 to 20 miles, represents journeys that would have taken at least 2 and up to 5 hours each way, and would therefore have been likely to have eaten up most of the working hours in a given day, especially if walking pace dipped below 4 miles per hour, which would be a fairly brisk speed when carrying goods. The third category, 21 miles and above, contains journeys of a minimum of 5 hours each way, and usually more, and would therefore have been difficult to complete both ways in a single day; in short, they would often have necessitated an overnight stay away from home as part of the task. Walking speeds would of course have varied from person to person, and across seasons and terrains. A small proportion of these tasks were done on horseback, with 7 per cent of tasks in the sample of 1,212 used in this section explicitly stating involvement of a horse. However, broadly speaking, these categories relate to part-day, full-day, and multi-day transport tasks, respectively.

For both women and men journeys of between 1 and 8 miles were by far the most common, with the distance of 2 miles being the most frequently undertaken. Nonetheless, longer full-day transport tasks accounted for roughly a quarter of inter-parish activities for both: it is clear that women were not limited to only short-distance, highly localised haulage work, as shown by their average transport task distance of 7 miles. Return journeys that could be undertaken within a day dominated for both women and men, as the identical mode and median distances travelled indicate. In fact, if all intra-parish tasks are assumed to involve distances of 20 miles or less (one way), they can be combined with inter-parish tasks of under 20 miles to show that 98.5 per cent of women's tasks and 93.3 per cent of men's tasks could be undertaken within a day. It seems that this factor, what could be achieved without the need to stay away from home, dictated the typical upper distances involved in everyday travel tasks. This explains why there were not major regional differences in average task distances. For instance, the average distance travelled to market for each region was very similar: 7.3 miles in the south-west, 7.6 miles in the north, and 7.3 miles in the east. The averages for all transport tasks were slightly lower in the south-west at 8.5 miles, compared to 11.2 miles and 11.5 miles in the north and east, respectively.

Men undertook a higher proportion of longer distance, multi-day tasks than women, who did so only rarely, and this is reflected in men's longer mean average distance travelled. Nonetheless, longer-distance tasks only represented a small proportion of men's transport work. It was three men who undertook our longest recorded journey, sailing 190 miles from Norfolk to Newcastle in 1627, and two men who undertook the second longest, carting 'sundry wares and goods' from Prestbury, Cheshire,

170 miles to London in 1632.[53] The longest distance recorded for a woman was in 1698 when the wife of Thomas Jackson went with her husband 50 miles from Sheffield to York to collect 'hardware' that they then took to the Thirsk fair.[54] Gender differences were more pronounced when it came to the types of tasks undertaken, as Table 3.7 demonstrates. Why did this division of transport labour prevail? One hypothesis would be that because men undertook the majority of longer-distance journeys, this explains their use of carts and horses, both modes of transport that women were rarely recorded using. However, although horses were used for many longer distance trips, 89 per cent of all horse-related transport tasks still involved distances of 20 miles or less. For carting tasks, this figure was 95 per cent: carts were only occasionally used for long-distance travel. In other words, these technologies were primarily used for the short and mid-distance day journeys that made up the bulk of transport work; men's domination of these subcategories was not a result of these tasks being intimately linked with the longer journeys.

Hierarchies of strength and skill are no more helpful in explaining men's dominance of tasks involving vehicles and animals. Women's carrying activities often involved them transporting goods on their heads over many miles, as we saw with Katherine Singard at the start of this section. In 1650 Joan Symonds bought three pecks of grain in Bridgwater, Somerset, a quantity that probably weighed about 45 lbs (20 kgs), and was recorded carrying it home on her head.[55] Carrying activities were not without risk: Agnes Parker of Chilton Cantelo, Somerset, was crossing a bridge in 1592 with a measure of hay on her head and a pot for milking in her hand, when she was tragically blown off the bridge by a gust of wind and drowned in a ditch.[56] Women were no strangers to physically demanding transport tasks; tasks that likely required more strength than driving a cart. It is clear women could and did have the necessary skills to cart, drove, or ride horses, as there are examples of them undertaking all of these tasks in the database. It is true that driving carts, riding horses, and droving livestock were all potentially dangerous activities: carting in particular features prominently in the coroners' reports of accidental death. But so too did collecting water from rivers and ponds, where drowning was a real risk, a task mainly performed by women and children. Nor is it clear that the male-dominated subcategories necessarily conferred higher status on the actor than moving goods on foot. Horse-riding did confer status, but not

[53] NRO, C/S3/26, 82–5; CALS, QJF/61/2, 51. [54] NYCRO, QSB/1699, 202, 207.
[55] SHC, Q/SR/82, 88–9. [56] TNA, KB/9/683b/185.

carting. Carting was low-status male work, typically performed by young men, servants, and labourers.[57] In short, whilst there was a clear division of labour by mode of transport, with women overwhelmingly moving goods on foot whilst men also employed carts and horses, and took responsibility for droving animals, there is no straightforward single explanation for why this was the case.[58]

3.4 Inside and Outside the Home

The spaces in which work took place are a neglected aspect of histories of work. We are currently experiencing a revolution in homeworking as digital technologies remove the need for co-locating workers in purpose-built offices. In this context, the wider implications of where exactly people work become apparent, including issues such as commuting times, the relationship between paid and unpaid work, and the supervision and motivation of workers. The work-task data allows a detailed examination of workspaces before purpose-built workplaces were widely adopted in the nineteenth century. It is a shorthand to say people worked at home in early modern England. In fact, the work-task data shows that the most common workspace was not inside the home or any other building, but outside. Further, many people worked in the homes of others, where they were often closely supervised. Thus, rather than people working 'at home', it is more accurate to say that work took place either at home, in some-one else's home, or from home.[59]

Early modern advice literature repeatedly asserted that women's work was located in the home, while men 'went abroad'. For instance, Edmund Tilney stated that the husband should 'go abroad in matters of profit', while the wife should 'tarry at home, and see all be well there'.[60] Gervase Markham offered more detail when he introduced his book, *The English Housewife*, a sequel to *The English Husbandman*, by stating that:

> having already … passed through those outward parts of husbandry which belong unto the perfect husbandman, who is father and master of the family, and whose office and employments are ever for the most part abroad, or removed from the house, as in the field or yard; it is now meet that we descend … to the office of our

57 See Section 2.3.
58 For similar findings from early modern Sweden, see Ågren (ed.), *Making a Living*, pp. 128–35.
59 Where 'from home' indicates that home is their 'headquarters', for example, in the case of agriculture and transport.
60 Tilney, *Flower of Friendship*, p. 120; the passage was repeated in Anon, *A Godlie Forme*, p. 168, a book republished at least nine times up to 1630.

English housewife, who is the mother and mistress of the family, and hath her most general employments within the house.[61]

The medieval terms 'husbondman' and 'huswife' both contained the 'hus' element, which referred to their responsibilities as householders. Only for huswives was this later modernised as 'house' and assumed to correspond with a duty of staying within the home as a housewife.[62] Yet women's work in early modern England frequently took them beyond the house: the work-task data not only offers many examples of this but allows the spatial differences between women's and men's work to be measured.

Only a handful of studies have looked in detail at the spatial relations of work inside and outside the home in early modern England.[63] Nonetheless, wider investigations into houses and the activities that took place within them have been exceptionally rich in recent decades. Matthew Johnson prompted a shift in the history of vernacular architecture away from typologies of surviving buildings and their construction techniques towards an appreciation of the wider social and cultural implications of the forms houses took.[64] The objects recorded in probate inventories have been used to reconstruct room-use, and more ambitiously to examine the practice of domestic activities such as cooking and commensality by Anthony Buxton.[65] Even more sophisticated is the approach taken by Tara Hamling and Catherine Richardson, combining evidence from surviving houses and objects with inventories, court depositions, and visual and literary sources to reconstruct the experience of living in early modern houses for people of middling status, including their work activities.[66] The work-task data can add to these approaches by showing how work within the house related to the wider landscape of work. This section looks first at the division of work between inside and outside, before moving on to examine work activities in different rooms within the house. The following section explores issues of privacy and supervision.

Table 3.9 classifies workspaces into three main categories: inside, outside, and unknown. Inside workspaces are further divided between the worker's own home, another person's home, non-domestic buildings, and inside spaces for which there is no further information.

[61] Markham, *English Housewife*. [62] An early example is Bullinger, *Golden Boke*.

[63] Flather, *Gender and Space*, ch. 3 and 'Space, place, and gender'; Whittle, 'House as a place of work' and 'Home and work'; Mansell, *Female Servants*, ch. 7.

[64] Johnson, *Housing Culture*; Johnson, *Houses*; Crowley, *Invention of Comfort*.

[65] Overton et al., *Production and Consumption*, ch. 6; Buxton, *Domestic Culture*, ch. 6.

[66] Hamling and Richardson, *Day at Home*, especially chs. 2 and 4; see also King, *Houses and Society*.

Table 3.9 *The proportion of work tasks located in different spaces*

	Own home (%)	Another's home (%)	Non-domestic building (%)	Inside – no details (%)	Outside (%)	Unknown (%)	Total tasks
Agriculture and land	2.9	1.7	0.1	0.3	89.9	5.0	2,635
Carework	20.9	42.6	1.6	3.0	25.5	6.4	564
Commerce	8.1	11.8	0.8	0.2	30.3	48.8	2,115
Crafts and construction	17.7	16.2	9.6	10.4	30.3	15.8	942
Food processing	25.7	19.1	9.6	6.1	21.9	17.6	607
Housework	39.3	13.6	0.5	1.6	37.3	7.6	748
Management	13.3	30.7	1.6	0.9	18.3	35.2	645
Transport	1.1	1.9	0.4	0.2	95.5	1.0	1,237
Other	15.3	26.8	3.8	9.6	33.8	10.8	157
Average	11.5	12.1	2.1	2.1	53.9	18.3	100.0
Adj. average	14.3	13.1	1.8	2.3	50.6	17.9	100.0
Total tasks	1,106	1,169	201	201	5,203	1,770	9,650

Notes: The adjusted average weights women's and men's work tasks at 50:50 using the x2.59 multiplier. These categories are more specific than those outlined in Section 1.2.3.

Specialist rooms and outbuildings, such as shops and barns, are treated as part of the domestic house, but gardens and yards are treated as outside in order to draw a sharp distinction between indoor and outdoor work. Own home was defined as the house in which the person undertaking the work task lived, thus servants doing work in their employer's house are counted as working in their own home, because most lived with their employer. As well as the raw figures, an adjusted average, in which women's and men's work is weighted equally, is provided because women's and men's work had different spatial profiles. The ability to identify workspaces varied according to the category of work task. Commerce and management tasks often had no details other than the transaction that took place, leading to particularly high proportions of unknown tasks; transport, on the other hand, typically took place outside, leading to very few unknowns.[67]

This analysis reveals three very distinctive features to the spatial distribution of work in early modern England. First, a high proportion of work

[67] Integral tasks are included in the analysis in this section as they had no clear impact on the results.

took place outside. This is partly because two large categories, agriculture and transport, were heavily dominated by outside work. However, it is also because other categories that were mostly inside also contained substantial proportions of outside work. Carework, for instance, often involved going to fetch a caregiver, equipment, or medicine, as well as sometimes administering care to people outside. Housework, as discussed in Chapter 5, involved laundry and water collection by and from wells, ponds, and rivers beyond the house. Commerce involved open air transactions at markets and fairs, as well as travelling to market. Within the crafts and construction category, construction involved groundworks, building houses, and maintaining roofs and the external fabric of buildings: all outside activities. A second striking feature is that almost as much work took place in other people's houses as in people's own homes, even when we treat servants as members of a household working at home. Thus, inside work was not necessarily taking place 'at home' but rather 'in houses'. Finally, very little work took place in dedicated inside workspaces. The non-domestic building category is largely made up of mills and churches. Mills were distinguished by the presence of large machinery for grinding corn or fulling cloth. Some mills were also homes, but the court evidence suggests most were not: for instance, a number of theft cases make it clear that no one slept at the mill.[68]

The differences between women's and men's workspaces are shown in Table 3.10. Men's work was more likely than women's to occur outside. Women were more likely than men to work in their own homes and in the homes of others. Yet there were also similarities. If the work tasks in unknown locations are discarded, 52.0 per cent of women's work took place outside. Conversely, 28.4 per cent of male work tasks with a stated location took place inside. These findings support the conclusions of Amanda Flather, that there was considerable overlap between male and female workspaces, and indeed, women and men often worked alongside each other.[69]

While court depositions often provide sufficient information to discern whether a work task took place inside or outside, more detailed descriptions of inside spaces were less common. When particular rooms are mentioned, they sometimes appear incidentally rather than as the location of a work activity. For example, John Okeford, employed as a sawyer by John Abbott of Semley in Wiltshire in 1600, noted that it 'being about noon' he was 'called in to dinner' and thus 'he was sitting in the kitchen of the same house at dinner' with three other people when defamatory

[68] Section 4.2 discusses a case where the miller only slept in the mill at Christmas time.
[69] Flather, 'Space, place, and gender'.

Table 3.10 *Gender and workspaces*

	Own home	Another's home	Non-domestic building	Inside – no details	Outside	Unknown	Total number
F tasks	555	412	30	72	1,159	458	2,686
M tasks	551	757	171	129	4,044	1,312	6,964
F (%)	20.7	15.3	1.1	2.7	43.1	17.1	100.0
M (%)	7.9	10.9	2.5	1.9	58.1	18.8	100.1
F (% of known only)	24.9	18.5	1.3	3.2	52.0	–	99.9
Men (% known only)	9.7	13.4	3.0	2.3	71.5	–	99.9

Notes: These categories are more specific than those outlined in Section 1.2.3.

words were exchanged.[70] The four most common room types mentioned in depositions that also described work activities were chambers, kitchens, halls, and parlours, in that order. 'Chamber' typically denoted an upstairs room in early modern England. Probate inventories show that such rooms were used for sleeping and storage.[71] The work-task data confirms this: tasks taking place in chambers most commonly involved caring for the sick and doing housework. For instance, Mary Hawkings nursed Mary Beard 'in the chamber where the said Mary Beard lay sick' in Wolborough, Devon, in 1670, while Elizabeth Thompson Dobson went 'into her master's chamber to make her master's bed' in South Kirkby in Yorkshire in 1600.[72] However, their use for storage meant that chambers were also mentioned in a wide range of other work tasks concerned with storing and fetching agricultural produce, foodstuffs, and textiles. William Pine 'going into a chamber at the house of Thomas Simpson his master to fetch down some apples' found a bundle of stolen clothes in Hatfield, Yorkshire, in 1677.[73]

The hall, parlour, and kitchen were the main downstairs rooms. A case from Great Elm, Somerset, in 1682, catches the movement of Joan Hearse through her employer's house, 'for she being in Mr Higdon's parlour she came from thence through the hall and was going towards the kitchen with a besom [broom] in her hand' when she was called to

70 WSHC, D1/42/18, *Abbat v. Clement als Browne*.

71 Overton et al., *Production and Consumption*, pp. 126, 133; see also Hamling and Richardson, *Day at Home*, chs. 1 and 6 for a more nuanced discussion.

72 DRO, Chanter 875, 60v–2v; DUIC, DDR/EJ/CCD/1/7, *Dorothy Glover v. George Craggs*.

73 WYAS, QS1/17/2, 3–4.

witness the tithes being settled.[74] In the medieval period and sixteenth century, the hall was the main living room. In small houses it might be the only room or exist alongside a buttery or kitchen. Many modest early modern houses that survive to the present day had three downstairs rooms, with the hall in the centre, and a parlour and kitchen or buttery on either side, as was evidently the case in Mr Higdon's house.[75] Architectural studies and probate inventories show that the hall almost always contained a hearth and was often used for cooking and eating. In the seventeenth century, however, cooking and eating increasingly took place in the kitchen.[76] Interestingly, we found no examples of cooking taking place in halls; instead, the most common activities were eating, drinking, and working.[77] Most of the work tasks, other than carrying and fetching, concerned textile work. Paul Dixon was engaged in his work as a tailor in the hall of Thomas Kennell's house in Christchurch, Hampshire, in 1591, while Thomas Kennell lay sick in 'an inner chamber within the hall of his house'. Oliver Eldridge was also present in Thomas Kennell's hall 'at breakfast', before going out to plough.[78] The hall was a location where female servants were found spinning, as in the case of Richorda Burden in Kenton, Devon, in 1617, and Maria Browning in Glastonbury in 1604.[79] Joan Foxwill was carding wool beside the fire of the hall in her own house at Venn Ottery in Devon in January 1558.[80] It seems that the hall provided a warm and relatively clean space suitable for these types of tasks.

In alehouses, the hall was the main drinking room. There is little indication that alehouses differed in internal structure and room nomenclature from other houses: the hall was used for eating and drinking, the kitchen or buttery for storing drink and preparing food, and the parlour for more select gatherings.[81] In normal dwelling houses, parlours were used to store items of value: cases mention items such as blankets, clothes, yarn, cloth, and a purse containing money being kept in chests or presses in the parlour from which they were fetched when needed. Mary Rawnforth went 'into the said Ellen Lambes parlour to borrow

[74] SHC, D/D/Cd/97, *Higdon v. Haglie.* [75] Brunskill, *Illustrated Handbook*, pp. 102–11.
[76] Overton et al., *Production and Consumption*, p. 126.
[77] We did not record cases which only contained non-work activities such as eating and drinking; these activities are evident because they also involved work by some of the people present.
[78] HRO, 21M65/C3/10, *Kennell v. Eldridge*; NRO, DN/DEP/8/7E, 107–9 also describes a tailor working in someone else's hall, in Suffolk, 1560.
[79] DHC, Chanter 867, *Pridham v. Combe and Scadlake*; SHC, D/D/Cd/36, *Soote v. Aplyn.*
[80] DHC, Chanter 855, *Colwill v. Foxwill.*
[81] See Section 5.3 for further discussion of alehouse work.

2 blankets' in Malton, Yorkshire, in 1694.[82] Two cases, one from 1557 and one from 1693, refer to making beds and sleeping in the parlour, a reminder that it could also serve as a bedroom.[83] Parlours were used for meetings of various kinds. A case from Lancashire in 1687 described several men gathering in the parlour of Chaddock Hall in Tyldesley to discuss issues relating to an inheritance.[84] At Shingham, Norfolk, in 1645 a group of men were seen entering a neighbour's parlour at night-time and meeting there by candlelight in suspicious circumstances; while in Wrington, Somerset, in 1551 the parlour was the location of a marriage proposal.[85]

Kitchens and butteries were used for storing and preparing food. The main difference between them was that butteries lacked a hearth, unlike kitchens where food was cooked in a fireplace. Architecturally, butteries predate kitchens as a common room in ordinary houses, but kitchens gradually became more dominant.[86] This transition was not evident in the work-task data: activities in kitchens were more common than those in butteries throughout the period. The range of tasks observed in butteries was quite limited, and were connected to fetching beer, storing meat, and folding linen. Activities in kitchens were more varied and suggest it was a room where members of the household often congregated. Two cases concerned incidents with guns. John Gaylarde, a servant, 'standing by the fireplace in his master's kitchen', was cleaning a fowling piece in Somerset in 1591 when it went off; while in Happisburgh, Norfolk, in 1684, Mary Gillam was in the kitchen of Thomas Chamberlaine, a yeoman, and while turned away, 'to wash a pot in a kettle over the fire', William Crow, a labourer, who had been standing holding a gun, shot her daughter-in-law, who was also in the kitchen.[87] Several cases mention eating meals in the kitchen, such as when John Kerry, a male servant, got himself some breakfast and sat down to eat it in the kitchen in Wellow, Hampshire, in 1573, and the case where workmen were called into dinner in the kitchen at Semley, Wiltshire, mentioned above.[88]

The kitchen was also a place where children were often present. For instance, Martha Dowling was sitting in her kitchen with her children when her husband came through from the butcher's shop adjoining to

[82] BI, CP.H.4349, *Office v. Helen Lamb*.
[83] Overton et al., *Production and Consumption*, pp. 126–32.
[84] LaA, QSB/1/1687, Easter, Info of James Hardman.
[85] NRO, C/S3/37, Info of Edward Skevington; SHC, D/D/Cd/6, 41–8.
[86] Overton et al., *Production and Consumption*, pp. 130–1; Pennell, *Birth of the English Kitchen*, pp. 40–5.
[87] TNA, KB/9/1038/205; NRO, C/S3/55A, Info of Sarah Gillam and Mary Gillam.
[88] HRO, 21M65/C3/9, *Bennys v. Cooper*.

tell her about a defamation that had taken place, in Chewton Mendip, Somerset, in 1694.[89] Lucretia Harward, a female servant, 'dressed up [tidied] the kitchen, made a fire, and attended up the children' in her employer's house in Bale, Norfolk, in 1637.[90] More traumatically, Elizabeth Balford, also a servant, was beaten by her master in the kitchen until his wife 'being big with child and having one under her arms did set the child down' and intervened, 'moved by the fury and cruelty of her husband', at Terrington St John, Norfolk, in 1621.[91] Other kitchen activities included storing and fetching cooking pots, pewter, and food; salting meat; and brewing. In terms of the work-task categories, chambers were generally spaces of carework, craftwork commonly took place in halls, parlours were used for management activities, and kitchens for food processing, while housework occurred throughout the house.

The evidence of work tasks disproves common generalisations about workspaces. Rather than work taking place at home, early modern work most commonly took place outside. This was true for women as well as men, although women were more likely to work inside than men. When working inside, people not only worked in their own houses but in the houses of others. Analysis of work inside houses shows that early modern room names related to distinct interior spaces where different types of activities were carried out.

3.5 Public and Private Spaces

Despite the much trumpeted 'spatial turn', the spatial dynamics of historical workplaces remain underexplored. The analysis of space is structured around several closely related binaries: the public and the private; outside and inside the home; openness and closure. Jurgen Habermas sparked the discussion of public and private, taking the public market places and private dwelling houses of Ancient Greece as archetypal examples.[92] Amanda Vickery laid the critical foundations for conceptualising public and private spheres in gender history, demonstrating that the idea of women being confined to the private sphere of the home while men were active in the public sphere was prevalent from at least the sixteenth century.[93] Lena Orlin has focused on the presence and absence of privacy in early modern homes, while the terms 'open' and 'closed' have been applied to late medieval houses by Matthew Johnson and

[89] SHC, D/D/Cd/106, *Culliford v. Cornish.*

[90] NRO, C/S3/31, Exam of Lucretia Harward, also discussed in the Conclusion to Chapter 5.

[91] NRO, C/S3/23, Info of Elizabeth Balford.

[92] Habermas, *Structural Transformation*, 'Introduction'.

[93] Vickery, 'Golden age'.

village topography by Stephen Mileson, and also much discussed in the context of European household economies.[94] 'Open' and 'closed' do not map precisely onto public and private, being closer to ideas of community and individualism, but they share many common features.

This literature draws attention to the categories into which work is instinctively and sometimes lazily organised by economic historians. Thus, women's work is assumed to take place mainly in the private sphere of the home and the dwelling house is assumed to be a private space visible (and audible) only to family members. A common reaction to the work-task data is to question whether housework and women's work are under-recorded because they took place in the home and thus go unobserved. Yet historians such as Orlin and Johnson have demonstrated the openness of early modern houses, which enabled neighbours to observe much of what went on within them. This was particularly the case in the sixteenth century, when windows were often unglazed, but remained the case throughout the period: walls were flimsy, doors were left open, and neighbours frequently entered each other's houses. For the poorer sections of society, houses were too small to offer much internal space, and activities spilled outside. Voices would have been more audible, inside and out, in the absence of the noise pollution that plagues modern industrial society.[95] While early modern moralists liked the idea of women being confined to the home, there is no evidence that this was put into practice, nor were women necessarily doing housework when they did work at home. Not only is spatial location a vital dimension of work, but work is also an important dimension of early modern spatial relations. For instance, Mileson argues that in the fifteenth century yeomen farmers achieved greater privacy by building larger houses set back from village streets. Yet if we also consider the organisation of work, it might be observed that increased land and wealth meant that such yeomen were also surely employing more servants. These servants lived and worked in yeomen's houses, undermining privacy on another level. Their economic functions made households permeable: the early modern home was not a private space in the modern sense.[96]

In modern society we assume a clear delineation between the private space of the home and commercial or public spaces such as shops and streets. In early modern England no such clear distinction existed. Houses could be places of commerce, as we see with alehouses, which are sometimes specifically referred to as dwelling houses despite offering

[94] Orlin, *Locating Privacy*, ch. 4; Johnson, *Housing Culture*; Mileson, 'Openness and closure'; Eibach, 'Das offene haus' [the open house]; Ågren, 'Households'.

[95] Hamling and Richardson, *Day at Home*, p. 38.

[96] Ågren, 'Households', p. 26.

hospitality to paying customers.[97] Shops, which could be workshops or places of commerce, or a combination of the two, were typically part of people's houses.[98] In a case from Exeter in 1617, a group of people including four men, two boys, and a woman were 'working on knives' in 'the shop of the house of George Rase', while two women were waiting to buy knives 'standing near the stall of the said shop', who all overheard defamatory words spoken.[99] This suggests a cutler's workshop within a house, with a street-facing window or stall for selling goods. Examples of weaving in which the location was specified all described the work room as a shop. Thus, Henry Turner was weaving 'in his own shop' in Westbury in 1662, while in Leeds in 1625 Thomas Whittaker was described as a weaver 'working of his hand' in another man's 'shop'.[100] A case from Ipplepen, Devon, in 1613 offers further detail about the domestic context of the weaver's shop. Walter Turpyn gave evidence that he and his son were 'in his shop weaving' when Ann Turpyn 'came unto this deponent's door'. The son described how his wife 'was sitting in the entry of the house' talking with their relative Ann Turpyn. Both men heard all the defamatory words spoken by Ann Turpyn to the wife/daughter-in-law, suggesting the weaving shop was just inside the doorway in the main part of the house.[101] This corresponds to Jane Whittle's reconstruction of a weaver's house in early seventeenth-century Uffculme, Devon, where the looms were located in the buttery adjoining the cross-passage and front door.[102] Probate inventories confirm that retail shops were normally part of dwelling houses. This was occasionally confirmed in depositions, as in a case of tobacco theft from Yeovil, Somerset, in 1650, in which Robert Myer described 'being at Mr French his house in Yeovil mercer he saw in his shop a roll of Virginia tobacco', or the case noted above in which a butcher came from his shop through to the kitchen to talk to his wife.[103]

Another way in which the distinction between domestic and public spaces was blurred was by the extent to which people worked in doorways, streets, and backyards where they could be clearly seen by neighbours and others passing by. Spinning and other textile work was often done in the doorway, which offered the benefits of better light and sociability. Maria Tong and Elizabeth Watson 'were sitting together at the good Mr Watsons door sewing' along with Mr Watson's servant Susan Dawson who was 'sitting also there with spinning' in Whittlesey,

[97] See Section 5.3. [98] See Section 8.3. [99] DHC, Chanter 867, *Wast v. Rafe.*
[100] WSHC, A1/110/1662T, 185; BI, CP.H.1704, *Rawdon v. Philip.*
[101] DHC, Chanter 867, *Bully v Turpyn.*
[102] Whittle, 'House as a place of work', pp. 142–4. [103] SHC, Q/SR/82, 52.

Cambridgeshire, in 1560.[104] Similarly, Joanna Edwardes was 'spinning at her turn in the entry of her master's house' at Shebbear in Devon in 1575, and Ellen Kates was 'sitting spinning at her mistresses door' in Pilgrim Street, Newcastle, in 1632, while Agnes Adams was 'sat carding wool at the door of Matthew Roberts' in Farleigh Hungerford in Somerset in 1532.[105] Two cases from Norfolk, from Neatishead in 1600 and Norwich in 1683, record women knitting 'in the street', outside their houses.[106] In addition, depositions often record women 'working' in their doorway, a term which was not specific enough to be included in the database: it is likely many were spinning or sewing.[107] Even those working inside saw activities in the street outside through open doors and windows. William Bishopp was looking out of the house 'where he was at work being a tailor by his occupation' in Seaton, Devon, in 1618 and witnessed a witchcraft accusation.[108] John Poddarde was 'working journey work with one Richard Care shoemaker dwelling in the Butcher Row in Salisbury' and 'sitting at his work in the shop of the said Richard Care' when he witnessed a deponent entering the shop across the street in 1565.[109]

Thus, streets were not only conduits for transport but places of neighbourly interaction. People looked out from their houses, worked in doorways, and went backwards and forwards engaged in daily chores like collecting water and milking, which took them outside several times a day. As most journeys were undertaken on foot, or while travelling slowly with carts or horses, travel was also much less impersonal than modern transport, giving people time to interact and observe what was going on around them. John Northen was 'going with seed corn of his master's into Wishford field to sow' along 'the highway lying above the town' when he witnessed a defamation in Great Wishford, Wiltshire, in 1588.[110] Anne Divine was 'milking in a certain ground of her father's … about 7 of the clock in the morning she saw a strange man' on the nearby highway, who suspiciously washed a bag in a stream at 'a certain place called Whistlebridge near Stoford' in Somerset in 1638.[111]

Some encounters led to assault or theft, but others were more friendly. In Cheshire in 1682 John Cooper fell from his horse in a lane leading from Church Hulme to Middlewich. He claimed he was attacked by a man in a periwig, but his neighbour, Sarah Beswick, deposed 'that she

[104] CUL, EDR/2/4, *Glapthorn v. Watson*.
[105] DHC, Chanter 859, *Rowland v. Padden*; DUIC, DDR: Consistory court depositions (loose), *Leach v. Dodds*; SHC, D/D/Cd/2, *Gylbarde et Adams*.
[106] NRO, DN/DEP/31/34, 433–9; NRO, DN/DEP/51/55, 184–5.
[107] This is one reason why spinning is under-recorded.
[108] DHC, Chanter 867, *Gibbs v. Courtis*.
[109] WSHC, D1/42/6, *Turley v. Mathew*.
[110] WSHC, D1/42/10, *Cowdrey v. Southick*.
[111] SHC, Q/SR/77, 38.

believes nothing but drink had hurt him'. A young man of 16 or 17 years of age, William Hulme, who did not know Cooper, had just passed him on horseback but looked back and saw Cooper's horse without its rider. He went back and caught the horse and tethered him 'upon a stoop at the pavement side'. At this point Sarah Beswick, travelling along the lane on her own errand, joined them and recognised Cooper, 'and finding him then sitting in the dirt said (in the name of God) goodman Cooper where have you been? Seems you have been with no good company that would let you come forth in this order'. She then, using his knife, 'scraped the dirt off his clothes'. With some difficulty he got to his feet, and with even more difficulty was helped back onto his horse, almost falling off the other side, before going off homewards down the lane swaying from side to side on his horse.

This case describes geographical locations in unusual detail, allowing the residence of all the actors, and the incident itself, to be identified on the modern map. John Cooper, a husbandman, lived at Bostock Hall, just north of Middlewich. He had argued with Robert Buckley of Wharton, who was also his tenant, and was slandered by Rebecca Saint, an alehouse-keeper from Cotton, just outside Church Hulme (now Holmes Chapel). William Hulme came from Church Hulme and was travelling to Middlewich. Sarah Beswick was a blacksmith's wife from Kinderton, which was where Cooper fell from his horse, 'in Sproston Lane over against Kinderton Park', also described as 'at the end of Kinderton Street and the lane end which goes towards Byley's Bridge'.[112] Despite the fact court depositions have disputes and crimes at their core, the world they depict is one of many-faceted interactions, involving people of all levels of wealth, engaged in an enormous range of activities. It is unlikely that the work-task data omits activities in private spaces for the simple reason that no space in early modern England – including domestic houses – was fully private. Despite the absence of large, specialist workplaces, work was typically carried out under the eyes of others – or at least with the likelihood it might be seen.[113] While people were often self-employed and might undertake tasks alone, they were nonetheless under observation and subject to the judgement of those around them.

3.6 Conclusion

By measuring and analysing the work tasks taking place in different locations this chapter has shown that the spatial distribution of work

[112] CALS, QJF/110/4, 87.

[113] There were some large, specialist workplaces, such as some mines, shipyards, and ironworks, but these were exceptions.

often confounds expectations. In aggregate, regional differences in work were muted, because the volume of commonplace tasks drowned out regional specialisms – although examples can be used to demonstrate that specialisms, such as coalmining in county Durham or lacemaking near Honiton in Devon – were present. Differences between work in towns and the countryside were more obvious. In this case, however, it is important to distinguish between the location where activities took place and where workers lived: there were higher rates of commerce in towns, but many of those engaged in commerce lived in the countryside; conversely, more workers engaged in crafts and construction lived in towns, but much of their work took place in the countryside. Travel was a significant form of time-use and integral to many forms of work. The great majority of journeys were short enough for people to undertake a return journey on foot in a single day, and the mode and median distances travelled by women and men were identical. Gendered differences of travel arose from men doing more of the comparatively rare multi-day journeys, and the fact men used a range of transport, while women typically travelled on foot. Both women and men were more likely to work outside than inside in early modern England. Despite exhortations in early modern literature for women to work in their own homes, only 25 per cent of their work tasks took place in this location. While domestic houses were by far the most common type of inside workspace, people almost as often worked in others' houses as in their own home. This, as well as the material culture of early modern houses, meant that houses were not private spaces in the same way as modern homes: they were physically and socially open. While people often worked on their own, the openness of houses, the slow pace of travel, and the familiarity of neighbours in small communities meant that few activities, including work, took place away from the observation of others.

4 Rhythms of Work

In late September 1662, Margaret Johnson, the wife of a butcher from Handley, Cheshire, sold drink to some of her neighbours, she 'having perry at her house'. Thomas Stockton, a 16-year-old servant, drank until he ran out of money, promising to pay Margaret back later. On St Luke's Day, 18 October, he returned, offering to 'bring her some apples' in compensation that night. Margaret accepted, but for 'fear of her husband', she had Thomas place the apples outside her house in the gorse-cote, a type of shed, about an hour before midnight. One week later, Margaret rose early on Saturday morning on 25 October about 'two hours before day' by her reckoning, or 'about four of the clock' according to her husband, Ralph. She set about various chores, driving away the swine 'which were at some straw' and looking to the horses. Informing her husband that the horses were missing from their yard, she then went into the village to light a candle 'about an inch longer than her middle finger', so that they might 'cut the meat down and ready it for the market'. Upon her return with the light, Ralph went looking for his horses, being 'absent about half an hour'. Margaret took advantage of his absence to move her apples from the gorse-cote 'into a loft above stairs in the said house, in a basket at twice or thrice carrying'. Ralph returned from his search for the horses empty-handed, but 'it being by this time daylight', his wife was able to point out their location under a neighbour's ash tree. Ralph then 'got his horses up and loaded', and 'about sunrising' the couple started the seven-and-a-half-mile journey to Chester market. While away, constables searched their house for goods stolen from the parish minister the night prior. They found the apples, and though these were unrelated to the crime at hand, Thomas Stockton would later confess to stealing them from his master.[1]

The rich depositions from this quarter sessions theft case reveal much about time-telling conventions and the seasonal, calendrical, weekly, and

[1] CALS, QJF/90/4, 70–1.

daily rhythms of work in early modern England. The darkness of early morning did not keep the Johnsons from their chores, but the lack of light and its provision through candles or daybreak clearly shaped their approach to their tasks. Such a busy early morning was probably not their daily norm, but rather due to weekly trends, as the married couple prepared and set out for a Saturday market in Chester. Three separate deponents described how work took place 'upon St Luke's day', a holy day when labour was ostensibly prohibited. Margaret's implicit involvement in perry and cider production and sale, like the Johnsons' butchery activities and trip to market, speaks to seasonal cycles of labour: the autumnal harvest and storage of fruit, and commencement of the winter slaughtering season, respectively. Moreover, Margaret's implied engagement in cider production, apparently hidden from her husband, and the married couples' division of Saturday-morning labour, demonstrate how temporal patterns of work could differ according to gender.

By drawing on cases such as this the work-task data allows for an exploration of the hourly, daily, monthly, and seasonal experience of work. In doing so, this chapter brings together two overlapping subjects central to the history of work – seasonality, and the working year/day – which have not received equal amounts of historiographical attention. Scholars have long recognised the highly seasonal nature of work in agrarian societies and its variance according to farming type and region.[2] Yet in other respects, the seasonality of labour has been taken for granted. Relatively few studies have considered its potential variance according to gender, occupation, status, or type of employment. Exceptions have been limited largely to urban contexts, construction, or the agricultural sector, with the seasonality of many other facets of rural labour and economy – like commerce, carework, or transport – left unexplored.[3] The common theme across this literature is a perception, or assumption, that work was intense during the summer, and lax during the winter – a pattern usually attributed to weather and the availability of daylight.[4] While the work-task data certainly does not disprove the winter-summer dichotomy, it enables a more nuanced appraisal of winter work and its contribution to the

[2] Hutton, *Stations of the Sun*; Jones, *Seasons and Prices;* Kussmaul, *General View*, pp. 1–45; Wrigley and Schofield, *Population History*, pp. 298–305. See also Section 3.1 on regional variation.

[3] Snell, *Annals*, pp. 15–66; Sharpe, *Adapting to Capitalism*, pp. 71–100; Flather, 'Space, place, and gender'; Woodward, *Men at Work*, pp. 135–42; Stephenson, *Contracts and Pay*, pp. 160–3 and 'Working days'. For early modern Sweden, see Gary, 'The distinct seasonality'.

[4] Sharpe, *Adapting to Capitalism*, p. 73; Snell, *Annals*, p. 19; Woodward, *Men at Work*, pp. 127, 135; Flather, 'Space, place, and gender', p. 351; Gary, 'Distinct seasonality', p. 3.

economy than proxy measurements like marriage seasonality or sources like farming and building accounts typically allow.

In contrast to seasonality, the early modern working year, week, and day have been central to various historiographical debates. For economic historians, estimating the number of days and hours worked in a year is crucial to building long-run wage series, and these in turn underpin narratives about changing standards of living, and the development of industrial and 'industrious' revolutions. More than just a key variable in calculations, the number of annual work days and hours lies at the heart of such narratives, many of which contend that worktime gradually increased in the early modern period, spurring economic change.[5] Part of the 'industrious revolution' theory of Jan De Vries, for example, postulates that workers gradually gave up holidays and leisure time in the latter half of the seventeenth century to increase their purchasing power for consumer goods.[6] Likewise, Hans-Joachim Voth's study of depositional evidence from eighteenth-century London suggests a decline in the observance of St Monday and religious holidays resulted in more annual work hours for industrialisation.[7]

Yet, aside from notable exceptions like Voth's time-use study, little empirical evidence has been offered to back up these economic grand narratives. Social and cultural historians' theories of time-use and its regimentation during societal transitions of reformation or modernisation have been built on similarly shaky ground. Most famously, E. P. Thompson argued that the rise of industrial capitalism in the eighteenth century fundamentally altered time-consciousness and discipline within the English workforce, with strict factory regimes based on clock-time supplanting the casual irregularity of traditional work patterns.[8] Although historians have since challenged and refined Thompson's argument, the assumption that premodern rural time regimes lacked sophistication, consistency, and clock awareness has lingered. In contrast, the work-task data shows women and men of early modern rural England were well-versed in clock-time and structured their workdays and weeks in strikingly regular ways.[9] In addition to providing robust empirical evidence for working

[5] For recent appraisals and summaries of this extensive literature, see Tiratelli, 'Working week'; Stephenson, 'Working days'; Gary, 'Distinct seasonality', and Section 0.1 of the Introduction.

[6] de Vries, *Industrious Revolution*, pp. 87–92.

[7] Voth, *Time and Work in England*, pp. 59–160 and 'Time and work in eighteenth-century London'. For estimates of days worked based on more traditional economic sources, see Woodward, *Men at Work*, pp. 125–35.

[8] Thompson, 'Time, work-discipline'.

[9] Hailwood, 'Time and work' presents results from an earlier iteration of this project. See also Tiratelli, 'The working week'.

hours and days that most other studies have lacked, depositional evidence can move the debates forward to consider variability across gender, occupation, employment arrangement, and sector.

4.1 Recording Time

This chapter addresses these issues in the literature, illuminating the common experience of rural 'worktime' to a greater extent than has been possible before. It does so in three sections, covering seasonality and the labours of the months; the working week and holidays; and the hours and phases of the working day. Such analysis is possible because, as the opening anecdote illustrates, deponents in the quarter sessions and church courts tended to situate their activities within rich timescapes, while coroners' inquests usually noted the date and time of accidental deaths. Month or date observations were most commonly linked to festivals – 'a week after hocktide' – and calendrical units – 'on or about Thursday sevennight last past'. Somewhat less frequently they were related to the weather – 'about the snow time about twelve tide' – or lifecycle events – 'the day of the christening of the said Mr Windham his child'. Witnesses might also use work itself as a touchstone, demonstrating labour's influence upon senses of time. References to cropping activities abound in the observations – 'haymaking time', 'latter end of wheat harvest' – while animal husbandry likewise left a mark – 'at sheep shearing time'. Commercial events such as 'fair time' and 'market day', or contracts of service and employment, also structured the timescape, while the day itself could be delineated in terms of clock-time, natural or fire light, phases of the day, and social events such as 'before evening prayer'.[10] As shown in Table 4.1, these observations can be aggregated into work-task subsamples according to different increments of time.

These incidental references to work, when systematically collected from depositions, hold many advantages over other historical sources of time-use and seasonality. They are closer to realities on the ground than proxy measurements based on marriage patterns or unemployment rates, or aspirational descriptions in labour legislation and literature. And they capture a wider range of tasks and experiences, especially those of women and servants, than financial accounts usually afford. Nevertheless, they do have limitations linked to the proclivities of respective courts and sources. As Table 4.1 shows, some time-use information, such as months and weekdays, was much more readily reported

[10] For more on the time-telling conventions recorded in depositional material, see Hailwood, 'Time and work'; Wrightson, 'Popular senses'.

Table 4.1 *Sources of evidence for worktime-use*

Type of time-use data included	% of tasks from quarter sessions	% of tasks from church courts	% of tasks from coroners' reports	Total tasks	% of all tasks
Overall sample	56.5	32.2	11.3	9,650	100.0
Month[a]	62.1	21.5	16.4	6,559	68.0
Weekday	63.0	12.9	24.1	4,331	44.9
Calendar date	59.7	9.3	31.1	3,361	34.8
Phase of day (e.g. morning)	58.2	16.7	25.1	2,236	23.2
Hour	43.1	12.3	44.6	1,256	13.0

[a] This count includes 'harvest time' data. This relates to tasks for which no specific month was given but were instead described as occurring during 'harvest time'. These tasks have been assigned specific months based on the distribution of harvest tasks for which there is month data, as explained in Appendix C. Without these additions there are 6,137 tasks with month data.

than others, and some sources were more likely to record certain types of information than others. This means that the subsamples of data used for analysis throughout this chapter draw on different proportions of material from each of the respective courts. That said, the proportions of each category of work observed in each subsample do not diverge significantly from the overall dataset, with the exception of very low levels of commerce reported for hours and phases of the day.

More potentially consequential are the ways in which crime, dating and time-telling conventions, and the judicial process might shape results in ways unconnected to actual rhythms of work. For example, certain hours, days, or months could be more prone to crime than others. Yet as explained in Section 1.2, all activities in the work-task dataset have been assigned an 'information status' based on how linked or 'integral' the task was to the court case at hand. Filtering out integral cases allows us to mitigate the temporality of crime as and when necessary: it decreases the number of late-night tasks in our sample; suggests there was little to no weekly pattern to crime; and points to an intense concentration of theft in November and especially December.[11] Accounting for time-telling conventions and the judicial process in our results – especially with regard to the monthly data – is a trickier business. To take the first issue, nearly

[11] The monthly average of integral tasks was 29 per cent, compared to 39 per cent for November and 42 per cent for December.

400 tasks in the dataset were described as happening in 'harvest time', rather than a specific month. This obviously creates problems for seasonality analysis based on the monthly distribution of tasks. Because it was customary to date autumnal activities in this manner – indicative of the cultural significance of the harvest – leaving this data out would seriously underrepresent tasks in that season, and especially the harvest fieldwork so central to early modern society.[12] Thus, we have assigned all undated 'harvest time' activities to specific months (largely July–September) based on the monthly distribution of harvest-related and 'harvest time' tasks for which we *do* have precise monthly data.[13]

The seasonality of the judicial process and deposition-taking presents an even more complicated problem. The majority of our month data derives from the quarter sessions, a court which, as the name implies, met seasonally: after Easter, Midsummer/Trinity, Michaelmas, and Christmas/Epiphany. While every effort was made to survey an equal number of session rolls across sample years, in the end depositions were more numerous for some quarterly sessions and particular months than others.[14] Across the whole year, these deviations were not extreme, but the potential effect on a time-use study becomes more cogent, given that the most overrepresented month, December, had nearly twice as many depositions as the least represented month, February; the equivalent of a random-hour recall survey making twice as many calls in one month as another.[15] Reasons for this might include discrepancies in session roll survival, a seasonality to legal business, and – as the December depositions suggest – criminogenic seasons.[16] Monthly weightings have therefore been applied to the quarter sessions tasks to create the effect of a more even distribution of sampled depositions across all months.[17]

[12] Evidence for the tendency to date harvest-related tasks in such a way can be found in the fact that specific months were recorded for only 37 per cent of fieldwork tasks, compared to the 64 per cent for all tasks. This discrepancy cannot be explained by the lower rates of date recording in the church court (tithe case) depositions: while 35 per cent of church court tasks had month data, only 22 per cent of the fieldwork tasks in that subsample did.

[13] A similar process was also applied to the much smaller number of activities dated only to 'Lent'. For more on how these 'harvest time' tasks were assigned, see Appendix C.

[14] Depositions dated to December, May, and June were overrepresented, while those dated to the Easter quarter (Jan–Mar) and August were underrepresented.

[15] For random-hour recall surveys, see Section 0.4 of the Introduction, and Section 1.4.

[16] For similar findings of December crime in eighteenth-century London, see Voth, *Time and Work in England*, pp. 63–5.

[17] Monthly weights were applied *only* to quarter sessions tasks, as the business of other courts was not as seasonally structured. Weighting approximates an even sample of quarter sessions depositions across the months. See Appendix D for more details on this methodology.

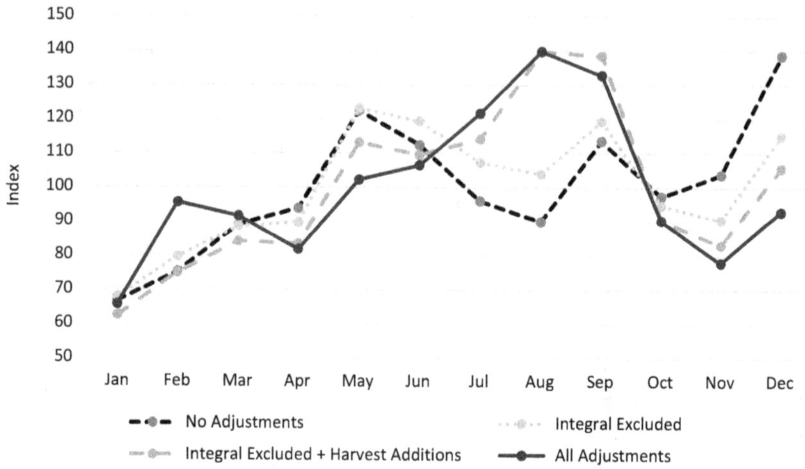

Figure 4.1 Seasonality of labour: an index of monthly tasks showing data adjustments.
Notes: 100 = monthly average. All Adjustments = Integral excluded, harvest additions, monthly weights, and female multiplier (x2.36). This differs from the standard multiplier as it is designed to give an equal number of male and female tasks with weighted monthly data attached.

Figure 4.1 shows the effect of applying adjustments – 'harvest time' additions, monthly weights, excluding integral, the female multiplier – to the monthly distribution of tasks. These adjustments, which have been applied to the seasonality analysis below unless otherwise noted, do not aim to 'fix' the data or present an infallible statistical picture, but they do account for various factors that might otherwise obscure or significantly distort seasonal patterns in the observed work tasks. We remain cautious about reading these results as precise indicators of overall work *intensity* in different months due to the sampling issues outlined above, but it is possible to make some meaningful observations about how the distribution of tasks varied through the seasons. Moreover, the great strength of this data is that it allows for comparisons of time-use across different types of work and groups of people. The rest of the chapter does just that, proceeding inward from the seasonal and monthly experience, through the pattern of the week, down to the phases and hours of the day.

4.2 Seasonality of Work

What was the shape of the working year in early modern England and in what ways did it vary? The adjusted data in Figure 4.1 provides the best

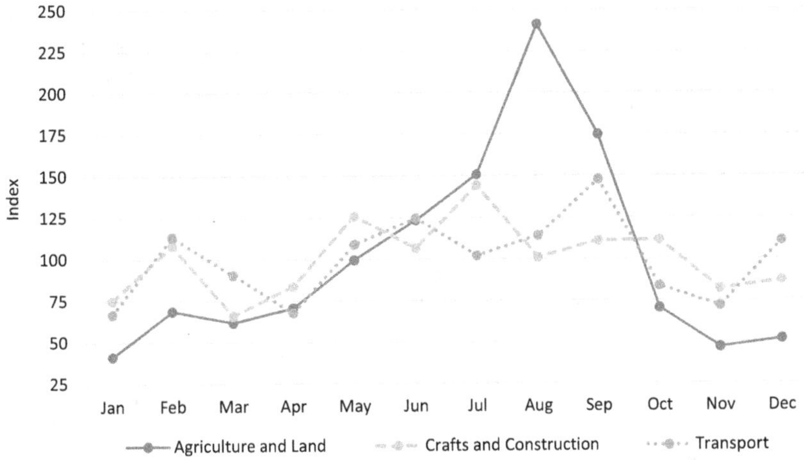

Figure 4.2 Summer work: indexed monthly distribution of agriculture, construction, and transport tasks.
Notes: 100 = monthly average. Harvest additions and monthly weights applied; Integral excluded; F adjusted (x2.36). This differs from the standard multiplier as it is designed to give an equal number of male and female tasks with weighted monthly data attached.

approximation of the frequency of work tasks across the months and quarters of a typical year. The highest concentration of tasks was observed in the summer quarter (July–September), the season of hay and cereal harvests, while the winter quarter (January–March) saw the lowest levels of activity. These trends fall in line with the oft-remarked discrepancy in labour and employment between winter and summer. The individual months, however, show variation within this general pattern. During the winter half of the year, for example, activity rose to notable peaks, nearing the annual monthly average in December, February, and March, with January exhibiting the only pronounced slump in work levels.[18]

More revealing than overall task numbers are the monthly distributions within particular work categories and subcategories. Figure 4.2 highlights those sectors with a pronounced peak in the summer half of the year, when as we would expect agricultural labour was at its most concentrated. Indeed, fieldwork, gathering food, and farm transport

[18] These January results parallel seasonal data from building and farm accounts. See Woodward, *Men at Work*, p. 136; Stephenson, 'Working days', p. 419; Whittle and Jiang, 'Gender, wages, and agricultural labour'.

tasks overwhelmingly took place in the summer quarter, with over 70 per cent of tasks in each category recorded during that period as workers mowed and made hay in July, reaped and gleaned corn in August and September, and spent all three months hauling in such harvests to storage. Yet other types of work contributed to the late summer peak in activity as well. A total of 30 per cent of observed craft and construction tasks took place between July and September, with building work, at 56 per cent, and groundworks, at 53 per cent – rather than general craftwork – proving particularly seasonal.[19]

Transport activity also reached its peak in the summer. Movement of goods was above average or at its height during the harvest quarter, especially when done by cart or horse, with 42 per cent and 47 per cent of such tasks respectively taking place in this period, as when John Blydes drove a cart 'laden with wheat to the Stokesby ferry' in Norfolk in 1594.[20] At the same time, it clearly depressed labour in other sectors. August's repertoire of tasks suggests that 52 per cent of people's time was devoted to agriculture during this prime harvest month, while most other work categories simultaneously fell around or below the average monthly distribution of 8.3 per cent.[21] Commercial activity in particular was at its lowest in August, while even the busy construction sector concentrated its summer work in July and September rather than August.[22] The participation of craftsmen in seasonal agricultural labour is explored further at the end of this section, but it is clear that priority was given to the harvest over other types of work, something dictated in the labour laws but rarely demonstrated empirically.[23]

While fieldwork and gathering were concentrated in the summer quarter, other tasks connected to the land – like fishing and hunting, digging marl/earth, and weeding – clustered in the spring. In contrast, animal husbandry represented a more constant and evenly spread tax on time and labour, appearing as one of the top subcategories in every single month of the year. But here as well activity was at its most concentrated in the spring and summer months, particularly May through July, and even more so when we take the harvesting of hay fodder into account.

[19] Compare to Woodward, *Men at Work*, pp. 135–42; Stephenson, 'Working days', pp. 418–20.

[20] TNA, KB/9/690b/241.

[21] The average monthly distribution of 100/12, or 8.3 per cent, is a useful comparative benchmark for assessing the seasonality of certain tasks. The average quarterly distribution is of course 25 per cent.

[22] The monthly distribution of days worked on St Paul's construction c.1700 shows interesting parallels, with peaks in June, July, and October bookending slight dips in August and September: Stephenson, 'Working days', p. 419.

[23] See Woodward, *Men at Work*, p. 138.

Much of this peak derived from the care and movement of sheep and cattle. The droving of livestock was at its height in the spring quarter, at 33 per cent, as people moved animals, especially sheep, from winter to summer pasturage. Sheep washing and shearing was overwhelmingly concentrated in the months of May and June – 83 per cent of tasks – while cow milking was more evenly spread throughout the summer half of the year, with 75 per cent of tasks in this period and just 25 per cent in winter. Of course, work on the land did not entirely cease as the weather turned cold. Autumn and winter quarters were characterised by ploughing and sowing and otherwise preparing the ground, and foddering of livestock reached its height in the barren months from January to March. Wood husbandry was likewise most heavily focused in the winter quarter, while people fetched wood and faggots for fuel most often during the three-month period from December to February, protecting their households against the cold. But although agricultural work certainly continued during the winter half of the year, it was a season more notably characterised by other sectors, as Figure 4.3 shows.[24]

Food processing in particular had an inverse relationship to summertime agricultural work, as people prepared and stored harvest produce for winter consumption. Threshing and winnowing at 70 per cent of tasks, milling at 67 per cent, and storage and preservation at 58 per cent were all at their height during the coldest half of the year. Butchery was at its busiest in the autumn quarter, at 38 per cent of tasks, when, as we saw from the Johnsons at the beginning of this chapter, October kicked off the winter slaughtering season. Like the harvest, this had knock-on effects in other sectors such as transport. Droving saw one of its peaks in the autumn quarter, as livestock was moved for exchange in meat markets. In November 1674, for example, the butcher William Cubbech bought a heifer in Setchey market, Norfolk, which he then drove homeward and slaughtered for sale at Lynn market in the first week of December.[25] This vignette highlights how food processing interconnected with commerce, another major wintertime sector.

Figure 4.3 conveys the relative aseasonality of commerce in its monthly distribution, aside from a modest trough in August and a very notable peak in December. Figure 4.4 looks more closely at the largest commerce subcategories, buying and selling, according to the types of goods transacted. This suggests that livestock purchases were only one factor in the commercial peak in December, and in autumn more broadly. Even when accounting for the potential distortions of December

[24] The seasonality of agriculture is discussed further throughout Chapter 6.
[25] NRO, C/S3/51, Info of Thomas Bell.

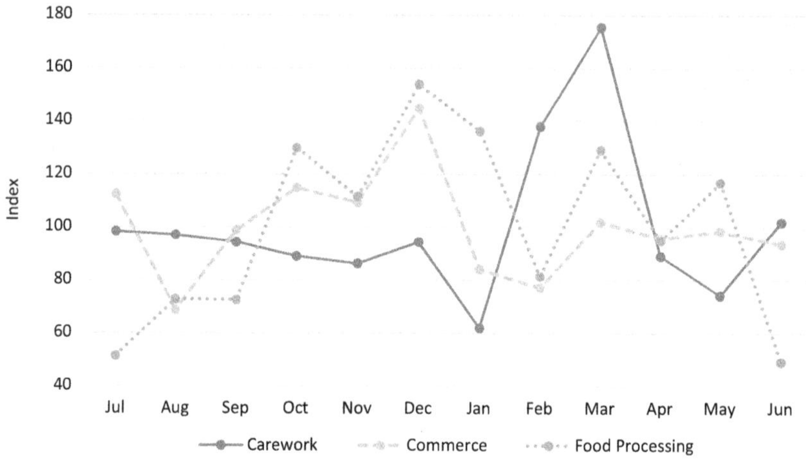

Figure 4.3 Winter work: indexed monthly distribution of carework, commerce, and food processing tasks.
Notes: 100 = monthly average. Harvest additions and monthly weights applied; while carework and commerce exclude integral tasks, food processing reflects raw numbers. This is because a large percentage of recorded food processing tasks (mostly butchery) were integral to criminal cases, as deponents slaughtered sheep under suspicion in the winter. Excluding these would render the food processing sample too small for robust analysis. While the raw pattern certainly reflects the seasonality of crime, and overrepresents sheep slaughtering in particular, it is reasonable to infer that it genuinely reflects seasonal trends in butchery intensity, as culprits responded either to their own needs or to economic demand. F adjusted for food processing (x2.58), for carework and commerce (x2.36). These differ from the standard multiplier as they are designed to give equal numbers of male and female tasks with weighted monthly data attached after filtering.

crime, the autumn quarter saw the highest proportion of commercial exchanges for most good types, and those transactions were of higher value on average.[26] These annual patterns of buying and selling derive partly from the seasonality of certain commercial spaces and events, like fairs and markets. Fair activities in the work-task dataset fall neatly in line with the monthly distribution of fairs recorded in Harrison's *Description of England*: there were very few in the winter quarter, 9 per cent, with most

[26] The trend is still pronounced after excluding integral tasks and adjusting for deposition numbers, and even the isolated church court data (where crime is less a factor) shows the same seasonal peak, with December and January accounting for 27 per cent of commerce activities. It seems clear this pattern is not an artefact of the sources.

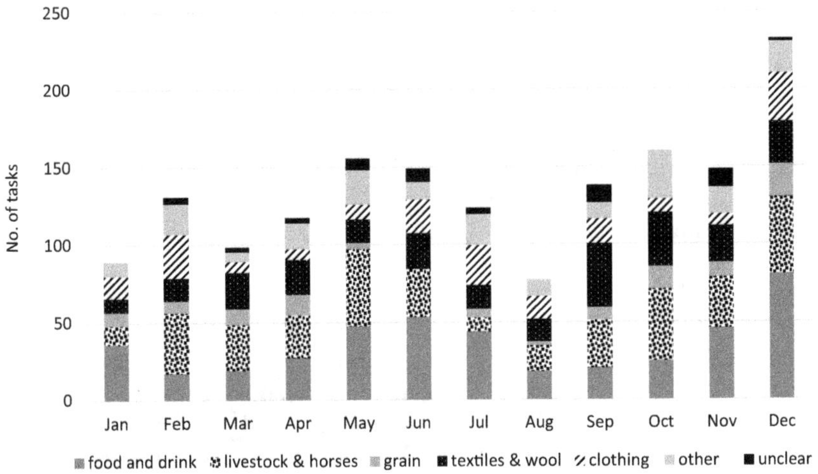

Figure 4.4 Seasonality of buying and selling: monthly distribution by good type.
Notes: Harvest additions and monthly weights applied; Integral included: the chart uses raw numbers for more robust analysis, since the shape and pattern of the commercial year remain largely the same even when integral tasks are excluded. F adjusted (x2.58). This differs from the standard multiplier as it is designed to give an equal number of male and female tasks with weighted monthly data attached. 'Other' includes books, tools, furniture, housewares, iron, fuel, silverware, and timber.

concentrated in spring, 31 per cent; summer, 33 per cent; and early autumn, 27 per cent.[27] Contrastingly, marketplace activity, while of course taking place weekly throughout the year, was much more intense during the autumn, 34 per cent, and winter, 32 per cent. Again, December played a leading role in this trend, accounting for 16 per cent of the market tasks, against the 8.3 per cent monthly average.

This commercial dominance of December, when buyers and sellers contracted 13 per cent of their business,[28] which was over 3 per cent more than the next busiest month, warrants further scrutiny. All major categories of goods were bought or sold at rates above the monthly average, but textiles, livestock, grain, and food were in particularly high demand. As we have already seen, the livestock and grain purchases were linked to the seasonality of food processing, with households preparing

[27] Harrison's fairs fell 10 per cent in winter, 35 per cent in spring, 36 per cent in summer, and 20 per cent in autumn. Harrison, *Description of England*, pp. 246–52.
[28] Excluding integral tasks.

for the long winter months ahead. But while some of the food and drink was undoubtedly salted or stored to ward off future dearth, much of it was intended 'for provision of [the] house in the holy days', as one Richard Hull of Thornton, Lancashire, put it in 1636.[29] Hull claimed that his father-in-law had procured and sent 'turkey … wheat flour puddings and fresh beef' as gifts, and others were similarly forthright in connecting transactions explicitly to Christmastide celebrations. The servant Winifrid Oliver of St Mary Bourne in Hampshire bought 'turkeys against Christmas' in 1630 at her dame's behest, while butcher Louis Spratly sold flesh from his stall in Southwark 'upon … twelfth eve' in 1597.[30] The Twelve Days of Christmas thus left their mark upon annual work patterns, not only in the sheer amount of food and drink transactions during the two months of December and January – over 29 per cent of the annual total – or the level of marketplace and financial activity but of course in the large proportion of labour devoted to processing and preparing such food for feasting. In terms of butchery, at 28 per cent of tasks, milling at 24 per cent, carrying goods at 24 per cent, and food preparation at 20 per cent, these two months were manic, with averages well above the two-month norm of 16.6 per cent, something witnesses not infrequently ascribed to the festive period. The miller of a water corn mill in Hulme, Cheshire, for example, explained in 1622 that he never slept in his workplace, except from 'about a fortnight before Christmas because of that time there is much grinding'.[31]

In light of this, it seems likely that December's high rates of theft, and of depositions, derived in part from the intense social pressures to feast, celebrate, and give appropriately during the holy season, alongside other crime factors like decreased daylight, fewer wage work opportunities, and winter privation.[32] Witnesses sometimes admitted to the desperate theft and slaughter of animals at Christmas to 'serve their great need', or because they 'wanted money to buy meat withall', while seasonal gift-giving was an oft-used excuse for ill-gotten gains.[33] Poverty, crime, and plenty thus all came to a head at the turn of the New Year. The cultural importance of Yuletide in early modern England is well documented, but less is known about the impact of the festive season upon work and the

[29] LaA, QSB/1/177, Examination of Richard Hull. Some examples of meat being salted down in December: CALS, QJF/51/4, 58; NAS, QSR/1/56, 32.

[30] HRO, 21M65/C3/12, *Mason v. Yates*; HALS, ASA8/8, 26–8.

[31] CALS, QJF/51/4, 52.

[32] On the argument that lower light levels were the prime driver behind winter crime, see Voth, *Time and Work in England*, pp. 64–6.

[33] DHC, QS/4/Box 5, 29; LiA, LQS/A/1/10, 121; DHC, QS/4/Box 24, Exam of John Crowdacott.

economy. Certainly, the evidence here suggests that Christmas' position at the centre of the commercial year is not unique to modern industrial society. Moreover, and like today, the early modern festival had wide-ranging effects on other economic sectors.

Carework is another work category in which the supposedly lax winter season was in fact a busy one. Even allowing for the smaller size of the subsample, Figure 4.3 demonstrates a significant seasonal trend in care tasks, with an intense peak concentrated in February and March. This primarily derives from work in midwifery, childcare, and healthcare, and correlates with prevailing demographic patterns of the time. Over a third of midwifery tasks, 35 per cent, were observed in just two months, February and March, more than double the two-month average and falling neatly in line with the pronounced peak in monthly recorded baptisms for England in the period 1540 to 1700.[34] Nursing and infant-care duties increased in line with this annual seasonal baby boom. If these transitional months from winter to spring were a time of new life, they were also a season of loss. Parish registers show a marked increase in burials starting in December and rising steadily to a crest in March and April, when the cumulative deprivations and diseases of winter exacted their final toll.[35] It is perhaps unsurprising then to find 37 per cent of healthcare tasks, attending to the sick and dying, in the three months of December, February, and March. Mary Davis, a covenant servant from Chelvey, Somerset, tended upon her master 'during the time of his sickness' and death 'in the month of December' in 1669, while Joanna Clark, a married woman of Waterford, Hertfordshire, was hired to care for a sick woman 'upon Shrove Tuesday' in 1596.[36] The picture of carework that emerges from this material is one of steady monthly labour punctuated by an exacting season when the symbolic clash of winter and spring – death and life – must have felt all too real.

Although the summer harvest was undoubtedly the greatest drain on time and energy relative to other seasons, the findings discussed here complicate the traditional narrative of an idle or lax winter. Between commerce, carework, and food processing and provision, men and women had plenty to keep them occupied in the cold months, and for several sectors this season was the busiest time of the year. But to be more precise, many historians characterise winter as a slack season specifically in terms of wage work and paid employment. It may be that

[34] Wrigley and Schofield, *Population History*, pp. 288–93, found the February-March crest to be very consistent and pronounced in comparison to other months of the year.

[35] Wrigley and Schofield, *Population History*, pp. 293–8.

[36] SHC, D/D/Cd/93, *Sharpe v. Barker*; HALS, ASA8/8, 11–3.

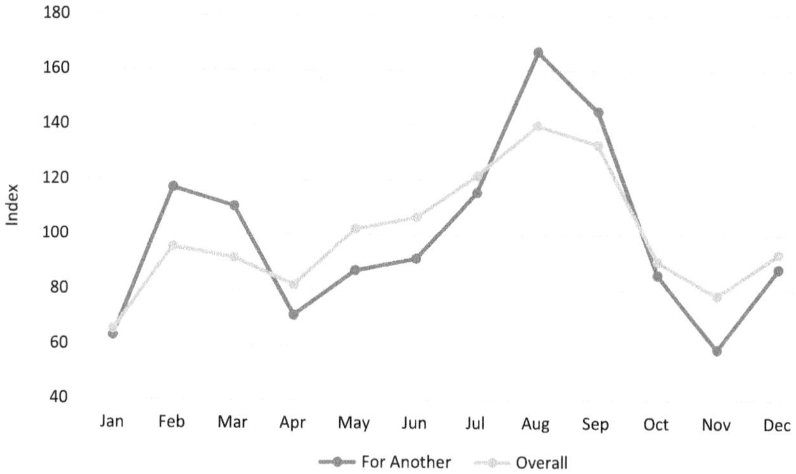

Figure 4.5 'For another' vs overall work: indexed monthly distribution of tasks.
Notes: 100 = monthly average. Harvest additions and monthly weights applied; Integral excluded; F adjusted (x2.58). This differs from the standard multiplier as it is designed to give an equal number of male and female tasks with weighted monthly data attached.

our more inclusive definition of work emphasises winter work, where traditional approaches have overlooked it. Commerce, for instance, was not usually waged work, though it of course generated income. Nevertheless, the seasonal distribution of 'for another' work, done for someone outside of the household, as well as the proportions of tasks that were done 'for another' each quarter, shown in Figure 4.5, suggest the importance of work for pay in the winter months.

In simple terms of distribution, there was an even more pronounced gulf between August and January for 'for another' work than for work overall, as the harvest generated maximum opportunity for waged labour. Beyond the harvest, however, more 'for another' tasks were observed in both the winter and autumn quarters than in the spring. Indeed, when we consider the percentage of quarterly tasks done for another, we find 48 per cent from January to March, above the 46 per cent for the harvest quarter.[37] Much of this winter work done for others fell in the categories of transport, food processing, carework, and housework; the latter three were sectors where women played an important role. Indeed, gender

[37] The monthly average across the year was that 42 per cent of all tasks were done 'for another', when the female multiplier is applied.

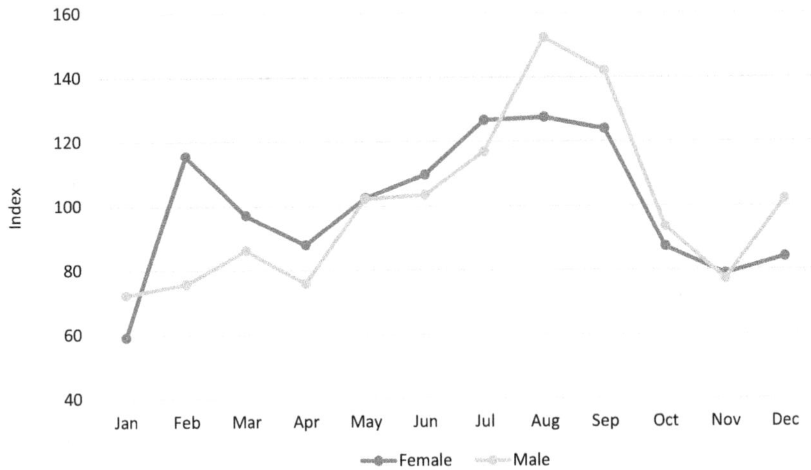

Figure 4.6 Gendered seasonality: indexed monthly distribution of male and female tasks.
Notes: 100 = monthly average. Harvest additions and monthly weights applied; Integral excluded; F adjusted (x2.58). This differs from the standard multiplier as it is designed to give an equal number of male and female tasks with weighted monthly data attached.

could shape seasonal patterns of work in significant ways. Yet to what extent and in what manner did men's and women's work overlap over the course of the year? At least in terms of the monthly distribution of tasks, Figure 4.6 shows relatively little difference between the genders. The key distinction is that more tasks were recorded for women in the first half of the year, with the opposite true in the second. Women's tasks substantially outnumber men's from February to April – 56 per cent against 44 per cent – when carework was at its height, while men's share of observed work tasks notably increased in August and September – 54 per cent against 46 per cent – when they played a bigger role in the grain harvest. Both genders participated in the end-of-year commercial boom, but men did 57 per cent of commerce activities in December, compared to the typical 50:50 commercial split between the genders. This partly sprang from men's involvement in larger transactions like livestock purchases, whereas buying and selling food and drink in the month of Christmas was more evenly divided between the genders.

Table 4.2 turns from task distribution to consider specific types of work. The highly gendered nature of the working year emerges in some predictable ways. Nonetheless, there were seasons when women and men worked in the same sector, highlighted by the italicised categories

Table 4.2 *Gender division of seasonal work: top categories and subcategories by quarter*

Women	Quarter	Men
Housework (30%), Carework (24%), midwifery (32), laundry (28), food and drink provision (22), childcare (16), *buy (16)*, carry goods (16)	Jan–Mar	Agriculture (34%), Transport (18%), animal husbandry (70), fieldwork (52), wood husbandry (34), *buy (29)*
Housework (25%), *Agriculture (23%)*, *animal husbandry (28)*, collecting water (27), childcare (26), food and drink provision (23)	Apr–Jun	*Agriculture (37%)*, Transport (20%), *animal husbandry (121)*, carting (69), hunting and fishing (48), financial (41)
Agriculture (33%), Housework (24%), *fieldwork (64)*, collecting water (34), food and drink provision (31), gathering food (24)	Jul–Sep	*Agriculture (52%)*, Transport (15%), *fieldwork (286)*, farm transport (157), animal husbandry (71), carting (71), buildings (58)
Housework (28%), Carework (18%), *Commerce (18%)*, food and drink provision (28), *buy (24)*, *carry goods (21)*, laundry (19)	Oct–Dec	Agriculture (28%), *Commerce (17%)*, Transport (17%), animal husbandry (73), sell (59), *buy (48)*, *carry goods (43)*

Notes: Harvest additions and monthly weights applied; Integral excluded. Overlap in seasonal work between the two genders is italicised. Top two work categories (given as a repertoire percentage) and top four subcategories (no. of tasks) are shown.

and subcategories in the table. Although the gender division of labour could still be stark within these broader subcategories, as discussed more fully in Chapter 6, men and women did work alongside one-another, particularly in summertime agriculture like May/June sheep shearing, June weeding, July haymaking, and August/September reaping.

Contrastingly, the winter quarter stands out as the season when the gender division of labour was most pronounced. With a relatively reduced workload, men focused on animal husbandry, ploughing, wood husbandry, and threshing. Women were particularly busy, partly due to the boom in carework discussed above but also because of the demands – and opportunities – of work in the housework category. Food provision, whether for household consumption or sale, was particularly intensive from December to February, when wives and female servants shouldered the brunt of festive responsibilities. Unsurprisingly, light and fire provision was a greater priority in the autumn and winter quarters, when women warded their households against the cold and dark. Lower temperatures and sunlight levels may have shaped the striking seasonality of laundry as well. Observed laundry work was at its ebb in the three months from November to January, when just 15 per cent of annual laundry tasks took place. A sudden and dramatic laundry peak in February and March, with 34 per cent of all tasks in just those two months combined, coupled with a smaller one in October, with 10 per cent of tasks, hints that women prepared in advance for the difficulties of the darkest months and then dealt with a washing backlog after them.[38]

The pre-eminence of housework, alongside carework, during the autumn and winter quarters supports Amanda Flather's argument that 'women spent most of the winter working in and around the house and yard, cooking, cleaning, and caring for children'.[39] Yet when we view our locational and seasonal data together, the spatial dynamics to the gender division of labour become more complex. Women were indeed more likely to work within or around their own household in the winter half of the year, when 37 per cent of their tasks took place there as opposed to just 22 per cent in summer.[40] During the darkest months, from November to January, housework took up the largest share of these labours, representing 51 per cent of their repertoire of work at home, followed by spinning, carding, and other textile work. But women still performed the majority of their wintertime tasks outside their own household. Notably, 72 per cent of winter carework took place away from the home, as did over 40 per cent of housework activities, with women venturing forth for water, light, and laundry. Nor were women's forays spatially confined to their own parishes: 21 per cent of women's work tasks took them outside their home parish, accounting for nearly 40 per cent of all inter-parish work travel. During the winter half of the year, it was certainly true that women stayed closer to home, but the difference was not drastic, with 18 per cent of tasks outside the parish against 23 per cent in summer. Moreover, women's out-of-parish work was above average in the autumn quarter, at 24 per cent, when they engaged heavily in commerce.[41]

Mixed-gender participation in the important commercial season complicates the narrative that 'for much of the winter different work in separate places kept contact between husbands and wives to a minimum'.[42] As the example of the Johnsons at the start of the chapter

38 North, *Sweet and Clean?*, p. 223. 39 Flather, 'Space, place, and gender', p. 351.

40 Based on the categories own household/outside the household explained in Section 1.2.3.

41 Out parish/in parish data is taken from the full dataset, excluding church court tasks since residency data is not as reliable. In the autumn quarter, nearly 50 per cent of women's commercial activity took place outside their resident parish, and they were responsible for 43 per cent of all out-parish commerce.

42 Flather, 'Space, place and gender', p. 351.

underlines, husbands and wives could work together to engage in the winter market boom. More generally, our location data shows that men, like women, spent the greatest amount of time working within or around the household during the winter half of the year, at 14 per cent against 9 per cent in summer. This household-based work reached a peak for men in December, at 19 per cent of their tasks, when, as Flather put it, 'they retreated to the house out of the cold and wet weather for a few weeks to mend tools and perhaps to weave some cloth'.[43] Men's household work in December, however, went far beyond craftwork. Their share of work within the household reached an annual high in the final month of the year, with a 40:60 male-to-female split, against an average of 30:70 across the year, an increase that came across almost all categories, including housework and carework. From the perspective of the spatial gender division of labour, December thus represented a winter counterpoint to the harvest months, with men and women more frequently working alongside each other in and near the home, as had been the case outside in the fields during July and August. William Cresey of Cheshunt, Hertfordshire, for example, dressed a slaughtered pig in his mother's house on St Stephen's Day 1590, which she then roasted for them to eat. Likewise, Laurence Farlton and his wife, of Newton, Cambridgeshire, pilled hemp together in their house on a December night in 1661.[44]

If gender influenced the seasonality of work, did occupations do the same? Table 4.3 breaks down and compares the quarterly working patterns of agricultural workers with those of artisans and tradesmen. What emerges are two quite distinct working years, which occasionally intersected or overlapped in character, just as we saw with women and men. As might be expected, agriculture and craftwork dominated the working years of the respective occupational groups. But the seasonality of work in adjacent sectors is more interesting. Chapter 2 explored the central importance of tertiary forms of labour like commerce to workers in the primary and especially secondary sectors. These results show that such tertiary engagement often fell along seasonal lines. For artisans and tradesmen, commerce, though of constant importance, became more pronounced in the autumn and winter, when the market for foodstuffs, textiles, and other wares reached its height. For agricultural workers, commerce took up the second-largest share of their time in autumn and spring, the two big quarters for livestock transactions. As we have seen already in this chapter, the summer harvest pulled in labour from diverse

[43] Ibid. [44] HALS, HAT/SR/2, 176; CUL, EDR/E10/110, 3.

Table 4.3 *Agricultural and craft occupations (male): top two categories and task distribution per quarter*

	Agricultural occupations[a] (555 tasks)	Artisan/Trade occupations[b] (654 tasks)
Overall	Agriculture (51%), Transport (16%)	Crafts and construction (30%), Commerce (19%)
Jan–Mar	Agriculture (52%), Transport (17%) 19% Distribution	Commerce (28%) Crafts and construction (27%) 20% Distribution
Apr–Jun	*Agriculture* (45%), *Commerce* (15%) 20% Distribution	Crafts and construction (32%), Management (15%), *Commerce* (15%), *Agriculture* (15%) 23% Distribution
Jul–Sep	*Agriculture* (64%), Transport (16%) 38% Distribution	Crafts and construction (38%), *Agriculture* (26%) 32% Distribution
Oct–Dec	Agriculture (36%), *Commerce* (19%) 24% Distribution	Crafts and construction (26%), *Commerce* (21%) 25% Distribution

Notes: Harvest additions and monthly weights applied; Integral excluded. Distribution = proportion of tasks per quarter. Overlap in seasonal work between the two occupational groups is italicised.

[a] Agricultural = yeomen, husbandmen, and agricultural trades.

[b] Artisan/Trade = artisans, commercial trades, and transport trades.

groups, like craftsmen, who were not otherwise heavily involved in agriculture. Yet while the fieldwork of tradesmen was largely seasonal, other agricultural activities like animal husbandry complemented their work repertoire throughout the year. Such evidence of by-employment or makeshift economies appears most stark, for both occupational groups, in the spring – the quarter when the overall proportion of 'for another' work fell to an annual low at 35 per cent.[45]

In contrast to husbandmen and artisans or tradesmen, the work experience of male servants and labourers showed relatively little variation through the year. It was dominated by agriculture and transport work, with little evidence of market activity outside the autumn quarter. That being said, some specific tasks did vary with the seasons, and often clearly extended from their particular employment arrangement. Labourers' tasks were more seasonal: threshing and wood husbandry in autumn and winter, carting and the digging of marl or earth in the spring,

[45] See Figure 4.5.

and harvest fieldwork and farm transport in the summer. Male servants shared in many of these tasks, but on the whole were more oriented to steady year-round responsibilities on the farms where they lived and worked. Animal husbandry was a constant, while their fieldwork and food processing tasks followed the seasonal cycle of ploughing, sowing, reaping, and threshing. Female servants experienced similar levels of seasonal variation to their male counterparts. Housework and animal husbandry dominated the whole year, but milking especially characterised the summer half, and food and drink provision the winter. Such gendered experiences of the working year emerge even more clearly when we consider the workweek and holidays.

4.3 Working Week and Year

If seasonal and monthly patterns shaped early modern work, so too did the rhythms of the week. Yet as Figure 4.7 suggests, the general distribution of tasks varied relatively little according to weekday for men and

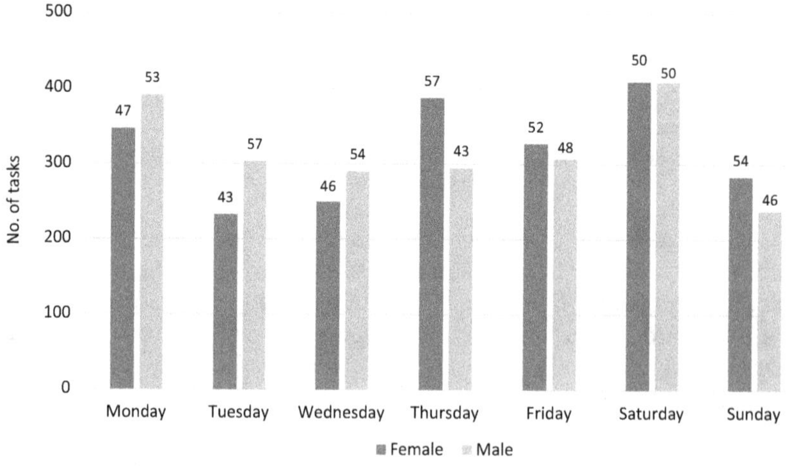

Figure 4.7 The gendered workweek: distribution and gender division of tasks per weekday.
Notes: Integral excluded. Removing integral tasks has a negligible effect on weekday distribution overall, but they are excluded here to demonstrate that these patterns are not a consequence of certain days being more criminogenic. F adjusted (x2.67). This differs from the standard multiplier as it is designed to give an equal number of male and female tasks with weekday data attached. Overall daily task total (F adjusted): Mon 737, Tue 536, Wed 539, Thu 683, Fri 634, Sat 818, Sun 521.

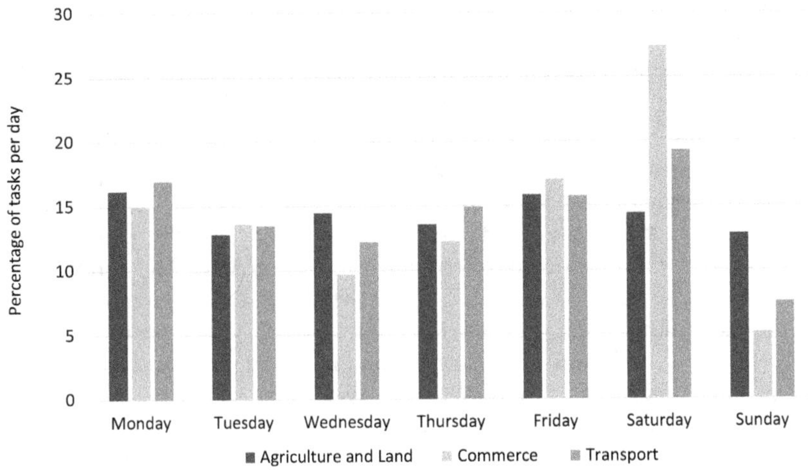

Figure 4.8 The workweek for agriculture, commerce, and transport.
Notes: Integral included as they have a negligible impact on weekday distribution. F adjusted (x2.67). This differs from the standard multiplier as it is designed to give an equal number of male and female tasks with weekday data attached. Task totals per category: agriculture and land (1,445 tasks); commerce (1,165 tasks); transport (862 tasks).

women alike. Men observed a fairly cyclical work pattern, with moderately lower midweek activity levels bookended by Monday and Saturday peaks in activity: there was certainly no 'St Monday' in evidence here. Women were busy on these two days as well, but their workweek was less straightforwardly structured. On Sunday, both genders performed fewer tasks, but this held greater contrast for men than it did for women. For the latter, just as many or more tasks were recorded on Sunday as on Tuesday or Wednesday. Yet, while the lines between 'days of rest' and 'days of work' were clearly more blurred for women, men still contributed significantly to Sunday work. Indeed, it is striking quite how much sabbath work the dataset captures overall – only slightly fewer tasks than that observed on Wednesdays. The character of Sunday labour is explored further below, but some of the general causes behind these weekday variations emerge when we break down the data according to work categories.

As Figure 4.8 shows, agricultural work was distributed evenly throughout the week, including Sundays. Conversely, commerce and transport fell off significantly on the sabbath day. Tasks within the latter two categories reached their height on Saturday, which was far and away the most common market day recorded in our dataset, across all regions.[46] Women in particular played a leading role in Saturday markets, on that day accounting for 59 per cent of commerce tasks, 56 per cent of management tasks, and performing their largest daily share of transport at 43 per cent. Market days more broadly, as catalysts for commerce and transport, brought variation to the workweek. At the beginning of this chapter, the Johnsons' preparations for a Saturday market in Chester demonstrated how these weekly events could lengthen the workday, as men and women rose early to travel to market towns and came home late. The cumulative impact of these differing work hours comes through in the data for 'phases of the day', discussed in Section 4.4, where Saturday exhibits the highest percentage of combined early morning and morning tasks per weekday, at 43 per cent, against a Monday-to-Friday average of 38 per cent. Not infrequently, deponents dated actions in relation to market days, and in general people seem to have had a keen awareness of when these events took place within their region. Witnesses' suspicions were sometimes aroused, for example, when individuals transported certain goods to towns when it was 'not the market day there'.[47] Some weekdays, like Wednesday, played host to markets less often than others, and this may partly explain the relatively lower number of overall tasks reported on such days in the dataset, as commerce and transport tasks in particular tended to be more common on market days.

The high level of activity on Mondays, however, is harder to explain. Although it was not a popular market day, Monday saw above-average activity in commerce, and in almost every other work category besides. These findings cast doubt upon the relevance of 'St Monday' as a traditional day off work in early modern England.[48] Certainly, if the phenomenon did exist, it does not seem to have been a rural one.[49] The strongest empirical evidence for St Monday comes from mid-eighteenth-century London, where Voth found that Sundays and Mondays were the weekdays with the lowest probability of observing people at work. He did not find equivalent evidence in a contemporary northern and more rural sample of depositions, and this complements other

[46] A combined total of 191 'at market' and 'go to market' tasks can be ranked per weekday as Saturday (48 per cent), Tuesday (18 per cent), Friday (11 per cent), Thursday (10 per cent), Wednesday (7 per cent), Monday (6 per cent), Sunday (0.5 per cent). Saturday's dominance as a market day in early modern England has not been much discussed.

[47] HALS, HAT/SR/8, 143. See also NRO, C/S3/12A, Exam of John Dobson.

[48] On St Monday see Tiratelli, 'Working week'; Reid, 'Weddings, weekdays, work' and 'The decline of Saint Monday', and Section 0.1 of the Introduction.

[49] See also Hailwood, 'Time and work', pp. 105–7; Hindle, 'Work, reward, and labour discipline', p. 270.

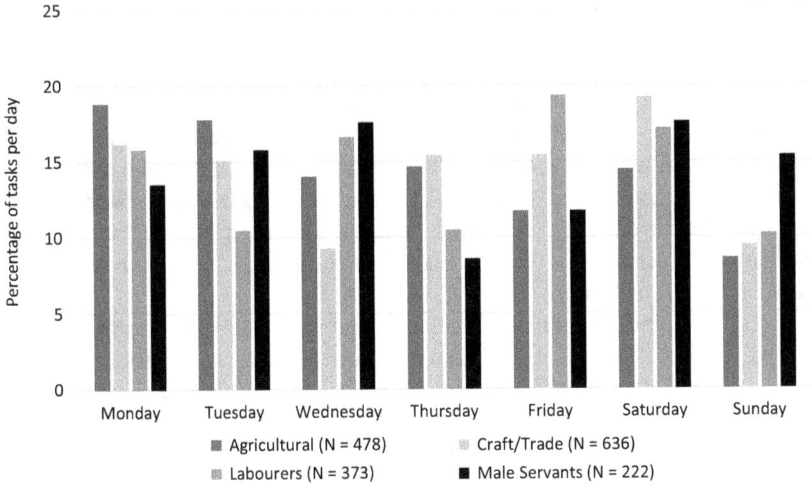

Figure 4.9 Occupational workweeks (male).
Notes: Integral included as they have a negligible impact on weekday distribution. Agricultural = yeomen, husbandmen, and agricultural trades (478 tasks); craft/trade = artisans, commercial trades, and transport trades (636 tasks); labourers (373 tasks); male servants (222 tasks).

evidence – especially literary evidence – that St Monday was an observance of urban artisans.[50] The work-task data suggests the observance may have been even more limited than this, perhaps extending no further than the metropolis. When we isolate those work tasks in the sample performed in large towns and market towns, it shows that Monday's work activity was above average even in these urban places.[51]

Furthermore, mapping the workweeks of different occupational groups, as shown in Figure 4.9, demonstrates that artisans, tradesmen, and labourers did not shy from work on Monday, any more so than agricultural workers and servants did. If anything, the opposite seems to have been true, with Monday seeing a flurry of activity across sectors as workers returned to their labours after a mandated day of rest. Moreover,

[50] Voth, *Time and Work in England*, pp. 85–93 and 'Time and work in eighteenth-century London'. On literary evidence of St Monday, see Thompson, 'Time, work discipline', pp. 74–6.

[51] Against a weekday average of 14.3 per cent, 17 per cent of tasks took place on Monday in both market towns and large towns. For early literary evidence of St Monday in seventeenth-century London, see discussion of the ballad *Mondayes Worke* in Hailwood, 'Sociability, work and labouring identity', pp. 15, 20.

when we survey the data for women and different male occupational groups, no single weekday emerges as an alternative 'day off' to St Monday. Certainly, breaking down the data in this way reveals some variation between different workers, although we must allow for the much smaller size of these occupational and gender subsamples. Notably, the number of recorded tasks is lower on Wednesday for artisans and tradesmen, and on Tuesday and Thursday for labourers. Overall, however, these findings suggest a regular six-day workweek prevailed across most sectors, with only a moderate dip in activity across most sectors on Sunday.

Economic and social historians' interests in St Monday and the length of the workweek derive from a broader concern with the number of days in the working year, and associated levels of income and 'industriousness'. For example, historians have often assumed a five-day workweek existed in preindustrial England when calculating annual incomes and standards of living from wage series. Likewise, Voth's findings of St Monday and its decline in London over the latter half of the eighteenth century fold into broader arguments that an increase in workdays during the early industrial period – due in part to a longer workweek – led to greater outputs. Yet grand narratives of economic change over time like these largely trade on a strict dichotomy between workdays and 'non-work' or leisure days, which the work-task data simply does not support.[52] The most obvious case in point can be found in the results for Sunday, the quintessential day of rest.

From the early medieval period through successive reformations, both canon and secular law decreed that the Lord's Day should be free from 'abusive pursuit of any servile occupations'.[53] Yet even on this day, when all but the most indispensable forms of work were ostensibly forbidden by law and custom, the work-task data shows that men and women did a substantial number of tasks. Certainly, they did more work than the 'nil' assumed in the calculations of 'workdays' which underpin most wage series. That being said, the types of work and forms of employment found on Sundays remain important factors to consider. Our inclusive definition of work, for example, may capture more sabbath activity than studies devoted solely to waged labour. Yet when we look at the percentage of tasks done 'for another' – those activities most likely to be remunerated – Sunday's proportion, at 36 per cent, is above the daily average

[52] See Clark, 'Review of *Time and Work*', p. 1123, for a similar critique of Voth's calculations of change in the working year length.

[53] Parker, *English Sabbath*, p. 21, quoting Archbishop Arundal's letter against the barbers of London in 1413.

of 32 per cent, and second only to Monday's of 37 per cent. These results suggest more remunerated or employed labour on the sabbath than other approaches to the history of work typically assume. One possible reason for this is that the work-task approach captures the work experiences of women and servants in much more detail than wage accounts.

To take servants first, we have already seen from Figure 4.9 that in the distribution of tasks across the week that male servants carried out, an above-average proportion of their tasks occurred on Sunday, at 15 per cent. Specifically, out of the four occupational groups displayed in Figure 4.9, male servants shouldered the lion's share of agricultural and transport work on the Lord's Day.[54] And so we find that William Bend, a servant from Parson Drove, Cambridgeshire, 'went to water two mares at the pond' on a 'Sunday morning' in 1664, and that Jacob Jackson of Hurworth, Durham, delivered his master's sheep after marking their ears on a Sunday in 1603.[55] Such evidence suggests that workers on annual contracts benefited less from the day of rest than those with more freedom and agency in their work schedules. Of course, this technically flew in the face of contemporary Sabbatarian commentary, which emphasised the responsibility of householders to furnish Sunday rest to those under their supervision, including even animals, 'so that they might have bodily refreshment and time for spiritual exercises'.[56] Servants and apprentices sometimes held their masters to account for dereliction of this duty, as in 1650 when shoemaker's apprentice Benjamin Hooper of Wells, Somerset, claimed he ran away 'because his master did make him work upon the sabbath days' in cleaning shoes, 'packing of wares', and running the shop.[57]

To judge from sabbath-breaking prosecutions in the church courts, Hooper's experience was shared by many servants.[58] Yet the proportion of all Sunday 'for another' tasks undertaken by servants was comparable to the proportion of 'for another' tasks they undertook on weekdays, so other forms of 'for another' work continued on this day too. The small number of examples of 'explicitly paid' sabbath labour are telling here, and do reflect Sunday's status as an important day of recreation. Thomas Westcott and William Philipps, for example, played the violin and cittern 'for a little money' late on Sunday night in 1691 at 'the house of Hanna

[54] Mansell, *Female Servants*, pp. 198–201, also found Sunday to be by far the busiest weekday for female servants. Our results for female servants show Monday as the busiest day, with Sunday comparable to other weekdays.

[55] CUL, EDR/E10/112, Info of William Bend; DUIC, DDR/EJ/CCD/1/7, 247v–51r.

[56] Parker, *English Sabbath*, pp. 30, 39.

[57] SHC, Q/SR/82, 72.

[58] See Emmison, 'Tithes, perambulations, and sabbath-breach', pp. 193–8.

Table 4.4 *Sabbath work: comparing weekday repertoires and gender division of labour*

	Monday–Friday average		Sunday	
	Repertoire (%)	% by F	Repertoire (%)	% by F
Agriculture and land	28.7	32.7	28.1	41.3
Carework	10.9	86.8	19.4	79.2
Commerce	11.2	48.3	6.2	59.8
Crafts and construction	7.9	22.0	5.0	18.7
Food processing	3.7	34.7	1.5	61.8
Housework	17.2	87.8	18.8	81.6
Management	4.1	39.9	9.7	38.5
Transport	15.1	28.7	9.7	19.1
Other	1.2	37.3	1.7	54.8
Total	100.0	49.0	100.1	54.4
Total tasks	3,129	49.0	521	54.4

Notes: Integral excluded; F adjusted (x2.42). This differs from the standard multiplier as it is designed to give an equal number of male and female tasks with weekday data attached. Saturday has been excluded from the Monday-to-Friday average because the high proportion of market-day commerce makes it distinct from the other days of the week.

Dyer who sold beer or ale' in Newton Poppleford in Devon.[59] Likewise, in 1637 Alice Alredd of Atherton, Lancashire, was paid in ready money and linens for serving 'so much drink and victuals as came to nine pence' to three men who came into her house 'upon Sunday'.[60] These examples hint at what is perhaps the most notable characteristic of 'for another' work on Sundays: that women did the majority of it, at 62 per cent. And while young servants bore the brunt of Sunday labour among male occupations, it seems married women took the lead here, performing a larger share of 'for another' female tasks compared to other weekdays. The relationship between gender, status, and sabbath work comes into sharper focus when turning to the categories of tasks most commonly performed on the day.

Table 4.4 compares Sunday's work repertoire to a Monday-to-Friday average, highlighting the distinct nature of sabbath activity. Sunday work was more characterised by housework and carework than other weekdays, with crafts and construction, commerce, and transport activity all subdued. Although the former two categories were still dominated by

59 DHC, Chanter 8299, *Westcott v. Johns*. This was also on St Luke's Fair Day.
60 LaA, QSB/1/182, 58–9.

women, men performed a larger share of such tasks on the Lord's Day than they did during the week. Agricultural work made up just as much of the repertoire on Sundays as it did Monday through Friday, but on the Lord's Day tasks overwhelmingly centred on animal husbandry, with a fairly even gender division of labour. In an illustrative example from Heacham, Norfolk, in 1624, John Orrman 'in the forenoon before divine service ... went to his cows which were feeding in a clay pit ... and there kept by a girl of his whom he sent away to church'. He stayed in the pit until noon, alongside Ann Elvun and Margery Eran 'who were there also feeding of their cattle', after which he then drove his cows homeward.[61]

For many men like John Orrman, the tending of livestock was the principal Sunday task, with a notable absence of the fieldwork, carting, farm transport, and other physical labour, which otherwise dominated the male workweek. Artisans generally seem to have set down tools as well, with the occasional exception of building work. Roofing was not an uncommon task on Sunday, and it was a dangerous one at that to judge from several coroner's reports. On a Sunday in 1527, for example, the labourer John Webbe met his untimely end while 'thatching roof at the house of John Colyns' in West Lavington, Wiltshire.[62] Thatchers, alongside carpenters, masons, and other builders, were also sometimes called upon to inspect damaged church structures on Sunday, occasionally quite far from their home parish.[63] This illustrates the willingness of parsons, churchwardens, and other church officials to engage workers in ostensibly prohibited sabbath work. Of course, some Sabbatarian commentators did make allowance for labour deemed necessary to the preservation of life and property, which might include building work.[64]

Compared to men, women must have noticed relatively little difference between Sundays and other weekdays, in terms of the character of their work and time-use. Caring for children, milking, or tending to livestock, and providing the household with food and water, were constant responsibilities, many of which fell into the 'preservation of life' category. Nevertheless, women's work patterns did shift in a few notable ways on their 'day of rest'. For one, laundry activities fell to a weekly low, likely due to the public and arduous nature of the work. Food and drink provision, on the other hand, rose to a high. As touched on above, this may reflect the recreational demands and money-making opportunities of the Lord's Day, over and above standard household subsistence. Indeed, what little

61 NRO, C/S3/24, Part 2, Information of John Houlton. 62 TNA, KB/9/506a/108.

63 BI, CP.G.3559, *Drax v. Jackson*; CP.G.1210, *Taylor v. Oakden*; CP.G.2792, *Churchwardens of York v. William Barton and Edward Eardley*.

64 Parker, *English Sabbath*, pp. 19, 31.

commerce did take place on the sabbath appears to have passed principally through the hands of women engaged in selling or buying food and drink. On a Sunday in November 1597, for instance, Mawde Leighe of Sidbury in Devon sold cheese to Joan Lugge, while in July 1632 Alice Baylie, the wife of a labourer, sold drink from her house in Poole Keynes in Wiltshire.[65] Thus, just as women picked up the slack left by reduced waged work for men in winter, they found ways to generate income and employment on the one weekday when labour was technically forbidden.

In contrast to prosecutions from church and criminal courts, which tend to capture the most egregious and publicly visible examples of profaning the Lord's Day with 'servile labour', our depositional evidence suggests a common attitude towards sabbath work, which was respectful yet pragmatic. Those activities most strictly condemned by authorities from the medieval period onwards – trading, travel, carrying burdens, craftwork – were mostly avoided, but this left an array of tasks that often stretched the definition of 'necessary'. What seems to have been readily understood by ordinary women and men as the chief Sabbatarian duty was that work should not disrupt or conflict with divine service. The innkeeper William Hellycar of Williton in Somerset, for example, refused to accompany Samuel Crustman, a weaver, in hunting fowl one Sunday in 1638 because 'it would be too far to go unto the said ground and return again at evening prayer'.[66] When witnesses did admit to Sunday labours, they might clarify that these happened 'after prayers in the afternoon', or 'a little before evening prayer'. John Houlton went to a common near Heacham, Norfolk, on a Sunday morning in 1624 to retrieve his grass-filled cart, but upon hearing the ringing of a bell he perceived it to be 'church time and so came away to church'.[67] These examples speak to a common belief that work should not sully worship but also a view that it was the sabbath *service* rather than the *day itself* which took priority. Thus, the modest decrease in work tasks observed on Sundays likely reflects those hours taken up with worship, and no doubt some recreation, rather than day-long abstentions from work.

The key conclusion is that men and women carefully honoured the sabbath, as they understood it, while also pursuing what work they could. Remaining completely idle one day out of every week was likely neither affordable nor realistic. Crucially, this balanced approach embraced opportunities for income generation and paid employment, especially for women, and this has far-reaching implications for our understandings of the early modern economy in England. For one, it underlines the

[65] DHC, QS/4/Box 5, Epiphany, 69; WSHC, A1/110/1632M, 185–6.
[66] SHC, Q/SR/77, 64–5. [67] NRO, C/S3/24, Part 2, Information of John Houlton.

Table 4.5 *Workdays vs holy days: comparing repertoires and gender division of labour*

	Workdays		Book of Common Prayer holy days	
	Repertoire (%)	% by F	Repertoire (%)	% by F
Agriculture and land	27.8	29.0	24.5	45.1
Carework	10.6	87.5	17.4	92.6
Commerce	10.0	52.8	17.3	29.5
Crafts and construction	8.4	17.1	2.6	0.0
Food processing	3.8	37.7	4.3	39.8
Housework	18.4	88.4	15.4	93.8
Management	3.9	44.0	4.3	39.8
Transport	15.9	31.6	12.8	39.8
Other	1.3	48.1	1.5	57.0
Total	100.1	49.0	100.1	56.1
Total tasks	2958	49.0	312	56.1

Notes: Integral excluded; F adjusted (x2.65). This differs from the standard multiplier as it is designed to give an equal number of male and female tasks with calendar date data attached. Workdays = tasks with calendar date data which did not occur on Sunday or a holy day. Holy day count excludes Sunday tasks.

systematic underestimation of women and servants' contributions in the literature. More broadly, it complicates those narratives and models which hinge upon the length of the working year and its change over time, for these often assume that every Sunday and holy day was a 'day off'. Indeed, our evidence for activities done upon holy days further undermines such binary understandings. Using a subsample of the work-task dataset for which we have full calendar dates, Table 4.5 displays the repertoire of work tasks done on those holy days (excluding Sundays) prescribed in the Book of Common Prayer of 1561. Publication of the latter capped off a series of reforms, begun in 1536, which culled dozens of traditional feast days from the calendar. Twenty-seven holy days, in addition to Sundays, were left upon which all 'lawful bodily labour' should be set aside for prayer and worship. As the core festivals of the church throughout our period, they provide a conservative but serviceable list to test the extent to which holy days were observed as days off work: a question central to theories of economic, and of course religious, change.[68]

[68] On calendar reform and popular response, see Hutton, *Rise and Fall*; Duffy, *Stripping of the Altars*; Cressy, *Bonfires and Bells*; Parker, *English Sabbath*. For a list of the 1561 Book of Common Prayer holy days, see Cressy, *Bonfires and Bells*, pp. 6–7. This conservative list excludes many customary holidays (e.g. Shrove Tuesday), Protestant additions (e.g.

While we must allow for a much smaller sample size where holy days are concerned, the difference in work repertoires between the types of calendar days is striking. Most obviously, commerce took up a much larger share of time on holy days compared to workdays, and especially compared to the Sunday repertoire presented in Table 4.4, where it was just 6.2 per cent. This relates partly to the close connection between fairs and traditional feast days, for at least 36 per cent of holy day commercial activities were associated with these major economic events.[69] Thus, Margaret Slater sold linens at a fair in Preston 'upon the feast day of Simon and Jude' in 1626, while the glover Francis Richardson ran a stall 'on Easter Monday … at Oxborough Fair' in Norfolk in 1627.[70] Yet even when we filter out 'fairtime' activities, commerce appears more pronounced on feast days, likely due to the celebratory demands they occasioned.

Commerce aside, the holy day and sabbath repertoires appear largely similar in terms of work categories and gender division of labour: housework and carework carried on while craftwork and transport abated, so that women were less likely than men to have a day off. Indeed, Thomas Tusser warned huswives in particular to 'forget not the feasts that belong to the plough'. He tasked them, alongside their servant maids, with providing 'flesh [and] corn … wafers and cakes … good cheer and welcome' to their employees on certain festive occasions, alongside twice weekly roast beef dinners on Sundays and Thursdays.[71] The only other pronounced difference between Sundays and holy days was the nature of agricultural work. Although it generally did not cease on either type of 'day off', on holy days agricultural work was characterised by a wider array of activity than the animal husbandry which dominated the sabbath.[72] One might therefore witness William Carter driving a cart within a Topcroft farm in Norfolk on St Stephen's Day 1571, or John Whitehead and James Booth ploughing a field in Idle, Yorkshire, on Lady Day 1696.[73]

Overall, this evidence suggests that holy days fell somewhere between Sundays and workdays in the estimations of working men and women, perhaps reflecting contemporary religious debates among church and

Bonfire Night), and those Catholic feast days in effect during the first half of the sixteenth century (e.g. St George), which in practice may have long survived abolition.

69 See list of fairs on traditional feast days in Cressy, *Bonfires and Bells*, p. 16.

70 LaA, QSB/1/17, 25–6; NRO, C/S3/26, Exam of Francis Richardson.

71 Tusser, *Five Hundred Points*, 75r-v.

72 On Sundays 60 per cent of agricultural tasks fell under animal husbandry. On holy days it was 36 per cent, comparable to 35 per cent on workdays.

73 TNA, KB/9/631b/184; WYAS, QS1/35/6, John Whitehead.

Table 4.6 *Prevalence of work on different types of holy day*

	Holy day tasks (%)	Annual holy days (%)	% Difference
Christmastide	14.0	17.2	−3.3
Eastertide	6.5	10.3	−3.8
Whitsuntide	13.7	13.8	−0.1
Saints' Days	36.3	34.5	+1.8
Quarter Days	29.5	24.1	+5.3
Total	100.0	99.9	0.1
Total tasks/days	336 (tasks)	29 (days)	n/a

Note: Book of Common Prayer (1561) Holy days. Christmas Day is placed in 'Quarter Days' alongside Lady Day, Midsummer, and Michaelmas, and cross-quarter days Candlemas, May Day, and All Saints. Christmastide includes the Feasts of Stephen, John the Evangelist, Holy Innocents, New Year, Epiphany; Eastertide includes Easter Sunday, Monday, Tuesday; Whitsuntide includes Ascension, Whit Sunday, Monday, Tuesday; Saints' Days includes Feasts of Mathias, Mark, Peter and Paul, James, Bartholomew, Matthew, Luke, Simon and Jude, Andrew, and Thomas. Holy day count includes Sunday tasks when the Sunday fell on a holy day.

state authorities. Should holy days be disregarded entirely, treated as equal to the sabbath, or divided into tiers with Sundays and the major feasts of Christ on top?[74] The work-task data suggests that the latter tier system prevailed in popular practice. Sorting holy day tasks into feast day categories, as in Table 4.6, shows that work was most prevalent on busy quarter days, and least during the chief festivals of Christ's life, Christmastide, and Eastertide.

Certainly, further research is needed into how such weekly and annual work patterns may have shifted over the course of two centuries of intense religious and economic change. Yet already these sabbath and holy day findings suggest a more nuanced relationship between work and traditional days of worship and leisure in early modern England than historians have typically allowed. Rather than a strict dichotomy between 'workday' and 'day off', there was a spectrum, within which men and women deployed different labour strategies for Sundays, holy days, and workdays. These strategies rarely resulted in a completely idle day off, and the extent to which they did was dependent on factors like gender, occupation, or age and marital status. Any attempt to measure the working week or year must grapple with these realities, just as it must account for the length and character of the working day itself.

[74] See Parker; *English Sabbath,* pp. 50–5.

4.4 Working Day

If the work-task data challenges ideas about the length and character of the early modern workweek and year, it also confronts assumptions about the rhythms of the premodern working day. Whilst E.P. Thompson and Jacques Le Goff characterised preindustrial agrarian work rhythms as erratic and irregular, more recent studies of working hours in the early modern period have found that regular workdays, with consistent start and end times, were widely observed.[75] Voth's influential study of increased industriousness in eighteenth-century London argued that the number of days worked went up, but that the length of the working day did not; and Hailwood's recent study of sixteenth-and seventeenth-century rural working hours argued that a regular working day was in place long before the arrival of industrial modernity.[76] This section builds on Hailwood's analysis of the south-west data, adding to it the north and east samples. The increased number of observations of work tasks taking place at specific hours, such as 'at two of the clock in the afternoon' or 'between three and four of the clock in the morning'; and within broader phases of the day, such as 'in the morning early', 'in the evening', allows for an examination not only of the distribution of work tasks across the day but of how this varied by gender, the seasons, types of work, and occupational groupings.

The basic outline of the working day can be seen in Figure 4.10. This plots the numbers of tasks recorded in the database for each hour of the day, excluding integral tasks, which were often linked to crimes, and therefore overrepresent night-time activity – and adjusted to give an equal total of male and female work tasks, resulting in a total of 1,487 tasks. The overall shape looks, in most respects, like a recognisably modern, 'classic' working day. There were the first stirrings of activity between five and eight in the morning, before a pronounced peak of busyness between eight and midday. The next two hours show a slackening of pace, which coincided with taking dinner, the main meal of the day in early modern England. The afternoon, from two through to six, saw further peak hours. Levels of activity then dropped, but here we can see one of the key findings that has been overlooked in previous studies: the importance of the evening as a time of work. Indeed, the hours between 6 pm and 9 pm witnessed lower levels of work than during the morning or afternoon peaks, but they were not a time when all the day's labour had come to an end.

75 Thompson, 'Time, work-discipline'; Le Goff, *Time, Work, and Culture*; Woodward, *Men at Work*; Stephenson, 'Working days'.

76 Voth, *Time and Work in England*; Hailwood, 'Time and work'.

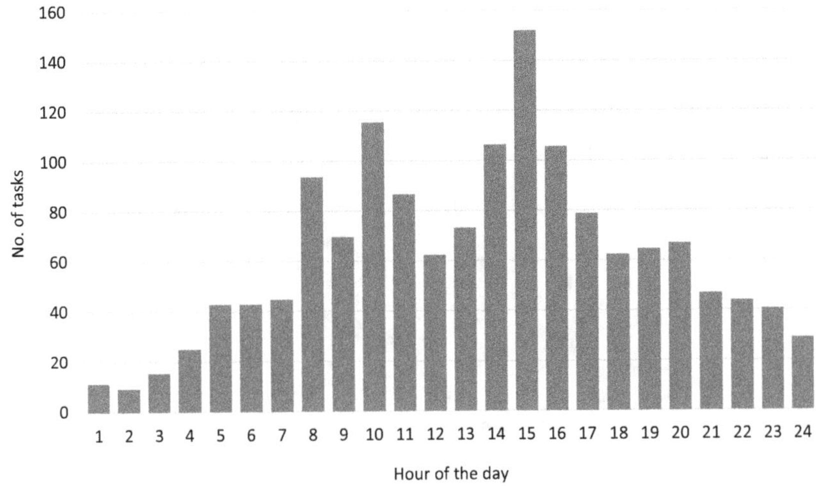

Figure 4.10 Tasks per hour.
Notes: Integral excluded; F adjusted (x2.58). This differs from the standard multiplier as it is designed to give an equal number of male and female tasks with hourly data attached.

The line between 'worktime' and 'non-worktime' thus was a blurry one. As with Sundays and holy days, this pattern is partly a result of the work-task methodology recording women's work, both paid and unpaid. As Figures 4.11 and 4.12 show, women's work was less confined to the 'peak' hours of the workday than was men's. For women, with the exception of a spike between 2 pm and 4 pm, work tasks were fairly evenly spread between 8 am and 9 pm, and there were also more tasks recorded in the two or three hours either side of this window than was the case for men. That said, Figure 4.12 shows that men also undertook a significant amount of 'off-peak' work tasks but in a lower proportion relative to 'peak' working hours.

It has been suggested that seasonality would have had a significant impact on the length of the working day in preindustrial society, with shorter daylight hours restricting the window in which to work.[77] As the above analysis has demonstrated, work tasks undertaken did change with the seasons, but the extent to which work rhythms did may well have been overestimated previously. By splitting the work-task data into two broad seasons – April to September; October to March – Figures 4.13 and 4.14

[77] Woodward, *Men at Work*, p. 127.

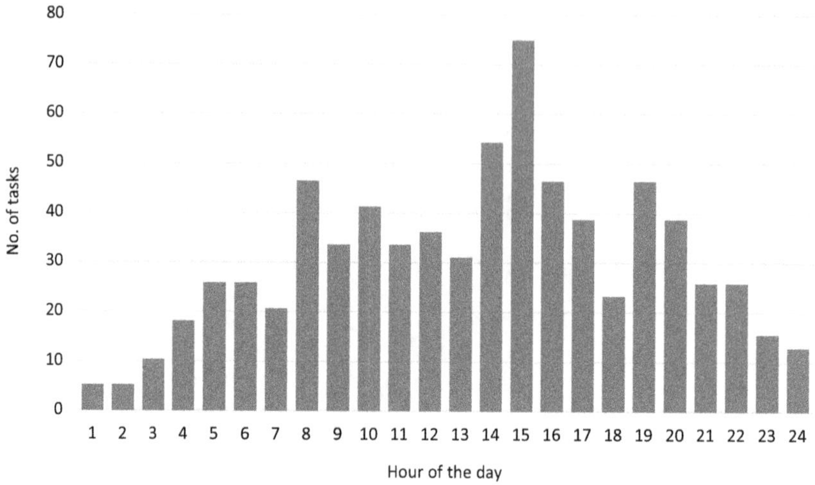

Figure 4.11 Tasks per hour by gender (female).
Notes: Integral excluded; F adjusted (x2.58). This differs from the standard multiplier as it is designed to give an equal number of male and female tasks with hourly data attached.

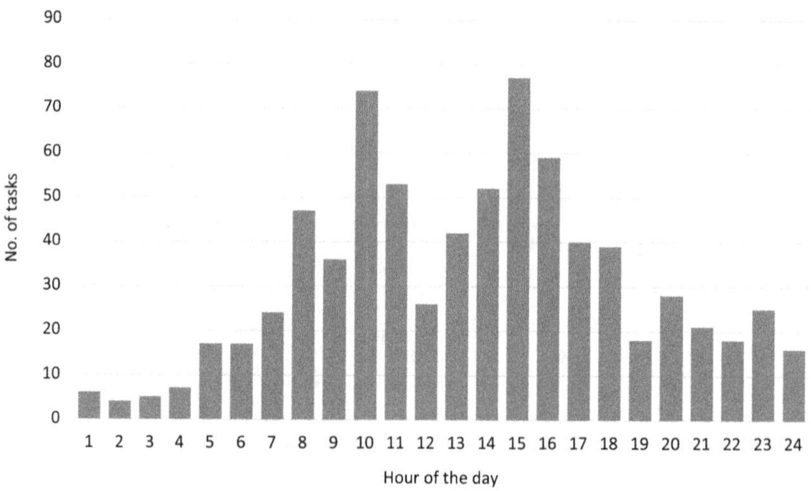

Figure 4.12 Tasks per hour by gender (male).
Notes: Integral excluded.

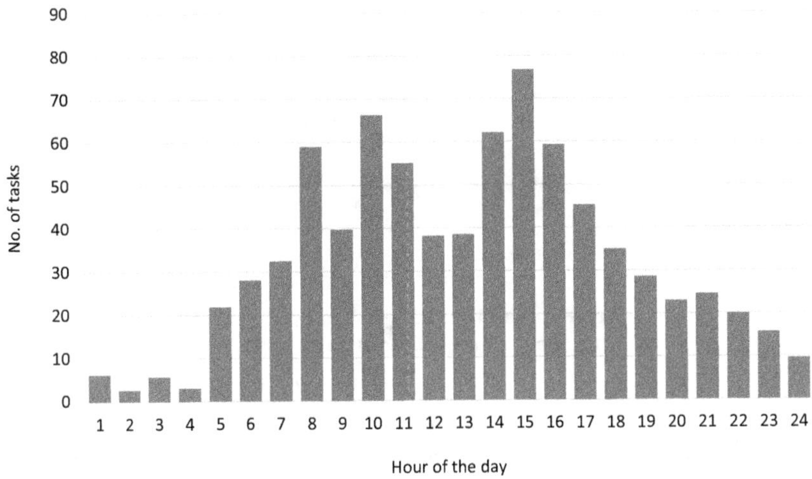

Figure 4.13 Tasks per hour in summer.

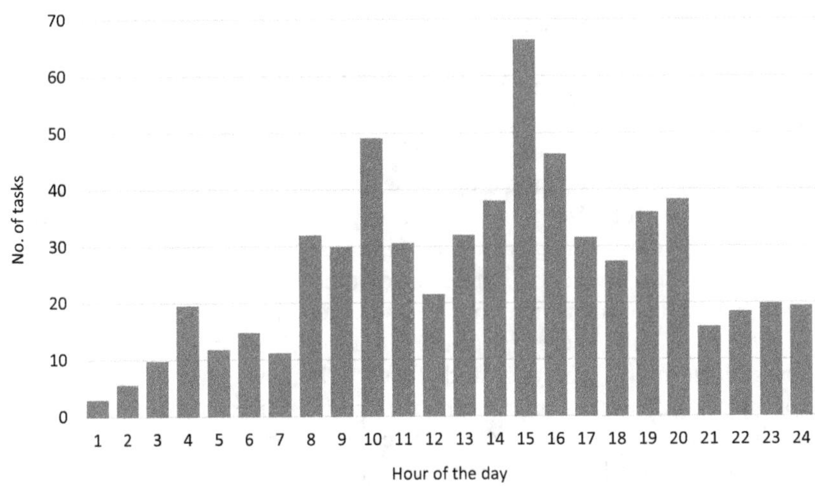

Figure 4.14 Tasks per hour in winter.
Notes: Integral excluded; F adjusted (x2.58). This differs from the standard multiplier as it is designed to give an equal number of male and female tasks with hourly data attached.

Table 4.7 *Tasks per phase of day*

	Tasks	%
Morning early (3–6 am)	130	5.6
Morning (6–12 am)	748	32.3
Afternoon (12–6 pm)	694	30.0
Evening (6–8 pm)	343	14.8
Night (8 pm–3 am)	396	17.2
Total	2,311	99.9

Notes: Integral excluded; F adjusted (x2.22). Differs from standard multiplier as it is designed to give an equal number of male and female tasks with phase-of-day data attached.

make it is clear that work activity did tend to start earlier in the summer, but there was not an earlier cessation to labour in the winter months; in fact, winter evenings were a period of considerable activity.

As Hailwood has previously argued, historians have overstated the extent to which early modern workers were dependent on good light levels to complete their work tasks. The example of the Johnsons at the start of the chapter shows how workers often made do with the light of a fire, a candle, or even the stars and moon, as well as relying on touch and feel.[78] But taking a closer look at what types of work were taking place during these evenings, and during other phases of the day, gives a better understanding of the long tail to the working day in early modern England. The number of tasks available for such an analysis can be increased by including not only those instances where a specific hour was recorded but also those where deponents referenced a broader 'phase of the day'. Using instances where deponents deployed both an hour and a phase, such as 'at seven of the clock in the evening', it is possible to determine which hour periods each phase statement generally referred to. Whilst there was some variation in usage, five key phases emerged from this analysis, and Table 4.7 shows the distribution of 2,313 work tasks across them. The pattern is similar to the hours analysis: the majority of work, at 62.3 per cent, is concentrated between the 'peak' work periods of morning and afternoon, 6 am to 6 pm, but a significant proportion also took place during 'off-peak' hours, especially during the evening.

What tasks took place when? In the summer months, the most common subcategory of evening task was animal husbandry, with 24

[78] Hailwood, 'Time and work'.

tasks, much of which involved checking on or moving animals that were out to pasture. In September of 1699, William Rowsell and his wife went 'in the evening' from North Curry, Somerset, to 'a moor called West Sedgemoor' and 'fetched out thence six ewe sheep and one weather sheep and drove them home'.[79] Other common tasks included fieldwork, with 20 tasks, and milking, with 16, which could be undertaken in the longer and warmer evenings. In the winter none of those activities featured prominently. At that time of year the top subcategory was carry goods, with 16 tasks, which included bringing home goods from market, taking wheat to the mill, and collecting hay and coals from nearby stores. These tasks are a reminder that the movement of goods was a time-consuming activity at all times of year, and was also one that could be undertaken in low light when necessary. Other activities that needed completing all year round also feature in the top five winter evening subcategories: locking doors and gates, food and drink provision, collecting water, and light and fire provision. The Cheshire servant Alice Smith would have known only too well that these housework tasks were not put on hold in the dark days of winter. When a man and woman arrived to lodge at her dame's Bowdon alehouse, one January evening in 1662, they first required food to be prepared, and then Smith did 'light a candle' for them, showed them to a bed chamber, and when they called for drink a short while later 'she went and brought them some'.[80] Similar tasks would have been carried out on evenings in all seasons across England's alehouses and domestic homes alike.

Whereas activities such as droving, carrying goods, and housework explain the busy evening work period, it is more surprising to find that as many as 17.2 per cent of tasks took place during the night. This is not simply a function of using depositional material that could often relate to nocturnal wrongdoing, as this number excludes integral activities that were closely linked to criminal activities. A closer look at subcategories is helpful here too and demonstrates that there were in fact many legitimate forms of work that could take place at night. Food and drink provision constitutes the largest subcategory, with 46 tasks. Much of this involved the preparation of food and serving of drinks to paying customers in the alehouse world of commercialised housework, where publicans clearly did not adhere to the 9 pm closing time stipulated in legislation from the period.[81] Animal husbandry, with 38 tasks, featured prominently, especially feeding. John King, a yeoman of Bishopstone, Wiltshire, was by no means unusual to be up at night 'about 12 of the clock to feed his horses'

[79] SHC, Q/SR/213, 6. [80] CALS, QJF/90/1, 118.
[81] Hailwood, *Alehouses and Good Fellowship*, p. 25.

in October of 1661.[82] He did so as he had 'a journey the next morning', and this was often a reason to make sure a horse was well fed at night: the Norfolk woolcomber John Thacker borrowed a horse in 1679 and was given by its owner 'a lock of barley to give his horse that night before he did take his journey' the following morning.[83] Journeys to fetch or carry goods were another common activity that took place at night. For those transporting yarn, clothes, and victuals on foot to and from suppliers, producers and consumers, an early start or a late finish to the working day was often required to fit in these time-consuming travels. Healthcare had a strong nocturnal dimension to it too. Attending the sick, dressing wounds, or giving medicine were all tasks that could be required at any time of the day or night, and very frequently the small hours were a time when those on their sickbed were especially vulnerable.[84] The prominence of both evening and night-time work in our data is not a 'fiction of the archive' created by using depositional material; rather, it demonstrates that when a broad definition of work is adopted, it becomes clear that the temporal rhythms required by many everyday tasks did not neatly align with daylight hours.

This was true for some forms of work more than others, and by grouping the various phases of the day into 'peak' (6 am–6 pm) and 'off peak' (6 pm–6 am) hours, it is possible to compare the temporal characteristics of different work categories, as shown in Table 4.8. Work most closely associated with craftsmen and artisans – crafts and construction, and the food processing of butchers, maltsters, and millers – had the highest concentration of work tasks within peak hours. In many respects these workers are the closest to modern industrial workers, often keeping set hours in their workshops so customers would know when and where to find them. But categories such as housework, and in particular care-work, were – as has been suggested above – much less bound to those peak hours. These patterns can also be identified by looking at the distribution between peak and off-peak work for broad occupational groupings, as in Table 4.9.

The experiences of male and female servants were very different: whilst the former may have had a certain degree of leisure time after the peak hours of the day, for the latter this was often when the working day was at its most demanding. Craftsmen and tradesmen had a stronger concentration of 'peak' hours than agriculturalists, but the most striking figure

[82] WSHC, A1/110/1662H, 208.

[83] NRO, C/S3/53A, Exam of John Thacker.

[84] Handley, *Sleep*, pp. 81–6.

Table 4.8 *Work categories peak vs off-peak hours*

	Tasks	% in peak hours (6 am–6 pm)	% in off-peak hours (6 pm–6 am)
Agriculture and land	725	67.1	32.9
Carework	230	40.0	60.0
Commerce	141	65.8	34.2
Crafts and construction	174	77.1	22.9
Food processing	86	81.9	18.1
Housework	504	58.3	41.7
Management	86	58.4	41.6
Transport	336	62.0	38.0
Other	29	49.4	50.6
Total	2,311	62.4	37.6

Notes: Integral excluded; F adjusted (x2.22). This differs from the standard multiplier as it is designed to give an equal number of male and female tasks with phase-of-day data attached.

Table 4.9 *Occupational groups peak vs off-peak hours*

	Tasks	% in peak hours (6 am–6 pm)	% in off-peak hours (6 pm–6 am)
Agricultural occupations (M)	167	56.9	43.1
Craft/trade occupations (M)	208	60.6	39.4
Labourers (M)	163	73.6	26.4
Servants (M)	98	67.3	32.7
Servants (F)	109	45.9	54.1

Notes: Integral excluded; F adjusted (x2.22). This differs from the standard multiplier as it is designed to give an equal number of male and female tasks with phase-of-day data attached.

here is that of labourers, who have the highest percentage of 'peak' work. If husbandmen had long hours of fieldwork and animal husbandry contributing to their off-peak work burden – more so than craftsmen – it may well be the case that labourers, with a lack of land and animals, had fewer tasks to attend to outside of the hours during which they could find paid day work. That said, paid work should not be conflated with work undertaken during the 'peak' hours of the day. For men, 'for another' work was concentrated in peak hours, at 62 per cent, but this still left 38 per cent of work done for others outside the household taking place in the evening and at night. For women, 'for another' work was actually more likely to take place during 'off-peak' hours, at 54 per cent, than during peak hours, at 46 per cent, reflecting the fact that housework and carework – even when taking place in the evening or at night – were very often undertaken by women for pay.[85]

Taken together, the work-task data shows that the rural working day was not entirely irregular or erratic. There were very clear 'peak' working hours during which the majority of work tasks took place. But there was not one uniform temporal pattern for all types of work and workers; men, and especially those engaged in artisanal or labouring work, performed a higher percentage of their work during 'peak' hours, whereas the labour of women was spread more evenly around the clock. Once again, these findings demonstrate the importance of an inclusive definition of work, and of decentring the experience of male artisans when understanding the full range of experiences of work in early modern England. What does appear to have been a unifying experience though is the undertaking of long hours of work. Even for groups of workers with a high concentration of their tasks in 'peak' hours, significant levels of activity in the evening and during the night were recorded. Even when all housework and carework are excluded from the analysis, and the overall totals of female tasks are not adjusted, adjustments that would bring our data more into line with the definition of 'labour force participation', the proportion of tasks undertaken during 'peak' hours only rises to 69 per cent, as opposed to 62 per cent in the more inclusive and adjusted data used above. In short, undertaking work tasks during 'off-peak' hours was common practice.

This has implications for debates about rising work intensity in our period. The work-task data, as discussed in Section 1.4, does not lend itself to the straightforward analysis of change over time within the period, and attempts to do so on this issue reveal no clear patterns. But there does not appear to have been significant scope for early modern rural workers to abandon a 'leisure preference' in order to work longer hours, as the working day was already long and arduous. That is not to say that a shift to different types of work might not have been a factor, of course, but there is little evidence in our data that rural workers lacked day-to-day industriousness in the first place.

4.5 Conclusion

Early modern work hinged upon seasonal, weekly, and daily rhythms, yet robust empirical evidence for these has often been lacking in histories of labour and economic change. The work-task approach goes some way in

[85] See also Section 5.3.

filling this gap, providing a mixture of reassuring results, novel findings, and overt challenges to received wisdom on the topic. The monthly distribution of tasks demonstrates familiar patterns of seasonality, with intense work in summer characterised particularly by harvest fieldwork, carting, and construction. Yet winter was not a season of idleness or markedly reduced work hours, as has often been reflexively assumed. Indeed, it was the major season of activity for certain sectors of the economy like carework, which responded to the excess of births and deaths in late winter, and commerce, which pivoted around the Christmas festival. The fact that women played key roles in such winter labour, often income-generating or paid, may explain its relative neglect in a literature that has prioritised the experience of the male wage worker. Certainly, winter commerce was a seasonal activity shared between men and women, and across occupations, in a working year often bifurcated according to identity. More well-known seasonal tasks such as spring weeding, June sheep shearing, and July haymaking also brought the genders together, but the grain harvest was unrivalled in mobilising men, women, children, husbandmen, and artisans alike.

While the seasonality of labour varied substantially according to sector, gender, and occupation, the working week did not. Men of most occupations and women observed fairly regular weekly schedules. Surprisingly, considering the emphasis placed on St Monday in the literature, Monday was the busiest day in terms of observed tasks. The other end of the week saw the commercial dominance of Saturday, the favoured weekday for markets in all three regions of our sample. Points of difference emerge, more intriguingly, around Sunday labour. Rather than a pronounced 'day of rest', the data reveals only a moderate decline in activity, comparable to other midweek days. This drop came in those sectors most targeted by Sabbatarian restrictions, like commerce, transport, or craftwork, while church-going commitments and recreation reduced the number of hours available for work tasks. Yet much sabbath work was done for others outside the household, suggesting that paid labour did not cease on the Lord's Day. Nor did it cease on holy days. Such festivals fell somewhere between Sundays and 'workdays' in terms of task repertoires, being especially flush with commercial activity linked to fairs and conviviality.

The working year which emerges from these findings is a complex spectrum rather than a binary model of workdays and 'days off'. The latter has underwritten many narratives of economic change, predicated upon longer workweeks and workdays, or fewer holidays. But such a formulation fundamentally misconstrues how early modern worktime was navigated in practice, undercounting the economic contributions of certain groups in the process. It was servants and women, for example, who were more likely to work on Sundays, holy days, and during off-peak hours, though they were not alone in doing so. Such blurred boundaries between work and leisure time do not reflect a lax or erratic work regime, as some histories have painted the preindustrial economy. Instead, the work-task approach has revealed a relatively stable early modern working day which, like the workweek, was long, and altered minimally across sectors and seasons. These results reflect an inclusive approach to the definition of work, which arguably gets much closer to reality than a fixation on day labouring for wages. The varied experiences thus captured allow a more grounded understanding of the nexus between work, industriousness, and the rhythms of everyday life in early modern England.

5 Housework and Carework

Four depositions from Wiltshire offer a taste of the variety of housework and carework in early modern England. A fortnight after Midsummer in 1566, Katherine Imber, the daughter of John Imber of Chittern, prepared 'a cream and posset' and invited her friends to share the food and drink in the hall of her father's house that evening and 'make merry'.[1] They included two women and a man who were servants in her household, and three men employed as servants by another wealthy farmer in the village. In a second case, from Leigh in 1632, Julianne Brookes reported how Alice, wife of George Burge, 'being then in labour of a child came unto her door and entreated ... [Julianne] presently to come unto her' to help deliver the baby, which she did. Later that day, Alice Smyth, a midwife from the next village of Ashton Keynes, visited the mother and child.[2] In a third case, from Salisbury in 1663, Mary Dyer heard that her neighbour's son was ill and asked him if he would like some bacon. When he said he would, she went to another neighbour to get some firewood and cooked the bacon for him in her chamber.[3] While in 1652, Mary Wilton of Brooke by Westbury described how Francis Rogers, a clothworker, 'did use to come diverse times to her house by reason she washed his clothes and the clothes of others that did work with him'.[4]

In each case, the people carrying out the varied care and housework tasks were female. In the database, these were the categories of work most heavily dominated by women. Adjusted figures show women undertook 86 per cent of housework tasks and 83 per cent of carework tasks, while no other category was more than 54 per cent female: for this reason and because both types of work are often subject to the same misconceptions, they are considered together in this chapter. Carework often involved helping neighbours, as it did in the cases of Julianne Brookes and Mary Dyer. Housework was often carried out by servants, but in the case from the Imber household, it was Katherine, the

[1] WSHC, D1/42/6, *Norton v. Imber.*

[2] WSHC, A1/110/1623T, 129.

[3] WSHC, D1/42/58, *Flower v. Dyer.*

[4] WSHC, A1/110/1653T, 174.

householder's daughter, who prepared the food to entertain a group of servants who were also her friends. Mary Dyer went to the trouble of lighting a fire to prepare food for someone outside her household: her neighbour's son. Housework and carework were frequently undertaken to earn money. This was the case for servants, but also for a woman like Mary Wilton who took in men's laundry. Some caregivers were skilled professionals, like Alice Smyth the midwife. Not one of these activities was carried out in private. Katherine shared her household with at least four other adults: her father and three servants. Tasks often spilled outside the boundaries of the house: Alice Burge had to call on a neighbour to get help when she was in labour; Mary Dyer left her house to get firewood; Francis Rogers took his clothes to another household to be washed.

Carework and housework are rarely studied as part of the preindustrial economy, yet these activities creep into historians' assumptions about other types of women's work. Thus, Broadberry et al. estimate that women carried out only 30 per cent of 'the total number of days worked in the economy' because 'child-rearing and household duties' took up the rest of their time.[5] Merry Wiesner-Hanks suggests that women worked closer to the home so that they could care for their children.[6] John Hatcher argues that female day labourers worked shorter hours than men because of 'the need to care for their families and to work in the house'.[7] Our findings show that women did most, although not all, of carework and housework. Yet this work did not dominate their work repertoires, combined making up 40 per cent of women's work tasks in the database.[8] However, the idea that such work was unpaid and undertaken only for family members should be challenged. Our evidence shows that it was often paid and frequently undertaken for people outside the immediate family.

Modern economic theory has created a raft of unhelpful assumptions about the place of housework and carework in the wider economy. In particular, unpaid housework and carework undertaken for family members are excluded from the definition of 'labour-force participation' and calculations of GDP.[9] In modern society such tasks have largely been the work of married women and take place within their own home, often as the only adult present. Historians frequently apply these assumptions to past societies. Where the economic importance of such tasks is

5 Broadberry et al., *British Economic Growth*, p. 348.
6 Wiesner-Hanks, *Women and Gender*, p. 119.
7 Hatcher, 'Women's work reconsidered', p. 194.
8 See Table 1.9.
9 Whittle, 'Critique of approaches'.

acknowledged, it is often as wives' unpaid 'social reproduction' or 'productive consumption' which allowed husbands to perform their income-generating work.[10] This chapter demonstrates that most of these assumptions are erroneous. It shows that a high proportion of early modern housework and carework was paid work or undertaken for people outside the family. It was not a specialism of married women: the amount of housework a woman did decreased after marriage. The carework women are recorded undertaking was more often skilled medical care than childcare. Early modern houses were rarely places of solitude or privacy in the same way as the modern home: walls were often flimsy, windows were not always glazed, doors were left open, and sound travelled further.[11] Servants and lodgers lived alongside family members. People were expected to know each other's business. Therefore, even a married woman undertaking housework and childcare in her own home was unlikely to have done so in solitude.

Housework and carework are modern terms. Meaning cleaning and tidying around the home, 'housework' did not come into common usage until the late eighteenth century.[12] The term 'carework' is even more modern, with 'careworkers' first coming into usage in the 1980s.[13] Ågren et al. have no such categories in their analysis of work tasks in early modern Sweden, placing such tasks in the categories of 'other specified work' and 'food and accommodation'.[14] We felt it was useful to create these categories precisely to address scholars' assumptions about this type of work. Our housework category is based on modern ideas of housework as encompassing cooking, cleaning, and provision of basic amenities (water, light, heat) within the home.[15] Nonetheless, the activities involved in such work have changed substantially over time. In early modern England the provision of water, lighting, and fuel loom large, and many activities, such as laundry, were often undertaken outside. Housework should not be confused with the early modern term 'housewifery', which encompassed a much wider range of tasks.[16] Our carework category includes childcare, education, nursing, and medical

[10] For example, McIntosh, *Working Women*, p. 3.

[11] Orlin, *Locating Privacy*; Johnson, *English Houses*; Hamling and Richardson, *Day at Home*. See also Section 3.5.

[12] OED online.

[13] OED online. There is an OED entry for careworker but not for carework. In this book we deliberately use the word 'carework', as opposed to the two-word form 'care work', to highlight the ways in which care and work are intimately connected.

[14] Ågren (ed.), *Making a Living*, pp. 29–34.

[15] Note that food processing is a separate category.

[16] Whittle and Griffiths, *Consumption and Gender*, pp. 26–48; Tusser, *Five Hundred Points*; Markham, *English Housewife*.

care. Early modern carework occupied an ambiguous position straddling unpaid labour borne out of obligation and duty, and care undertaken by professional medical practitioners and teachers.[17] While carework undertaken by women is often overlooked and assumed to be unpaid or of little monetary value, carework by men, particularly as tutors and medical professionals, tends not to be discussed in terms of care. Our carework category deliberately ignores these divisions.

For historians and economists, key issues are whether housework and carework were paid or unpaid and undertaken within or outside the family unit. In early modern England servants were considered part of the family, which was commonly understood as a group of people living and eating together.[18] However, servants were also paid workers employed under contract. The overarching categories of work as located in 'own household' or 'outside the household' used in the work-task database include servants as part of the household.[19] In this chapter, however, finer distinctions are made to explore the relationship between housework, carework, and the labour market. As a consequence, in this chapter 'family' refers to co-residents related by blood or marriage excluding servants.

Studies of domestic material culture and technology emphasise the extent that housework has changed over time, particularly in the nineteenth and twentieth centuries. In her classic study, Ruth Schwartz Cowan argued that the adoption of labour-saving technologies such as cooking ranges, piped water, and eventually vacuum-cleaners and washing machines did not lead to a significant decline in the amount of time women spent on housework but instead higher standards of cleanliness and cookery were adopted.[20] More recently, Harms and Gershuny have shown that across the twentieth century the time married women in rural America spent on housework did actually decrease substantially but was substituted with increased time spent on childcare rather than paid work.[21] Just as expectations about housework increased in the nineteenth century, so expectations around childcare rose significantly during the twentieth century, with increased focus on the child's psychological and educational development. These studies demonstrate that housework and carework have changed significantly over time, due both to changes in domestic material culture and technology, and wider cultural expectations and norms. Consequently, modern assumptions should not be applied uncritically to the early modern world. The work-task data

[17] Although see Shepard, 'Care'. [18] Tadmor, 'Concept of the household-family'.
[19] See Section 1.2.3, on these categories. [20] Cowan, *More Work*.
[21] Harms and Gershuny, 'Housework'.

provides an opportunity to explore the nature of housework and carework in early modern England before the transformations that took place from the eighteenth century onwards.

The chapter is structured to address the three main misconceptions about early modern housework and carework. The first section explores the location of such work, showing that the majority was located outside or undertaken in other people's houses. The second section looks at who performed housework and carework, in terms of not only gender and marital status but also age, social status, and occupation, demonstrating that workers varied according to task. The final section examines the balance between paid and unpaid housework and carework, and shows that paid housework was common and most carework was performed for people outside the family.

5.1 Location

Housework spilled outside the house and outside the family, showing that the conceptualisation of housework as a private, unpaid activity undertaken reciprocally within the family is inappropriate for early modern England. Table 5.1 details housework tasks that had locational information and shows that 41.1 per cent took place outside, while only 28.0 per cent took place in the worker's own home, here defined as house or outbuildings belonging to husband, wife, or parents of children.[22]

Water collection and laundry work tasks had particularly high proportions of outdoor work. The great majority of water sources were outside, requiring trips beyond the house. Water collection undoubtedly took up a great deal of time in early modern society, with people making several trips each day to fetch water. However, 80 per cent of the water collection tasks recorded were associated with accidental death. This is a stark reminder that the chores of housework were not necessarily risk-free indoor tasks. People slipped or tripped and fell into wells or bodies of water. Of the 113 water collection work tasks recorded, water was most commonly fetched from a well or a pond.[23] Only 10 work tasks recorded collecting water from a river or stream. Eight cases offered more various sources including a castle moat at Wressle in Yorkshire; a mill dam at Cranworth in Norfolk; 'the town ditch' at Fen Ditton in Cambridgeshire; a street conduit at Totnes in Devon; and a single case mentioning a water

[22] Integral tasks are included in the analysis in this chapter, but the categories of housework and carework only contained very small proportions of the integral tasks in the dataset: see Table 1.8.

[23] Well = 48 and pond = 41 tasks, respectively.

Table 5.1 *The location of housework*

	Own house (%)	In master's house (%)	Another's house or building (%)	Outdoors (%)	Location not stated (%)	Total tasks (no.)
Attend guests	53.8	23.1	0.0	23.1	0.0	13
Cleaning	14.3	32.9	21.4	24.3	7.1	70
Collect water	0.9	2.7	2.7	79.6	14.2	113
Food/drink provision	39.6	14.2	19.2	19.2	7.9	318
Laundry	11.1	4.3	4.3	61.5	18.8	117
Light/fire provision	26.5	23.5	20.6	29.4	0.0	68
Locking doors/gates	29.5	13.6	18.2	36.4	2.3	44
Misc. housework	40.0	60.0	0.0	0.0	0.0	5
% of all tasks	25.4	13.9	14.2	37.3	9.2	748
% of all tasks with known location	28.0	15.3	15.6	41.1	0.0	679
Total tasks (no.)	190	104	106	279	69	748

Notes: 'Own house' includes stables and barns, work by nuclear family; 'in master's house' includes work by servants or for a master or mistress; 'another house or building' includes other people's houses and churches. These categories are more specific than the own household/outside the household distinction used elsewhere in the book: see Section 1.2.3.

pump at Fakenham in Norfolk in 1637.[24] Wells and ponds were often near houses, described as being 'in the garden', 'in the messuage', 'by the house', or 'in the home close'. For instance, Dorothy Blakey of Mitton in Yorkshire in 1668 described how at 'about nine of clock in the night, she being about to fetch water at a well before the house door where she dwelleth, heard a great noise in the street'.[25] Many were explicitly public, such as the 'town well' at Hambledon in Hampshire, where Alice Benstead exchanged defamatory words in 1581.[26] Very occasionally, a well was described as being 'in' someone's house, such as when Dorothy Felder was 'in the house of William Felder at Binstead taking a bucket of water out of a well' in Hampshire in 1564.[27] However, such phrasing leaves it unclear if the well was actually indoors, or in the backyard.

The need for substantial quantities of water and fresh air for drying meant that laundry work also often took place outside: 62 per cent of

[24] TNA/KB/9/550/93; TNA/KB/9/631b/189; TNA/KB/9/1040b/586; DHC, Chanter 8299, *Mayne v. Webber*; NRO, C/S3/31, Info of Richard Cademan, Ruth Chapman, and Margaret Tomson.

[25] WYAS, QS1/7/2, 2/15–16, 3/4.

[26] HRO, 21M65/C3/8, *Bensted v. Pratt.*

[27] TNA/KB/9/610a/111.

117 laundry work tasks took place outdoors. Most laundry tasks recorded were concerned with washing and drying clothes, although a few relate to folding or putting away linens, preparing to wash, and starching. The term 'wash', as it was used in depositions, encompassed both washing clothes in heated water, and scrubbing and rinsing them in the cold water of ponds and streams, or next to wells. The large houses of wealthy owners might have specialist wash houses, such as the wash house of Mr Roger Fortescue at Buckland Filleigh in Devon, where two maids were busy washing in 1620.[28] Less high status was the 'backhouse' where Katherine Newman was doing laundry when a man came and asked if she would wash his shirt, in Norfolk in 1661.[29] More commonly, washing, presumably involving hot water, was done 'in the yard' or near the house.[30] Cold-washing and rinsing was done by a source of water and was often a sociable activity. In 1600, Joanna Drew was 'at the washing stock' at Erlestoke in Wiltshire when she witnessed a defamation; similarly in 1596 Elizabeth Trees was with Maud Grove 'washing at the well' when she heard defamatory words spoken in St Germans, Cornwall.[31] Only very occasionally are details of the washing process described. Cicely Large was collecting fuel to 'heat her lye' in preparation for washing in Norfolk in 1625, lye being the alkaline solution used to wash linens.[32] The process of steeping and washing linens in lye was known as bucking. In 1653, Mary Smokeham of Brinkworth, Wiltshire, described how 'having made an end of rubbing and bucking of clothes of her said masters', some were then stolen.[33]

When the types of clothes being washed were specified, they were most commonly linens. Personal cleanliness in early modern England depended on linen underclothing being regularly washed.[34] In contrast, woollen outer-clothing was more likely to be brushed down than laundered. There was only one example of an explicitly woollen item of clothing being washed, and that was newly acquired second-hand. In a 1682 case from Cheshire, Elizabeth Moores recounted washing a woollen waistcoat along with her linens, and incidentally describes how laundry was fitted in around her other work:

> About Midsummer last past she was pulling flax at Ralph Walley's in Leftwich … at which time Elizabeth the wife of … Ralph gave this examinant a waistcoat of woollen cloth, the body being a red colour and the sleeves of a brown colour, a

28 DHC QS/4/Box 24, Easter, 41. 29 NRO C/S3/44, Info of Katherine Newman.

30 For example, WSHC, D1/42/61, *Stumpe v. Brown*; HALS, ASA8/8, 92–4.

31 WSHC, D1/42/18, *Halswell v Walker* DHC, Chanter 864, *Dyer v. Lankey*.

32 NRO, C/S3/26, Exam of Elizabeth Mann. 33 WSHC, A1/110/1653M, 249.

34 North, *Sweet and Clean?*

few days after, this examinant washed the said waistcoat and afterwards laid the … waistcoat, a smock and some other small linens upon her hemp yard hedge to dry, in the evening coming home from her labour she went to the hedge … to take her clothes into her house and then missed her waistcoat and a handkerchief which she suspected had been stolen.[35]

Like Elizabeth Moores, most people dried their washing on hedges. Of the 50 work tasks related to drying clothes, 32 described clothes being hung on hedges to dry. Others described clothes left in fields, gardens, and yards, which may also relate to hedges. Only one case described a cord or line being used to hang out washing, while another described a wood-rack being used, and a third 'pales' round the house yard – presumably a wooden fence. A single case referred to drying clothes by a fire, and those were wet stockings still being worn by their owner.

Other types of housework tasks were less likely to take place outside, but nonetheless surprisingly often took people beyond their own house. Rising early in the morning and going to bed after dark required the light of a candle, and both candles and the means of lighting them were sometimes in short supply. In the case from Handley in Cheshire, which introduced Chapter 4, Margaret Johnson had to walk from her house to the nearby village to get a light.[36] Fuel was a precious resource, and fires were not necessarily kept alight overnight or during the day. Katherine Vinton conveyed this economy when she stated that 'she usually maketh fire in one corner of the said chimney and that the chimney is very little' in Devon in 1640.[37] As a consequence, just as people sometimes went to light candles, they also went to their neighbours' houses to fetch fire, as when Anne Boothe 'went out of her own house to one William Sutton's house being in distance from this informant's house about two roods to fetch some fire' in Lancashire in 1637.[38] Cooking could take people beyond the home. Alice Glover declared that she 'made two chaps of bread … and that they were baked at the house of Thomas Hawkins of this borough, baker' in Devizes, Wiltshire, in 1632.[39] Nor was food necessarily eaten indoors. In 1575 William Selleck recounted how 'about some 45 years past when he was but a little boy able to carry into the field a bottle and a bag with provision for work folks … [he] carried bread and cheese to the workmen at mowing of the corn that was then grown there' in a Somerset tithe case.[40] When Gryffyn James was working at

[35] CALS, QJF/110/4, 90. [36] CALS, QJF/90/4, 70–1.
[37] DHC, QS/4/Box 43, Baptist, 2, 1.
[38] LaA, QSB/1/186, 50. See also HRO, 21M65/C3/10, *Bull v. Anderson* (Hants 1591); LiA, LQS/A/11/10, 63 (1642); DHC, Chanter 864, *Drue v. Reede* (1593–8); LiA, LQS/A/1/6, 105 (1634).
[39] WSHC, A1/110/1632E, 108. [40] SHC, D/D/Cd/55, *Bilbie v. Shute*.

Limington in Somerset in 1607, his wife brought 'bread and beer' to him travelling approximately 1.5 miles from neighbouring Ilchester.[41]

While the most common location of housework was outside, followed by a person's own home, carework showed a different distribution. Carework most frequently took place in someone else's house, accounting for 52 per cent of carework activities with known locations, followed by carework outside, accounting for 24 per cent. Only 16 per cent of activities took place in the worker's own home, with a further 4 per cent carried out by servants.[42] The final 5 per cent took place in other types of buildings. None of the depositions recall care in institutional buildings such as hospitals. Non-domestic buildings included churches and a single instance of childcare in a nunnery but predominantly refer to school buildings. Deponents' descriptions of schoolhouses demonstrate the blurred boundaries between schools and homes. The Smith family, Francis Smith Senior, his son Francis, and his wife Anne, all taught Latin grammar and testament from their 'private house' in 1678 in Devizes, Wiltshire, and when the schoolhouse in Kirkheaton closed for 12 weeks over winter in 1693, the schoolmaster Thomas Blyth taught the students in his own home.[43]

The location of carework varied by gender. A larger proportion of men's carework, 40 per cent, was performed outside, compared to only 16 per cent of women's. Men were more frequently noted fetching medicine and healthcare professionals, as well as aiding intoxicated individuals home. While travelling home to Tadcaster in Yorkshire in 1663, Hugh Davis encountered the priest, Mr Holt, who was so 'much overtaken with drink ... that he fell from his horse three several times'. Hugh helped Holt back onto his horse twice 'whereupon he stayed about 30 yards and fell down again'.[44] However, rather than women working mostly in their own homes, they most commonly performed carework in other people's houses: this accounted for 58 per cent of their carework, compared to 38 per cent of men's.[45]

The high percentage of female carework tasks undertaken in other people's homes was influenced by the inclusion of paternity cases that record work connected to childbirth. Midwifery made up 35 per cent of the carework carried out by women in other's homes. Midwives were

[41] SHC, Q/SR/2, 23–4.
[42] Out of 564 carework activities, 509 indicated spatial location.
[43] WSHC, D1/42/61, *Office v. Smith*; BI, CP.H.4378, *Office v. Thomas Blyand and John Preston*.
[44] BI, CP.H.5509, Office v Holt. A similar case from Cheshire is described in Section 3.5.
[45] 18 per cent of women's carework was in their own home, compared to 11 per cent of men's.

expected to persuade unmarried mothers to name the child's father during labour and report his identity to parish officials.[46] Sheilagh Ogilvie excluded paternity suits from her work-task dataset in *A Bitter Living* to avoid it being overwhelmed by descriptions of midwifery.[47] They are included in the work-task database because of the rich detail they provide about healthcare and childcare. Of the 124 midwifery work tasks recorded, 78 per cent came from paternity cases. These paternity cases were uneven geographically, and were particularly common in Cheshire, which provides 41 per cent of midwifery work tasks. It could be argued that midwifery is overrepresented because of its centrality in this particular type of case. It accounts for 32 per cent of women's carework tasks recorded in the database, and is the largest carework subcategory for women, just higher than healthcare at 31 per cent.[48] Nonetheless, it should be noted that between 100,000 and 150,000 children were typically born each year in early modern England, the great majority attended by a midwife of some kind.[49] The diary of the Kendal midwife Elizabeth Thompson reveals the heavy workload of rural midwives. Elizabeth worked in and around the rural communities of Kendal in the mid-seventeenth century, servicing an area within approximately 10 miles of Kendal and delivering 81 babies in 12 months in 1672/3, as well as 89 the next year.[50] The contested births in paternity suits only capture a fraction of the workload of midwives.

Depositions point to the longevity of care provided by midwives either side of birth. Elizabeth Walker in Hedgefield, Durham, in 1567 recalled care prior to the arrival of her baby when 'a midwife came to her and drew her breath 2 or 3 days before her labour'.[51] The midwife Francesca Flower attended Mary Wyatt in her labour in Priston, Somerset, in 1693, and though she missed the delivery of the baby did 'tend her in her child bed' for six weeks, a prolonged period of carework for a mother and baby.[52] The birthing chamber was a significant female space of work. Though we do not include the emotional labour of those simply present as witnesses to the birth as 'gossips', paternity suits capture the perfunctory work related to births such as fetching healthcare, lighting candles, providing drink and food, and tending to the infant immediately after the birth.

In contrast, childcare is somewhat under-recorded but appears across all spatial categories. One important reason for this is likely to be that

46 Gowing, *Common Bodies*, pp. 160–2; Wilson, *Ritual and Conflict*, pp. 26–7.
47 Ogilvie, *Bitter Living*, p. 29. 48 See Appendix B.
49 Wrigley and Schofield, *Population History*, pp. 496–8.
50 Ashcroft (ed.), *Diary of a Kendal Midwife*. 51 DUIC, DDR/EJ/CCD/1/2, 80v-1r.
52 SHC, D/D/Cd/106, *Wyatt v. Wyatt*.

childcare was often undertaken in combination with other tasks. But secondly and related to this, it also reflects the fact that less time was dedicated to childcare in early modern England than we might expect. Young babies were left in cradles or carried in arms, and toddlers were watched while people engaged in other activities. From the age of five onwards, children were expected to engage in work of their own and quickly became relatively independent. Much of the childcare described in the database implies that childcare was in fact subsumed within other day-to-day work tasks and activities. Children were mentioned incidentally when carried in arms or strapped to the body. At Bishopstoke in Hampshire in 1564, Agnes Abram had attended a Lady Day supper with her husband and because she 'had a child in her arms she could not go so fast as the rest' and as a consequence witnessed a couple exchange marriage vows.[53] Ann Wright was 'working in a garden' and 'standing by with a child in her arms' when a man attacked her with a rake, injuring her child, at Patrick Brompton, Yorkshire, in 1685.[54] Judith Wilkinson, 'a poor wandering woman', carried a 'little child' upon her back in Prescot, Lancashire, in 1666.[55]

Childcare was often performed alongside other work activities. In 1532, Isabel Ballard of Stow Cum Quy, Cambridgeshire, took her one-year-old daughter Agnes to the malthouse where she placed Agnes on the straw in front of the kiln whilst she climbed the kiln to stir the malt. By misfortune, the fire in the furnace spread to the straw causing burns to Agnes' arm and face.[56] Alice Adam of Sawbridgeworth, Hertfordshire, was carrying a six-month-old boy as she fetched water from the well in 1564.[57] In 1543 Elizabeth Crome of Norwich sat her one-year-old child in a small chair by the fire to stay warm whilst she 'was busy around the house'.[58] Children often appeared alongside their parents as they ran errands outside the home: 38 per cent of the childcare recorded in the work-task database was performed outside the household.[59] Mrs Bradford 'took up her child in her arms and went to a smith's shop' in Keynsham, Somerset, in 1682.[60] Marion Symondes of Shipdham, Norfolk, was followed by her one-year-old daughter as she went to a neighbouring house to lend a shovel in 1564.[61] When it was not possible to combine tasks, women switched from one to the other. In 1618 in Huntspill, Somerset, Agnes Pople put her children to bed and then

53 HRO, 21M65/C3/3, 215–8. 54 NYCRO, QSB/1685, 232.
55 NYCRO, QSB/1/1666, Info of John Newton. 56 TNA/KB/9/521/142.
57 TNA/KB/9/610b/267m. 58 TNA/KB/9/560/197.
59 Using the categories explained in Section 1.2.3.
60 SRO, D/D/Cd/97, *Bradford v. Browning*. 61 TNA/KB/9/610b/160.

headed out to the fields to gather thistles and teasels for brewing, 'having no fit time to go by day for that one of her children was sick in an ague'.[62]

Even when women worked in their own home, they were not necessarily caring for family members. Wetnursing and care of the sick provided money-earning opportunities. In 1570 in Marlborough, Wiltshire, Margaret Byde housed Elizabeth Ryves for four or five days to heal her of 'the pox'. She was paid 20s 'for her pains' in healing Elizabeth and offered medical advice to Elizabeth's husband who appeared to have contracted the illness himself after 'sleeping with a strange woman'.[63] In 1676 Marie Beere opened up her home in Bradford on Tone, Somerset, to a man named Holmes whom she 'tabled' for the course of his illness.[64] Research on early modern healthcare has explored the place of the home in the wider healthcare economy. Strocchia has stressed the interconnectedness of domestic medicine with the wider medical economy; householders were required to purchase ingredients from the market and medical knowledge circulated from practitioners into the home.[65] Medical knowledge was a key element in early modern definitions of housewifery. Elaine Leong has shown women to have engaged with medical texts and to have acquired and adapted knowledge to their own household use.[66] The closeness of food preparation to medicinal preparation meant medical care and the production of medicines and remedies required similar skills and were both mastered by women; as Margaret Pelling notes, 'in its double nature, sacred and profane, medicine resembled food and drink; there was no dividing line between medicines and nourishment'.[67] The work-task database captures some female production of medicines: Ellen Holt was reported to 'get savin at diverse places' and to have 'made medicines' in Childwall, Lancashire, in 1626, and Christian Aske tended to her sick husband at their home in Ryther, Yorkshire, in 1593, and made him almond milk, a traditional remedy known for its medicinal properties.[68]

Medical knowledge was acquired in and percolated through rural communities. In 1619 Joan Whitfield of Watchet, Somerset, claimed 'she could make a medicine that could cure the green sickness and that she was taught it of surgeons and physicians which came unto the house where she dwelt'.[69] Women also appear giving medical advice from their

[62] SRO, Q/SR/33, 135. [63] WSHC, D1/42/7, *Ryves v. Ryves.*
[64] SRO, D/D/Cd/97, *Parsons and Shute v. Holmes.*
[65] Strocchia, 'Introduction', pp. 497–8.
[66] Leong, 'Making medicines' and '"Herbs she persueth"'.
[67] Pelling, 'Occupational diversity', p. 486. See also, Stobart, *Household Medicine.*
[68] LaA, QSB1/26, 54–5; BI, CP.G.2852, *Aske v. Aske.* [69] SHC, Q/SR/33, 5–6.

own homes after being sought out by their neighbours. At Wallsend in Northumberland in 1565, Katherine Fenwike went to one Pereson's wife seeking advice for her sick child 'taken with the fever'. Pereson's wife told her, 'The child should be washed in the water ... upon a Friday at night and that on the morrow the fever should be gone and the child should risen healthier'. Fenwike paid Pereson's wife 3d 'for her pains'.[70] The home was permeable to the medical knowledge of skilled practitioners, shared book knowledge from wealthier households, and the ingredients and practices available through the marketplace. Where women performed carework within their own home, this was not always for their own family but often provided as a service for others.

Examining the location of housework and carework does not reveal what we might expect. Carework most often took place in other people's houses. Housework and carework were commonly undertaken outside. Both activities frequently involved neighbourly cooperation: light, fire, fuel, and oven space were borrowed from other households nearby; neighbours were called on to provide medical help and advice. Rather than the provision of housework and care being the isolating experience it had become by the twentieth century, early modern descriptions of this work are full of social interactions.[71]

5.2 Who Performed the Work?

Of the nine main categories of work task analysed in this book, housework and carework are the most heavily dominated by female workers. Housework was the only major category in which all subcategories were also female dominated.[72] However, a closer look at housework and carework reveals a more interesting story. The analysis in Chapter 2 demonstrated that housework made up a larger proportion of young women's work repertoires than that of married women: it accounted for 59 per cent of the work tasks carried out by girls aged less than 15, and 30 per cent of those by young female adults aged 15 to 24, and only 14 per cent of women aged 25 to 44. For never-married women, housework accounted for 24 per cent of tasks compared to 18 per cent of married women's. Carework shows an inverse pattern: it made up 8 per cent of the work repertoires of women and girls aged under 25, 22 per cent for women aged 25 to 44, and 38 per cent for women aged 45 and older.[73] These profiles suggest that the performance of housework had more to do with age and power within the household than marriage, and that

[70] DUIC, DDR/EJ/CCD/1/2, 36v-8r. [71] Oakley, *Sociology of Housework*.
[72] See Appendix B. [73] Tables 2.4 and 2.8.

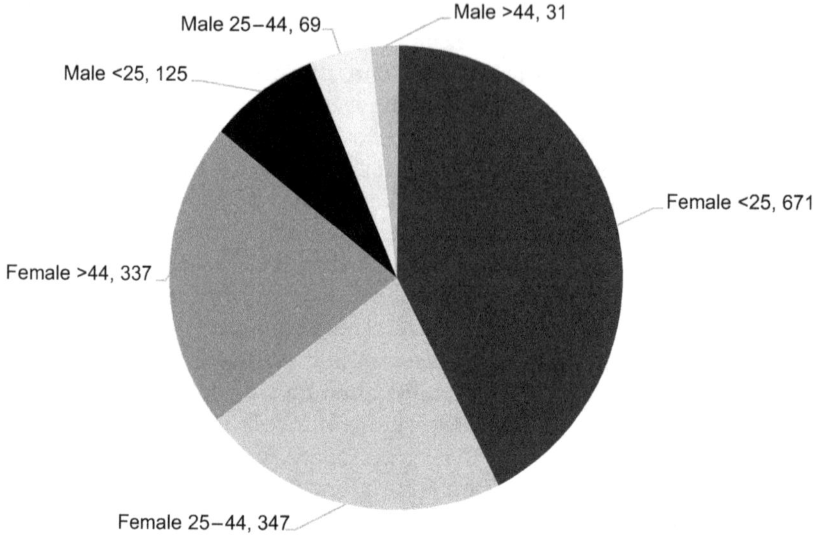

Figure 5.1 Who did housework: a breakdown by age and gender.
Notes: Age data was only available for 109 of the 523 housework work tasks carried out by women, and 36 of the 225 tasks carried out by men. The proportions falling into different age and gender groups where age was stated were applied to the remaining work tasks. The figures for women were then adjusted (multiplied by 2.59).

carework involved skills which were accumulated with age. This section looks in more detail at who carried out these work tasks, paying attention to the circumstances in which they were undertaken by men and the types of women who performed them. For housework it is argued that status was as important as gender. For carework, childcare in particular is examined, showing that only a third of childcare was performed by parents for their own children, mostly by mothers, and even this took up less time than is often assumed, and was frequently combined with other activities.

Figure 5.1 explores the type of people who did housework, divided according to gender and age. Girls and young women made up the largest group of workers carrying out housework. Women aged 25 to 44, who were most likely to be married and have young children–the group that some historians assume did housework–were responsible for only 22 per cent of tasks, while a similar proportion was carried out by older women aged over 44. Men's participation was not insignificant, accounting for 14 per cent of the total. Age was even more important for men, with more than half of the housework done by men carried out by boys and young men under the age of 25. This means that in total, young people carried out more than half of all housework tasks. These findings show that rather than being the preserve of married women, housework was typically allocated to young people. This was partly because it was relatively unskilled work that nonetheless required energy and exertion, but it was also surely related to this work having little status. Householders, women as well as men, offloaded these tasks onto their subordinates: children and servants, most commonly to young women.

Amongst the subcategories of housework, laundry was the most female dominated. Only five work tasks out of 117 were done by men. Three of these are ambiguous: a man who hung up his clothes (possibly not because they had been washed, but just to store and air them), a case where a man stood by a fire to dry his stockings, and another case in which a man removed his stockings from a rack where they had been drying.[74] Only two cases definitely relate to men doing washing. In a coroner's report from Northamptonshire in 1552, James Nycols is described as 'washing his clothes in a pond having soiled his shirt and breeches with his own excrement because of his illness, the great lax', the unusual detail perhaps inserted to explain why a man was doing laundry in public.[75] In the other, John Burwell 'did hang out 4 flaxen shirts in a close not far from his house ... and also a parcel of flaxen yarn in the garden belonging to his said house' in Great Bowden, Leicestershire, in 1696. Given he was described as a 'flax dresser', it is likely these activities were connected to his occupation.[76]

There was more male participation in other cleaning activities than in laundry.[77] The cleaning subcategory contains a wide range of tasks. Some are what could be considered classic housework: 16 related to making beds, 9 to washing and scouring dishes and pots, 9 to cleaning rooms, and 6 to sweeping. Other tasks included cleaning windows, chimneys, wells, shoes, and cheesecloths; wiping and dusting furniture; emptying chamber pots, throwing other things out (waste disposal), and shovelling dunghills. It is amongst these heterogeneous activities that male work is mostly found. The only two examples of emptying chamber pots both relate to men carrying out the task, one employed in an inn, the other using the opportunity to throw the contents on someone he disliked.[78]

[74] LaA, QSB/1/284, 97; NRO, C/S3/20, Exam of Edward Reynolds.
[75] TNA/KB/9/1004/97. [76] NAS, Unorganised Box, Exam of John Burwell.
[77] Adjusted figures: 15 per cent of cleaning tasks by men.
[78] SHC, Q/SR/77, 143 (1638); SHC, Q/SR/82, 132.3 (1650).

Laundry work and cleaning activities showed different age structures as well as differences in workers' gender. Laundry was more likely to be undertaken by married women and women over the age of 25; cleaning was commonly left to younger workers.[79] The low status of everyday cleaning tasks was emphasised in a dispute concerning a gentry family from Terrington St Clement in Norfolk in 1659. Elizabeth Richars lived with her married brother, John, who was under bond to support her with 'sufficient meat, drink, clothes, apparel, firing etc.' until she married, and then to pay her £100 dowry. She complained to the justices of the peace that not only was John violent and insulting, throwing things at her, kicking and striking her, and calling her 'an ugly creature to look on', but he also 'did command [her] to wash the dishes which she did. And he would have [her] to be at his wife's command'. Elizabeth's argument, it seems, was that she was being treated like a servant. John seemed to agree with her about the status of washing dishes, as in his defence he said that he 'did never but once command her to wash the dishes'.[80]

Another commonplace activity reserved for subordinate members of the household was fetching and lighting candles. Mary Bower sent her son and daughter to a neighbour's house to get a candle in Devon in 1597, and in two Somerset examples Alice Goole carried a candle upstairs for her master's son in 1616, while in 1668 Edith Parker was called in by her master to witness a document but first lit a candle and carried it to him.[81] In contrast, male householders called for others to light candles for them: as when in Devon in 1639 William Holcombe was called upstairs 'to the chamber of his said master to light a candle'.[82] Or in Norfolk in 1614 where Steven Harrise came home from working on the common at eight o'clock at night, and 'went near his house and called for a light' so that he could 'go dress his horse'.[83] This is a reminder that who undertook a task was determined by status as well as ability. While it may have been inconvenient for male householders to light their own candles in these cases, their disinclination to do so was surely more about enacting their superior status than a lack of ability or skill in candle

79 The data shows that 49 per cent of laundry by women was done by women specified as married or widowed, compared to 36 per cent of cleaning work; in the 20 tasks where age was specified 65 per cent of laundry was done by women over 24. For cleaning out of 14 tasks with age noted, 71 per cent of workers were under 25.

80 NRO, C/S3/44, Info of Elizabeth Richars.

81 DHC, QS/4/Box 5, 58–61; SHC, Q/SR/29–31, 99–100; SHC, D/D/Cd/93, *Searle v. King*.

82 DHC, QS/4/Box 43 and 44, Epiphany, 15.

83 NRO, C/S3/20, Exam of Steven Harrise.

Table 5.2 *Gender division of labour in food and drink preparation*

	F tasks adj.	M tasks	Total tasks	% by F adj.
Kill/prepare poultry	57	47	104	54.8
Fetch ingredients	21	3	24	87.4
Cook food	186	31	217	85.7
Bring/fetch food	36	3	39	92.4
Draw/serve alcohol	150	30	180	83.4
Serve food	39	6	45	86.6
Other	16	3	19	83.8
Total	505	123	628	80.4

Notes: adj. = adjusted (x2.59).

lighting, just as Elizabeth Richars was reluctant to do the simple task of washing up.

Food and drink preparation is the largest subcategory within housework, and also the subcategory with the largest number of tasks done by men. Table 5.2 breaks this subcategory down further into 'sub-subcategories' and shows that all were heavily dominated by women except killing and preparing poultry. This group of tasks was closely related to the butchery subcategory in food processing, which was even more male dominated.[84] Like butchery, killing poultry was most often recorded in theft cases in which the stolen animals were quickly consumed.

Nonetheless, cooking was one form of housework that men seemed to have been less uncomfortable taking part in. This can be broken down even further: men made up 35 per cent of those roasting meat or fish compared to between 8 and 12 per cent of those engaged in baking, boiling, and unspecified cooking, using adjusted figures. However, some men were even observed standing over the cooking pot. Occasionally, this was explained by circumstances. Robert Griffine stole a sheep, butchered it and 'put part thereof into the pot over the fire to make broth and some provision for his wife being great with child and three children' at Knook in Wiltshire in 1622.[85] Other instances seem more casual, although still possibly connected with animal theft, as when a neighbour came round to borrow a sleekstone and found 'Peter Stubbes standing by the fire side, and tending a pan over the fire, where was a pullet boiling' at Rostherne in Cheshire in 1602.[86] A case from Willoughby with Sloothby in Lincolnshire in 1634 seems to relate to (perhaps adolescent)

[84] See Appendix B. [85] WSHC, A1/110/1622E, 231. [86] CALS, QJF/31/2, 66.

boys deciding to cook when others were absent. It describes how a Jane Alderman

> sent her son to fetch fire at some neighbour's house, and perceiving he stayed long she went to the house of … Remegious Tompson, the said Tompson and his wife being then at church, and there she found her son who with … Tompson his son [who] were making of an oatmeal pudding, and being made he brought some milk to eat it withall, and so she stayed to take part with them.[87]

This case, in which two young men cooked a meal for a married woman, hints at the way in which we need to revise our understanding of housework in early modern England. It was a task that more often fell to the young rather than married women, who were busy with a plethora of other, often more skilled, tasks.[88]

Married women's childcare work is often assumed to shape their other activities, but surprisingly little research has examined how early modern childcare was undertaken in practice. Women performed 92 per cent of all childcare recorded in the database, but almost half of the childcare tasks recorded were either explicitly paid, carried out by servants, or undertaken for people outside the household.[89] This hints at the complexities of the relationships that supported childcare in early modern society. Linda Oja, exploring the evidence for childcare in seventeenth- and eighteenth-century Sweden, identified a hierarchy of child-carework tasks, with the most constricting, demanding, or dirty tasks being taken on by women or employed carers.[90] Breaking down the childcare tasks in the work-task database according to the relation of the care giver shows the disparate roles played by parents in the bringing up of their children. Only a third of childcare was performed by parents for their own children, and almost all of that was done by mothers. This carework was varied: mothers are described dressing their children by the fireside, holding and carrying children, tending to their sick child at the bedside, seeking medical advice, and nursing and feeding their children. In Baddiley, Cheshire, in 1671, Jane Broster's mothering was described by other deponents thus: she 'did often give the said child suck and was also very careful and tender of it'.[91] Nursing a child was often used as a term to describe a stage of motherhood. In Kirby Knowle, Yorkshire, in 1662, Grace Wetherell was described as 'with child and had another in her

[87] LiA, LQS/A/1/6, 105.
[88] An observation originally made by Clark: *Working Life*, p. 11.
[89] A total of 124 childcare tasks were recorded; 60 of these were 'for another', of which 9 were by servants, 8 explicitly paid (not servants), and 43 done on terms unspecified.
[90] Oja, 'Childcare and gender'.
[91] CALS, QJF/100/1, 58–9.

arms that she had to nurse'.[92] What Oja has termed the 'confinement' of childcare is found in mothers' descriptions of their work. In Mottram, Cheshire, in 1671, Katherine Higginbotham described nighttime care rituals as she awaited her husband's late return 'having then a young child sucking on her, which was in bed, and it crying', adding that she breastfed her baby 'to still it'.[93]

Fathers appear performing childcare infrequently. Linda Oja found fathers' parenting and carework to be 'supplementary' to a mother's care. Fathers were on 'stand-by' and relieved mothers where necessary but their engagement in childcare was an exception rather than expected or constant.[94] Amongst the work tasks collected, there were just five examples of fathers performing childcare for their own children. In the only instance of disciplining a child, a father admonished his son for playing cudgels: he 'rebuked his son, and gave him correction', and removed his game.[95] In a case of disputed paternity from Christleton, Cheshire, in 1672, Randal Gill held his child when the mother refused to pick up her baby without a promise from Gill for his financial support, the baby having been born out of wedlock.[96] When performing healthcare for their children, fathers were more frequently involved in the fetching of care and supplies or arranging for others to care for their children than physically tending to their own child. In Merriott, Somerset, in 1689, John Lawrence fetched a pot of ale from the alehouse for his daughter, who was sick at home.[97] In 1656 in Wigan, Lancashire, George Collier sought a nurse for his child on one occasion and took his son to be christened on another.[98]

However, the majority of the childcare recorded was not performed by parents. Where non-parents can be identified as having familial bonds, it was typically in the context of long-term care for a child. Two cases detail grandmothers providing long-term care for their illegitimate grandchildren. Aunts are mentioned in two cases caring for small infants, one of whom was employed as a wet nurse in her brother's house after the death of his wife. In most childcare tasks, however, it was simply not possible to identify a relationship between the child and the carer. Some were wetnurses, as discussed in the next section, or transporting children to wetnurses. Only 7 per cent of childcare work tasks were explicitly performed by servants, although other work tasks were performed by people who may have been servants. For instance, in 1598 Mary Mills, spinster,

92 BI, CP.H.2656, *Hammond v. Wilson*. 93 CALS, QJF/100/2, 92.
94 Oja, 'Childcare and gender', 85. 95 NRO, C/S3/23, Examination of Thomas Lewes.
96 CALS, QJF/100/1, 81–2. 97 SHC, Q/SR/176–80, 5–6.
98 LaA, QSB/1/1656, Michaelmas, Examination of William Mather.

of St Thomas, Exeter, described her 'master and dame' going out for the day leaving their six-month-old son in her care, and whilst he was sleeping in his cradle in the afternoon Mary asked Hugh Darke, a 'groom' or male servant, who was sitting by the fire, to 'see unto it' while she went on an errand.[99] Some servants undertaking childcare were children themselves. The ten-year-old servant Elizabeth Michell was deemed able to milk cows, make beds, do 'any other ordinary work about the house' and 'attend children' in Gittisham, Devon, in 1674; while John Cowton from Whalley in Lancashire was 11 years old when he 'waited upon his [master's] children to school' in 1629.[100]

Charmain Mansell's detailed study of the carework in the testamentary suits of Hereford church courts illustrates the complex networks of carers that provided care in the home; close family were just one node of potential carers and instead Mansell identifies a range of family members, employers, employed carers, and unrelated kin who cared for the sick.[101] Despite this mixed economy of care, the majority of caregivers in the work-task database were women. There are some variations between subcategories; men performed a greater proportion of tasks in the education subcategory, at 61 per cent, and appear more frequently in the 'other care' subcategory where carework was described in broad terms and often referred to physically aiding others to travel.[102] Three-quarters or more of the tasks in the remaining carework subcategories were performed by women. While housework was allotted to the young, as discussed above, the importance of carework for women increased with age.[103] Age seems to have been more important than marital status: carework made up 23 per cent of widowed women's repertoires, but 38 per cent of those of women aged over 44.[104]

Historians have tended to explain women's dominance of housework by the fact women with young children were restricted to working in or close to the house. The work tasks show that housework and childcare were often delegated to others. When women did care for their own children, they were not confined to the house, and often did so alongside other work tasks. Mothers certainly did do childcare and this was particularly onerous when caring for young babies, but non-relatives also undertook this care. Care of older children is rarely recorded, largely because they became workers themselves from a young age. Housework

[99] DHC, QS/4/Box 5, 8–9.
[100] DHC, Chanter 880, Eveleigh v Tucker; CALS, EDC/5/1684, 26.
[101] Mansell, 'Reconstructing the labour of care'.
[102] See Appendix B. Female-adjusted figures.
[103] Men's involvement in carework remained low throughout the lifecycle; see Table 2.6.
[104] See Tables 2.8 and 2.4.

in particular seems to have been regarded as a demeaning form of labour that signified subordinate status. Men did take part in these activities but seem to have avoided them when they could. Often these tasks were done by paid workers.

5.3 Paid Work

The final misconception that needs to be addressed is the idea that housework and carework were predominantly forms of unpaid work that women did for their own families. In Chapter 2 we showed that 78 per cent of the carework observed in the work-task data was performed 'for another', meaning it was either paid work or performed by a non-family member.[105] The percentage for housework 'for another' was lower at 44 per cent, but still substantial and similar to the proportion of agricultural work done 'for another'. This section explores the ways in which such 'for another' work was carried out. It looks at the evidence for casual wage labour performing laundry and cookery for other households, and at the way alehouses offered commercialised housework. Analysis of paid carework examines wetnursing, and the balance between licensed and unlicensed healthcare practitioners. The proportion of 'for another' carework carried out by women was only slightly lower than the proportion carried out by men, 76 compared to 83 per cent, indicating that much of women's carework was paid. Given that women made up 98 and 75 per cent of those providing midwifery and other healthcare services respectively, this is important to bear in mind.[106]

Table 5.3 takes a closer look at the contexts in which housework was undertaken 'for another'. Work by servants is a significant subcategory of work 'for another', but this was not the only context in which housework was undertaken for pay, given servants only carried out 38 per cent of all housework done 'for another'. Alehouses were another important institution for the provision of commercialised housework, dominated by attending guests as we might expect. Alehouses provided much of the food and drink provision 'for another', but there was commercial provision in other contexts too. A great deal of 'for another' work seems to have been women carrying out tasks on a casual basis for people outside the household: much of this work must have been paid but also might have been carried out in exchange with neighbours, or as acts of kindness.

Laundry work offers a good example. Although the total proportion undertaken 'for another' is not especially high, many work tasks were

[105] See Table 2.2. [106] See Appendix B. Female-adjusted figures.

Table 5.3 *Housework undertaken 'for another'*

	Total tasks	'For another'		By servants		In an alehouse	
		no.	%	no.	%	No.	%
Attend guests	13	12	92.3	2	15.4	12	92.3
Cleaning	70	42	60.0	20	28.6	6	8.6
Collecting water	113	22	19.5	20	17.7	0	0
Food and drink provision	318	165	51.9	40	12.6	67	21.1
Laundry	116	47	40.5	21	18.1	0	0
Light and fire provision	68	40	58.8	18	26.5	3	4.4
Locking gates and doors	44	27	61.4	13	29.5	3	6.8
Miscellaneous housework	5	3	60.0	2	40.0	0	0
Total	747	358	47.9	136	18.2	91	12.2

Notes: 'For another', 'by servants', and 'in an alehouse' overlap, so the three categories add up to more than the task total. 'By servants' is a subset of 'for another'. Many of those working in alehouses were servants. Alehouses include inns and fair-booths.

explicitly undertaken for people outside of the household, or for pay. Laundry was often done by female servants, but women did other types of paid laundry: 12 of the 56 laundry washing tasks include details that make it clear washing was sent out to others as a form of paid work. As well as the case of Mary Wilton described in the introduction to this chapter, examples include Agnes Eldridge who did washing for 'the gentlemen attending on the Earl of Hertford' and went to collect the wages owed to her in Amesbury, Wiltshire, in 1621; Margery Reader who was 'hired by Mr Walter Paynes wife to wash her linen' in Bury St Edmunds, Suffolk, in 1600; Elizabeth Bexwick who in 1627 'came unto the house of Isabel Gilbodye of Stretford … widow, and brought her a linen apron which she washed for the said Isabel' in Manchester; Joan White who in 1661 was called 'to the common well of the said town' by Elizabeth Beales servant to Anthony Cates of Little Walsingham in Norfolk who 'delivered her certain pieces of linen to wash for her'; and Ellena Bowman from Barnstaple in Devon who in 1576 declared she 'getteth her living by washing and spinning'.[107]

Cookery and related food processing also presented opportunities for casual work. For instance, in Wiltshire in 1551, it was stated that the mother of a witness, Joan Drue, 'doth much resort unto the parson's house and doth the parson's work as in brewing and baking and making of his malt and such other service' on a daily basis rather than as a live-in

[107] WSHC, A1/110/1622H, 165; NRO DN/DEP/31/34, 371–2; LaA, QSB1/27, 82–3; NRO, C/S3/44, Exam of Elizabeth Beales; DHC, Chanter 859, *Ward v. Stapledon.*

servant. There are numerous examples of people cooking for other households, such as William Cooke's wife and Edith Sadler, who went 'to dress meat for Mr Pope's supper' at his house at Moorlinch in Somerset in 1566; William Putt, who 'dressed [a] … marriage dinner' for a couple in Devon in 1555; and Joan Ware, who in Somerset in 1637 'dressed a dinner at George Lawrence his house in Crewkerne … and after dinner carried home a pot to the house of Maurice Game'.[108] Johanna Smith from Hampshire stated in 1573 that she witnessed a dying man's wishes as 'she did dress his meat and drink and was in his house before with him'.[109] A case from Winwick in Lancashire described how in 1626 Jane Gaskell 'had flour upon her head; and that she went unto the house of Henry Litherland; and there would make pies of the said flour'.[110]

Running an alehouse or inn offered another way to generate income from housework. Such establishments not only sold alcohol but commonly offered heat, light, food, and lodgings, providing what was in essence commercialised housework.[111] The payment for overnight lodgings was not only for the use of a room but the labour of cleaning it, laundering the sheets, and making the bed, just as it is in a hotel today. Men and women provided alehouse housework, although women predominated, taking responsibility for 78 per cent of such tasks using the adjusted figures. Research by Amy Burnett shows that although it was men who most often held alehouse licences, it was more commonly married women who did the work of running them.[112] A wide range of establishments are recorded in the work-task data, from booths at fairs selling food and alcohol, to well-established inns, such as the Catherine Wheel at Winchester, the Half Moon at Guildford, or the White Hart at North Curry in Somerset. Village alehouses were typically known by their owner's name. Given other houses were also referred to in this way, it is sometimes only possible to identify alehouses by the activities taking place within them. For instance, in a case from Ely, Cambridgeshire, in 1614, the witness recounted that:

> yesterday in the afternoon he came into the house of Thomas Awsten and there found in the house drinking these three persons viz Robert Clerk Steven Baker and Peter Whitby … And the beer being found fault with the goodwife desired this examinant to help her in breaching of a new vessel.[113]

[108] SHC, D/D/Cd/12, Personal Response of William Cook; DHC, Chanter 855, *Seck v. Hopill*; SHC, Q/SR/77, 11.

[109] HRO, 21M65/C3/5, *Creshill v. Palmer*.

[110] That is, she was carrying the flour on her head. LaA, QSB/1/18, 34.

[111] On the varied functions of alehouses see Hailwood, *Alehouses and Good Fellowship*, ch. 1.

[112] Burnett, '"His wief the chiefe doer of it"'.

[113] NRO, C/S3/19, Examination of Robert Clerk.

Descriptions of men arriving at a house and demanding alcohol indicate that the establishment was an alehouse. For instance, Henry Lucas described how, at Leyland in Lancashire in 1626, 'about a month before Christmas last … there came to this examinant's mother's house [a diverse company, who] knocked at the door (this examinant and all the whole family being then in their beds) and demanded to come in to drink, whereupon [he] did rise and let them in and filled them ale'.[114] More excessively a 1598 case from Cheshunt, Hertfordshire, recounted that:

> the Monday morning after by day break the company [of drinkers] came down the stairs and there they fell to drinking afresh and so they drank as he guessed about forty pots and after they went over the way to William Cordole's house and there they did drink a kilderkin of beer where they tarried almost two hours and after in their coming back they killed a goose of John Law's and brought the goose with them to Bull's house and as he thinketh Monday paid 12d for the goose which goose was roasted.[115]

Bringing your own food and asking it to be cooked was not unusual. For instance, in 1620 at Brixham in Devon, Joan Frend described how 'there came to [her] … house a poor walking man of Berry Pomeroy and requested [her] … to roast a couple of pilchards the which she granted him'.[116] Nor were lodgings only provided in larger inns. Another case from Devon in 1620 recorded how a man came as a guest to the common tippling house kept by Alice Sanders of Sampford Peverell, 'and desired to have lodging and [was] … showed a chamber by a girl of the house'.[117] Similarly, Alice Smith recounted how a man named Richard Goseling and an unknown woman came to her dame's alehouse late in the evening, and after eating the woman asked Alice 'to show her a bed, for they would stay there that night and [she did] … light a candle and showed her a bed' in Bowdon, Cheshire, in 1662.[118] It was maid servants, sent to clean rooms after guests had left, who often discovered property had been stolen and damaged, as did the maid servant 'going to make the said bed' at an inn at Bishops Cannings in Wiltshire in 1631.[119]

If housework could be income generating, the same was even more true of carework. By definition, carework involved the provision of work by one person for someone else. Because of this, it allows the relationship between those two people to be inferred and demonstrates that the carework recorded in court depositions typically involved provision of care outside the immediate family. Table 5.4 provides more detail,

[114] LaA, QSB1/25, 31. [115] LiA, HQS/A/1/1688, Midsummer-Boston, 17–23.
[116] DHC, QS/4/Box 24, Easter 4–5. [117] DHC, QS/4/Box 24, Epiphany 3.
[118] CALS, QJF/90/1, 118. [119] WSHC, A1/110/1632H, 175.

Table 5.4 *Carework undertaken 'for another'*

	Total tasks	% undertaken 'for another'			% with no evidence task undertaken 'for another'
		Explicitly paid	Service	Unspecified terms	
Childcare	124	6.5	7.3	34.7	51.6
Education	25	8.0	4.0	60.0	28.0
Healthcare	211	15.6	6.2	60.7	17.5
Midwifery	124	0.8	1.6	95.2	2.4
Other care	80	2.5	10.0	72.5	15.0
Total	564	8.2	5.9	64.2	21.8

showing the subcategories of carework divided according to work that was explicitly paid, performed as part of service, or 'for another' but with terms unspecified, as well as work that was not obviously 'for another' – either taking place within the family or without any details provided. Childcare was the only subcategory of carework which was not dominated by work 'for another'. Only a small proportion of work tasks 'for another' had explicit evidence of payment for the work: the proportion was highest for healthcare at 15.6 per cent. Servants carried out a relatively small proportion of carework. Most carework tasks fell into the category of 'for another' but with terms unspecified: they were outside the family but the terms of payment are not stated. Much of this must have been paid work, but some could have been reciprocal and charitable.

Care for the elderly could be given in expectation of inheritance, childcare could be reciprocal between family and neighbours, and healthcare could be given as an exchange of knowledge and learning. When the elderly widow Joan Fargeson died in Cambridge in 1594, Agnes and William Clarke and their son attested to the ongoing care they provided Joan in her last months, delivering her weekly 8d allowance, caring for her, dressing her by the fireside, and preparing medicinal drinks using nutmeg, ginger, spices, and bread. They appeared in a testamentary case claiming that in return for their care, 'having been very troublesome' to the Clarke family, Joan had verbally promised them all her worldly goods.[120] The Clarke family utilised the terminology at court that Charmian Mansell identified as that most commonly used to describe patterns of paid work, 'taking pains', which implied that the

120 CUL, EDR/2/19, *Clarke v. Jackson.*

care provided had been given in expectation of remuneration.[121] Care where terms were unspecified reflects these blurred obligations where remuneration was not explicit but could be expected, and make up the largest proportion of 'for another' carework for both men and women.

As discussed in Section 5.2, although the home was an important site of medical healthcare, 52 per cent of the healthcare work tasks recorded in the work-task database were performed outside of the actor's own household.[122] Many of those providing care away from their own home did so to make a living. Testamentary cases often record ongoing care: in 1687 Agnes Hanford was described as employed by the son of Margaret Kempe with the sole purpose of providing care to his mother during her declining health, in Cruwys Morchard in Devon. He paid Agnes a wage and maintained her diet.[123] In Odiham in Hampshire in 1631 as a man lay sick, Ann Phillips, along with a second woman, were hired to sit and watch him, and witnessed his visitors in his final days.[124] In death, bodies were cared for in the home. In 1631 in Hillington, Norfolk, Margaret Wilson and Jane Betts were requested by Thomasine Tye to attend the house of Robert Tye to prepare the body of Alice Fendick. The two women stayed with Alice's body during the night and the following day removed her clothes and wound her body in sheets ready for burial.[125]

The two largest subcategories of carework, healthcare and midwifery, recorded professional practitioners with occupational descriptors such as doctor, surgeon, apothecary, physician, and midwife, who were likely to be paid for their work even when this was not explicitly stated. The extensive literature on medical provision in early modern England has focused primarily on licensed practitioners, male and female, and men who can be identified by their occupational titles.[126] The work-task data provides examples of licensed doctors attending patients, but also evidence of healthcare being provided by many people who had other occupations or were unlicensed, the majority of whom were female.[127] At her bedside in Sandford, Devon, in 1617, Margaret Heydon was attended by Mr Doctor Wescombe with his apothecary and one 'Trowte of North Tawton who is accompted to be a physician and to have done

[121] Mansell, 'Reconstructing the labour of care'.
[122] Using the categories explained in Section 1.2.3.
[123] DHC, Chanter 8299, *Kempe v. Kempe*.
[124] HRO, 21M65/C3/12, *Phillips v. Thornton*.
[125] NRO, C/S3/28, Exam of Margarett Wilson.
[126] See Webster (ed.), *Health, Medicine and Mortality*; Porter (ed.), *Patients and Practitioners*; Mortimer, 'Triumph of the doctors'; Jenner and Wallis (eds.), *Medicine and the Market*.
[127] Reinforcing the arguments made in Nagy, *Popular Medicine*.

people good and money was paid to them'.[128] In Runcorn, Cheshire, in 1627, a surgeon, Mr Jesup, was credited with saving the life of a young man who, being 'unable to make water', visited Mr Jesup who 'with an instrument did or had taken forth of his yard a quart of the filthiest matter or corruption that ever he saw'.[129] Yet it was a clergyman, Mr Hooke, who served his ministry in Stibbard, Norfolk, who doubled up as a medical expert in the 1610s. Dorothy Rutland carried her mother's 'matter' to Mr Hooke for him to view and give his advice on her health, and John Durrant recalled that Mr Hooke 'did prescribe and minister physic to her this deponent's mother'.[130] Percival Slake of Prescot, Lancashire, admitted in 1637 that he had attended Robert Bushell in his illness where he administered physic and that he had 'given physic to diverse others theretofore but had no licence or toleration from anyone to do so'.[131]

It is particularly striking that three-quarters of healthcare (not including midwifery) was provided by women who neither received licenses nor were given medical occupational titles. Some of these women openly asserted their skills. In 1605 Joanna Stukelie in Yeovil, Somerset, claimed that she 'hath skill in physic and surgery and … used the same and received money of such as she hath helped and healed but saith that she hath no license to do so'.[132] Others clearly charged for their services, such as 'one Bond's wife of Saxthorpe' in Norfolk, who charged 40d for healing Thomas Abraham alias Sleth in 1557.[133] The case of Earth Bickley reveals a market for medical advice and care provided by women. When Earth was sexually assaulted in Crediton, Devon, in 1597, her husband Richard spoke to the wife of Ellis Basse 'for the helping and curing of her [Earth]'. She examined Earth and noted that 'that she had been very badly used' but required a higher payment than Earth's husband could afford. Instead, he 'procured and appointed one Joan Browninge widow to help her, who had her in cure almost half a year before she was cured'. The attacker, Robert Aileston, who was also Richard's employer, 'did pay and deliver money to [Richard] to recompense her for the curing of her'.[134]

Midwives were exclusively female before the eighteenth century.[135] This was the only medical occupation for which women were commonly licensed, although not all practising midwives were licensed. There were

[128] DHC, Chanter 867, *Heydon v. Heydon*. [129] CALS, EDC/5/1634, 39.
[130] NRO, DN/DEP/37/40, 17–20. [131] LiA, QSB/1/182, 50.
[132] SHC, D/D/Cd/36, *Wood v. Fonstone*. [133] NRO, DN/DEP/7/6A, 166–7.
[134] DHC, QS/4/Box 5, 32–3, 45–6. Earth is an unusual Devon name, derived from the local saint, St Urith.
[135] Wilson, *Making of Man-Midwifery*, p. 1.

97 midwives recorded in the database, who ranged in age from 18 to 80 with a median age of 48. Almost half of midwives, 49 per cent, had no marital status recorded. Nearly a third of the recorded midwives were described as married; eight were married to a husbandman and other spousal occupations included bricklayer, clerk, draper, weaver, inn-holder, butcher, glazier, and baker.[136] Just five of the midwives, 4 per cent, were never married and all were older women, aged 42 or older. Widows made up 16 per cent of midwives – appearing at a greater frequency in the work subcategory of midwifery than any other in the dataset. They had an age range of 28 to 60.

Midwives attested to their experience and expertise. Isabella Rowell of St Oswald, Durham, was called to a labour in the city in 1598, 'being a midwife and often employed in the like case'.[137] Elizabeth Antrobus, a resident of Knutsford, Cheshire, in 1682, was a 'professed midwife'.[138] Elizabeth Yong testified that despite being a 'very poor woman', she was 'much used for a midwife' and her clientele included 'the substantial parishioners' of Muchelney, Somerset, in the early 1600s.[139] In part this language reflects the official role granted midwives in the courts as experts in their field to grant access to the bodies of suspected women in the legal process. For example, as was common practice, the midwife in Winsham, Somerset, in 1659, Sybell Kingston, was called upon to search the body and breasts of Elinor Partridge at Master Bovett's house before 'diverse other women', as Elinor was suspected of having recently borne an illegitimate baby.[140] In 1674, midwife Elizabeth Twise, then aged 80, recalled taking her licence in the mid-1630s before the Bishop of Lichfield's chancellor 'for the employment of a midwife'. She did 'take her oath faithfully to perform that office and has ever since practised the same in that neighbourhood'.[141] The use of promissory oaths to officiate midwives was a long-held practice recorded in early sixteenth-century church visitations. Taking a licence to practice midwifery could be costly. Records of licensing agreements in the Chester courts show an initial fee of 18s 8d was paid for a license whilst licenses in London varied between £1 and £2, with subsequent payments made at annual church visitations to continue to practise.[142] The practice required midwives to attest to their professionalism with the written testimony of the women they had

[136] See Thomas, 'Early modern midwifery'. The midwives in the database were of lower status than in his study, probably because we included unlicensed practitioners.
[137] DUIC, DDR/EJ/CCD/1/5, 102r-3r. [138] CALS, QJF/110/1, 49.
[139] SHC, D/D/Cd/36, *Waggott v. Baker*. [140] SHC, QSR/98, 140–1.
[141] CALS, EDC/5/1674, 3.
[142] Harley, 'Provincial midwives', p. 30., Evenden, *Midwives of Seventeenth Century London*, pp. 22–30.

already assisted in birth. Elizabeth Twise was already an experienced and professional midwife, aged 50 when she took her oath in the 1630s.

At times the role of midwife is less clearly defined. In Freshford, Somerset, in 1617, Margaret Tucker was awoken at midnight to 'help deliver Mary Widdon of child', and Katherine Tompson was 'called to the travail' of Hannah Lake in Sandbach, Cheshire, in 1682.[143] Neither claimed to have been a midwife by profession. In other cases, it is apparent that women acted as midwife out of necessity. Similarly to the case described in the introduction to this chapter, Martha Lane was called 'to the groaning' of Mary Wyatt where she delivered Mary's baby 'in the absence of a midwife', who was called for but did not arrive in time in Priston, Somerset, in 1693.[144] At Winterbourne Monkton in Wiltshire in 1670, Mary Eatwell assisted the vicar's maid in her labour, 'having some skill in the mystery and cunning of midwifery', a skill that was confirmed 'by some of the women of the parish'.[145] Licensed medical professionals were not absent from the rural care economy, but the depositions too show the ways in which non-licensed practitioners provided expertise in care.

In contrast to healthcare and midwifery, a small percentage of childcare, 15 per cent, was either explicitly paid or performed by servants. Nonetheless, care of infants and particularly wet nursing could provide an income for women. Of the six explicitly paid work activities performed by women in the category of childcare, four describe wet nursing newborn babies and a further two strongly suggest that wet nursing was involved as part of 'nursing and keeping a child' for a prolonged period of time. In total 12 women were recorded working as wet nurses caring for other people's infants. We know considerably less about the arrangements for wet nursing in England compared to continental Europe, where foundling hospitals in urban centres employed wet nurses to feed abandoned infants and maintained records of their employees.[146] For England, Valerie Fildes has suggested that during the seventeenth century wet nursing in the home could be a regular and lucrative form of employment, particularly in the rural parishes surrounding London.[147] Wages from wet nursing could be significant: Amy Erickson has calculated the annual costs for raising children maintained by the parish to be roughly £5 per annum in the seventeenth century but rates varied by region and authority.[148] The accounts of the Le Strange family show that they paid their wet nurses, who were women in local farming households, £5 4s per annum in the

[143] SHC, Q/SR/33, 127–9; CALS, QJF/110/3, 90. [144] SHC, D/D/Cd, 106.
[145] WSHC, D1/42/61, *Office v. Bransdon.* [146] Sarti, *Europe at Home*, p. 166.
[147] Fildes, 'The English wet-nurse'.
[148] Erickson, *Women and Property*, pp. 50–1; Crawford, *Parents of Poor Children*, p. 127.

1620s.[149] Our evidence suggests similar rates of pay. A married woman with the surname Pitler was paid £5 per annum to wet nurse the son of a yeoman in Congresbury, Somerset, in 1668; while Julianne Blunt took in an infant to nurse for the payment of 17d a week (£3 13s 8d a year) in North Curry, Somerset, in 1619.[150] However, it is likely that some of these agreed wages were not intended to cover the full costs of raising a child. Many of the wet nurses lived close-by to the infant's family and received further help such as when in 1686 Ann Linsey visited her child at the home of its wet nurse and carer, Jenet Anderton in Myerscough, Lancashire, where she delivered 'several parcels of linen' and cloth.[151]

Where details are given in the depositions, aside from the two wet nurses working in service, wet nursing was performed in the home of the wet nurse. Out of the 12 wet nurses recorded, nine were married women, two were widowed, and one (who worked in service) was never married. None of the wet nurses were described as employed by parish officials or doing the work in receipt of parish poor rates. One case did record an infant who was put out to nurse by a parish – 'at the charge of the town of Sutton [Cheshire]' – but failed to mention who was employed as the wet nurse.[152] Instead, the wet nurses described in the depositions appear to be mainly married women contracted privately. Their husbands were typically husbandmen or artisans. The work of caring for infants could carry on beyond the period of breastfeeding. Helen Katherine received 4d weekly for the bringing up of the young Thomas Abraham over the course of seven years in Norfolk in 1550; Alice Knowles in Derby in 1682 was paid 16d per week for the first quarter for nursing and keeping a child and £3 per year thereafter.[153] Janet Anderton of Lancaster did not claim to be paid explicitly for her work, but did wet nurse and keep a child as a 'tabler' for Ann Linsley in 1686.[154]

The examples of wet nurses also illustrate some of the inequalities of the care economy. In the case from Congresbury in Somerset already mentioned above, the wife of John Pitler was well paid at £5 per annum for the nursing and caring of Samuel Cannoway. But upon the death of Samuel's father, the terms of the arrangement broke down and John Pitler pleaded poverty in his deposition, 'for that this informant being a very poor man, and hath a great charge of his own cannot maintain the said Samuel but must leave him to the parish'. The wage earned by his

149 Whittle and Griffiths, *Consumption and Gender*, pp. 170–2.
150 SHC, Q/SR/111, 41; SHC, Q/SR/33, 95.
151 NYCRO, QSB/1/1686, Info of Joshua Gervis.
152 CALS, QJF/110/2, 87.
153 NRO, DN/DEP/7/6A, 166–7; CALS, QJF/110/2, 87.
154 LaA, QSB/1/1686, Midsummer, Info of Joshua Gervis.

wife for nursing did not, he claimed, cover the cost of tabling Samuel in their home and his care compromised that of their own children.[155] In 1698 Agnes Hargreave of Keighley gave a testimony at the Wakefield quarter sessions in Yorkshire in a case of disputed paternity. Her sister Margaret Hargreaves was, she recalls, 'a spinster and servant or wet nurse to a child of one John Shakleton'.[156] Margaret had been working in service for a year in the Shakleton household during which she became pregnant with the child of her master John Shakleton. Soon after the birth of the baby, Margaret did 'turn away from the said bastard child and left the same to the charge of the town of Keighley', moving to live close to her sister. Margaret was given 30s by John Shakleton, and gifts of butter at 5lb a time, presumably for her to sell, but her requests for consistent maintenance were refused. As a consequence, she left her baby with the parish so she could pursue productive labour, seeking work elsewhere to support herself.

Rather than assuming simplistically that women's productive labour was reduced by marital and maternal duties, we can instead look to the complex networks of care that sustained women's productive work as well as the ample opportunities specialist knowledge in care provision granted them for paid employment.[157] Even carework that confined women to the home could provide opportunity for gainful employment: wet nursing and tabling young infants was a valuable source of income that could provide competitive wages for women.[158] There were many opportunities to earn income from carework and housework in early modern England. Such work was dominated by women, but it was not separate from market relations. Indeed, with little state provision and attitudes to care that allowed everything from breastfeeding to care of the dying to be performed by non-family members, such work was probably more monetised in early modern England than in some more modern economies.

5.4 Conclusion

Examining housework and carework task-by-task perhaps fails to convey the way workers experienced these tasks, which were fitted in amongst other activities. This is captured in a rare testimony describing a day's work by a female servant, Lucretia Harward of Bale in Norfolk in 1637. Accused of stealing money from a fellow servant, her defence was that she had been too busy to go into the man's room where the money had been hidden in a handkerchief. It was harvest time, and Lucretia and

155 SHC, Q/SR/111, 41. 156 WYAS, QS1/37/8, Agnes Hargreaves.
157 Shepard, 'Care', p. 57.
158 Fildes, 'English wet-nurse', pp. 42–4., Sarasúa et al., 'Nursing babies'.

another maid were brewing beer and baking bread for the harvest workers as well as seeing to their usual chores. Her description vividly conveys the need to juggle multiple activities in a busy household:

> [S]he was employed in tending the copper, the other maid being then busy in the same room; she further saith that she went into the house to fetch the maid her dinner and forthwith returned again with the same and then without any intermission set on liquor for the mixing of paste which took her about one hour's time, that done she forthwith gave attendance upon the heating of the oven and also in helping the maid to save her beer which was in danger to be lost, about the house next she repaired instantly into the kitchen again which she dressed up …, attended upon the children, and then by reason of the other maid's employment, went a-milking.

This chapter has sought to overturn three pervasive assumptions about housework and carework: that it took place within people's own homes, was predominantly carried out by married women, and was unpaid work. Instead, we show that much of housework took place outside, while carework is most often observed taking place in other people's houses. Only the care of young infants was predominantly carried out as unpaid work by mothers – overwhelmingly married women, but this did not restrict women to the home. Housework was most often undertaken by young unmarried people. Carework was dominated by healthcare which typically involved the care of people from outside the household. Much of housework and carework was paid work: although explicit evidence of payment is only recorded in a minority of cases, the performance of work for non-family members demonstrates the doing of such work outside of a family household was commonplace.

Exploring specific examples of the tasks involved in housework and carework in-depth, as this chapter has done, uncovers a new history of these forms of work. Close examination of housework tasks and who performed them suggests status was more important than gender: housework was left to the young and subordinate. Women's predominance amongst those doing housework had more to do with their subordinate position than the 'convenience' of women combining housework with other forms of women's work. In contrast, responsibilities for carework increased with age, but the carework described in court depositions was rarely routine childcare; instead, it was often skilled healthcare and midwifery. The work-task data captures the grassroots delivery of medical care, predominantly provided by women for people from outside their household. Just as other forms of work changed over time, so did housework and carework. Twentieth-century assumptions about housework being unpaid work carried out by married women within the privacy of the home cannot be applied to early modern England.

6 Agriculture and Food Production

In the harvest of 1611, four wage workers set about reaping wheat in 'two little pieces of ground' belonging to Edward Hayward in Ryecroft, an open field in Redbourn, Hertfordshire. They were a 22-year-old servant, Anne Godman, who had been employed with Edward since the previous Christmas; Richard Byrch, a 45-year-old labourer who was hired by Hayward for a single day; Richard Black, a 33-year-old husbandman, hired by Hayward as a 'harvestman' since Midsummer; and Thomas Black, a 23-year-old husbandman employed as a 'month's man' and Edward's distant cousin. Part way through the day, with the reaping almost complete, Hayward took Richard Black and Thomas Black 'to other business elsewhere and left the said Richard Byrch and Anne Godman to bind and shock the same wheat'. Each shock of wheat contained 15 sheaves, and there were 117 sheaves in total. At 7 in the evening, Richard and Thomas returned with Edward's horse and cart and loaded up the wheat, being careful to leave the tithe, consisting of 12 sheaves, in the field. They 'carried … home' the rest of the wheat to Edward's barn. Soloman Barton, passing by the field the next morning, saw the 12 tithe sheaves standing in the field. Philip Barker, the deputy of Francis Sylles, who owned the tithes, had spoken to the workers while they were loading the wheat but decided to come back the next day rather than waiting. By the time he returned some of the wheat was missing. As a consequence, the four workers were called to the church court the following November to give evidence, recounting in detail that one day's work.[1] Tithe disputes are a particularly rich source of evidence about agriculture and coastal fishing, but many other types of cases also provide snippets of evidence offering a window into the work activities involved in the largest sector of the economy: food production and the management of landed resources.

This chapter explores a set of related production activities. Most of these, such as agriculture, fishing, and food processing, involved the

[1] HALS, ASA8/8, 134–5.

production of food. Others, such as woodland management and cutting turf, relate to closely connected forms of land management and the provision of land-based resources such as fuel. Occupational descriptors suggest farming remained the most common male occupation in early modern England up to 1700.[2] The existing history of early modern agriculture is dominated by evidence from three types of sources, each of which has weaknesses that the work-task data can correct. Probate inventories provide details about the economies of individual farms, but they do not reveal who exactly carried out the work of farming.[3] Farming advice books offer stylised depictions of the division of labour between women and men, but it is unclear how far these conventions were actually followed.[4] The wage accounts of large farms frequently reveal details of the work undertaken by labourers paid by the day or task, but such documents are rare and a-typical, relating only to the large farms run by or for wealthy, literate owners.[5] They also leave us in the dark about the work carried out by the many servants employed, because their tasks are rarely described. The work-task data is valuable because it allows the whole cross-section of farms to be viewed, from smallholders with a single cow, to small family farms and large farms with gangs of workers, and they reveal who exactly was doing what. A further bonus is that work patterns recorded in court depositions go beyond farms into the realms of shared resources such as commons, woods, and bodies of water, providing an overarching view of rural labour.

Women's role in agriculture has been the subject of many contradictory generalisations and thus is a particular focus of this chapter. The work-task data shows that 39 per cent of male work activities fell into the category of agriculture and land, which includes farming and fishing, while a further 4 per cent involved food processing. For women the equivalent figures were 20 per cent and 4 per cent. Overall, the adjusted figures show that women undertook just over a third of work in the agricultural and land category, and 42 per cent of food processing.[6] Previous assessments of women's involvement in agriculture have ranged from Keith Snell's assertion that 'there is abundant supportive evidence for a very wide range of female participation in agricultural tasks before

[2] Shaw-Taylor and Wrigley, 'Occupational structure', p. 59; Wallis et al., 'Structural change', pp. 871–2; see also Table 1.1.

[3] Overton et al., *Production and Consumption*, pp. 33–86; Whittle, 'Housewives and servants' and 'Enterprising widows'.

[4] For Fitzherbert's *Boke of Husbandry*, see excerpts in Goldberg, *Women in England*, pp. 167–8; Tusser, *Five Hundred Points*; Markham, *The English Housewife*. For a careful assessment of such evidence, see Roberts, '"To bridle the falsehood"'.

[5] Whittle and Jiang, 'Gender, wages, and agricultural labour'.

[6] See Table 1.6.

1750', to Marjorie McIntosh's exclusion of agricultural work from her study of working women because it was 'less directly related to the money economy', and thus judged of little interest.[7] More commonly historians have repeated summaries drawn from early modern farming advice books, noting that farmer's wives produced 'food, drink, and clothing for their households ... [they] tended small livestock, such as hens and ducks. They planted kitchen gardens, and processed fruit from orchards'.[8] Such descriptions are not wholly inaccurate, but they lack sufficient detail and underplay the flexibility and range of female farm labour.

Only a handful of articles have sought to reconstruct the historical gender division of labour in agriculture. Most famously Michael Roberts examined harvest labour, showing that while only men mowed with the scythe, women took part in other activities including harvesting with a sickle.[9] Amanda Flather used court depositions from rural Essex to reconstruct the interlocking work patterns of women and men more generally across the seventeenth century.[10] Our findings confirm the conclusions of both these approaches. Less reliable is A. H. Smith's argument arising from analysis of one Norfolk gentleman's farm, that 'men's work and women's work was "sexually exclusive"'.[11] Also problematic is the recent assertion of Alesina et al., that in historical 'plough societies' women work in the home rather than in agriculture.[12] England was certainly a 'plough society' by their definition, but this did not lead to the exclusion of women from agricultural work. We find that the gender division of labour was flexible and women's participation in agriculture was significant. Alesina's approach is related to another strand in the history of gendered work in agriculture contrasting arable and pastoral regions. It has been suggested that women found more work in pastoral agriculture.[13] Recently, Voigtländer and Voth developed an elaborate theory based on the assumption that married women worked in arable agriculture and unmarried female servants in pastoral agriculture and thus the switch to more pastoral agriculture after the Black Death encouraged women to delay marriage and led to the development of the European Marriage Pattern.[14] The inaccuracy of these generalisations has been pointed out by Edwards and Ogilvie.[15] In this chapter, the

[7] Snell, *Annals*, p. 52; McIntosh, *Working Women*, p. 5.
[8] Mendelson and Crawford, *Women in Early Modern England*, pp. 265, 304. See also McIntosh, *Working Women*, p. 3.; Johnson, *Houses*, p. 51, for similar generalisations.
[9] Roberts, 'Sickles and scythes'.
[10] Flather, 'Space, place, and gender'.
[11] Smith, 'Labourers [Part II]', p. 377.
[12] Alesina et al., 'Origins of gender roles'.
[13] Snell, *Annals*, pp. 45, 49; Goldberg, *Women, Work, and Life Cycle*, p. 355.
[14] Voigtländer and Voth, 'How the west'.
[15] Edwards and Ogilvie, 'Did the Black Death'.

agricultural work patterns of female servants and married women, and women's involvement in arable and pastoral agriculture, are compared.

Tithe disputes offer some of the most detailed descriptions of agriculture and food production, providing 30 per cent of the work tasks in the agriculture and land category. The process of tithing awarded a tenth of produce from the land (and sea) to the tithe owner. Originally tithes supported the parish clergy. However, even before the Reformation, tithes were often appropriated by advowsons – people or institutions who received tithes and appointed clergy to parishes, and thus often fell into private hands.[16] Tithe collection led to disputes which were heard in the church courts. This was particularly the case in the half-century, 1550 to 1599, following the Reformation. Of the 143 tithe cases that provided evidence of work tasks in the database, 59 per cent came from this period. In total the 143 tithe cases provided evidence of 1,117 work tasks, of which 801 fall into the agriculture and land category. Nonetheless, agricultural work is a large category, and much of the evidence comes from other types of cases: theft, accidental death, and a whole range of miscellaneous cases provide valuable evidence. For food processing, theft cases yielded two-thirds of the work tasks collected. As such, integral tasks are generally included in the analysis in this chapter, as they capture many important forms of agricultural and food processing work that would otherwise be overlooked.

The chapter is divided into four main sections. The first provides an overview of the farm economy and the types of people undertaking agricultural work. This is followed by three sections looking in turn at arable agriculture, livestock husbandry, and work on or in commons, woods, and water. The processing of food and other resources is considered in the relevant sections: thus milling, malting, and brewing are discussed in relation to arable farming, butchering and dairying with livestock, and fishing and fuel with commons, woods, and water.

6.1 Farm Economy and Workers

Early modern England had a system of mixed agriculture in which the raising of crops was combined with keeping livestock.[17] The most common grains were wheat, barley, oats, and rye. In addition, peas, beans, and vetches were grown as field crops, while turnips and rapeseed started to appear in the second half of the seventeenth century. The most common livestock were sheep and cattle. Sheep provided wool, mutton,

[16] Outhwaite, *Rise and Fall*, pp. 23–4; Emmison, 'Tithes, perambulations, and sabbath-breach'.

[17] See Overton, *Agricultural Revolution*; Thirsk (ed.), *Agrarian History*, Vol. 4.

and tallow; while cattle were kept for milk, beef, and hides.[18] Oxen and horses provided traction for ploughing and pulling carts. Vegetables and fruit were cultivated in gardens and orchards, adding an essential element to diets. A tithe case from Pewsey in Wiltshire from 1675 reported, for instance, that Anthony Godman had 'a small garden plot belonging to his house in Pewsey' in which was grown 'a few pot herbs' and 'sometimes a few cabbages for the use of his family and sometimes a few beans, but no peas, turnips or carrots'.[19] Animals such as pigs and poultry were another important source of food and income.

Maintaining yields of grain and other crops relied on land being kept in good heart. Manure was either collected and spread on the fields, or animals were grazed on the land when it lay fallow and spread the manure themselves. Thus, in Worstead, Norfolk, in 1528, a servant named William Chamber drove a cart 'laden with dung to his master's land to unload it there', while in Weston Zoyland, Somerset, cows were put to graze on the grass that had grown beneath the corn in the open field between harvest and the start of ploughing in October 1583.[20] Rotations also helped to maintain crop yields. At Wherwell in Hampshire in 1558, a classic rotation was described involving three large common fields in which local farmers each owned strips of land. One field was sown with wheat, one with barley, and the third 'lay for a summer field' – a fallow where sheep were grazed.[21] Peas, beans, and vetches were valued not only because they were used as food or animal fodder but because they replaced some of the nutrients extracted by other crops, thereby increasing soil fertility.[22] Another method for maintaining fertility was 'convertible husbandry'. This involved alternating pasture and arable over a longer period: pasture was cleared, ploughed, and then cropped for several years before being put back down to pasture again. Two cases from Devon record this process: groups of men and women were engaged in 'burning beat' and 'righting beat' at Mr Halewood's ground in South Molton in 1620, and at North Petherwin in 1593.[23] Beat-burning had been practised as part of convertible husbandry in Devon since the medieval period and involved burning the vegetation off rough pasture to prepare it for ploughing.[24]

18 Tallow was used to make candles, the most common source of lighting.
19 WSHC, D1/42/61, 190v–6v.
20 TNA/KB/9/508/162; SHC, D/D/Cd/20, *Bowne v. Seller.*
21 HRO, 21M65/C3/8, *Gattenbye v. Twyne.*
22 By fixing nitrogen in the soil. See Overton, *Agricultural Revolution*, p. 16–7.
23 DHC, QS/4/Box 24, Baptist, 17; DRO, Chanter 864, *Lawrie v. Pope.*
24 Fox, 'Farming practice', pp. 309–10; see also Pinchbeck, *Women Workers*, p. 53; Sharpe 'Time and wages', p. 66. Carew mentions the practice in Cornwall in 1602, Carew, *Survey of Cornwall*, p. 34.

Table 6.1 *The most common farm-based work tasks*

	F tasks adj.	M tasks	Total tasks	% by F adj.
Harvesting crops	155	317	472	32.9
Sheep farming	96	311	407	23.6
Farm transport	70	313	383	18.3
Milking	231	8	239	96.7
Hay harvest	75	128	203	37.0
Cattle farming	91	117	208	43.7
Prepare ground	18	171	189	9.6
Caring for horses	52	130	182	28.5
Wood and hedge husbandry	16	175	191	8.8
Threshing and winnowing	52	119	171	30.3
Total	856	1,789	2,645	32.4

Notes: adj. = adjusted (x2.59). Farm-based activities from agriculture and land, and food processing, categories. Wood husbandry and hedging are combined. Cattle farming does not include milking. Harvesting crops does not include hay.

Table 6.1 shows the most common farm-based work activities, breaking down some of the larger subcategories in Appendix B, such as fieldwork and animal husbandry. Adjusted figures are used for female work tasks to represent women's contribution more accurately. This offers an overview of the most labour-intensive activities on the early modern farm. In arable agriculture the most demanding processes were preparing the ground (which included ploughing), harvesting, and threshing crops. Animal husbandry also required large quantities of labour, although that labour was spread more evenly throughout the year. The hay harvest was an essential adjunct to keeping livestock, providing fodder over the winter. Farm transport encompassed the movement of crops and animals within the farm: common and time-consuming activities often overlooked in descriptions of agricultural labour. Trees and hedges were managed to provide timber for building and bundles of wood (faggots) for fuel, while well-maintained field-boundaries were essential to keeping livestock. Women dominated milking and are well represented in most categories. Only in farm transport, preparing ground, and wood husbandry, did their participation fall below 20 per cent of work tasks.

Men whose main occupation was farming adopted a variety of titles. Table 6.2 shows the categories of agricultural work undertaken by men with different occupational descriptors. Yeomen were wealthier farmers, although below the gentry in status. Husbandmen were generally family farmers: men with smaller farms that were nonetheless sufficient to

Table 6.2 *Agricultural repertoires of types of male farm workers*

	Yeomen repertoire (%)	Husbandmen repertoire (%)	*Agricola* repertoire (%)	Labourer repertoire (%)	Male servant repertoire (%)
Fieldwork	26.5	38.5	46.3	29.8	22.5
Animal husbandry	46.8	29.0	17.1	21.5	45.4
Farm transport	11.4	17.9	24.4	16.9	17.9
Wood and hedges	3.8	7.2	8.1	11.8	3.8
Other agricultural	11.4	7.5	4.1	20.0	10.4
Total	99.9	100.1	100.0	100.0	100.0
Total tasks	79	335	161	255	240

provide a living for their family.[25] Some husbandmen also worked for wages. The Latin term *agricola,* or farmer, was also used in some church court records.[26] Wage workers are represented by labourers and servants.

Husbandmen and *agricola* did the highest proportion of fieldwork: the *agricola*'s proportion is possibly inflated by the fact they only appear in the church courts, and thus often in tithe cases concerned with bringing in the harvest. Yeomen and male servants did higher proportions of animal husbandry; indeed, the agricultural repertoires of male servants were remarkably similar to those of yeomen, although servants did a higher proportion of farm transport. Labourers undertook a wide range of tasks and were particularly likely to do wood husbandry and hedging. Thus, for instance, two labourers, John Chescombe and John Henckocke, were paid to 'make and repair the hedge of the churchyard' at Newton Valence in Hampshire in 1523.[27] Labourers also did noticeably more 'other' tasks. Two-fifths of these involved digging marl and clay, which was likely to have been paid work, but tasks such as collecting fuel, hunting, and gathering food related to their own smallholding economy.[28]

25 On yeoman and husbandmen, see Shepard, *Accounting for Oneself*, pp. 240–7.

26 For most analysis in this book, the term 'agricola' has been translated and categorised as husbandman, as the frequency of its use in the church courts suggests it was more commonly used as a Latin equivalent to this than the rarer terms yeoman or labourer. Here, however, it is treated in its own right to allow for a more in-depth analysis of its meaning.

27 HRO, 21M65/C3/2, *Churchwardens of Newton Valence v. Aldwyn and Hardinge.*

28 There were 51 other agriculture and land activities by labourers: 20 digging marl or clay, 12 hunting or fishing, 11 collecting fuel, and 4 gathering food. Servants hunted and fished to a similar extent but collected fuel and gathered food less often.

Table 6.3 *Agricultural repertoires of different types of women*

	Single women and spinsters repertoire (%)	Servants and maids repertoire (%)	Wives repertoire (%)	Widows repertoire (%)
Fieldwork	12.3	20.4	24.6	35.3
Animal husbandry	32.1	24.5	23.9	26.5
Milking	29.6	38.5	18.1	5.9
Gathering food	8.6	5.1	18.1	11.8
Other agricultural	17.3	11.5	15.2	20.6
Total	99.9	100.0	99.9	100.1
Total tasks	81	78	138	34

Apart from servants, women were typically described by their marital status rather than occupations. Women, like men, were heavily involved in fieldwork and animal husbandry, but the next most common subcategories were milking, and gathering food. Servants, maids, spinsters, and single women were mostly, but not always, younger women.[29] While servants and most maids were paid employees, the occupational status of spinsters and single women is unclear. Some may have been servants, but their pattern of work differed, suggesting that many were unmarried women living with their parents and working either on the family farm or for day wages. All types of women were involved in all the categories of agricultural work shown in Table 6.3, but the emphasis of their work differed. As a proportion of agricultural tasks, servants did the most milking, single women the most animal husbandry, wives the most gathering – which included gleaning – and widows the most fieldwork. Together, milking and animal husbandry made up more than 60 per cent of servants' and single women's agricultural work, compared to 42 per cent of that of married women. Of all types of women, widows' pattern of agricultural work was closest to that of men, suggesting some of these women were managing farms without much male labour. Tables 6.2 and 6.3 are a reminder that work was divided not just between men and women, but between family farmers and wage workers, and between unmarried and married people. Even amongst wage workers, servants and day labourers had different work patterns and skill sets.

Agricultural work was strongly seasonal.[30] Our evidence supports Flather's conclusion that gendered work patterns varied across the year, sometimes overlapping but often occupying women and men in different

[29] Mansell, 'Variety of women's experiences'. [30] See also Section 4.2.

activities.[31] In animal husbandry, women were most heavily involved in milking and care of cattle, while men dominated sheep farming. In May and June, however, men and women worked together to move, wash, and shear sheep. Women's involvement in these labour-intensive tasks seems to have been more common in communities of the south-west. In Stogursey, Somerset, for instance, 'at sheep shearing time … about the beginning of June' 1603, Marie, the wife of William Bitford, worked alongside other men and women 'at sheep shearing in the barn' of her husband.[32] Men and women also worked side by side in the fields as the summer progressed, making hay together in July and harvesting cereal crops in August and September. Gleaning corn in the late summer was largely the preserve of women. Fruit harvest, on the other hand, saw a more even division – 51 per cent female – as in Somerset in August 1681, when the tailor Thomas Clarke worked 'at Cloford with his wife and son George in an orchard … gathering of apples'.[33]

Running a farm required the mastery of many interlocking activities and a wide range of skills. Male servants were particularly prominent in animal husbandry, and male labourers in wood management and hedging and ditching; female servants and unmarried women dominated milking, and married women were prominent amongst the gleaners. Yet these were differences in emphasis rather than specialisms. All types of agricultural workers took part in the main areas of farm work: fieldwork and animal husbandry. The varied seasonal work tasks and peaks of labour demand in the summer meant that agricultural workers had to be multiskilled and flexible.

6.2 Field Crops

The frequency with which different field crops were mentioned in work tasks is shown in Figure 6.1. 'Corn' was a catch-all term for grain crops. Wheat was valued as a bread corn: high-quality white bread was always made from wheat. Barley, although sometimes made into flour or added to pottage, was primarily used to make beer. Oats, which were a hardier crop than wheat, were eaten throughout the north of England as the main food grain, in the form of oatcakes or porridge.[34] Oats were sometimes brewed into ale in the west of England, a famously unpleasant drink.[35]

31 Flather, 'Space, place, and gender'.
32 SHC, D/D/Cd/36, *Ecclestone v. Huishe*.
33 SHC, D/D/Cd/97, *Masters v. Hill*. For further analysis of seasonal patterns of work, see Section 4.2.
34 On cultivation, see Overton, *Agricultural Revolution*, Chs. 2 and 3; on consumption, see Muldrew, *Food, Energy*, ch. 2.
35 Carew, *Survey of Cornwall*, p. 35.

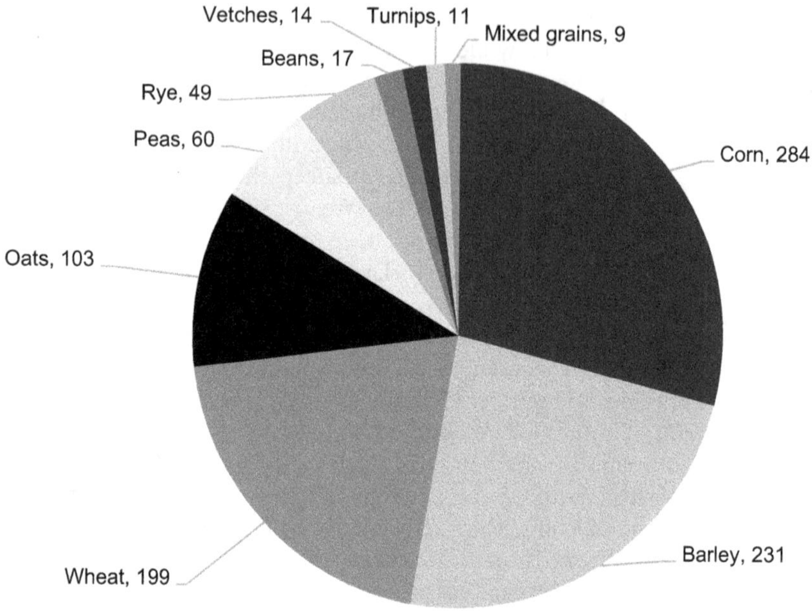

Figure 6.1 Field crops mentioned in work tasks.
Notes: Graph shows the number of work tasks in which each crop was mentioned.

Jane More was malting oats ready for brewing 'in the granary of her husband's house … in which there was a malt kiln, with her servants Mary Hayward and Christiana Osmond' in West Coker, Somerset, in 1598; Mary passed a sieve full of oat malt to Jane, 'and as she carried the sieve to empty it in the granary her feet slipped due to weight of the sieve'.[36] Throughout the country, oats were also valued as fodder for working horses, the main form of traction and transport. Rye was another hardy grain which would grow on thin sandy soils and in upland regions. It was sometimes sown as a mixture with wheat. Rye was a bread grain, often mixed with wheat for cheaper forms of bread. Peas are highly nutritious and were valued as human food used in pottage and the cheapest form of wholemeal bread, but also as animal fodder.

The cultivation of field crops followed an annual cycle that notionally began and finished each year at Michaelmas (29th September). Wheat and rye were sown in the autumn from August to November, while

[36] TNA/KB/9/700a/78.

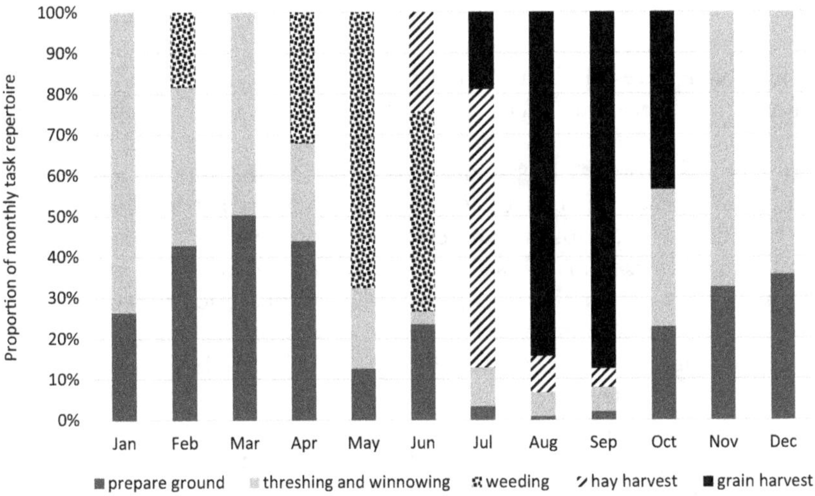

Figure 6.2 Seasonality of arable and harvesting tasks.
Notes: Harvest additions and monthly weights applied: for an explanation of these, see Appendices C and D. F adjusted (x2.58). This differs from the standard multiplier as it is designed to give an equal number of male and female tasks with weighted monthly data attached.

barley, oats, beans, and peas were sown in March and April.[37] Figure 6.2 demonstrates how key tasks were spread unevenly over the year with the preparation of ground (mostly ploughing) and threshing and winnowing dominating the winter months, weeding occurring in spring and early summer, and haymaking and the grain harvest concentrated in the busy months of July, August, and September. Food processing had an inverse seasonal distribution to agricultural fieldwork and animal husbandry. As discussed in Section 4.2, the majority of threshing and winnowing, milling, and food storage and preservation took place in the coldest six months of the year. Tasks were also gendered, with more female involvement in the summer tasks of weeding, harvesting, and gleaning.

Ploughing was an overwhelmingly male activity. The only example found of a woman engaged in ploughing was Margaret Parsons, a female servant who helped to plough a field in WestonZoyland, Somerset, in 1551.[38] Ploughing was not the only preparatory process, however. Land that had been out of cultivation was stubbed, grubbed, or cleaned of

[37] Of 11 sowing activities with month specified, there were 4 in August or September, 3 in October or November, and 4 in March and April.
[38] SHC, D/D/Cd/6, [?] v Symes.

'briars, brambles, bushes, weeds, thistles, and nettles'.[39] Fields were spread with manure and marl. Digging marl, clay, chalk, sand, and top soil, which were all used to improve the quality of soil in fields and gardens, had peaks in May and June, and again in November, fitting around the more urgent work of the harvest, and avoided when the ground was frozen.[40] In Devon and Somerset, the spring-sown barley land was 'hacked' or 'balled' as well as manured, which appears to refer to breaking large lumps of heavy clay soil before sowing.[41] This was done by teams of workers. At Rewe outside Exeter in March 1636 at least five men were 'hacking barley land'; while in Brean in Somerset two men and a woman were 'at work viz. at balling of barley land' in April 1584.[42] After sowing, ground might also be rolled. This could be hazardous: all the examples come from the coroners' reports into accidental death. The roller was a heavy piece of wood, drawn by either one or two horses, used to flatten the ploughed soil. When Thomas Lorkyn was rolling a field at Ickleton in Cambridgeshire in March 1524, 'he struck the horse on the head and the horse pulled him to the ground, struck him with its feet and ran the roller over him'.[43]

In northern and eastern England sowing was a male activity, but it was more mixed in south-west England. Out of 37 examples of people sowing crops, the six women recorded all came from Devon and Somerset.[44] Ivy Pinchbeck implied that women's involvement in planting peas and beans was an eighteenth-century innovation, yet two cases record women setting peas and planting beans in fields in the mid-seventeenth century in Somerset and Devon, and bean planting had been dominated by women in the medieval period.[45] Three cases recorded women sowing corn. At Shute in East Devon in 1672 a whole family, including two women, shut up their house for the day because they were in the field sowing corn.[46] Weeding was commonly done by women: only 8 of the 28 weeders recorded were men.[47] While weeding vegetable gardens might begin as early as February or March, field crops were weeded

[39] Quoting from a Hertfordshire tithe case of 1592: HALS, ASA8/8, 8–11.
[40] Of 49 cases with month specified, there were 1 in January to March, 24 in April to June, 7 in July to September, and 17 in October to December.
[41] In the south-west 'to ball' was to 'shower blows upon', while hack could also mean 'to strike'. See also English Dialect Dictionary Online [website].
[42] DHC, Chanter 866, *Hedgland v. Page*; SHC, D/D/Cd/20, *May v. Pearce.*
[43] TNA/KB/9/503/57.
[44] When adjusted, this suggests 16 female work tasks, with 33 per cent of sowing undertaken by women.
[45] Pinchbeck, *Women Workers*, p. 60; Rogers, *History of Agriculture*, Vol. 1, p. 281.
[46] DHC, Chanter 875, *Farrant v. Cox.*
[47] When adjusted, these figures are 8 men and 73 women.

between April and June. A case from Cornwall in 1595 referred to the period between Whitsun and Midsummer as ‘weeding time’.[48] Weeding was typically done in groups and seems to have been an occasion for sociability and gossip: 16 of the 28 workers taking part in weeding were recorded in cases relating to defamatory gossip. For instance, five women were ‘weeding in the ground of William Zeager within the parish of Broadclyst’ in Devon in 1617, when ‘Agnes Voysy and Margaret West fell at variance between themselves’ and Agnes slandered Margaret saying ‘John Holmead did lye with thee in Mr Moores shippon and the boys did look in through the door and make a game of it’.[49]

In late June the busiest period of the year began, with first hay harvested and then grain. The hay harvest is described in the next section. Harvesting grain sometimes began as early as late July in southern England but was normally concentrated in the second half of August and the first three weeks of September, occasionally stretching into early October. Of the grain harvest tasks that recorded the month of activity, 6 per cent took place in July, 54 per cent in August, 33 per cent in September and 7 per cent in October.[50] Crops were harvested with sickles and scythes and then bound into sheaves and stood up in shocks, stooks, or pooks, before being transported back to the farm for longer-term storage.[51] Scything was a less careful method of harvesting and mowers were accompanied by rakers who gathered up the cut stalks for binding.[52] Once the harvest had been cut and stacked, gleaners scoured the fields for ears of corn that had been missed. Table 6.4 shows the gender breakdown of these harvesting tasks. Aside from gleaning, reaping and raking used the highest proportion of female labour, while mowing with a scythe was a male-only task.

The different verbs used to describe the two harvest technologies, ‘mow’ for scythes, and ‘reap’ or ‘shear’ for sickles, allow the distribution of the two technologies to be explored. Between 1500 and 1700 the scythe was predominantly used to harvest barley and oats, as well as peas and vetches, and was used in all the regions studied. Snell argued that use of the scythe to harvest wheat as well as barley and oats decreased women’s participation in harvest work from the mid-eighteenth century onwards, a conclusion recently confirmed by Joyce

[48] DHC, Chanter 864, *Trevetheck v. John.*

[49] DHC, Chanter 867, *Holmeade v. Voysie.* A shippon is a barn. Two female weeders giving evidence were both aged 60.

[50] Only eastern England recorded October harvests.

[51] Shocks referred to wheat, as did stooks, although in the north to barley and oats as well; pooks referred to barley, oats, peas, and sometimes hay.

[52] On harvesting methods, see Roberts, ‘Sickles and scythes’.

Table 6.4 *Gender division of labour in the grain harvest*

	F tasks adj.	M tasks	Total tasks	% by F adj.
Reap/shear	60	82	142	42.3
Mow	0	33	33	0.0
Rake	13	18	31	41.9
Bind	21	53	74	28.4
Stack	28	52	80	35.0
Glean	91	12	103	88.3
Total	213	250	463	46.0

Notes: adj. = adjusted (x2.59). These figures are lower than 'harvest crops' in Table 6.1 because not all harvest work was described in detail and some involved non-grain crops.

Burnette, who noted that while the sickle persisted longest in northern England, the scything of wheat was widely adopted between 1750 and 1850, squeezing women out of the harvest workforce.[53] For the period before 1700 we found only one case of the scythe being used to harvest wheat, from Axminster in Devon in 1634.[54] Sickles were used to harvest all types of grain. It was the normal way of harvesting wheat, and rye was only ever harvested with a sickle. Reaping barley with a sickle was recorded not only in Cheshire in 1555 but also in Norfolk in 1627 and 1642, and shearing (reaping) oats was recorded in County Durham in 1602 and Yorkshire in 1663.[55] The scythe and sickle had existed side by side as alternative technologies for many centuries, and the respective qualities of the two tools were likely well understood. The scythe saved labour, allowing grain to be harvested more quickly, but it was wasteful, leading to more grain being dropped in the field; it also required the highest-paid form of male labour. The sickle ensured less grain was wasted and could be wielded by both women and men. The choice of which to use therefore depended on the available labour force and the priorities of the farmer.

In contrast to Snell's pessimistic picture, Pinchbeck argued that women's involvement in agriculture increased in the late eighteenth century, working with new crops and techniques.[56] The new crops of the 1500 to 1700 period did not necessarily involve women's labour. In the dataset, only men were recorded sowing and 'drawing' (or pulling)

[53] Snell, *Annals*, p. 50; Burnette, 'Wages and employment', pp. 684–5.
[54] DHC, Chanter 866, *Farmers de Axminster v. Burridge*.
[55] CALS, EDC/2-6, 79–81; NRO, C/S3/26, Exam of Thomas Chapman; NRO, C/S3/33, Info of John Rowling; DUIC, DDR/EJ/CCD/1/7, 257r–8r; BI, CP.H.5994, *Scott v. Cote*.
[56] Pinchbeck, *Working Women*, pp. 59–62.

turnips, which appeared in the late seventeenth century. It was men who cut woad leaves to harvest them in Hampshire in 1579, but women who were engaged in picking saffron in Cambridgeshire in 1582.[57] Gardening, with only 15 recorded activities, was dominated by men (12 male tasks against 3 female), despite the insistence in early modern husbandry books that this was a female activity.[58] Early modern commentators such as Gervase Markham characterised fieldwork, on the other hand, as the responsibility of the male husbandman, but this generalisation overlooked the significant contribution of women.[59] Some tasks were more strongly gendered than others: men dominated ploughing and threshing, while women dominated weeding and gleaning. Harvesting required everyone's labour. Only men mowed, but the workers who reaped or sheared crops with a sickle and bound them into sheaves were mixed. As a consequence, women made up a third of the workers harvesting crops, and of those engaged in growing and harvesting crops overall.[60] It is wrong, therefore, to characterise arable agriculture as the province of men alone.

Grain crops were removed from the field with stalks attached. Before the crop could be used or sold it had to be threshed (beaten with a flail to dislodge the grains from heads of corn) and winnowed (tossed into the air to separate grain and chaff). Table 6.5 shows that threshing was largely undertaken by men, whereas winnowing was a mixed activity. In fact, as discussed in Section 3.1, the gender of winnowers was strongly regional: female in the west of England and male in the east. For instance, Agnes Clement was sent for 'to winnowing, whilst that the wind did serve' at John Peyrce's house in Midsomer Norton in Somerset in 1607, announcing on arrival, 'I am come to winnow your corn'; whilst in Tickhill in Yorkshire in 1690, it was a man, Matthew Taylor of Moorehouse, who 'was windowing [winnowing] wheat at Mistress Rowleston's house'.[61]

Malting, the process by which barley or other grains were prepared for brewing (by soaking in water, allowing the grain to sprout, and then roasting gently in a kiln), was an activity undertaken by women and men. As we saw in the case from West Coker in Somerset discussed above, there it was a wife and two female servants who malted oats in 1598.[62] In a case from Cambridge in 1525 the workforce was male: in the

[57] HRO, 21M65/C3/8, *Gary v. Cooper*; CUL, EDR/2/19, *Stookes and Chapman v. Robson.*

[58] The database also contains six men with the occupation 'gardener'. The adjusted figure would be eight women.

[59] Markham, *English Husbandman* and *English Housewife.*

[60] Fieldwork category minus haymaking. Female-adjusted figures.

[61] SHC, Q/SR/3, 18; WYAS, QS1/29/4, Anne Travis.

[62] TNA/KB/9/700a/78.

Table 6.5 *Gender division of labour in processing of field crops*

	F tasks adj.	M tasks	Total tasks	% by F adj.
Threshing	10	98	108	9.6
Winnowing	39	14	53	78.5
Malting	16	6	22	72.1
Milling grain/malt	23	47	70	33.2
Total	65	118	183	35.4

Notes: adj. = adjusted (x2.59). Threshing and winnowing are lower than the figures in Table 6.1 because some tasks involved cleaning peas and lentils, not shown here.

brewhouse of Ralph Bicardike, Thomas Brankeston and William Bicardike carried a barrel of boiling wort while Clement Ferror was stirring malt in mash vat of boiling liquid.[63] Markham tried to make sense of this mixed picture by saying of malting: 'this office or place of knowledge belongeth particularly the housewife; and though we have many excellent men maltsters, yet it is properly the work and care of the woman, for it is a house work'.[64]

Grain had to be milled into flour, and malt was also milled before brewing. Milling was one of the few truly industrial processes in the English countryside. Mechanised watermills and windmills had replaced the labour of hand-milling corn with a quern in the medieval period.[65] Corn tended to be milled in small batches as flour keeps much less well than unmilled grain. The transport category shows roughly equal numbers of women and men carrying corn to the mill: 18 women and 15 men.[66] Nor was mill-work an exclusively male affair: 33 per cent of milling work tasks were undertaken by women.[67] Some cases relate to customers helping to grind their own corn or malt, while others relate to women married to male millers. A defamation case from Moorlinch, Somerset, in 1605 recorded Joanna Tintyinge and James Allen, who were both servants of Alexander Walton, gentleman, visiting the house of Agnes Salter for 'grinding certain malt in a mill of the said Salter's', implying that Agnes Salter was running her own mill.[68]

The baking of flour into bread and other foods was undertaken both for household consumption and as a commercial occupation. Of the 15 work tasks that record people baking, 13 were done by women and

[63] TNA/KB/9/501a/40.
[64] Markham, *English Housewife*, p. 180; discussed in Roberts, '"To bridle the falsehood"'.
[65] Langdon, *Mills*. [66] Female-adjusted total. [67] Female-adjusted percentage.
[68] SHC, D/D/Cd/36, *Hucklebridge v. Salter.*

Table 6.6 *Gender division of labour in making alcoholic drinks*

	F tasks adj.	M tasks	Total tasks	% by F adj.
Make malt	16	6	22	72.1
Fetch ingredients	16	3	19	83.8
Brew beer	62	10	72	86.1
Make cider	0	4	4	0.0
Other (malt & brew)	5	2	7	72.1
Total	99	25	124	79.8

Notes: adj. = adjusted (x2.59).

2 by men. In seven cases they were baking bread, four relate to pies, and four tasks to other or unspecified baking. The gender balance was reversed for people with the occupation of baker: 3 were women and 11 men. The most common activity undertaken by people described as bakers was selling bread (7 instances). Only one of the bakers, Joan Mundyn of Cornwood in Devon in 1673, was actually recorded baking. Joan, who appeared in a long and complex church court case relating to a disputed will, also ran an alehouse, and is described purchasing malt, taking corn and malt to the mill, and selling bread and beer, as well as baking.[69] Brewing was part of a subset of food processing activities concerned with making alcoholic drinks. Judith Bennett has described how brewing ale, a female-dominated activity in medieval England, developed into male-dominated beer brewing in early modern England.[70] All 11 people with the occupation 'brewer' in the database were men. However, as Table 6.6 shows, women remained heavily involved in beer production.

Despite generalisations in early modern farming advice books about fieldwork being a male domain, women were actively involved in many areas of crop production. Processing grain into foodstuffs also involved both women and men: although men dominated the occupations of 'baker' and 'brewer', women dominated the work of baking and brewing.

6.3 Livestock

With an estimated 0.93 million cattle and 16.75 million sheep in England in 1600, animal husbandry was dominated by sheep and cattle.[71] Table 6.7 shows a breakdown of the main tasks related to farming

69 DHC, Chanter 875, 68v–84r. 70 Bennett, *Ale, Beer, and Brewsters*.
71 Broadberry et al., *British Economic Growth*, p. 106.

Table 6.7 *Gender division of labour in animal husbandry*

	F tasks adj.	M tasks	Total tasks	% by F adj.
Care of cattle	91	117	208	43.8
Milking	231	8	239	96.7
Care of sheep	67	247	314	21.3
Shearing sheep	28	64	92	30.4
Care of horses	52	130	182	28.6
Care of pigs	21	11	32	65.6
Care of poultry	49	20	69	71.0
Other animals	10	25	35	28.6
Hay harvest	75	128	203	37.0
Provide fodder	5	9	14	35.7
Total	629	759	1,388	45.3

Notes: adj. = adjusted (x2.59). Other animals = goats, rabbits, dogs, fish, bees. Provide fodder is for unspecified animals only – otherwise included in care of that animal.

livestock by gender of worker. This table includes milking and the hay harvest, a more expansive definition of livestock farming than the one used in the animal husbandry subcategory in Appendix B. This shows that women were more involved in pastoral farming than arable, carrying out 45 per cent of work tasks compared to 32 per cent for arable farming. However, this difference depends largely on how each type of farming is defined, with the classification of milking being crucial.[72] Rather than pastoral farming providing more employment for women, it is the presence of milk cattle and dairy production that led to higher demand for women's work in comparison to crop production. Without milking, women's contribution is 35 per cent – much closer to the level for arable farming. Nonetheless, this proportion demonstrates that women's involvement in keeping livestock was not confined to milking and raising poultry as some early modern advice books suggest.[73]

While fieldwork was heavily seasonal, concentrated particularly in the summer months, animal husbandry required constant work that was more evenly spread over the year. Nevertheless, as Figures 6.3 and 6.4 demonstrate, animal husbandry had a seasonality of its own, varying according to the type of animal and task concerned. The demands of

[72] The percentage of work tasks by women in animal husbandry including milking and haymaking is 45 per cent, and in arable production excluding haymaking and threshing and winnowing is 32 per cent. Including threshing and winnowing makes little difference to the arable proportion (32 per cent); excluding hay from animal husbandry also has little impact (47 per cent). Totals are adjusted figures in all cases.

[73] For example, Markham, *English Housewife*.

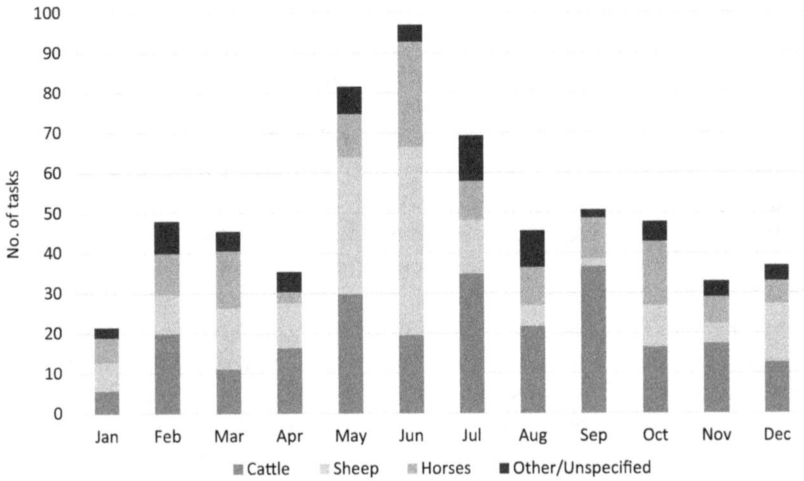

Figure 6.3 Animal husbandry: monthly distribution by animal type. *Notes*: Harvest additions and monthly weights applied: see Appendices C and D; Integral excluded; F adjusted (x2.36). This differs from the standard multiplier as it is designed to give an equal number of male and female tasks with weighted monthly data attached.

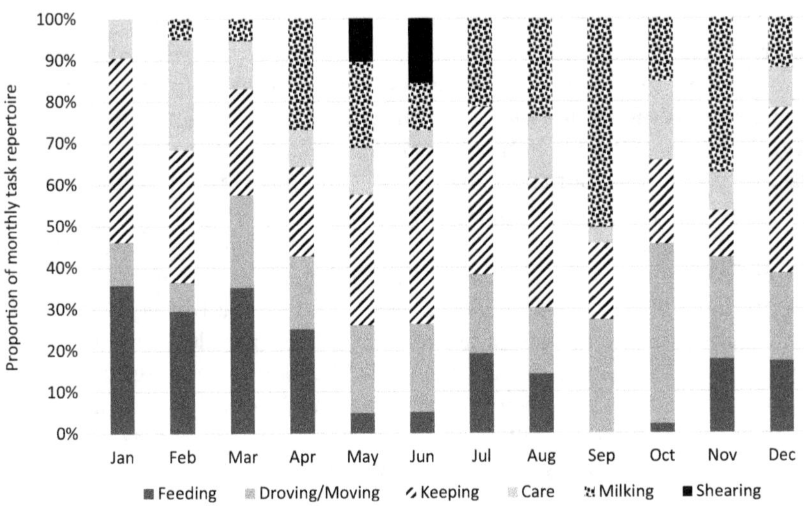

Figure 6.4 Animal husbandry: monthly repertoires by task type. *Notes*: Harvest additions and monthly weights applied: see Appendices C and D; Integral excluded; F adjusted (x2.36). This differs from the standard multiplier as it is designed to give an equal number of male and female tasks with weighted monthly data attached.

livestock farming were most intense from May to July, particularly if the hay harvest, shown in Figure 6.2, is also taken into account.

Much of the summertime peak in animal husbandry derived from the care of sheep and cattle in particular. Out of these, sheep washing and shearing was by far the most seasonal, with 83 per cent of these tasks concentrated in the months of May and June. Milking had a less pronounced but distinctive seasonality, with 75 per cent taking place in the summer half of the year. However, the production of these two resources, wool and milk, can only partly account for the summer peak in activity. The droving of livestock was also at its height in the spring quarter, with another bulge in the autumn. Most droving was related to sales, often at markets and fairs, but some movements related to animals grazed well away from home, perhaps on a seasonal basis. For instance, Richard Burge, who came from Spaxton near Bridgewater, pastured sheep on a 'parcel of ground' he rented on the Somerset coast at Brean 20 miles away, and then drove them to Bristol market, a further 30 miles, in June 1678.[74] Droving fell to a low in the winter quarter, when foddering reached its height. During these barren months, feeding, alongside the general maintenance or 'keeping' of beasts, became the most time-consuming livestock husbandry activity.

Table 6.8 explores the tasks involved in farming cattle. Women's almost total monopoly of milking was a distinctive feature of their farmwork in early modern England.[75] Our findings confirm women's domination of milking, although 8 out of 97 of milking work tasks were carried out by men. Five of these work tasks relate to men helping women, or being with women when they were milking, such as William Marten, who was described as 'going homewards from milking with his wife' in a tithe case at Wembdon, Somerset, in 1632.[76] Thomas Hesketh went with his wife 'to milk their cow' at Halsall in Lancashire in 1626.[77] Less ambiguous, although still open to interpretation, was William Ridwood of West Pennard in Somerset's statement in 1670 that 'he doth live by his labour and doth milk two cows', which appears to describe his work activities but might refer to his source of income.[78] The only clear case involved two men in Griston, Norfolk, who milked a cow belonging to another man in 1615: this was only detected because the farmer's wife noticed the cows were giving less milk.[79] Women went outside to milk, with the phrases 'went to milking' and 'came from milking' occurring repeatedly.

[74] SHC, Q/SR/138.1, 28–9. [75] Valenze, 'Art of women'.
[76] SHC, D/D/Cd/75, *Still v. Seaward.* [77] LaA, QSB/1/18, 36.
[78] SHC, D/D/Cd/93, *Farr v. Billingsley.*
[79] NRO, C/S3/20, Exam of Symon Wyndwood.

Table 6.8 *Gendered patterns in cattle farming*

Task type	F tasks adj.	M tasks	Total tasks	Types of cattle cared for	F tasks adj.	M tasks	Total tasks
Care	26	8	34	Unspec./mixed	36	55	91
Move	31	38	69	Male cattle	0	19	19
Feed	16	43	59	Female cattle	272	42	314
Keep	18	28	46	Calves	3	9	12
Milk	220	8	228				
Total	331	125	436		331	125	436

Notes: adj. = adjusted (x2.59). 'Care' includes medical care but also searching, rescuing, and cleaning; feeding includes providing fodder and water and leading to pasture; keeping includes many unspecific entries regarding 'looking to' or 'tending' cattle, as well as tethering and housing. Care of calves was only noted when calves were not with cows.

The regularity of these movements allowed one William Masters to commit adultery with Marie Allen in Pawlett, Somerset, in 1621 while his wife was 'at milking' and before her servants 'came from milking'.[80] Sometimes the cows were brought closer to the farmstead for milking, but in other cases women went to fields, passing neighbours on the way, as when Isabel Worthington 'was going to milk' one Friday morning and passed 'James Bullor stood at his own door' in Standish, Lancashire, in June 1657.[81] Trudging in and out to the fields at the beginning and end of each day was a time-consuming activity but one that refutes the idea of women working at home. As we have seen, it was a task often given to young unmarried women.[82]

It is clear from Table 6.8 that women's involvement in caring for cattle extended well beyond milking and included looking after herds of cows in the fields, leading them to water, feeding them hay, and droving and fetching them. The most significant difference between men's and women's work was in the type of cattle cared for. It was almost always men who cared for male cattle (bulls and bullocks), while women looked after cows, calves, and mixed groups. It is perhaps unsurprising that women's work extended beyond milking to other care activities for herds of milk cows, given the close relationship that the twice-daily milking of small herds was likely to entail. Where farms specialised in fattening bullocks for beef, women's involvement would have been much lower.

[80] SHC, D/D/Cd/55, *Masters v. Atyates*.

[81] LaA, QSB/1/1657, July, Exam of Isabel Worthington.

[82] See Table 6.3.

The processing of milk into butter and cheese was an indoor task rather than an outdoor one. This distinction was drawn with regard to Mistress Wood of East Anstey in Devon in 1686, who was described as 'not entrusted nor did concern herself with the management of her husband's estate or outdoor affairs' but did engage in 'the making of butter and cheese and such like'.[83] Fourteen work tasks recorded people making butter or cheese: all were women. The relatively small numbers recorded stem from a lack of detail about who carried out this task. Tithe cases sometimes required the amount of cheese produced to be stated but rarely specified who made it. A man from Selborne in Hampshire in 1564 was unusual when he stated that it was his wife and maids who typically made 30 cheeses from the milk of 8 kine (milk cows) each year.[84] Elizabeth Creston described how she was set to 'stir the butter' by her mistress, and did so for at least two hours, to explain why she had not observed what her mistress was doing with one Tom Wilmot in an upstairs chamber at Priddy in Somerset in 1617.[85] On the Somerset levels, some women ran dairies that were separate from the main farm. Anthoine Pearman was employed by a man who took her 'from Sanford to Burnham to a tenement which he had there and appointed her there to look to his dairy' in 1615. Similarly, Joan Buckland kept a dairy at Stenning in Stogursey in 1605.[86] A much larger number of work tasks recorded butter and cheese being transported and bought and sold. These tasks were also majority female, with 83 per cent carried out by women. Even when men were involved, traces of women's work are often evident. Jarred Doon reported going to Newcastle to sell 'all the butter and cheese his wife made' each week in a testamentary case in 1570.[87]

The hay harvest was essential for the survival of livestock, particularly cattle, over the winter months when low temperatures meant grass did not grow, and even covered it with snow. Examples of hay being fed to cattle, horses, sheep – and in one case from Norfolk, rabbits – are concentrated in the winter months between November and April. Such hay would have been harvested the previous summer, mostly between late June and mid-August, when it was mown with a scythe and then 'made' or dried in the field.[88] In a tithe dispute in Somerset in 1632 John Clement described haymaking in Woodberrie Meade in Camerton. After mowing, it 'lay on the ground for some few days', and then was tossed

[83] DHC, Chanter 8299, 22v–8v. [84] HRO, 21M65/C3/3, 256–7.
[85] SHC, Q/SR/33, 109–10.
[86] SHC, Q/SR/33, 77; SHC, D/D/Cd/36, *Ecclestone v. Huishe*.
[87] DUIC, DDR/EJ/CCD/1/2, 122r–4r.
[88] There was also some hay harvested in September, likely representing a second crop: four such cases were recorded in the south-west and two in the north.

and 'made up into small cocks' or heaps, and 'so stood some two or three days in such cocks'. Next, it was loaded onto a wain, with a maid raking after the wain to catch stray pieces, and carted back to the farm. The tithe hay, 'every tenth cock', was left in the field, and soon after was 'made up into greater cocks' by a man and his wife employed by the tithe owner. However, it was left too long in the field 'till by means of foul weather the same was spoiled and worth little or nothing', having originally been worth 10s.[89] The purpose of haymaking was to dry the cut grass so that it could be stored for later use. Wet hay rotted, as this case indicates. The necessity of good weather could delay and prolong haymaking, meaning that it sometimes overlapped with the grain harvest, intensifying labour demand in August.

While mowing was always done by men, haymaking – the raking, tossing, and heaping – was done by both men and women. Smith found that haymaking was an exclusively female task in late sixteenth-century Stiffkey in Norfolk, but the work-task data, and household accounts that record payments to haymakers, shows that it was a mixed task.[90] The adjusted figures indicate almost equal numbers of female and male haymakers: 67 and 62 respectively. Mowing was more strenuous, but haymaking required more work: Henry Best says two haymakers were needed for each mower 'as there are many things that belong to the tifting of hay, as spreading and sometimes turning, raking and cocking, throwing together and casting into the great cock'.[91] Using the adjusted figures, this is almost exactly the proportion of work tasks: 62 mowing tasks to 129 in haymaking.

There were many more sheep than people in early modern England.[92] The quarter sessions reveal sheep to have been particularly criminogenic: small enough to steal easily, but relatively high value. Of 339 animal husbandry work tasks drawn from theft cases, 186 relate to sheep, compared to 53 concerning horses, 39 to cattle, and 34 to poultry.[93] Women's involvement in sheep husbandry was lower than in cattle farming, yet they were nonetheless involved in all the aspects shown in Table 6.9. Where sheep were milked, this was done by women. Only four

89 SHC, D/D/Cd/75, *Hodson v. Love.*

90 Smith, 'Labourers [Part II]' p. 377; Whittle and Jiang, 'Gender, wages, and agricultural labour'.

91 Woodward (ed.), *Farming and Memorandum Books*, p. 34. Best provides a detailed description of early-seventeenth-century haymaking in Yorkshire, pp. 33–40.

92 4.1 million people and 16.75 million sheep: Wrigley and Schofield, *Population History*, p. 208; Broadberry et al., *British Economic Growth*, pp. 106.

93 There were also 10 cases relating to pigs, a few that mention dogs, and one relating to bees.

Table 6.9 *Gendered patterns in sheep farming*

Task type	F tasks adj.	M tasks	Total tasks	% by F adj.
Keep/feed	18	117	135	13.3
Drove/move	28	80	108	25.9
Shear	28	64	92	30.4
Mark	10	39	49	20.4
Wash	8	7	15	53.3
Medical care	3	4	7	42.9
Milk	10	0	10	100.0
Total	105	311	416	25.2

Notes: adj. = adjusted (x2.59). Droving relates to movement within the farm only, as longer-distance droving was recorded within the broader category of transport, not agriculture and land.

instances were noted, three from Hampshire in the late sixteenth century, and one from Ulverston, Lancashire (now Cumbria), where Dorothy Holmes sent her son 'to fetch in the ewes' so that she could milk them in 1636.[94] The busiest time of the sheep farming year was when flocks were washed and shorn, as depicted in the sixteenth-century English drawing shown in Figure 6.5. Only two cases of women washing sheep, from Wiltshire and Yorkshire, were recorded. Both came from coroners' reports of accidental death, suggesting the hazards of a task undertaken in rivers and streams. All our examples of female sheep shearers came from Devon and Somerset, such as Anne Josse and Wilmotta Smallridge, both married women, who deposed that 'they did shear ... yearly 50 sheep' for one Westcott of Holcombe Burnell, three years in a row from 1632 to 1634, in a Devon tithe case.[95] However, other types of evidence record female sheep shearers elsewhere in southern England, as well as for the medieval period.[96]

Farming advice books placed pigs and poultry under the care of housewives, as animals that were raised close to the house, and often fed with the waste from food processing and cooking.[97] Sometimes, these animals were even found inside the home. In 1651 John Wills of Sheepwash in Devon recounted how he came home at four in the

[94] LaA, QSB/1/176, 37–8. [95] DHC, Chanter 866, *Garnett v. Westcott*.

[96] Clark, *Working Life*, p. 62; Goldberg, *Women, Work, and Life Cycle*, pp. 139–40; Rogers, *History of Agriculture and Prices*, Vol. 1, p. 266.

[97] See, for instance, Fitzherbert, *Boke of Husbandry* (1523) in Goldberg, *Women in England*, p. 167. Advice on keeping pigs and poultry was still being given to housewives in the eighteenth century: Ellis, *Country Housewife's Family Companion*; Verdon, '"Subjects deserving"'.

Figure 6.5 Washing sheep.
Notes: Thomas Fella (compiler), *A booke of diveirs devises and sortes of pictures, with the alphabete of letters, deuised and drawne with the pen* (manuscript, 1585, 1593-4, 1622), f.51v. Call no. V.a.311. Image no. 23640. Folger Shakespeare Library.

afternoon and found 'within his house two hens or pullen walking and picking crumbs on the table board'. He was accused of stealing them but said they wandered in through a hole in the door.[98] In a dispute over pig ownership at Otterhampton in Somerset in 1679, Rachael Pilcorne fetched a pig from a neighbour's barn where it was being kept and put 'him in her dwelling house'. Elizabeth Score, who believed the pig was hers, then assaulted Pilcorne, and 'took the pig out of the house and carried him away and put him in her own dwelling house where she yet detained him'.[99] Table 6.7 shows that pigs and poultry were mostly, although not exclusively, cared for by women. Some work tasks fit the stereotype of the farming advice books as work allotted to housewives. For instance, Jane Whittell 'was desired by the wife of Christopher Asley to keep her two ducks and one drake, until such time that their corn was gotten in … [but] the said ducks were strayed away from her house' in Leigh, Lancashire in 1637.[100] However, it is notable that neither pig nor poultry keeping was strongly gendered: both men and women were involved.

Live animals provided milk, eggs, honey, wool, and in the case of horses and oxen, traction. But most animals were also kept for their meat. Quarter sessions cases relating to the theft of animals often also describe how they were killed, and sometimes how they were cooked. In 1614, when Margaret Harward of Tilney cum Ilsington in the Norfolk fens was challenged by a constable who found mutton baking in the oven of her house, she said it was 'parcel of the ewe of her husband's that was drowned … and she baked it not before that day and … she herself did flay the sheep'.[101] Similarly in Sherston Magna in Wiltshire in 1641, when asked what had happened to a pig, suspected of being stolen, one Palmer's wife 'answered that the said pig was killed and dressed by her'.[102] These cases demonstrate that women could butcher animals if they needed to. Yet the occupation of butcher was exclusively male, and indeed the great majority of work tasks recording the butchering of animals for red meat were undertaken by men – 260 compared to only 98 by women.[103] Butchering showed a distinct seasonal pattern. The traditional start to the slaughtering season was the Feast of St Martin (11 November), as livestock owners reduced their flocks and herds to save fodder during winter, and meat was purchased in preparation for Christmas.[104] The autumn quarter accounted for 38 per cent of butchery

[98] DHC, QS/4/Box 55, Easter, 9. [99] SHC, Q/SR/140.3, 12.
[100] LaA, QSB/1/190, 54.
[101] NRO, C/S3/19, Exam of Robert Howling and John Harward.
[102] WSHC, A1/110/1642H, 183. [103] Female-adjusted figures.
[104] See Section 4.2.

work tasks. The flurry of activity began in October and rose to an annual peak during December. Lent, when red meat could not be sold, brought a trough in March, before numbers rose again in April and May as the new season's animals became available. The lowest levels of butchering were in July and August: perhaps because hot weather made meat difficult to preserve and other foodstuffs were plentiful.

While pastoral farming is often characterised as employing more women than arable agriculture, historians are rarely specific about the tasks women or men were involved in. The work-task data confirms that pastoral agriculture made more use of women's labour, but the difference is not as great as is sometimes assumed and was largely the consequence of women's responsibility for milking. It should also be remembered that almost everywhere raising crops and livestock existed as symbiotic activities within individual farms. Husbandry manuals, which ignored women's labour caring for cattle and sheep, have also caused historians to underestimate the range of women's work tasks. Conversely, tasks such as haymaking and poultry keeping, often characterised as female, frequently involved male labour, underlining the flexibility of agricultural work patterns.

6.4 Commons, Woods, and Water

The rural economy depended on other resources which lay beyond arable fields and enclosed pastures. This section examines three of these: common pasture, woodland, and water (both freshwater and the sea).[105] All were characterised by complex sets of rights which governed uses and users in early modern England. These rights have been discussed in detail elsewhere.[106] Much less evidence is available about the types of work that these resources enabled and the workers who carried it out.[107] Debates around eighteenth-century enclosures present a picture of poorer households depending on the commons, with women and children earning or saving precious resources while men worked for wages.[108] As Andy Wood points out, in earlier periods the use of the

105 The common land discussed in this section excludes common arable fields and hay meadows.

106 Thompson, *Customs in Common*, pp. 97–184; Neeson, *Commoners*; Wood, *Memory of the People*; Bowen and Brown (eds.), *Custom and Commercialisation*; Winchester, *Common Land*.

107 For instance, Woodward's classic, 'Straw, bracken and the Wicklow whale', is more focused on resources than workers.

108 Snell, *Annals*, pp. 138–227; Humphries, 'Enclosures, common rights, and women'; Neeson, *Commoners*; see also Shaw-Taylor, 'Labourers, cows, common rights'.

commons was more socially varied. It was not only the poor who grazed their animals upon the common and collected fuel but also the members of wealthy and middling rural households.[109]

In addition to parish-level commons, the regions studied contained several extensive areas of common land. These included the upland moors of Dartmoor and Exmoor in the south-west, and the Pennine moorlands of Lancashire and Yorkshire. There were also lowland moors and fens, which were only partly drained in this period; most famously the fens of Lincolnshire, Cambridgeshire, and Norfolk but also the Somerset 'moors' or fens, and areas of lowland 'moss' in Lancashire and Cheshire.[110] Woods, although not extensive, were scattered across the countryside. These were often carefully managed as renewable resources. There were also areas described as 'forest': technically these were areas where forest law applied, protecting deer for hunting, although many, such as the New Forest, were areas of wood.[111] Of the counties studied, all except Wiltshire, Hertfordshire, Cambridgeshire, and Northamptonshire had sea coasts, providing opportunities for maritime fishing and gathering.[112]

Work concerning commons, woods, and areas of water is examined here using two main approaches. The first is to focus on the type of place and observe the activities carried out there. The second is to analyse the types of work that are likely to have been carried out in these environments: gathering food and fuel, wood husbandry, and hunting and fishing. Neither approach offers a complete picture. Many records of work tasks provide little indication of their exact location. Added to that, terms such as 'common' and 'moor' had multiple meanings and uses, which make some descriptions ambiguous. There were 235 work activities recorded as carried out in, or associated with, commons, moors, and fens. These activities indicate that such land was mostly rough pasture but could also be marsh or woodland. Women carried out 33 per cent of the 235 work tasks.[113] The majority of the work activities, 73 per cent, involved livestock-related activities, including caring for animals, moving them, buying and selling livestock, and butchery. Of the 35 butchery tasks recorded in connection to common land, the animals had either died on the common or been stolen from it. Most of the actual

[109] Wood, *Memory of the People*, p. 158.

[110] Fox, *Dartmoor's Alluring Uplands*; Ash, *Draining of the Fens*; Croot, *World of the Small Farmer*; Shannon, 'Risks and rewards'.

[111] Rackham, *Trees and Woodland*; Williamson et al., *Trees in England*; Warde, *Invention of Sustainability*, pp. 58–101.

[112] Fox, *Evolution of the Fishing Village*; Johnson, 'Economics of shipwreck'.

[113] Female-adjusted figure.

butchering took place at home, as when Oliver Nabb confessed he had taken two sheep from the common next to his house and 'killed them being forced to do so through hunger and want', in Bury, Lancashire, in 1643.[114] However, some butchering did take place opportunistically on commons. A group of four women from Sibsey in Lincolnshire were gathering wool in the fen in 1652 when they found a dead sheep 'with the eyes and entrails pulled out and not knowing whose it was they cased it and divided the skin and carcass amongst them'.[115]

Of the 83 work tasks that were related to keeping livestock on the common, 49 related to sheep, 23 to cattle, 5 each to horses and geese, and one to a pig. The pig, in a slightly comic case from 1674, was taken by its owner, a husbandman named Thomas Kithingman, to Leeds market. He failed to sell the animal and as he returned home the pig became tired, so Thomas left it on Shadwell Moor. Unsurprisingly, when his maid was sent to collect it the next morning, it had gone. It turned up later, dead, hanging in a butcher's shop in nearby Thorner.[116] In a number of cases, those caring for livestock on the commons were children and young people. In 1691 near Boston in Lincolnshire, John Wright had a cow and calf 'with about a score of other cattle' on 'the Eight Hundred fen wherein [he] hath right of common', and where his son was 'looking to the cattle'.[117] In the fens at Wisbech in Cambridgeshire in 1661, three siblings, 'Michael Dixon the younger and Mary Dixon his sister and one Richard Dixon his brother', were observed 'driving eight sheep upon the common', which were claimed to be stolen.[118] At Little Fransham in Norfolk in 1637, William Bluncall put his geese upon the common under the care of 'Widow Topping's daughter', who brought the geese home.[119] While at Wilmslow in Cheshire in 1672 a boy, Thomas Bradford, was responsible for 'driving Mary Royle's geese to the common'.[120] John Harnay of Gidleigh in Devon, who was 'sent to Dartmoor to see his master's flock of sheep' in 1669, was most likely a servant.[121] John Elton of King's Somborne in Hampshire described himself as a servant, keeping the sheep of a Mr Russell 'upon the Cowards Common', during a period from 1596 to 1598.[122]

Activities within the subcategories collecting fuel and gathering food, shown in Table 6.10, might be expected to take place on common land. In fact, Figure 6.6 shows that only 12 out of these 211 work tasks were

[114] LaA, QSB/1/285, 50. [115] LiA, LQS/A/1/13, 37. [116] WYAS, QS1/13/4/2, 9.
[117] LiA, HQS/A/1/1691, Info of John Wright. [118] CUL, EDR/E10/109, 7–16, 21–2.
[119] NRO, C/S3/31, Info of William Bluncall. [120] CALS, QJF/100/3, 58.
[121] DHS, QS/4/Box 84–5, Easter, 8–9. [122] HRO, 21M65/C3/11, 198–201.

Table 6.10 *Gender division of labour in collecting fuel and gathering food*

	F tasks adj.	M tasks	Total tasks	% by F adj.
Cut wood	0	14	14	0.0
Gather/fetch wood	49	43	92	53.3
Cut/fetch gorse	0	5	5	0.0
Dig/fetch turf	0	12	12	0.0
Fetch dung	3	0	3	100.0
Pick vegetables (cultivated)	10	8	18	55.6
Pick fruit (cultivated)	23	23	46	50.0
Glean grain	91	13	104	87.5
Collect honey	10	0	10	100.0
Collect wild plants/food	26	11	37	70.3
Total	212	129	341	62.2

Notes: adj. = adjusted (x2.59).

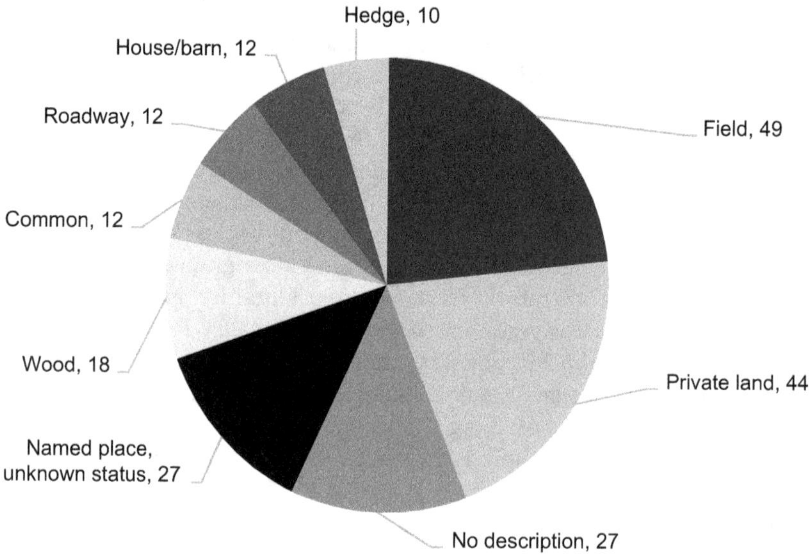

Figure 6.6 The location of collecting fuel and gathering foods.

clearly specified as taking place on commons, all of which related to collecting fuel. No tasks related to gathering food were described as taking place on a common. This was in part because many of the food-gathering activities either related to gathering cultivated fruit or vegetables, or to gleaning arable fields for dropped grain: both of these activities were more likely to take place on land belonging to specific people (private land).[123]

In some cases the status of the land, and thus legality of the activity, was under dispute. This was particularly true of hedges. Collecting firewood from hedges, or 'hedge breaking', was frequently forbidden and subject to fines in local by-laws.[124] Of the 10 work tasks that recorded gathering resources from hedges, all implied disputed ownership. Four related to gathering fruit: two from plum trees that grew in hedges, and two from currant bushes where the fruit hung over the hedge from a garden. Three tasks related to a group of women who raked hedges for barley as well as gleaning – presumably gathering stalks of grain that had fallen from the farm carts. The final three related to taking wood from hedges. An attempt to discredit Robert Stuckye of Muchelney in Somerset in 1604 described him as a 'very poor man and one that hath wasted his estate and that doth use now and then to cut a stick out of other men's hedges'.[125] At Collingbourne Ducis in Wiltshire in 1570 Elizabeth Blansdon argued with two building workers at a parsonage over whether 'certain hedge wood' was taken from their employer's hedge.[126] George Gilmore, accused of stealing bits of wood in Wiltshire in 1653, said he 'had cut them out of a hedge'.[127] Some activities that took place in roadways had similar implications, as when Elizabeth Hunt claimed she 'did take two pieces of a rotten tree in the Kingsway which was found' in Bradford on Tone in Somerset in 1679, and Robert Lawrance of Merriott, also Somerset, in 1668, who 'took up wood in the highway', both arguing that the wood was not stolen.[128]

Table 6.10 shows interesting patterns of gendered work, although the small numbers mean these should be treated with caution. For instance, while all the examples of cutting turf related to men, other sources record women's involvement in drying and transporting peat for fuel in the late seventeenth century.[129] The division between cutting or digging fuel (male) and collecting and fetching it (mixed, with a slight predominance of women) does seem significant. On the other hand, gleaning, and collecting wild foods and plants, were mainly undertaken by women.

[123] Gleaning was a disputed customary right on private land: see King, 'Customary rights', pp. 469–72.
[124] McIntosh, *Controlling Misbehaviour*, pp. 84–8.
[125] SHC, D/D/Cd/36, *Waggott v. Baker.* [126] WSHC, D1/42/7, *Rives v. Blansdon.*
[127] WSHC, A1/110/1653M, 246.
[128] SHC, D/D/Cd/106, *Colthurst v. Hayse*; SHC, Q/SR/111, 2–3.
[129] For example, the wage accounts of Sarah Fell, relating to Swarthmoor in Lancashire (now Cumbria) in the 1670s: see Penney (ed.), *Household Account Book*.

The plants collected included weeds to feed to pigs, thistles and teasels for brewing, cowslips and primroses, herbs to make 'rosa solis' (a type of cordial), crab apples and bullaces, nuts and acorns.[130] Fruit, however, was mostly gathered in orchards, which were overwhelmingly private. The vegetables that were 'gathered' – rather than harvested in the fields – included turnips 'fetched' from a field, and cabbages from a winter garden. The majority, however, relate to fresh peas, or 'peascods'. In 1632 in Wiltshire, a man's wife 'did gather a capful [of peas] and no more' as part of an allowance to top up her husband's wages.[131] Edith Prankett gathered half a quart of peas, before they were taken off her by a man who was later accused of stealing them, in Somerset in 1618.[132] A boy was more clearly in the wrong when he was found to have 'plucked [peas] off from horses carrying tithe peas', also in Somerset in 1668.[133]

Wood husbandry and hedging were two distinctly male work activities. Together 181 tasks were recorded in these two subcategories of which only six were undertaken by women. England had few extensive tracts of woodland and trees were a valuable resource, growing both in woods and as part of the hedgerows that enclosed many fields, and used for fuel and timber. The most common tasks recorded were felling trees, accounting for 50 work tasks, and lopping wood from living trees, which accounted for 43. Coroners' reports into accidental death provided 40 per cent of these tasks, including 56 per cent of tasks that involved felling trees, and 65 per cent of lopping wood, highlighting the dangers involved. For example, John Spycer was hired to work in Castle Camps park in Cambridgeshire in February 1565 and was sent 'to cut certain branches of the trees to feed the animals there in the extreme or snowy weather … he went to a oak tree with a hatchet in his hand and climbed it but stood on a small or slender bough to cut another branch growing a little higher', when the higher branch fell knocking him to the ground.[134]

As well as felling trees and lopping wood, a range of commonplace but less dangerous tasks are recorded: making faggots, cutting felled wood, maintaining hedges, and making fences. Just as women's group work weeding in the fields provided a setting for defamation, so did men's hedging work. John Carter 'was at hedging or making of a hedge with Richard Skerne … one William Towker did work by the further side of the hedge' when defamatory words were exchanged in Brixham, Devon, in 1559.[135] Less frequently recorded tasks included making charcoal, cutting rushes or reeds, brambles or 'thorns', and bracken, and cutting

[130] Also unspecified 'flowers'. [131] WSHC, A1/110/1632M, 195.
[132] SHC, Q/SR/31, 12. [133] SHC, Q/SR/111, 107–8. [134] TNA/KB/9/610b/169.
[135] DHC, Chanter 855, *Welthine Hazzard v. Richard Skerne.*

twigs to make brooms. Here there was some involvement of women, engaged in tasks such as cutting rushes and sedge, gathering birch twigs and brambles to make brooms, and making 'wyth kidds'. This last activity, which took place in an unnamed Lincolnshire parish in 1656, involved cutting and bundling pliable willow twigs, which were used for rope.[136] Wood husbandry was concentrated in the winter and spring, which together accounted for 64 per cent of the tasks carried out, and reached a low point in the summer, with only 14 per cent. Collecting fuel followed a similar seasonal pattern, although people fetched wood and faggots most often during the three-month period from December to February.

In contrast, hunting and fishing was concentrated in the warmer spring months. Poaching (illegal hunting and fishing), like other forms of theft, was not recorded in the work-task database when it was the cause of prosecution. Thus, the hunting recorded was either legal or its legality was not the main issue of the case. As a consequence, cases of accidental deaths were the most common source of hunting and fishing work tasks, providing 32 per cent. Tithe cases were also a valuable source of evidence, particularly for fishing, providing a further 21 per cent. Like wood husbandry and hedging, hunting and fishing was overwhelmingly the work of men. Only two women are recorded: Jane Felde caught coots in a pond in her father's garden at Hitchen in Hertfordshire in 1511, and Jane Coper who fished in the tidal channel at Salthouse in Norfolk in 1571.[137] Catching freshwater fish was the most common type of activity in the hunting and fishing subcategory accounting for 40 per cent of tasks, followed by catching and scaring wild birds at 22 per cent, catching sea fish at 16 per cent, and hunting and trapping rabbits at 13 per cent. The remaining 9 per cent fell into a miscellaneous category. The most hunted birds were rooks and crows: they were killed as a nuisance to farmers, for sport, and in the case of chicks, sometimes for food.[138] Other birds mentioned included kites, owls, ravens, magpies, jays, wild ducks and geese, herons, woodcocks, partridges, and martins. Rabbits or conies were kept in protected warrens but still had to be caught by the warreners, typically using nets with dogs or ferrets to flush the rabbits out. Rabbits did not respect boundaries and were also hunted by those with neighbouring land, or illegally. Unusually Richard Smyth of Axminster, Devon, was shooting rabbits in a hedgerow with a bow and arrow in 1515.[139] The miscellaneous hunting tasks included six cases of unspecified

[136] LiA, LQS/A/1/15, 206. [137] TNA/KB/9/459/9; TNA/KB/9/629b/281.

[138] Fifteen work tasks related to rooks and crows, while no other bird was mentioned more than three times.

[139] TNA/KB/9/966/66.

hunting, four cases involving park keepers protecting game, three of catching moles, one of catching polecats, and one of setting a dog on a sheep to kill it. Deer featured only in the activities of park keepers. In two separate but related cases from Northamptonshire in 1671, two pairs of keepers reported watching for deer and poachers in Astell Park and Whittlewood Forest.[140]

Freshwater fishing most often involved catching eels, but trout, carp, pickerel, lampreys, and perch are also mentioned. Fish were typically caught in nets, sometimes from boats and sometimes from the bank or wading into the river or pond. Occasionally more detail was provided: at Mary Tavy in west Devon in 1690 'the said William Mare was in the water fishing and David Mare was by the side of the river assisting', at a place called St Mary's pool 'towards the lower end of the said pool with a net hanging on a long pole (which this deponent doth believeth was a net commonly called a Tramell)'.[141] Kettle nets and bow nets are also mentioned, along with pots lying in the water to catch fish in a mill pond and traps called 'leapes'. Three cases mentioned angling or using an angling rod. One man caught a fish (a pickerel) with a hook on a piece of string, while another described using his hands.

The examples of sea-fishing in the database are geographically uneven. Of the 27 tasks recorded, 23 come from south Devon, and predominantly from a set of tithe disputes ranging in date from 1556 to 1662.[142] Eleven of the 27 tasks originate in 3 related tithe disputes from Torbay parishes dating from 1594 to 1595 and are exceptionally interesting. In 1595, William Ball described how in the last 12 years he had 'hath set out for Newfoundland' each year. Balthazar Bounde outdid this stating that 'about 30 years ago he … did begin to travel to Newfoundland and continued the same every year (unless he was pressed into the queen's ships) by the space of 13 years together … he and the rest of his company did always pay the tithe of the Newfoundland fish brought home by them in barques or ships'.[143] A string of men from the neighbouring parishes of St Marychurch, Tor Mohun, and Cockington made similar statements, noting that the ships returned from Newfoundland at the end of August, and the tithe of preserved fish was paid each Easter. Some named the ships they sailed in, such as the 'Judith of Stonehouse', 'a ship of Plymouth', 'the Grace of Dartmouth', and 'a ship of Poole [Dorset] called the Royal'. These depositions make clear the international scope of fishing by this date.[144] Closer to home, but still

[140] NAS, QSR/1/61, 7–14. [141] DHC, QS/4/Box 127, Info of Degory Howey.
[142] Fox, *Evolution of the Fishing Village*, offers a study of coastal fishing in this region.
[143] DHC, Chanter 864, *Carye v. Wheeler*. [144] Ibid., and *Carye v. Saunder et al.*

travelling widely, Philip Croppe sailed in one Thomas Seyes' boat of Exmouth, catching mulwell, pollock, and ling off Scarborough in the North Sea in 1559, and herring off Great Yarmouth in Norfolk in 1560.[145] In 1614 Thomas Grant described how he 'used the trade of fishing with his 3 boats and nets and hooks' and he 'himself or such fishermen as he hath employed therein' caught 'pilchards, plaice, hake, bream, [and] haddock [and] landed them at East Teignmouth, sold the bulk to fish "jowkers" and divided the rest amongst the company'. He paid his tithes in nearby Bishopsteignton rather than East Teignmouth.[146]

The Vicar of West Alvington's claims that the local fishermen of South Huish and Malborough were short-changing his tithes in 1556 led to a detailed account of how coastal fishing was organised and paid in that locality. John Hinxton, the owner of two fishing boats and a seine net, landed 12,000 mackerel in June that year, along with 64 porpoises, together worth £33 6s 8d. The fishermen went to sea in groups of 4 or 5 boats, and each boat had a crew of 5 or 6 men. These included men such as 60-year, old John Gerves, and were variously described as a company, servants, labourers, and mariners. Custom dictated a complex division of the catch between boat and net-owners, crew-members, the local manorial lord, and the church. Members of the community gathered on the shore to see the catch divided and observed the fish being sold. The nub of the dispute was that the vicar did not receive one-tenth of the catch. Hinxton instead paid the tithes of mackerel and porpoises following practices used 'for at least forty years', which dictated that the catch was first divided in half with half going to the lord of the manor. The other half was divided between the men who drew in the seine net: 'if there be forty men drawing they shall have forty parts'. The vicar received only 'so much as one man hath'.[147]

The wide range of activities surveyed in the section is a reminder that although arable and livestock farming had the primary claim on labour in rural England, many work activities related to other resources were fitted into the seasonal cycle. It was not just the poor but those of all levels of wealth who made use of commons, woods, and water, providing extra pasture and fodder, fuel, timber, and wild foods. The activities reveal a 'taskscape' of rural England and beyond where every piece of land, tree, or water served a useful and often carefully managed purpose for the

[145] DHC, Chanter 855, *Farmers of Kenton v. Phillip Croppe.*

[146] DHC, Chanter 867, *Lyle v. Grant.*

[147] DHC, Chanter 855, *Vicar of Alvington v. Hinxton.*

local population, and workers ranged from children looking after geese on the common to crews of men sailing to Newfoundland.[148]

6.5 Conclusion

The work-task data reveals much about agricultural labour and food production in early modern England that has previously been hidden. Existing studies of agricultural labour have had to rely on the wage accounts of large farms, farming advice books, and probate inventories to investigate the profile of workers and tasks undertaken. Work tasks allow the previously hidden activity within family farms and food processing businesses to be retrieved, as well as work outside the farm using common resources. They suggest a more overlapping and flexible division of labour than was previously appreciated and reveal the significant role of women as agricultural workers. Women carried out more than a third of total agricultural work tasks, undertaking both paid work as servants and labourers, and unpaid work on their own farms or farms of family members. Food processing tasks reveal a majority female workforce in brewing and baking, despite the male predominance in the occupations of brewer and baker; butchering tasks were more male but nonetheless show that women were capable of butchering sheep and pigs.

As the Hertfordshire tithe case discussed in the chapter's introduction illustrates, farms depended on a varied workforce of men and women, family members, and workers employed on a variety of contracts. The work patterns of yeomen, husbandmen, labourers, and male servants were characterised by differences in emphasis rather than radically different work repertoires. Yeomen and male servants did a higher proportion of work with animals, husbandmen more crop cultivation, and labourers more wood husbandry than other male workers. Similarly, the agricultural work of female servants, wives, and widows had contrasting but overlapping profiles. Servants did more milking, wives more gleaning, and the work profiles of widows were closer to those of men. Women's higher participation in pastoral farming was almost entirely due to female dominance of milking; with milking excluded, their participation rates in pastoral and arable husbandry were similar at around a third. Errors made by historians and economists seeking to characterise the rural labour force often stem from a failure to appreciate the flexibility of farming and the workforce. If insufficient male mowers were available, harvests could be brought in by women using sickles; if insufficient

148 Ingold, 'Temporality of the landscape'.

female servants were available to milk a dairy herd, wives, daughters, and female labourers could also be deployed, or cows sold to reduce the labour demand; when widows found themselves without a husband's labour, they not only employed male servants but also undertook some majority-male tasks themselves. The art of good husbandry and housewifery was thrift.[149] That meant ensuring that no resources, from land, labour, and livestock, to woods, hedges, and water, went to waste: the work-task data provides ample evidence of this system in motion in early modern England.

149 See especially, Tusser, *Five Hundred Points*.

7 Crafts and Construction

In April 1661, Thomas Chapman, broad-weaver of Studley, Wiltshire, bought some Spanish white wool from a local clothier, which he took to Edward Baylie of Trowbridge to be dyed. After Chapman 'mixed … and broke' the dyed wool himself, his wife and sister spun it into yarn; he later took this to the shop of another broad-weaver of Studley, who wove it into cloth for Chapman on his loom.[1] Nearly a century earlier, in 1564, three local artisans were contracted to patch up the dilapidated vicarage of Bradford St Peter, Yorkshire. The slater William Dockley was hired to make repairs to the building 'in stone', while 84-year-old wright John Hayre and 50-year-old carpenter Thomas Hayre were paid £8 and bound to do the same 'in timber work'.[2] In the same county, about hay harvest in 1669, John Corker of Rotherham, cobbler, came to the shop of blacksmith James Tomson in Whiston to sell pieces of scrap iron, which he had received in payment for 'mending shoes for the workmen' and their wives at a Rotherham forge. Tomson, then being sick, directed his journeyman servant John Oldfield to weigh and pay for the iron, some of which the journeyman and Tomson's apprentice Richard Carr 'presently wrought up' in the shop.[3] Unlike Tomson and his servants, James Fisher and Thomas Oxenham of Ottery St Mary, Devon, carried out their craftwork away from the household. In 1614, the two tailors worked at their trade some 10 miles distant 'in the house of Mr John Stone of Luppitt', alongside Stone's daughter Dorothy, who sat 'near the window … making bone lace'.[4]

These four episodes illustrate the range of craftwork and construction captured in the work-task database, and how it can speak to the experience of industry in early modern England. The various steps of textile production delineated in Chapman's case imply a sharp but not immutable gender division of labour in England's largest industry. As the case

[1] WSHC, A1/110/1662T, 185. [2] BI, CP.G.1164, *Taylor v. Oakden.*
[3] WYAS, QS1/9/2/2, 3–4; QS1/9/2/3, 1–2.
[4] DHC, Chanter 867, *Follett v. Stone and Tottle.*

from Devon suggests, this extended to the process of turning textiles into clothing. Women like Dorothy were more likely to engage in the making of lace, stockings, and underclothing, while men like James Fisher could pursue the professional trade of tailoring, associated with outerwear production. The latter dichotomy highlights how the apprenticeship system excluded women from many industries, like those of building, smithing, and shoemaking referenced above. John Oldfield and Richard Carr grant some insight into the realities of this training system in a master craftsman's household, revealing the delegation and division of commercial and artisanal tasks. Apprenticeship for seven years was mandatory for rural crafts like blacksmithing under the Statute of Artificers, but this case suggests the law was not always strictly followed; Carr only served apprentice to Tomson 'for the space of three years' before he became a smith in his own right. In addition to issues of gender, occupation, training, and regulation, all of these cases bring to light the fine details of industrial or manufacturing work in the countryside, from workplace to employment and wage arrangements.

This chapter explores these themes using the tasks in the crafts and construction category of the work-task dataset. This includes mining and quarrying, building and construction work, working with wood and metal, mill maintenance, textile and clothing production, and other miscellaneous forms of manufacture. Work in this category was the most sharply gendered in the dataset, often being the remit of men with specialist occupations, described as craftsmen or artisans, who entered those occupations via apprenticeship. Textile and clothing production are the two largest subcategories, and the only subcategories in which women outnumbered men: these are examined in detail below. Building and construction, a form of work that dominates studies of wages and living standards, as well as some detailed studies of employment practices, are also given particular attention. In contrast to textile and clothing production, women were almost entirely absent from this subcategory.

To understand the sharp gender division of labour in craft production, it is necessary to consider how people entered these forms of work, and, conversely, how they were excluded from some occupations. In early modern society, apprenticeship was the dominant means of entering specialist occupations. The 1563 Statute of Artificers made it illegal to enter 'any craft, mystery or occupation' without serving a seven-year apprenticeship, although the extent to which this was enforced remains unclear.[5] Apprenticeship registers from guilds in large towns indicate

[5] Statutes of the Realm: 5 Elizabeth, chapter 4, clause 24. On enforcement, see Davies, *Enforcement of English Apprenticeship*.

that girls were only rarely apprenticed, although the apprenticeship of women became more common in the late seventeenth and early eighteenth centuries in London and elsewhere.[6] How apprenticeship was organised away from large towns remains poorly documented, although private apprenticeship agreements must have been common. Craft apprenticeships should not be confused with pauper or parish apprenticeships, compulsory unpaid work placements which were organised for orphans and the children of the labouring poor.[7] However, the records of charities and overseers of the poor suggest there was always a range of apprenticeship agreements: high premiums were paid to enter profitable trades and crafts, smaller premiums to enter occupations with more limited prospects, while householders might be paid to take on parish apprentices.

Much of the literature about apprenticeship in economic history stresses its role in human capital formation, seeing apprenticeship as an investment by parents in training that improved their children's future standard of living.[8] Yet Ogilvie's gendered perspective on guilds and apprenticeship emphasises the darker side of this system, which seems to have excluded women from profitable occupations.[9] It is notable that England's labour legislation, the main method for regulating apprenticeship outside of large towns, did not explicitly restrict women from apprenticeship, but nonetheless the work-task data confirms that women are notably absent from apprenticed crafts. There were alternative routes for women to participate in craft occupations. Non-apprenticed training allowed women to become skilled in crafts such as spinning, plain sewing, lacemaking, and stocking knitting. Women who married craftsmen might help to run their businesses, and ultimately run the businesses themselves after their husband's death. Yet as the work-task data on artisans' wives makes clear, even if a woman ran a blacksmithing or carpentry business or contributed to the financial management tasks necessary to run businesses, she did not undertake the metalworking or woodworking.[10]

Historians studying work in early modern crafts and industry have relied primarily on wage accounts, occupational descriptors in parish,

[6] Snell, *Annals*, pp. 270–319; Ben-Amos, *Adolescence and Youth* pp. 133–45; Gowing, *Ingenious Trade*.

[7] Fisher, 'Bound to the Soil (Part I)' and 'Bound to the Soil (Part II)'; Wallis, 'Apprenticeship in England'; Lane, *Apprenticeship in England*, pp. 71–83; Dunlop and Denman, *English Apprenticeship*, pp. 248–60.

[8] Mokyr, 'Economics of apprenticeship', offers a summary.

[9] Ogilvie, *Bitter Living*, pp. 320–52, esp. 329–31 and *European Guilds*, pp. 232–305.

[10] See Table 2.18 for the repertoires of artisans' wives.

legal, and probate records, and records of labour law enforcement.[11] For certain types of industries, like mining, the records of specialist courts have also proved valuable.[12] Together these sources, while rich, tend to prioritise large building projects and enterprises, exclude the contributions of women and workers engaged in non-apprenticed trades, and privilege occupational designations over the actual experience and practice of work. The work-task data can cast light on some of these blind spots, but it is of course shaped and sometimes limited by the type and provenance of the depositions used to collect it. The largest share of textile, clothing, and metalwork-related tasks, for instance, comes from quarter session theft cases, with defamation cases from the church courts making up the second-largest source. In contrast, the source profile for building, woodwork, and groundworks is made up predominately of coroners' reports into accidental deaths and church court cases related to ecclesiastical property, such as pew disputes and vicarage dilapidation cases.

There are also some forms of industrial labour which the work-task approach has been less successful at recording. Very few mining and quarrying activities have been collected, totalling less than 0.5 per cent of all male tasks. However, this is likely an accurate reflection of the small size of the sector relative to the national labour force, as well as its highly localised nature.[13] More concerning is the underrepresentation of spinning in the dataset. Craig Muldrew has estimated that carding and spinning made up between 50 and 65 per cent of the labour required to turn wool into cloth, depending on the type of cloth, during the period.[14] Spinning and carding activities combined make up around 43 per cent of the total (female adjusted) textile production tasks in the database; somewhat less than might be expected.[15] The reason for this underrepresentation is not wholly clear, but it is likely that spinning was so ubiquitous as to be hardly worth comment in testimonies. It is also a consequence of it frequently being described simply as 'work'. When in

[11] See for example Stephenson, *Contracts and Pay;* Airs, *Tudor and Jacobean Country House;* Woodward, *Men at Work;* Muldrew, '"Th'ancient distaff"'; Keibek and Shaw-Taylor, 'Early modern rural by-employments'; Thirsk, 'Industries in the countryside'; Davies, *Enforcement of Apprenticeship.*

[12] See for example Wood, *Politics of Social Conflict.*

[13] This aligns with CamPop's findings that 'in 1600 only around 0.3 per cent of the adult male labour force were miners': 'Share of the labour force in mining', CamPop, Economies Past [website].

[14] Muldrew, '"Th'ancient distaff"', pp. 504–5.

[15] This total excludes integral tasks, which inflate the number of 'gather wool' tasks, but also bring the percentage of 'spinning' down. Female multiplier applied; without the multiplier, spinning tasks make up 26 per cent of textile production, excluding integral.

1679 Mary Skatt of Warminster, Wiltshire, described herself and 'other neighbours sitting at their doors at work, as is custom in summertime', they were probably spinning, but this is never specified.[16] Nonetheless, as the example of the actions of Chapman's wife and sister at the start of the chapter shows, the depositional evidence does pick up illuminating details about spinning, and these are explored in greater depth below. Tasks like spinning, which were almost wholly done by non-apprenticed women, throw light on the tangled ideas of specialism, skill, and gender, which shaped craftwork during this period. The rest of the chapter works to unravel this web, starting with an overview of artisanal occupations, apprenticeship, and their relationship to work tasks in the category of craftwork and construction.

7.1 Occupations and Apprenticeship

The Statute of Artificers aimed to restrict most crafts to specialists trained via a seven-year apprenticeship, but to what extent did rural reality reflect these rules? Men with craft occupations account for nearly 65 per cent of craftwork tasks performed by male workers.[17] Figure 7.1 breaks down these artisans into categories, according to the character or materials of their industry.[18] Makers of textiles, clothes, and leather products together form the largest proportion, while artisans linked to food (food processors and millers) and construction (builders and many woodworkers such as carpenters) make up sizable groups as well.[19] These proportions align well with other occupational surveys of the period, suggesting that the work-task sample is largely representative of craftsmen in the English population as a whole.[20]

Also illuminating here is the strong correlation between craftwork and the recording of occupational descriptors. Overall, witnesses or scribes were much more likely to note occupational descriptors when craftwork was involved, even incidentally in a case, as opposed to other activities such as agriculture or transport. Occupational descriptors were recorded

[16] WSHC, D1/42/61, 136. See also DHC, Chanter 867, *Bully v. Turpyn.*

[17] When workers lacking any descriptors are included, artisans account for around 50 per cent.

[18] Integral tasks have been excluded because they inflate the number of food processors (specifically butchers).

[19] Millers might be involved in textile production (fulling mills) instead of or in addition to grain milling, but such details are rarely provided in the sources.

[20] See CamPop's 'The share of the labour force in the secondary sector', Economies Past [website]. The work-task percentages line up well with CamPop's shares of adult male labour force c.1600, although the work-task results record significantly more builders when carpenters are included in the tally. See also Sections 1.1 and 2.4.

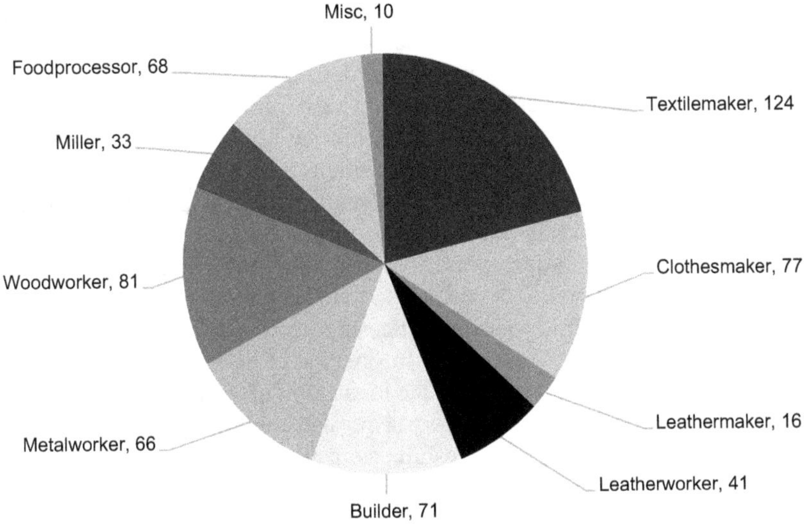

Figure 7.1 Male artisan actors in the dataset.
Notes: Integral excluded. The graph categorises those male actors (individuals who performed a work task) with artisanal occupations, according to the character or materials of their industry. Textilemaker includes comber, cardmaker, clothmaker, clothier, draper, dyer, feltmaker, flax-dresser, fuller, roper, and weaver. Clothesmaker includes button-maker, fringe-maker, hatter, hosier, sheet-maker, stockinger, and tailor. Leathermaker includes currier, fellmonger, skinner, and tanner. Leatherworker includes cordwainer, glover, saddler, and shoemaker/cobbler. Builder includes bricklayer, dauber, glazier, hellier/thatcher/slater/tiler, mason, millwright, plumber, and waller. Metalworker includes bellfounder, brasier, cutler, farrier, furbisher, ironmonger, nailor, pewterer, pinmaker, smith (black, gold, lock, white), tinker, and tinner. Woodworker includes carpenter, cooper, joiner, ploughwright, sawyer, shipwright, turner, and wheelwright.

for 72 per cent of male craftwork and construction tasks compared to 57 per cent of male tasks overall. Upon describing craft or building work, deponents often volunteered how they or the worker was 'a joiner by trade', 'a goldsmith by his occupation' or 'wrought at his trade of a weaver to which he had been apprentice'.[21] This pattern implies that witnesses deemed occupational details more relevant in such cases,

[21] SHC, D/D/Cd/75, *Needes v. Harris*; DHC, Chanter 859, *Buller v. Denys*; Chanter 875, *Osborne v. Andrewes*.

reflecting a popular association of craft labour with skilled occupations, as well as a desire to justify artisanal work with relevant qualifications. After all, even the seemingly incidental description of labour associated with regulated trades or crafts could have legal implications for witnesses, because practising a trade without apprenticeship remained a target of public presentments and private informants throughout the period.[22] Indeed, while the data points towards high rates of apprentice-training in rural craftwork, craft activities performed by those who were not apprenticed may be underrepresented due to the influence of the labour laws. Whatever the reality of craftwork, the *idea* that it should be specialised, male, and entered via apprenticeship seems to have been deeply embedded. Most crafts, trades, or 'mysteries' of early modern England were inextricably interwoven with the institution of apprenticeship, as the first step and primary means to acquiring skills and credentials.

In the prototypical apprenticeship, teenage boys were bound to live, work, and train with a master craftsman or tradesman for a set number of years. Upon graduating to the rank of journeyman, they would then labour for wages, in a position similar to an annual servant, until they accumulated enough capital to establish their own household and trade as a master. While medieval guilds and companies had long regulated trade and craftwork in urban communities through this mechanism, the 1563 Statute of Artificers made a minimum seven-year apprenticeship mandatory across the kingdom. Yet because most source material on apprenticeship derives from civic guilds and corporations, very little scholarship has explored its experience in the countryside, where the majority of English craftsmen resided.[23] It is here that the work-task database provides a valuable perspective. About 86 per cent of the work tasks attributed explicitly to apprentices or artisan servants in the task data took place outside the guild-dominated large towns. This section gives a quantitative overview of this evidence, followed by a qualitative exploration of artisanal training in rural contexts.

While apprentices, journeymen, domestic servants, and labourers were all discrete types of workers employed by tradesmen, contemporaries did not always honour these distinctions with precise terminology. In building and farm accounts, for example, craftsmen's assistants were often simply described as their 'men' or 'boys'.[24] Similar issues of ambiguity

[22] Davies, *Enforcement of English Apprenticeship*, pp. 77–107.

[23] Wallis, 'Apprenticeship in England', esp. p. 248, n. 2. According to the estimates of Wrigley, *People, Cities, and Wealth*, p. 170, around 22 per cent of the total English population in 1600 was 'rural non-agricultural', while just 8 per cent lived in urban areas.

[24] Woodward, *Men at Work*, p. 40; Whittle and Griffiths, *Consumption and Gender*, p. 227.

hamper the identification of apprentices and journeymen in the depositional evidence. For example, in a case from Somerset in 1668, some witnesses described Augustine Sellwood as a servant to locksmith Thomas Dryer, while others, Sellwood included, used the word 'apprentice'.[25] The broad 'servant' designation may thus obscure additional apprentices in the sample. As is explored in more detail below, even when workers were explicitly described as apprentices, the possibility remains that they were parish apprentices, rather than traditional craft apprentices. Identifying journeymen and tradesmen's servants is fraught for similar reasons. Deponents very occasionally testified as a 'journeyman' or spoke of doing 'journey work' of a certain trade, but it is often difficult to discern the exact employment arrangement.[26] More frequently, people might be described as both a servant and a 'cutler', for example. This implies journeyman status but not necessarily employment with a master tradesman. In other cases, they were defined more explicitly as the servants of tradesmen, but we cannot be certain they were also journeymen. Moreover, details on servants' masters and their occupations were not always supplied, so again the 'servant' occupational descriptor may hide further examples.

Given this ambiguity, it is likely that the 26 male apprentices and 31 male tradesmen's servants specified in the database represent a minimum. Yet despite the small size of the sample, it aligns well proportionally with contemporary population estimates. Apprentices make up 1 per cent of male workers in the task data. Wallis found that in c.1710 apprentices who paid premiums were around 12 per cent of England's male teenage population, which itself made up 4 per cent of the total male population at that time.[27] The sample is large enough to compare the respective work-task repertoires of apprentices and journeymen and explore how their work experiences overlapped and differed. Table 7.1 situates these within a larger spectrum of established artisans, farmers, and agricultural servants. Apprentices were observed doing a wide array of activities, and though they did more craftwork than agricultural workers, it made up a relatively small share of their repertoire, compared to established craftsmen. Apprentice engagement with craft labour is explored further below, but these results suggest that they contributed to their masters' trades primarily through tertiary activities like commerce.

25 SHC, Q/SR/111, 47–8.

26 For examples, see WSHC, D1/42/6, 1v (1564); D1/42/6, *Turley v. Mathew*, 31 (1565); NAS, QSR Unorganized Box 1694–1696, Info of Griffith Knight, Exam of Anne Adams (1696).

27 Wallis, 'Apprenticeship in England', p. 256; Lee and Schofield, 'British population', pp. 22–3.

Table 7.1 *Work repertoires of male servants and apprentices compared*

	Artisans repertoire (%)	Artisan servants repertoire (%)	Apprentices repertoire (%)	Agricultural servants repertoire (%)	Farmers repertoire (%)
Agriculture and land	13.1	20.4	36.6	43.7	44.6
Carework	1.6	2.0	0.0	1.8	2.5
Commerce	28.9	16.3	26.8	6.3	21.0
Crafts and construction	27.4	26.5	9.8	6.3	4.5
Food processing	8.3	18.4	0.0	9.2	5.8
Housework	1.8	6.1	9.8	5.2	1.7
Management	6.8	0.0	4.9	6.0	6.1
Transport	11.2	10.2	9.8	20.2	12.9
Other	1.0	0.0	2.4	1.3	0.9
Total	100.1	99.9	99.8	100.0	100.0
Total tasks	1,264	49	41	382	1,165

Notes: Artisans = manufacturers and food processors. Farmers = yeomen, husbandmen and agricultural trades. Artisan servants = servants of artisans, journeymen artisans, and artisans also labelled servants. Agricultural servants = all male servants except those labelled artisan servants. Integral included due to small sample sizes.

Illustrative examples include the aforementioned Augustine Sellwood, who helped set up and attend his master's 'standing' or stall at 'the fair day at Taunton', or the plumber's apprentice from Wellingborough, Northamptonshire, who ran his master's shop and bought lead in October 1664.[28] More surprisingly, a large share of craft apprentices' time seems to have been devoted to agriculture. In September 1668, for instance, carpenter's apprentice Isaac Ashly gleaned corn in a close in Fakenham, Norfolk, while Radulphus Grub, a tanner's apprentice from St Albans, Hertfordshire, corked hay during the harvests of 1586 and 1587. Before the Dissolution, William Stratford likewise made, loaded, and carted hay during the eight years he served as apprentice and then servant to a blacksmith in Hursley, Hampshire.[29]

Table 7.1 shows that as apprentices became journeymen, the agricultural share of their repertoire decreased, while the craftwork increased. Their repertoires thus became more closely aligned to those of established

[28] SHC, Q/SR/111, 47–8; NAS, QSR/1/36, 46–7.

[29] NRO, C/S3/48, Info of Edward Reynolds; HALS, ASA8/6, 22–7; HRO, 21M65/C3/11, 454–67.

artisans, as they acquired specialised skills. Yet as the example of William Stratford suggests, agricultural labour continued to play a significant role in the working lives of artisanal servants as they transitioned out of apprenticeship. This may speak to the makeshift economies which precarious journeymen relied on for their survival. But it also further illuminates the contours of artisanal by-employment discussed in Section 2.5. Not only did many rural artisans participate in the agrarian economy themselves, but they relied on their servants and apprentices to shoulder a large amount of the household's agricultural labour, with examples ranging from the watching and foddering of livestock, to the reaping and transportation of crops.[30]

Although agriculture clearly remained an important source of work as artisans progressed through life, apprentices' large repertoire share in this sector derives partly from the presence of parish apprentices in the sample. Both the Statute of Artificers and the Poor Law Acts of 1598 and 1601 empowered parish officers to bind children as apprentices to local householders as a means of poor relief. Most of these apprentices were bound in husbandry or housewifery, effectively serving as unpaid servants in exchange for maintenance. While the majority of the apprentices in the dataset had craftsmen for masters, agrarian pauper apprentices can occasionally be identified. Waren Aren, for instance, was apprenticed to a husbandman in Cruwys Morchard, Devon, for whom he 'led a horse before the plough' in 1660.[31] Girls were also frequently bound by the parish, and the few female apprentices positively identified in the dataset likely fell into this category. From the age of 10, Elizabeth Michell acted as 'servant or apprentice' in the household of John Tucker of Gittisham, Devon, where she was 'able to milk the cows, make beds, attend children or any other ordinary work about the house'. Witnesses in the latter defamation case from the 1680s praised Michell's work ethic, saying she 'very well deserved her meat and maintenance'.[32] Such a positive outlook on parish apprenticeship was rare in the court records. Examples of controversy and resistance appear more regularly, usually in response to the forcible removal of poor children from their families, or their compulsory placement with an unwilling householder.

While parish apprenticeships and traditional apprenticeships in trade and manufacture were distinct, they shared an ostensible purpose of training and skill acquisition in a contractual exchange for labour. Most of historians' knowledge about training and how such arrangements

[30] For examples, see WYAS, QS1/13/4/2, 12–3, QS1/13/4/ 3, 5–6; HRO, 21M65/C3/11, 389–92; NRO, DN/DEP/29/31, 164–8.

[31] DHC, QS/4/Box 66, Epiphany, 22.

[32] DHC, Chanter 880, *Eveleigh v. Tucker*.

were brokered comes from urban guild contexts and London in particular.[33] Young men often came from far afield to find a master in cities, with contracts arranged through paid premiums and the exact terms of service delineated in written indentures.[34] To what extent was this urban model replicated in the countryside? It is difficult to track the geographic origins of rural apprentices, but anecdotal evidence suggests that many, like servants, came from nearby locations, and mostly from within the same county. Examples of father-and-son teams among builders and textilemakers suggest some rural apprenticeships stayed in the family, while others took a place only slightly further afield. Hugh Bincks, for example, the son of a thatcher from Middleton, Norfolk, travelled about 10 miles to be bound to a thatcher in Oxborough in 1659.[35]

Some arrangements deviated from the traditional or statutory format. During the 1580s and 1590s, Nicholas Duke of Romsey, Hampshire, agreed to 'teach … his trade of shoemakers occupation' to at least two different men, neither being described as 'apprentice'. John Hopkins came from Glastonbury, Somerset, to lodge with Duke for six months training, while Thomas Brown, former servant to a gentleman, paid £5 to 'practice and exercise to learn that art' in the shoemaker's house.[36] These men were not of the typical age or background for an apprentice, and the brief terms imply a crash-course education. Even in more straightforward cases of trade or parish apprenticeship, flexibility towards rules and norms, particularly the length of term, can be discerned. At the beginning of this chapter, we saw how Richard Carr was apprenticed for only three years before he became a blacksmith, while Henry Bincks' indenture stipulated a nine-year term. Similarly, in the 1680s the 10-year-old Elizabeth Renshawe was bound to a chapman in Sutton, Cheshire, for just five years, shorter than the usual term for a female parish apprentice.[37] Despite these exceptions, entries into rural apprenticeships broadly followed the classic urban or legal model; the few apprentice ages recorded in the sample fell between 16 and 24, in line with averages from London, while contemporary craftsmen sometimes spoke of 'serving their seven years'.[38]

As we have seen, apprentices spent much of their term doing tasks outside their contracted trade. Yet there are occasional glimpses of

[33] Wallis, 'Apprenticeship and training'.

[34] Lane, *Apprenticeship in England;* Wallis, 'Apprenticeship in England'; Rappaport, *Worlds within Worlds,* pp. 291–322; Woodward, *Men at Work,* pp. 53–64.

[35] NRO, C/S3/44, Indenture of Hugh Bincks.

[36] HRO, 21M65/C3/11, 371–4.

[37] CALS, QJF/110/2, 84–5.

[38] NRO, C/S3/26, Exam of William Johnson. On the average ages of apprentices, see Rappaport, *Worlds within Worlds,* p. 295; Woodward, *Men at Work,* p. 56.

artisanal learning in progress. In an interesting case from Kingsdon, Somerset, dated to May 1630, Amy Logget retrieved her daughter from the house of Elizabeth Salapay 'who taught her to make bonelace', because Elizabeth was too sickly to 'attend her work' that day. The episode illustrates how girls could acquire skills in craftwork outside the formal apprenticeship system, through periodic tutelage from other women.[39] For apprentice boys who lived permanently with their masters, craftwork tasks were often menial and supervised, suggestive of the piecemeal attainment of skills.[40] The servants of blacksmith James Tompson, as introduced at the beginning of this chapter, weighed and paid for iron 'by his directions'. It was only when Tompson became ill that apprentice Richard Carr took a leading role with customers, stored purchased goods, and worked iron pieces in the forge. John Rindge of Wisbech, Cambridgeshire, likewise showed an ability to 'dye some parcels of [cloth] ware' in his master's vats in 1655 but got into trouble for doing so 'without his privity or knowledge'. When Thomas Parker of Puckington, Somerset, attempted 'to strike at the anvil' in 1650, he did so under the watchful eyes of his master, who beat him when he failed to carry out the task successfully.[41]

Once an apprenticeship formally came to an end, the master–servant relationship might nonetheless continue. Journeymen were expected to work for annual wages until they could establish their own trade, and their old master's household was a convenient place to do so. In the early 1530s, blacksmith William Stratford stayed on with his master in Hursley, Hampshire, for an eighth year after completing his apprenticeship. Likewise, Tamnell Vines of Wisbech, Cambridgeshire, served his former master 'as a journeyman' for about two years before he 'set up the trade of a dyer for himself' in the 1650s.[42] Vines was an undeniable success, ascending from apprentice to householder in short order, but it is doubtful that his was the common experience. Donald Woodward has found that relatively few journeymen builders ever attained the rank of master in northern cities and towns.[43] While the evidence for rural journeymen is limited, examples speak to a lingering dependence on

[39] SHC, Q/SR/29–31, 55–6; for a similar case of teaching bone-lace making see Carter, 'Work, gender, and witchcraft', p. 10. On training for girls in London, through apprenticeship or otherwise, see Gowing, *Ingenious Trade*, pp. 137–77.

[40] For similar findings: Lane, *Apprenticeship in England*, pp. 76–9; Earle, *Making of the English Middle Class*, pp. 95–100.

[41] CUL, EDR/E10/1654–5, Depositions of Francis Atmore, Tamnell Vines, John Rindge; SHC, Q/SR/82, 134.

[42] HRO, 21M65/C3/11, 454–67; CUL, EDR/E10/1654–5, Depositions of Francis Atmore, Tamnell Vines, John Rindge.

[43] Woodward, *Men at Work*, pp. 69–72; see also Rappaport, *Worlds within Worlds*, p. 335.

wage work and a peripatetic lifestyle, bouncing from master to master.[44] One example comes from the deposition of a Norfolk miller in 1627. Born in Stoke,[45] William Johnson was 'apprentice with … a miller at Fincham and served his 7 years' before serving a miller 'about London' for two years. He then settled down and married in Wighton, Norfolk, but did not establish his own trade. Rather, he spent eight years serving 'the miller there about three quarters of a year'. Since then, he had 'not served any except two or three days sometimes to help millers'.[46] Apprenticeship did not necessarily guarantee long-term stability and success in the countryside, any more so than it did in the cities. It was, however, the established and accepted means for training in most rural craft industries, particularly in building and workshop-based trades. The next section explores the working experience of the former group in more detail.

7.2 Construction Work

Construction work lies at the heart of many debates in premodern economic and social history. The wages of building craftsmen and labourers provide the backbone of long-run wage series, while social historians have delved into the organisation of labour and labourers on large civic and gentry building works. Such efforts have focused mostly on urban construction, or large rural projects that left rich financial records.[47] Much less has been said of rural construction in general, and particularly its day-to-day forms. While this section touches upon building works funded by the church or wealthy landowners, its novelty lies in illuminating smaller-scale and everyday experiences, as captured primarily in the craftwork and construction subcategories of building, woodwork, and groundworks, in the work-task data.[48] Donald Woodward has argued that 'building craftsmen stand out more clearly than any other group of manual workers in early-modern England', and the work tasks

[44] Examples of journeymen working in other men's households and moving between service contracts: WSHC, D1/42/6, 1–2v (1564), Turley v Mathew (1565); HRO, 21M65/C3/11, 371–4 (1592); WYAS, QS1/25/5, Deposition of Thomas Balderson (1686).

[45] Probably Stoke Ferry, Norfolk.

[46] NRO, C/S3/26, Exam of William Johnson.

[47] For wage series studies relying on building workers, see Phelps Brown and Hopkins, 'Seven centuries'; Allen, 'Great divergence in European wages'. On urban construction, see especially Woodward, *Men at Work*, and Stephenson, *Contracts and Pay*. For examples of larger rural construction projects, see Voth, 'Time and work in eighteenth-century London', 47–50; Jiang, 'Wage labour and living standards', pp. 161–212; Airs, *Tudor and Jacobean Country House*.

[48] Groundworks includes digging foundations, ditching, diking, and road and bridgework.

in these construction-related subcategories confirm this.[49] As this section explores, construction work distinguished itself from other rural sectors and forms of craftwork in three key ways: the forms such labour took and who did them, the ways in which employment was arranged and organised, and its geographic and spatial dynamics.

Perhaps the most prominent characteristic of construction work was its male-dominated nature. Out of 306 construction-related tasks in the dataset, women carried out only three. These were in ancillary roles, as when Alice Burge carried thatch up a ladder to a thatcher working on her house in Ashton Keynes, Wiltshire, in 1632, or Emmyne Thompson worked with her husband to 'build a little cote' in a field of Hatton, Cheshire, in 1661.[50] As discussed in the previous section, the apprenticeship system played a crucial role in excluding women from construction industries. The building and woodwork tasks in the dataset suggest a striking degree of specialisation relative to other forms of labour. Respectively 60 per cent and 58 per cent of tasks in these categories were completed by men with corresponding (and apprenticed) occupations like masonry or carpentry.[51] Yet women were equally excluded from groundwork activities, which did not require apprenticeship. The one exception, and the third example of a woman participating in construction, was Elizabeth Sweeting. She helped turn water into its correct course in Monksilver, Somerset, in September 1670.[52] Groundworks were much less the product of specialised labour, most tasks being done by servants, labourers, and husbandmen. Thus, apprenticeship was not the sole factor keeping women on the outside. It is likely that broader societal attitudes, customs, and gender norms shaped the building labour force.

To the extent that skilled craftsmen were involved in groundworks, contributing just 8 per cent of the tasks in the subcategory, they were employed in building bridges, wells, and waterways. Mason Richard Loe helped construct Lymford bridge, Cheshire, in 1672, with several other masons called upon to value the cost of raising a second arch in the structure. Similarly, the carpenter John Sutton was hired by 'the Adventurers' in May 1693 to 'mend the locks' near Burr Lane in Spalding, Lincolnshire, after rioters pulled them down.[53] In practice, these roles were often supervisory, and much of the work was carried out

[49] Woodward, *Men at Work*, p. 51.

[50] WSHC, A1/110/1632T, 129; CALS, QJF/90/2, 145–6.

[51] In comparison, 34 per cent of all craftwork tasks and 18 per cent of textile production were done by workers with corresponding occupations.

[52] TNA, KB/9/985/20.

[53] CALS, QJF/100/1, 97; LiA, HQS/A/1/1693, Midsummer-Spalding, 21.

by non-specialists, like the two teams of labourers who fell into dispute over a 'piece of diking work between ditches' near Sutton, Cambridgeshire, in October 1637.[54] From the reign of Mary and Philip onwards, repairing highways and roads became a statutory requirement for local landholders, who had to contribute equipment and labour on appointed days.[55] Thus, we find the tucker or fuller Thomas Pollard 'shovelling gravel in the king's highway according to statute' near Poulshot, Wiltshire, in 1556, and various husbandmen involved in the tangential tasks of digging up gravel and sand from pits throughout the period.[56] Husbandmen and labourers were likewise occupied in the digging and cleaning of ditches, work that formed 22 per cent of the groundworks subcategory and was essential to the maintenance of byways and boundaries. Labourer William Patterické recalled 'ditching and fencing' in his youth, as 'part and parcel of the common fields of Sutton' in Yorkshire when they were enclosed in 1506; while in June 1567, two husbandmen of Chedzoy, Somerset, 'lay out ditching work for the whole parish'.[57]

As Figure 7.2 shows, building work encompassed a larger range of tasks than groundworks and was largely linked to specialised work with particular materials. Nonetheless, craftsmen did not act alone. Labourers made up the second largest group of building workers with occupational descriptors and were visible at each stage of construction.[58] Carpenters like Richard Mylsent and Richard Russe erected 'a new frame of a house' in Kirtling, Cambridgeshire, in August 1567, while in February 1598, labourer Thomas Burnand fell to his death whilst 'standing on a ladder and trying to pull out one of the rafters' in an 'old house belonging to William Fairfax, esquire' of Steeton in Yorkshire.[59] Timberwork like this supplied the frame of most buildings in early modern England. Brick, stone, and plaster often accented the fabric and walls of houses, or provided essential features.[60] Bricklayer John Tyffyn, for example, used scaffolding to 'build a chimney at the house of William Woodeward' in Eltisley, Cambridgeshire, one September day in 1532. At the other end of the period, August 1693, dauber Edward Cowles worked together

[54] CUL, EDR/E10/1637, Info of John Johnson.
[55] Tait (ed.), *Lancashire Quarter Sessions Rolls*, pp. xxvii–xxix.
[56] TNA, KB9/589a/84; see also TNA, KB9/985/86; NRO, DN/DEP/29/31, 26–8.
[57] BI, CP.G.2194, *William Herrington v. Francis Atlay*; SHC, D/D/Cd/12, Thomas Myche.
[58] Out of 170 building tasks, 22 per cent were done by workers without specified occupational descriptors. Of the remainder, building craftsmen did 78 per cent, labourers 13 per cent, and husbandmen, servants, and other tradesmen 9 per cent.
[59] TNA, KB9/621/125, KB9/1040b/171.
[60] On early modern building techniques, see Johnson, *English Houses*, pp. 20–41.

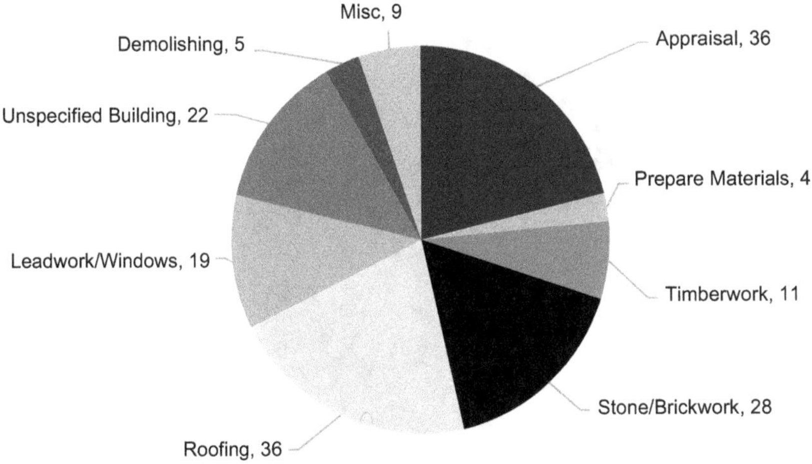

Figure 7.2 Types of building task.

with wool-comber Thomas Leader in 'striking of a wall' at 'Roger Lidster's at Scoulton', Norfolk.[61] Stonework was more prevalent on church and gentry building projects. Masons Christopher Roswell and William Babb, for instance, toiled alongside labourer Henry Langlie for 'the worshipful Mr Henry Waldron of Sear at his place at Isle Brewers' in Somerset in 1604.[62]

Roofing demonstrated a similar hierarchy of materials according to status. Thatch was more widely used on common dwellings and outbuildings, like the 'roof of John Wenne's stable' in East Dereham, Norfolk, from which the improbably aged thatcher John Wynde (at 106 years old) fell in 1543.[63] Slate and tile protected the houses of the wealthy, like gentleman Thomas Lynne of Bassingbourn, Cambridgeshire. He employed tiler Thomas Manfeld to repair his roof in 1544.[64] Leadwork, however, was almost exclusive to ecclesiastical structures in the work-task data. The minister of Westhoughton, Lancashire, employed plumbers to 'lay lead upon the roof' of the chancel around 1634, while glazier John Dye cut 'new sheet lead … which came from London' for the parish church of Stanhoe, Norfolk, around Lammas 1683.[65] Leadworkers like these straddled the line between site-based building and workshop-based metalwork. Examples can be found of plumbers buying and selling lead

[61] TNA, KB9/523/94; NRO, DN/DEP/53/58A, *Jane Tooly v. Mariam Lidster*.
[62] SHC, D/D/Cd/36, *Webb v. Rowswell, Virum, and Feminam*. [63] TNA, KB9/556/126.
[64] TNA, KB9/562/52.
[65] CALS, EDC/5/1664, 69; NRO, C/S3/55, Info of Robert Turffe, Info of John Dey.

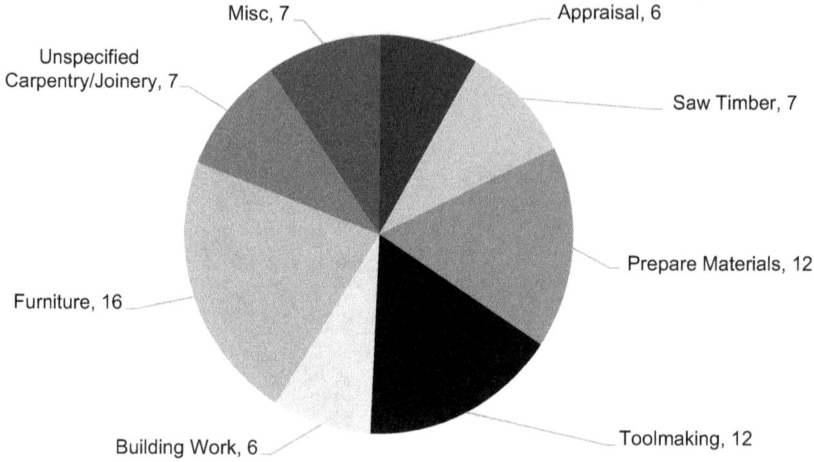

Figure 7.3 Types of woodwork task.

in their shops, as well as soldering and casting it.[66] The latter represents one of the few types of metalwork demonstrably associated with construction in the dataset. While smithing was essential to urban building projects, the work-task results for rural metalworking reflect a prioritisation of agrarian needs, with horseshoeing and the mending of agricultural tools at the fore.[67] As explored below, many builders resided in towns, so they may have had their tools mended or furnished closer to home.

Like metalwork or building, woodwork was a highly specialised category of labour. Yet as Figure 7.3 shows, tasks were not confined to construction proper. Carpenters were the most common type of woodworker and building craftsman in the database, but only 57 per cent of their craftwork tasks were directly linked to building work. The other 43 per cent entailed tasks such as sawing timber and preparing wood for future projects, making and mending tools for themselves or others, and crafting interior furnishings. All of these activities overlapped with other woodworking trades, those of sawyers, ploughwrights, and joiners. While this was a traditional source of conflict among civic craft guilds, adaptability seems to have been essential in the countryside. Carpenter Roger Francken, for instance, worked alongside sawyer Thomas Lacye 'about

66 DHC, Chanter 866, Gard de Winkleigh (1634); NAS, QSR/1/36, 46–7(1664).

67 Woodward, *Men at Work*, pp. 21–2. The production or mending of farm tools and housewares made up 35 per cent of metalwork tasks in the database, horseshoes 18 per cent, and leadwork 9 per cent.

Midsummertide' 1587 in 'squaring and sawing of timber' for Master John Sallmon of Barton Stacey, Hampshire.[68] The making of pews usually came under the purview of joiners like William Revell, who contracted to lengthen two seats 'in the south quire of the parish church of Ordsall, Nottinghamshire' in 1684.[69] Yet, carpenters were also employed to do the same in parishes around the country, suggesting necessity and availability could trump specialisation.[70] Tool making and mending was the woodworking activity least bound to a skilled trade. For instance, in September 1621, the weaver Edward Stephens cut hay staves for himself; husbandman Nicholas Holloway fashioned a log into a ladder in 1618; and yeoman Thomas Coulthurst 'made a plough' from parts of three ash trees he felled in 1636.[71]

Before any construction began, workers might appraise the structure and give estimates, gather necessary tools and materials, and occasionally demolish pre-existing fixtures. Not unlike building work today, these preparatory activities were an essential and time-consuming part of the process, making up around a quarter of the tasks in both the building and woodwork subcategories. Church court cases regarding the dilapidation of ecclesiastical property provide most of the work-task examples of appraisals. Diverse groups of builders would be summoned to give opinions and costings on repairs, as in July 1685, when the cleric of Bramerton, Norfolk, hosted a mason and bricklayer, two carpenters, two daubers, and a thatcher to 'view the dilapidations' of the chancel, 'parsonage buildings … dwelling house and barn'.[72] Estimates would follow, as when Thomas Allen the dauber reported back to the minister of Bolton, Cumberland, in January 1663 that no less than £8 would 'make good the plastering, raddling and daubing, and stone walls … needful to be done in and about the house and out housing' of the vicarage.[73] With an average age of 42, these appraisers were clearly consulted for their experience and expertise. Such consultations, however, were not limited to large-scale projects, as one example from Cheshire in 1612 typifies. On a Wednesday in July, labourer Raffe Nickson went to carpenter Raffe Aston's house in Over and 'asked him to make two bays of a back house for his father'. He requested the carpenter come to the house in Middlewich in a few days to discuss 'taking on the said work'. But when Aston arrived, Nickson Senior seemed to think better of the plan,

[68] HRO, 21M65/C3/9, *Sallmon v. Sallmon.*
[69] BI, CP.H.5153, *Sidney Wortley v. Henry Halfhead and Samuel Woodhouse.*
[70] For example, see DUIC, DDR/EJ/CCD/1/9, 71v–77r (1593); NRO, DN/DEP/53/58A, *Eliam Cooper v. Churchwardens of Hingham* (1680).
[71] WSHC, A1/110/1622H, 162; SHC, Q/SR/33, 126; LaA, QSB/1/181, 34–5.
[72] NRO, DN/DEP/51/55, 3–39. [73] CALS, EDC/5/1664, 50.

claiming, 'this is a busy time; I am not armed to build yet'.[74] Once all parties *were* armed to build, however, negotiations over the organisation of labour and materials could begin.

The rates of craftwork tasks done 'for another', for those outside the household, were notably high: they stood at 79 per cent for building and 71 per cent for woodwork, well above the rates for craftwork as a whole at 54 per cent and an overall rate of 35 per cent amongst all tasks. Moreover, a relatively large amount of these 'for another' tasks were explicitly paid: while only 5 per cent of overall tasks and 10 per cent of craftwork tasks were explicitly paid, percentages rise to 16 per cent for building work and 27 per cent for woodwork. These findings speak to the waged nature of most construction labour, the very thing that has made it so useful to economic historians. Individuals and householders of course could make repairs or alterations to their own properties. Thomas Popeblant, for example, worked alongside two carpenters to repair his house in St Albans, Hertfordshire, in the autumn of 1609, while George Panier of Ilchester, Somerset, stopped up a hole in a wall of his family's dwelling in 1650.[75] Yet an analysis of building task employers suggests such do-it-yourself labour accounted for only 10 per cent of activity. A larger proportion, 16 per cent, were wealthy landowners like Master Marmaduke Theakston, who hired carpenter Anthony Candill to build a house in Hunton, Yorkshire, in 1693.[76] Parish churches were the biggest employers by far, at 40 per cent of building tasks, although these numbers are inflated somewhat due to the centrality of church fabric to dilapidation cases in the church courts. Nonetheless, setting such cases to the side still leaves a rich range of ecclesiastical construction projects, encompassing the setting up of altars, the repairing of belfries, the knocking down of interior walls, re-tiling of roofs, and the replacement of lead guttering.[77]

The remaining 25 per cent of employers largely represent ordinary people of middle-to-low status who likely contracted much of the construction work in the countryside.[78] Heather Swanson has argued that for most builders in preindustrial England, life must have been a 'constant round of repairing doors, windows, roofs, and pavements' which

[74] CALS, QJF/90/2, 63. [75] HALS, ASA8/8, 120–2; SHC, Q/SR/82, 207, 210.
[76] NYCRO, QSB/1694, 174–5.
[77] For example, see DUIC, DDR/EJ/CCD/1/2, 170v–171r (1570); TNA, KB/9/1071/unnumbered (1546); DHC, Chanter 868, *Bartoe v. Lambert* (1663); NRO, C/S3/55, Info of Robert Turffe, Info of John Dey (1683); C/S3/50, Exam of John Spurrell, Info of Richard Harmer (1672); SHC, Q/SR/77, 35 (1638).
[78] For this analysis of building-task employers, 9 per cent were unclear.

surviving financial records fail to capture.[79] Certainly, the depositional evidence speaks to this parade of everyday small jobs. Mason John Ewens spent September 1585 helping to 'heal or tile' the house of a tradesman named Potter in Basingstoke, Hampshire, also filling with mortar 'certain brakes and holes in the inside of the walls' of his shop. William Thurlbye was 'retained in service for the day' in July 1563 to build and mend a chimney in clay on the roof of fellow husbandman Robert Brown of New Sleaford, Lincolnshire. Carpenter John Smart busied himself 'upon a Saturday morning' in November 1631 setting up a wall plate in the house of his brother-in-law, husbandman Thomas Greene of Bratton, Wiltshire.[80] Smart sent Greene 'to the house of Christopher Butcher in Milborne for carpentry tools to do the same', while Greene's wife brought him a candle to see the work.

As this last example highlights, construction hinged upon specialised tools and materials and was often a group effort combining skilled and unskilled labour. Indeed, group work was more prevalent in construction than other types of industry in the dataset: while 26 per cent of overall and 28 per cent of craftwork tasks were done in groups, building work, groundworks, and woodwork show much higher rates at 41 per cent, 43 per cent and 36 per cent, respectively. These high rates of group work speak to the organisation of construction under building firms or teams. However, the dataset contains little evidence of the large contractors characteristic of late seventeenth- and eighteenth-century London, and the dense networks of accountants and surveyors, suppliers and carriers, teams of craftsmen and labourers (both directly employed and subcontracted) responsible for the great projects of St Paul's Cathedral or Westminster Abbey.[81] Group work rates and worker numbers were highest for church and gentry construction projects.[82] Even for larger builds like these, however, firm sizes coincide with Donald Woodward's findings for northern towns: 'most master craftsmen worked with only one or two permanent employees, taking on unskilled labour as required'.[83] Small family businesses and especially father–son teams were common, like the helliers John and George Hawkins, who worked 'on a house of Mr Aske's in Somerford Magna about healing the same with tiles' in Wiltshire in September 1670. Extra labour was not limited

[79] Swanson, *Building Craftsmen*, p. 31.
[80] HRO, 21M65/C3/9, *Exoll v. Smyth*; TNA, KB/9/607b/143; WSHC, A1/110/1632H, 176.
[81] Stephenson, *Contracts and Pay*, pp. 115–8.
[82] Out of 135 combined building and woodwork tasks done for churches or wealthy and landowners, 53 per cent were done in groups.
[83] Woodward, *Men at Work*, p. 25.

to men described as labourers either. The glazier John Dye hired butcher Robert Turfe off-and-on during the month of August 1683 to help cut the lead for the church in Stanhoe, Norfolk.[84]

Payment was often negotiated at the level of the firm or team. In a typical case, the churchwardens of Bradford, Yorkshire, paid three masons together the 'sum of £46 for repairing the mason work of the said church' in 1664.[85] One key factor in such remuneration was the responsibility for building materials, which could be supplied either by the contractor or the client. As in London and other urban communities, rural arrangements varied widely depending on the size and complexity of the project.[86] While clients were more likely to contribute materials when the job was large, and contractors when it was small, this was no fixed rule. The church of Southrepps, Norfolk, hired a plumber to mend the chancel in May 1672, purchasing '8 hundred one quarter and 4 pounds of lead', which was sent 'in a cart to the house of … John Spurrell in Aylsham' to be worked. Yet plumbers Daniel Hole Senior and Junior were paid for both workmanship and materials in 1634 when they received £10 'for their labour and charge thereabout' in the 'soldering, casting, and laying lead upon the church' of Winkleigh, Devon.[87] Such sourcing and provision of materials was typical for relatively small jobs, as when carpenter Henry Wilson of Norton in Yorkshire was paid £5 6s 8d to 'find timber' and provide 'timber workmanship' for a new bell frame in St Denys of York in 1593.[88] However, small employers could also foot the supplies. One day in 1673, Richard Stronge of Downton, Wiltshire, stopped the bricklayer Sylvester Fry in the street 'to be speak him to do some mason work for him at his house his materials being all ready and Fry did promise to come to the said Stronge to do the same'.[89]

One similarity between rural and urban construction is that craftsmen often contributed their own tools to the job. Less can be said with confidence about labourers and other unskilled workers, but the fact that most depositional evidence places building tools in the hands of established tradesmen is suggestive. Many builders stored tools and materials near or at their current place of work, rather than their homes. Carpenter

[84] WSHC, D1/42/61, *Aske v. Butcher*; NRO, C/S3/55, Info of Robert Turffe, Info of John Dey.
[85] BI, CP.H.4952, *Thomas Ledger and Gervase Dickson and others v. William Pickles.*
[86] Woodward, *Men at Work*, pp. 44–51; Stephenson, *Contracts and Pay.*
[87] NRO, C/S3/50, Exam of John Spurrell, Info of Richard Harmer; DHC, Chanter 866, Gard de Winkleigh.
[88] BI, CP.G.2792, *Churchwardens of York v. William Barton and Edward Eardley.*
[89] WSHC, D1/42/61, *Stronge v. Fanston.*

Table 7.2 *Crafts and construction: spatial dynamics*

	Tasks in own household	% of tasks in own household	% of tasks occurring in rural parishes	% of actors' parishes of residence that are rural parishes	Location vs residence
Buildings	16	9.9	65.3	46.7	+18.6
Clothes and shoes	57	50.4	44.1	48.1	−4.1
Groundworks	3	5.0	64.4	62.7	+1.7
Metalwork	38	58.5	51.2	49.3	+1.9
Mill maintenance	2	13.3	51.7	47.1	+4.7
Mining/quarrying	0	0.0	60.0	64.3	−4.3
Other maintenance/ manufacturing	7	26.9	65.9	53.1	+12.8
Textile production	82	50.0	65.5	61.5	+4.0
Woodwork	6	10.0	65.3	54.8	+10.4
Total	211	30.2	59.3	54.0	+5.4
Overall database	1,301	16.4	60.6	63.5	+1.8

Notes: The 'own household' category here is based on the own household/outside the household distinction made in the database for all tasks where a location can be discerned, and as explained in Section 1.2.3. It includes shops or workshops as part of 'own household'.

Edmond Wallingham of Foulsham, Norfolk, for instance, worked for John Browne of Terrington on 21 November 1618, leaving in Browne's barn that Saturday night 'certain tools which he did use about his trade, viz three wimbles, a Flemish former or chisel, and a handsaw'. These were all stolen over the weekend, the thief selling them on to another carpenter of Tilney.[90] Similarly, Robert Kensey, a carpenter from the market town of Prescot in Lancashire, came to his work some 3 miles distant in Burtonwood on Monday 12 June 1637, having left 'his work tools' in the barn of Henry Lanchisheires 'on Saturday night before by and with Lanchisheires consent and leave'.[91] Examples like these speak to the spatial dynamics that made rural construction work peculiar: its location outside and sometimes far from the household, and the interplay between town and country.

Table 7.2 summarises the geographic and spatial features of construction tasks in the dataset, as compared to other craftwork. The locational distribution of work done in and around the actor's own household

[90] NRO, C/S3/21, Exam of John Dawlton.

[91] LaA, QSB/1/186, 47. For another example of tool use, see DHC, Chanter 875, 68v–84r.

compared with that done outside the household is particularly striking, if unsurprising. While over 50 per cent of workshop-based tasks like textile production or metalwork took place in their own household, a large majority of building, groundworks, and woodwork did not, reinforcing qualitative trends already discussed. Masonry, carpentry, and groundworks mostly took place on-site and away from home. Those tradesmen who did have shops, such as plumbers, glaziers, or joiners, split their time between home and the job site.[92] Thus, we see the plumber John Spurrell working on lead in his house in Aylsham and moving it in stages to the church building-site in Southrepps throughout the summer of 1672.

Building workers like Spurrell often travelled outside their parish of residence to work. This is demonstrated by comparing the resident parishes of workers with the parishes where tasks took place. Indeed, building workers did around 50 per cent of their work 'out of parish', far more than the average for craftwork of 17 per cent or the overall sample of 29 per cent.[93] These tendencies were especially pronounced in property appraisal. Only two of the six experts brought in to view the decayed properties of Master Tuckfield of Morchard Bishop, Devon, and value repairs, for example, were from that parish.[94] This speaks to the finite supply of building tradesmen in the countryside and the consequent demand for their labour. It was a supply which varied by trade. Carpenters, for example, were somewhat less likely to travel out of parish than other builders, likely because they were more numerous and better distributed throughout the countryside.

While much construction work entailed travel, the distances involved in such cases were usually manageable in a day. Analysing those building tasks done outside the worker's parish of residence returns a maximum distance of 45 miles, when the carpenter Robert Colman of Norwich travelled to 'judge and estimate' what the repairs of Walsoken church, Norfolk, might cost the parishioners in 1682.[95] But setting aside the few outliers like these, the average distance travelled when workers left their own parish was 5 miles from home to work.[96] Perhaps more interesting

[92] See also Woodward, *Men at Work*, pp. 118–9.

[93] These calculations exclude data from church court depositions. The time-lag between work task and testimony in these courts means the worker's given residence might not reflect residence at time of activity. However, the church court data does show broadly the same trends.

[94] DHC, Chanter 866, *Tuckfield v. Beare* (1637).

[95] NRO, DN/DEP/51/55, 72–83.

[96] Church court cases excluded. Only one task was allowed per person so as not to inflate distances due to workers carrying out multiple tasks. The resulting dataset included 50 tasks. Maximum distance 45 miles, minimum 1. The two distances over 20 miles were removed as outliers, resulting in an average distance of 5 miles. Mode and median were both 3 miles. See also the analysis of distances in Section 3.3.

was where builders like Robert Colman called home. Table 7.2 also compares the parish sizes where craftwork tasks occurred, with the resident parish size of the craftworkers who did those tasks. Groundworks were majority rural and so were the people doing this work. Metalworking tasks were 49 per cent urban, as were 51 per cent of their practitioners. Yet, discrepancies were far greater for the buildings and woodwork subcategories. While 65 per cent of both building and woodwork tasks took place in rural parishes, for respectively 47 and 55 per cent of those tasks the workers hailed from market towns or large towns. These results bolster Donald Woodward's findings of 'substantial movement of building workers between towns, and between town and country' in northern England.[97] Indeed, a further breakdown of 'out of parish' building tasks suggests that labour flowed from town to country more than in any other direction.[98] In this way towns played an outsized role in rural construction networks, relative to other types of craftwork. It was this feature, alongside its general mobility, high degree of waged group work, and specialisation, which set the industry apart. But if construction was male-centred, urban-skewed, and the domain of apprenticed trades, textile and clothing production was the opposite, as the next sections explore.

7.3 Textile Production

Textile manufacturing's position as early modern England's largest and most influential industry emerges strongly from the work-task data. When commerce and transport tasks are factored in, as much as 7 per cent of the overall sample relates to the industry or the cloths it produced, while production activities themselves make up 27 per cent of the craftwork category.[99] The related industry of clothing/apparel production accounts for another 20 per cent of craftwork, and an additional 4 per cent of the total sample. This section and the next examine the work experiences within these two dynamic industries during a period of growth and change. This first analyses the production of cloth, reviewing the materials used and products created in manufacture, the stages to production, the gender division and organisation of labour, and regional

97 Woodward, *Men at Work,* p. 164.

98 Building 'out of parish' tasks totalled 64. Rural to rural (30 per cent); rural to town (8 per cent); town to town (17 per cent); town to rural (45 per cent). For the 73 'in parish' building tasks, 55 per cent were rural, 45 per cent were urban.

99 Textile production (254); buy/sell textiles and wool (317) and transport of textile materials (93). The total of buy/sell tasks for textiles and wool combined differs from that in Table 8.2 as the latter uses a female multiplier to calculate the gender division of labour.

and spatial differences in the industry. The following section covers the making of clothing from textiles and leather, examining the variety of products made, the gendered nature of their manufacture, the balance between production for the household and the commercial market, and the distinctions between making and mending.

Textile production as captured in the dataset was predominantly concerned with woollen cloth: about 85 per cent of the textile raw materials mentioned in tasks relate to woollen cloth production, indicative of its national dominance as an export industry during the sixteenth and seventeenth centuries.[100] Linen production was less in evidence, and only in particular regions, as is discussed below.[101] It is interesting, however, to compare production-side references to raw materials and industry, with product-side references to finished cloths in the task data. The latter shows a more even split between linen and woollen products than found in the raw materials. Out of 152 mentions of cloth in the dataset, 27 per cent were woollen, 24 per cent were linen, 2 per cent were mixed, with the remaining 47 per cent unspecified.[102] Yet the greater prevalence of linen here speaks more to its importance as an imported and traded good, than as a product of local manufacture. Almost all the craftwork production references to 'linen cloth', for example, relate to its bleaching or whitening, rather than its weaving.

The database does, however, capture a few direct references to linen weaving in early modern England. In 1652, John Wood of Stockport in Cheshire spent the month of August weaving linen cloth, while in 1694 John Clarkson of Thirsk in Yorkshire testified that some 'raw linen web 20 yards long' was of 'his own working having his own name also marked in it'.[103] Both of these men styled themselves 'linen-websters', as did a further eight male workers in the dataset. Women were unlikely to be given such occupational descriptors, but their involvement in linen weaving and processing is suggested nonetheless by a witness from Melling, Lancashire, in 1637, who stated that Ellen Bottle:

[100] References to textile production raw materials were tallied from tasks in the textile production and buy/sell subcategories, and the transport category, yielding 416 references, or 172 when integral tasks are excluded due to the overrepresentation of wool and fleeces. The proportions of the latter 172 were wool (57 per cent), skins/fleeces (7 per cent), woollen yarn (6 per cent), unspecified yarn (but likely to be woollen) (15 per cent), flaxen yarn/thread (4 per cent), and flax/hemp (11 per cent).

[101] A contrast to the dominance of hemp and flax spinning, rather than wool spinning, found in criminal cases of eighteenth-century northern England: Styles, *Dress of the People*, p. 139.

[102] References to cloths derive from the textile production and buy/sell subcategories, and the transport category, with integral tasks included.

[103] CALS, QJF/80/3, 30; NYCRO, QSB/1695, 169–70.

did buy for her mother Jane Bottle some two pounds of hemp of one Richard Ratcliffe his wife and did borrow almost a pound of flax of Edmund Martin his wife, and this examinant's mother, with … [Ellen] did spin the said hemp and flax and afterwards did warp the same yarn with one Edmund Martin [webster].[104]

Alongside the Bottles, one spinster from Crediton, Devon, confessed to working 'a breadth of Rosterne' (a type of linen cloth) in 1610.[105] Yet there is more evidence of women's involvement in earlier stages of linen-making, during the processing of flax or hemp.

According to Gervase Markham's guide to good housewifery, the first steps in processing, after pulling or harvesting the flax or hemp crop, were to let it stand or ripen, before submerging the stalks in water for several days.[106] Once removed from the water, dried, and sorted, the stalks would be 'pilled', 'riven', or broken to remove the rind from the fibres. In December 1661, Laurence Farlton of Newton in Cambridgeshire and his wife came under suspicion of theft because they did not follow this order of tasks. They were accused of 'pilling large hemp' in their house at a late time of night, and before taking the necessary step of having their 'hemp watered'. While households might process their own crop in this way, the labour could also be subcontracted. Around Hallowmas 1630, Alice Fendicke, an old woman of Hillington, Norfolk, was hired by esquire Richard Hovell to rive 'ten sheaves of hemp', earning 'so much for every stone riving'. After the stalks were sufficiently broken came the final steps before spinning, collectively described as 'dressing'. These included beating or scraping the fibres with a 'swingle' to soften them, before 'heckling' or combing them in preparation for spinning. Elizabeth Walley, a husbandman's wife, was 'swingling to … [flax] at her barnside in Leftwich' in Cheshire in November 1682.[107] The locations of these tasks highlight the regional nature of English linen and hemp production, as discussed in Section 3.1. Nearly all references to flax materials and linen weaving derive from the northern counties of Lancashire, Cheshire, and Yorkshire, while hemp cultivation is attested in Cambridgeshire and Norfolk. The one direct mention of cotton wool comes from Manchester in 1627, when linen-weaver John Shawe pawned four or five pounds of the stuff to Ellen Gorton for 12d.[108]

While the English woollen and linen industries differed in scale and regional spread, they shared a similar gender division of labour.

[104] LaA, QSB/1/190, 47. [105] DHC, QS/4/Box 16, Easter, Exam of Christian Slee.

[106] Markham, *English Housewife*, pp. 155–61.

[107] CUL, EDR/E10/110, 3; NRO, C/S3/28, Exam of Margarett Wilson, Exam of Elizabeth Leake, Info of Robert Tye; CALS, QJF/110/4, 90.

[108] LaA, QSB/1/27, 78. This case and Manchester textile manufacture are discussed in Section 3.1.

Table 7.3 *Gender division of labour and location of textile production*

	Tasks	% by F adj.	% of tasks in rural settlement	% of tasks in urban settlement
Process flax/hemp	10	52.6	100.0	0.0
Gather wool	48	51.6	80.4	19.6
Clean wool	14	82.3	64.3	35.7
Card/comb	10	79.5	80.0	20.0
Spin	57	99.3	66.7	33.3
Wind yarn	8	60.8	37.5	62.5
Organise	21	50.9	81.0	19.0
Transport	5	100.0	40.0	60.0
Dyeing	18	56.4	55.6	44.4
Weave	42	25.9	54.8	45.2
Finish textiles	15	15.6	46.7	53.3
Other	6	72.1	16.7	83.3
Total	254	68.9	65.5	34.5

Notes: adj. = adjusted (x2.59). The task totals used for the first, third, and fourth columns are unadjusted.

As Table 7.3 shows, women dominated or were heavily involved in most preparatory stages of production while men controlled the weaving, fulling, dyeing, and shearing or dressing of cloth. Proportionally, the male-dominated finishing tasks account for 21 per cent of the adjusted total, with the remaining 79 per cent devoted to preparation and organisation. This generally corresponds to the time and labour distribution recorded in early modern records. A report from Yorkshire in 1588, for example, estimated that manufacturing a Kersey (a type of woollen cloth) required 60 people with 77 per cent devoted to the preparations of sorting, carding, and spinning. Producing 86 pounds of broadcloth required a similar number of workers, with around a 70:30 split between preparatory and other processes.[109] The intensive labour required to prepare wool for weaving, and women's dominance of these processes, explains the high proportion of women's work in textile production. The work-task data allows the organisation of production, and the gendered roles within it, to be examined in some detail.

Wool for cloth production was either imported or harvested from indigenous flocks during the shearing season. Even the labouring poor who did not own sheep collected stray wool as a supplementary source of

[109] Muldrew, '"Th'ancient distaff"', p. 504.

income, as when three widows and one married woman of Sibsey, Lincolnshire, spent a Tuesday in May 1652 'in the fen gathering wool'.[110] As well as collecting and weighing of wool, women were the primary workers behind its cleaning and sorting.[111] When Christine Cooper of Whitchurch, Hampshire, received a batch bought by her clothier husband at 'shear time' in 1580, she 'culled out about 7 todds of very coarse and feeble tarry tegs … scouring and dressing 6 or 7 pounds of wool in each todd'. Likewise, Joyce Berry of Brinkworth, Wiltshire, washed the wool pulled off a dubiously sourced sheepskin in 1642, before laying it out to dry in the garden.[112] The next step was carding or combing the wool to prepare it for spinning. Only three tasks in the dataset describe combing, the technique necessary to make yarn for worsted or the lighter, fashionable 'new draperies'.[113] All were done by men like Henry Smith and Thomas Billington, who worked together in the 'combing trade' in a 'workhouse' or workshop in Kettlestone, Norfolk, in 1679.[114] In contrast, nearly all carding tasks were done by women, such as Agnes Adams of Farleigh Hungerford, Somerset, who overheard a defamatory exchange while 'sat carding wool at the door of Matthew Roberts' in 1532.[115]

Spinning wool into yarn was the last major stage of preparation and was done almost exclusively by women. Craig Muldrew has demonstrated the amount of labour needed to produce enough yarn for the early modern industry's needs, and indeed spinning accounts for the largest number of textile production tasks in the dataset, 37 per cent of the adjusted total.[116] Alongside carding, it provided an important source of income for women and their families. At least 37 per cent of women's spinning and carding tasks in the sample were done 'for another' outside the worker's household, or for an employer.[117] Often explicitly waged,

[110] LiA, LQS/A/1/13, 37. The 'gather wool' category in Table 7.3 relates to this type of activity, not sheep-shearing.

[111] On the processing of wool, see Markham, *English Housewife*, pp. 146–52

[112] HRO, 21M65/C3/8, *Weke v. More*; WSHC, A1/110/1642E, 174.

[113] On the distinctions between old and new draperies, see Muldrew, '"Th'ancient distaff"', pp. 502–3; Coleman, 'An innovation and its diffusion'.

[114] NRO, C/S3/53A, Info of William Smith; See Muldrew, '"Th'ancient distaff"', p. 503.

[115] SHC, D/D/Cd/2, Gylbarde et Adams.

[116] When carding and combing are included, this figure rises to 43 per cent of all textile production tasks. These calculations exclude integral tasks which, due to the overrepresentation of wool-gathering tasks, bring the spinning proportion down to 33 per cent.

[117] This is likely an underestimation as it is often unclear for whom spinning was being done.

arrangements could take many forms.[118] Annual servants might be expected to spin as part of their usual duties, but medium-term contracts were also made.[119] In 1649 Ann Bishop of Martock, Somerset, was hired to spin some wool in the house of Edith Ferrice of Long Sutton in Hampshire for one month and no longer 'for which she was to have a penny a day and meat and drink'. Spinster Elizabeth Cayton lodged in the house of Edward Robinson of Garstang in Lancashire for two weeks, 'spinning for wages' with his wife in November 1636.[120] The deposition of 20-year-old Joanna Pittman of Cullompton, Devon, grants particular insight into the flexibility of these arrangements. She 'did spin at the house of the said Joan Bennett and her husband of Kentisbeare by the week' in 1634, employed for

> five weeks to spinning and had 6d her wages, and then she went from them, and now for these six weeks last past she hath also by the week used to spin with them again for the like wages but may go from them at every week's end if she please.[121]

Although most women in these temporary employments were young and/or single, wives and widows accounted for 48 per cent of spinning and carding tasks.[122] Householders like these could also earn wages on a casual basis, contracted to spin a set amount of wool, sometimes with the help of other family members. In 1629 in North Molton, Devon, Grace Fisher, the parish clerk's wife, and her children spun 'some coloured wool … of one Tooker of Tiverton', receiving '1/2 a pound for waste upon every 10 pounds that … [they] did spin for him'. In addition to this contractual work, Grace 'and her household' used the 'twickings and waste' in combination with wool acquired elsewhere to spin 4¾ pounds of yarn, which was then sold to one John Thorne.[123] This example demonstrates how women and children might spin yarn for sale on the commercial market, at their own organisation outside clothier networks, and thus supplement household income. Alternatively, they might use the yarn for their own household or cottage industry. As we have seen at

[118] See Zell, *Industry in the Countryside*, pp. 165–8 for a useful summary of these different arrangements.

[119] Examples of servants spinning: HRO, 21M65/C3/8, *Hewes v. Wayte* (1579); DHC, Chanter 866, *Flood v. Tucker* (1635); CALS, QJF/31/2, 66 (1602); QJF/100/4, 70 (1671). See also Mansell, *Female Servants*, pp. 189–93.

[120] SHC, Q/SR/82, 181–4; LaA, QSB/1/177, 32.

[121] DHC, Chanter 866, *Bennett v. Deymont*. This case and others like it are discussed in more detail in Mansell, *Female Servants*, pp. 157–9.

[122] Out of 62 spinning or carding tasks done by women, with 34 per cent done by never-married women (or those likely to be so) and 18 per cent done by women of unknown marital status. 'Likely never married' includes 'never-married' women, servants, and those at or below 25 years old.

[123] DHC, QS/4/Box 32, Epiphany, 24–5, 34.

the beginning of this chapter, the weaver Thomas Chapman's wife and sister spun yarn for the household's own production, while Joan Stephens, wife of a husbandman in East Harptree in Somerset, spun 15 pounds of wool 'to make clothes for herself and her children' in 1650.[124]

Once the yarn had been spun, it was typically women who ferried the product back to contractors, sold it at market, or took it to weavers to be made into cloth, with women performing 84 per cent of such tasks.[125] Their embeddedness in the industry made them savvy commercial operators and experts in quality control: well placed, as Gervase Markham put it, 'to bridle the falsehood of unconscionable workmen'.[126] When Mary Dawdon, a married woman from Masham in Yorkshire, 'did run eleven pounds of woollen yarn with one James Thompson … weaver' in the middle of August 1695, she was not pleased with the product she got back.

> [It] being fine wool she did expect to have again 8 yards of fine cloth, the list of the said run web being all white, but … Thompson did bring this informant a much coarser woollen web with a black list, being very certain that it was not her web, her own web only wanting 3 pounds for wool … [but this one] did want 5 pounds wool.[127]

Astute as they might be in judging the final product, women like Mary were largely uninvolved in the later stages of weaving and finishing cloth. In addition to the female linen weavers mentioned above, only two women were found directly involved in the weaving process. Agnes Fenton of Ridge in Hertfordshire spent 'a certain workenday after Whitsuntide … in the afternoon … working on a weaver's loom with her husband being a weaver' in a shop which they occupied in 1556.[128] In 1627, Margery Chamlett, a married woman of Rochdale, Lancashire, testified to making cloth out of some wool which she and her husband acquired.[129]

As with other industries explored in this chapter, apprenticeship appears to lie behind women's exclusion from weaving and other finishing tasks like fulling. Both show a high degree of specialisation in the dataset, with professed textilemakers (all being male) carrying out at least 50 per cent of tasks, or 71 per cent when workers without a given

124 SHC, Q/SR/82, 195–7.
125 Women performed 47 out of 56 (adjusted) tasks involved the buying, selling, or transport of yarn.
126 Markham, *English Housewife*, p. 152.
127 NYCRO, QSB/1696, 123.
128 HALS, ASA8/2/13, 20–3.
129 LaA, QSB/1/31, 53–4.

occupational descriptor are excluded.[130] Skilled artisans such as these could organise their labour, or be organised, in different ways. Some, like the Fentons or the Chapmans, operated small-scale cottage industries to which family members contributed. Walter Turpyn of Ipplepen in Devon spent a September day in 1613 with his son William 'weaving in their looms' in his shop and home while William's wife sat at the threshold, possibly spinning. On a Saturday in March 1637, Richard Bury likewise wove 'all day till sun setting ... in his father's house' in Hopwood, Lancashire.[131] Within these family enterprises, it is difficult to discern if sons and other relatives served formal apprenticeships. Yet there is certainly evidence of weavers employing journeymen and other servants, some of whom may have been apprentices, in their workshops. Richard Brooke and John Hobson, for example, were fellow servants who spent 25 March 1696 'weaving in a chamber' of their master's house in Idle, Yorkshire.[132] Edward Lacey likewise was 'a journeyman weaver' working in the house of weaver Richard Fortune of Seend in Wiltshire in 1564. Established weavers might employ each other on a more casual basis as well: in the 1590s in Devon weaver and married man Richard Bickley was often hired as 'an ordinary workman to weave dozens and kerseys for one Robert Aileston of Crediton ... weaver', with his wife fetching the required yarn from Aileston.[133]

As independent tradesmen, weavers provided bespoke services for their neighbours and the wider community.[134] But they might also be employed in larger enterprises and embedded in networks and fashions of international trade. Thomas Chapman, for example, purchased Spanish white wool from a clothier of Trowbridge named Robert Pinchin, with which he produced a lighter 'Spanish medley' cloth, no doubt to meet 'new market demands'.[135] Over the course of the period, clothiers like Pinchin increasingly brought the various stages of textile production under their management and control, a process often described as proto-industrialisation.[136] Under the putting-out system, clothiers might subcontract weavers to produce cloth *en masse*. Clothier John Smith of Haydon in Somerset, for instance, 'did employ one

[130] Out of 42 weaving tasks, 41 per cent were done by workers with no descriptor. For comparison, see Zell, *Industry in the Countryside*, p. 169.

[131] DHC, Chanter 867, *Bully v. Turpyn*; LaA, QSB/1/183, 88, 90–1.

[132] WYAS, QS1/35/6, Deposition of John Whitehead and David Burke.

[133] WSHC, D1/42/6, 1–2v; DHC, QS/4/Box 5, Easter, 32–3, 45–6.

[134] On such provincial and bespoke trade, see Styles, *Dress of the People*, pp. 135–51, esp. 140.

[135] Quotes from Coleman, 'An innovation and its diffusion', p. 428

[136] See for example Zell, *Industrial Countryside*; Mann, *Cloth Industry*.

George Foweracres and Edward Foweracres, weavers, to weave his cloths' in May 1650, accusing them of embezzling his yarn when they delivered broadcloth to him. Clothworkers Richard Duland and Matthew Prince, however, were under more direct supervision 'in the house of Richard Folwell … of Beckington clothier … being there at work with others' in Somerset in 1668.[137] Clothiers also collected, cleaned, and weighed wool, before putting it out to spinners for processing.[138] Companions from Frome in Somerset, widow Mauld Drap and Alice Yeomans, a weaver's wife, were contracted to a veritable web of clothiers in 1618. Drap received '6 and 20 pounds of wool to spin into yarn of her Mr Henry Albyn', while Yeomans received '8 and 20 pounds of wool … from her Mr Jeffery Cogswell clothier'. But they both ran afoul of authority when Drap lent Yeomans some of Albyn's wool, so she could spin it up and settle a debt for 'her Mr Blackborowe a clothier' of Wells.[139]

Clothiers might also direct the dyeing and finishing of textiles, often with the help of specialists. In February 1699, clothier William Bond of Oakhill in Somerset 'brought some wool to George Downe … dyer … and did help dye the same and put it on the barrow'.[140] 'Dyeing in the wool' like this was a preparatory stage, but cloth could be dyed as a finishing process as well. Either way, it was technically an apprenticed trade. The limited depositional evidence shown in Table 7.3, however, suggests a more equitable gender division of labour prevailed in practice.[141] Spinster Jane Browne of Covenham in Lincolnshire, for example, was hired to spin wool and 'lit' or dye it green, blue, and white in July 1630. Rebecca Harris operated on a larger scale: 'two pieces of narrow cloth' were sent to her in Wakefield in Yorkshire in April 1674, 'one piece whereof … to be dyed red and the other to be dressed and pressed'.[142] 'Dressing' refers to the final stage of production, usually done by shearmen, when the nap of rough wool was raised and the cloth smoothed. Women were also involved or even took the lead in the separate process of bleaching or whitening linen.[143] On a Sunday morning in July 1566, spinster Grace Caype went 'to a pit to whiten some linen webs' in Keelby, Lincolnshire. Similarly, spinster Margaret Chawner was ordered by 'her Mistress Entersely' to water 'three pieces of linen cloth

[137] SHC, Q/SR/82, 114, Q/SR/111, 69.
[138] For an example of a clothier weighing wool, see HRO, 21M65/C3/11, 302–10.
[139] SHC, Q/SR/33, 122–3. [140] SHC, Q/SR/211, 11.
[141] As does Markham, *English Housewife*, pp. 147–9.
[142] LiA, LQS/A/1/3, 123; WYAS, QS1/13/4/2, 19, QS1/13/4/3, 1.
[143] Of the four linen bleaching or whitening tasks recorded, two were done by women.

bleaching in the said Entersley's yard' in Weaverham in Cheshire around May Day 1661.[144]

If women were sometimes involved in the dyeing process, they were excluded almost entirely from fulling, when heavy woollen cloth, 'scoured by fuller's earth, was thickened by the fuller or tucker, who steeped and battered it in a vat of urine'.[145] Such specialists operated water-powered mills to mash the cloth with wooden stocks, causing fibres to constrict into a thick fabric. Clothiers were the most substantial customers of fullers, although smaller, local operators must have been common as well. In a defamation suit from 1577, for example, husbandman Humphrey Vynycombe of Stoke Canon in Devon testified to the honesty of Lawrence Tucker, who had been 'tucker [fuller] of his cloths by the space of these 11 years last past'.[146] Michael Zell summarised the three main types of fullers as mill owners, miller leasers, and wage workers.[147] Another case of a family-run business provides an example of the former. John Hagley either leased or owned a fulling mill in Tiverton in Devon during the 1620s, operating it with his two sons John and Gilbert. Hugh Mortymer's experience of fulling work was probably the more common. In November 1629 he 'wrought with a tucker named John Shorte about 9 days and then not liking his wages departed from him … and came to South Molton' in Devon.[148]

Most of the work-task evidence of fulling comes from Devon and other counties of the south-west, with a few tasks from Yorkshire. These demonstrate the regional variations in cloth production that can sometimes be discerned in the dataset. Fulling was an essential step for the 'old draperies', where warp and weft were woven loosely and had to be thickened. Worsted and the similar 'new draperies' of the seventeenth century did not require fulling, as the cloth was 'given its strength by the weaver, and its smoothness by cloth finisher'.[149] Old draperies remained dominant for longer in the west of the country, while 'new draperies' flourished in East Anglia, the location of worsted's namesake (Worstead, Norfolk). Such regional cloth industries are reflected in the task data, with 74 per cent of textile production for the eastern region occurring in

[144] TNA, KB/9/1013a/44; CALS, QJF/90/1, 143–4.
[145] Ramsay, *English Woollen Industry,* p. 10. See Zell, *Industry in the Countryside,* pp. 179–82 for a good summary of fulling processes.
[146] DHC, Chanter 859, *Tucker v. Tyler.* Tucker was a West Country term for fuller. See 'Tuck' in English Dialect Dictionary Online [website].
[147] Zell, *Industry and the Countryside,* p. 180.
[148] DHC, QS/4/Box 32, Baptist, 60–2 and Epiphany, 33.
[149] Muldrew, '"Th'ancient distaff"', p. 502.

Norfolk or Lincolnshire.[150] On a broader scale, the dataset shows textile production was less ubiquitous in the east than in the south-west and north.[151] And at the more local level, there were clear spatial patterns to the stages of production, as Table 7.3 conveys. Spinning and other preparatory stages were overwhelmingly rural, 73 per cent of such tasks taking place outside of towns.[152] The specialised weaving, dyeing, and especially fulling tasks were more evenly split between town and country, with 47 per cent performed in the former, and especially market towns. Towns became even more central to production as cloth was turned into clothing.

7.4 Clothing Production

The making of clothing, footwear, and bedding encompassed a wide range of specialist crafts. These are shown in Table 7.4, largely organised according to the product made. In noticeable contrast to the textile industry's 65:35 per cent rural/urban split, 56 per cent of overall clothing production activities took place in towns. Moreover, 63 per cent of the buying, selling, and transport of finished clothing goods occurred in urban communities. Nonetheless, the location of clothing tasks did vary according to the item, and large towns, which have received the bulk of attention from historians, accounted for relatively few. Leather tanning and outer-clothing manufacture were noticeably more urban, while the mending of clothes, and the making of lace and stockings, were more likely to occur in the countryside.

Leathermaking and the tailoring of outerwear were male dominated as well as urban. Alongside feltmaking and shoemaking, they represent the only apparel tasks with little or no participation from women in the dataset. In common with other forms of craftwork where women were noticeably absent, men with specialist occupations dominated, completing 64 per cent of the work tasks, or 79 per cent when excluding workers without an occupational descriptor. Leather-making processes were spread across different trades. Skinners and fellmongers bought and prepared the skins, tanners processed them into leather, which curriers

[150] In contrast, tasks from Norfolk or Lincolnshire make up 56 per cent of the entire eastern sample.

[151] Textile production made up 18 per cent of all eastern craftwork tasks, in contrast to 31 and 30 per cent for the south-west and north, respectively. This calculation excludes integral tasks and coroners' reports, the latter being overrepresented in the eastern sample and complicating direct regional comparisons.

[152] This includes all categories of textile production in Table 7.4 apart from dyeing, weave, finish textiles, and other.

Table 7.4 *Gender division of labour and location of clothing and shoemaking*

	Tasks	% by F adj.	% of tasks in rural parish	% of tasks in urban parish
Accessories	15	87.7	20.0	80.0
Bedding	6	72.1	40.0	60.0
Felt	2	0.0	0.0	100.0
Stockings	16	100.0	53.3	46.7
Lace	6	100.0	66.7	33.3
Mending	8	88.6	85.7	14.3
Outer clothing	50	33.0	33.3	66.7
Shoes	15	0.0	60.0	40.0
Tanning	16	0.0	18.8	81.3
Underclothing	20	95.9	50.0	50.0
Other	4	72.1	0.0	100.0
Sewing, unspecified	6	100.0	33.3	66.7
Tailoring, unspecified	21	0.0	76.2	23.8
Total	185	64.4	44.1	55.9

Notes: adj. = adjusted (x2.59). The task totals used for the first, third, and fourth columns are unadjusted.

dressed and coloured: these divisions were reflected in the dataset, with skinners buying and selling, tanners working the hides, and fellmongers doing both. However, leatherworkers like glovers might process materials too. Indeed, 31 per cent of the tasks done by glovers in the database involved the buying of skins, as in May 1680, when James Ellery bought one for 2s 8d and 'put it into his tan pit'.[153] For the most part, however, shoemakers, saddlers, and other leatherworkers concentrated on the manufacture, mending, and selling of leather goods. Trade could be bespoke or ready-made. Shoemaker John Callway of St Columb, Cornwall, 'went to the fairs to sell shoes' in 1557, while Samuel Shenton went to the shop of cordwainer James West of Leigh upon Mendip in Somerset in 1619, to have him widen a pair of boots.[154] Such workshops and the tools they held could be a valuable resource for the community, beyond the direct services of the tradesman. For instance, on 30 August 1679, labourer John Nightingale of Greens Norton in Northamptonshire spent all of his Saturday in the shop of

[153] DHC, QS/4/Box 103–4, Midsummer, Info of James Ellery.
[154] DHC, Chanter 855, *Callway v. Plewige*; SHC, D/D/Cd/55, *Allen v. Ray*.

shoemaker Thomas Kerwood, buffing one pair of shoes and mending another for his wife.[155]

Tailors and shoemakers were both workshop-based artisans and traders, but in other respects they differed substantially. For one, tailors often laboured away from their household and shop. Tailors in the dataset only did 19 per cent of their craftwork tasks in their own household, as compared to 78 per cent for leatherworkers.[156] Shoemakers and other leatherworkers were less numerous and more likely to be based in market towns and cities. Tailors were more ubiquitous; many lived in the countryside but did much of their business, both craftwork and commerce, in towns.[157] But tailors also often worked in their customers' houses, wherever those might be. As Danae Tankard has pointed out, there was a certain hierarchy to the location of work: tailors would have travelled to the homes of wealthy patrons, while poorer customers, like husbandman's wife Joan Cowling of Washfield in Devon, might send 'shag and stuff ... to one Edward Manley a tailor in Tiverton to be made into a coat for her child' in 1660.[158] Nevertheless, the depositions turn up examples of tailors working in the households of more humble clients as well. In a 1604 case discussed in the introductory chapter, Robert Lane of Wellow worked in nearby South Stoke, Somerset, and 'being a tailor by his occupation ... diverse times wrought in the same parish at many men's houses'. John Read worked 'at one goodman Mann his house at Thorpland' in Norfolk one Saturday in February 1661, when 'he missed about a yard and three quarters of taffety ribbon ... and about half a quarter of an ounce of silk' which he had left in a bag 'upon the hall table' the night before.[159]

While tailors specialised in the making of outer clothing like waistcoats, gowns, breeches, and suits, they did not monopolise its manufacture to the same extent as shoemakers or glovers did leather goods. Leatherworkers accounted for 63 per cent of leatherworking tasks, while tailors did 48 per cent of outerwear tasks. Married women in particular might follow the example of Mary Ivory, a gardener's wife from North Mimms in Hertfordshire, in making outer garments themselves. In 1681

[155] NAS, QSR/1/95, Info of William Leeke.

[156] For craftwork tasks done with a known location. Using categories explained in Section 1.2.3.

[157] Fifty-nine per cent of tasks where residence was known were done by rural tailors. Only 51 per cent of tailors' tasks were done in a rural parish, suggesting some movement into towns for work.

[158] Tankard, *Clothing in Seventeenth Century*, pp. 53–4. DHC, QS/4/Box 66, Michaelmas, 32.

[159] SHC, D/D/Cd/36, *Reade v. Hedges*; NRO, C/S3/44, Info of Samuel Mann.

she fashioned a 'piece of damask into a pair of sleeves for her own wearing', before lining 'her own riding hood' with the remainder of the fabric.[160] Yet it was in categories of clothing production other than leather and outerwear that women truly dominated. Overall, they accounted for at least 64 per cent of clothing production in the dataset, when adjusted figures are used. They were responsible for the making of all lace and stockings, nearly all underclothes, and the majority of clothing accessories and bedding. Women dominated these crafts, which did not require formal apprenticeships; but why these activities remained largely unapprenticed while others did not remains unclear. One possible interpretation might associate men with professional production for the market, and women with fashioning goods associated with the household and family. Certainly, there was a high degree of specialism and 'for another' work, at 61 per cent, among male apparel producers. Yet, while evidence of women producing for their own household is not hard to find, evidence of market-oriented activity also throws this simple dichotomy into question.[161]

In a typical case of household industry from 1693, Anne Brown testified that four shifts 'of her own spinning and making' and belonging to herself, her husband, and two children had been stolen from a hedge in her backyard in Sandhutton in Yorkshire.[162] Underclothing like this was the most common item made at home, but other needs might be met through the repurposing of second-hand goods. Sarah Marley of Liverpool bought two horse cloths from Sarah Digle in March 1666 for 18d, cutting up one of them to 'make her husband a frock'. Similarly, Annis Potter, the wife of a slipper-maker from Witchford in Cambridgeshire, used a child's blanket to 'sew part her petticoats' in 1655.[163] The previously mentioned damask sleeves of Mary Ivory illustrate the versatility of such second-hand items: Mary later gave or sold them 'to Thomas Chessam ... for Sarah Chessam the daughter of James Chessam ... of Essendon', and when one of the sleeves wore out, the other was 'made into a neckcloth' and passed on to Thomas Chessam's own daughter Mary.

As the latter example suggests, it is too simplistic to equate men's clothing work with commerce and women's with the household during this period. Much of women's apparel production was done for remuneration

160 HALS, QSR/19, 95.

161 Market-oriented clothing production was certainly the norm in seventeenth-century London: Shepard, *Accounting for Oneself*, p. 220; Gowing, *Ingenious Trade.*

162 NYCRO, QSB/1694, 178.

163 LaA, QSB/1/1666, April, Info of Edward Alcock; CUL, EDR/E10/1655, Info of Annis Gaul.

or the commercial market, particularly lacemaking and stocking knitting. Indeed, out of all female clothing production tasks, at least 48 per cent were performed for individuals outside the household. Moreover, as is explored in Section 8.1, women accounted for 58 per cent of selling clothing tasks (adjusted) in the dataset. It is difficult to know how many of these items were made by the sellers themselves or represented second-hand trade. But women like spinster Agnes Parsons were not uncommon; when she was accused of stealing bone lace from the market stand of Agnes and John Bowden in Taunton, and selling it on at the nearby stand of spinster Joan Gilford, she claimed to have 'made some of that kind' and bought the rest legitimately.[164] For Parsons, or seamstresses like Florence Band of Stockleigh Pomeroy, Devon, and Agnes Hope of St Albans in Hertfordshire, needlework may have been their primary occupation.[165] Single woman Catherine Padgot of Norwich claimed outright to earn 'her living by filling bobbins and sometimes by sewing' in 1693, while Margaret Roads similarly made 'her living by making of Bonelace' in the 1640s.[166] Roads was the wife of a 'wandering ballad-maker' and likely had an atypical lifestyle. For many married women or widows, sewing and knitting, like spinning, may have been supplemental work.[167] In 1631, labourer's wife Elizabeth Leake of Hillington in Norfolk hired Thomasine Tye, also married to a labourer, to knit a pair of stockings for her child. Cordwainer's wife Christian Slee of Crediton, Devon, bought a 'breadth of Rosterne' made by Thomasine Greene for 10d in October 1610.[168]Afterwards she 'made the same up to a falling band and sold the same to … Peter Joseph's wife for 12d'; Peter was later spotted wearing it. Widow Katherine Gyles of East Bradenham in Norfolk, meanwhile, had a standing arrangement with Thomas Armstrong around 1614, in which he 'put wool to her to spin … and she did use to knit his stockings'.[169]

If the gender division of the clothing industry did not spring principally from the commercial orientations of production, there were other telling distinctions. There was, for example, a clear gender divide between the mending of used clothes and the making of new ones. As we have already seen, women were more likely to repurpose used clothing and materials.

[164] SHC, Q/SR/29–31, 95–7.
[165] DHC, Chanter 859, 322r–324v (1577); HALS, ASA8/8, 5 (1595).
[166] NRO, DN/DEP/53/58A, *Ex Officio v. Georgina Rose*; HALS, QSR/7, 153–4. For similar examples, see Shepard, *Accounting for Oneself*, pp. 174–7.
[167] Shepard, *Accounting for Oneself*, pp. 176–7, 218–21.
[168] NRO, C/S3/28, Exam of Margarett Wilson, Exam of Elizabeth Leake, Info of Robert Tye; DHC, QS/4/Box 16, Easter, Exam of Christian Slee.
[169] NRO, C/S3/19, Info of Katherine Gyles, Exam of Thomas Armstrong.

They were also much more likely to mend damaged or worn apparel. Arrangements could be ad hoc or standing. Joan Elliot of Compton Chamberlayne in Wiltshire patched William Jeay's breeches when he came to her house wet and bedraggled 'about Christmas' in 1599, while William Jepton of Ecclesfield in Yorkshire employed Anne Whitley 'for three years ... by times' in the 1680s to mend his stockings and 'do such odd things for him'.[170] Men were capable of mending clothing, but the two examples of this in the dataset are revealing. The labourer Hugh Trapp did not go to church one Sunday morning in 1630 but stayed home in Brockley, Somerset, 'to mend his clothes'. The tailor John Gibson of Kirby Hill in Yorkshire was hired by George Raper to do the same in 1693. Yet Gibson was apparently so destitute that 'he refused and bid ... [Raper] get them mended where he would and at that time went into the country a begging and refused to work his trade'.[171] As with the well-known socio-economic separation between shoe menders (cobblers) and shoemakers, poverty and low status seem to have been the key factors, rather than gender alone.[172] In this way, a hierarchy of clothes, and not just materials, may have helped shape the gendered nature of clothing production: new and public trappings of wealth and rank (furnished by male tradesmen) were at the top, while old or intimate garments (furnished by women) were underneath.[173]

7.5 Conclusion

Judith Bennett argued that women's work largely remained 'low-status, low-paid, and low-skilled' during the early modern period.[174] The work-task evidence for rural textile and clothing industries, however, suggests some qualifiers are needed. Regarding pay, clothing production and spinning were major sources of income which, as Craig Muldrew has shown, could sometimes outstrip male earnings during the late seventeenth and early eighteenth centuries.[175] Nor was such work necessarily low-skilled. Spinning, knitting, sewing, and lacemaking all required training, in some cases extensive. In practice, the distinctions between tailors and seamstresses were not simply about the type of work done and form of training; they were also social and semantic. As Table 7.4 shows,

170 WSHC, D1/42/18, 23b–28bv; WYAS, QS1/25/10, Deposition of Anne Whitley.
171 SHC, Q/SR/62, 53–4; NYCRO, QSB/1695, 175.
172 On the nominal socio-economic division between shoemakers and cobblers, see Hobsbawm and Scott, 'Political shoemakers', p. 101; Porter, 'Cobblers all', p. 45.
173 For more on the gendered production of underclothing, see North, *Sweet and Clean?*, pp. 178–207.
174 Bennett, *History Matters*, p. 62.
175 Muldrew, '"Th'ancient distaff"', pp. 520–2.

all tasks described simply as 'sewing' were done by women, while 'tailoring' tasks were only done by men. Yet, tailors did quite a lot of sewing, as when Thomas Williamson of Winwick in Lancashire went 'to one Robert Rigbie's house webster there to sew being a tailor by profession'.[176] Women were largely excluded from apprenticed trades in these industries as they were in others. But the result did not keep them from attaining the necessary skills to practice such crafts. Instead, it barred them from the prestige and access to business that came with these trades, which in turn further shaped gendered attitudes towards craftwork. While women increasingly entered formal apprenticeships in mantua making and tailoring in late-seventeenth-century London, and elsewhere during the eighteenth century, the work-task results suggest that rural tradesmen, and society in general, jealously guarded access throughout the sixteenth and seventeenth centuries.[177]

Textile and clothing work thus epitomises the complex ways in which early modern craftwork was gendered and otherwise organised in the English countryside. While craft guilds did not control and regulate trade in market towns and villages, apprenticeship nonetheless played a major role in structuring rural industry. Although idiosyncrasies can be demonstrated, the apprenticeship system was the chief means of acquiring artisanal skill and recognition throughout the period. These trades remained the overwhelming preserve of men, despite a lack of legislation explicitly barring women from apprenticeship. However, such exclusion did not prevent women from acquiring advanced training and skills, and indeed numerical dominance, within the textile and clothing industries. Nor were women barred from industry solely on the basis of apprenticeship and specialisation; certain types of construction, like groundworks, were low skill yet male dominated. As we have seen elsewhere in this book, gender often intersected with status and other customary ideas in determining who did what work and why.

If groundworks and textile and clothing production are any indication, it is too simplistic to equate craftwork and construction with specialisation during this period. Nonetheless, for many categories of industry, specialised tradesmen performed the majority of work tasks. This was so for certain stages or segments of textile and clothing production, like weaving, fulling, shoemaking, and tailoring, but was particularly pronounced for woodwork, metalwork, and building. Yet, even in construction, artisans did not work alone or completely monopolise labour. They

[176] LaA, QSB/1/1667, October, Info of John Jenkinson, Exam of Thomas Williamson.
[177] On the rise of female apprenticeships see Snell, *Annals*, pp. 270–319; Gowing, *Ingenious Trade*, pp. 55–98.

worked alongside servants and labourers, but also, as some specific examples have shown, butchers, wool-combers, or husbandmen. Thus, specialisation alone, as communicated through occupational descriptors, tells only part of the story of craftwork in the English early modern economy. Moreover, it does not capture adequately women's contribution to industry, or the overall division of craftwork between self-employment/household production and the labour market. The work-task findings suggest that specialist craftsmen did much of their work 'for others', as one might expect. But a substantial amount of women's craftwork was directed outside the household as well.

8 Commerce and Money Management

At the end of November in 1580, Agnes More visited the shop of Richard Wright in the parish of Pullen St Mary, a small market town south of Norwich. She went with the intention of buying two yards of kersey fabric, but whilst in the shop was shown by Richard Wright a remnant of kersey measuring two and a half yards, which he claimed 'was a good one' and that the additional half yard might be 'good store for her' with many uses including making 'a pair of calyengs for a boy'.[1] Persuaded, Agnes purchased the kersey and an additional three-quarters of cloth to line a pair of hose for one of her boys. She agreed to pay 5s 2d for the cloth in total, 22d of which was paid in coin and a further 3s 4d on credit, which was entered into Richard Wright's debt book. The transcribing of the debt was witnessed by Richard's wife, Elizabeth, and Francis Kerison, soon to be Agnes' son-in-law. Sometime in August 1581, Agnes sent her daughter to the tailor's shop tendering the outstanding debt. When her daughter arrived Richard Wright refused to take the payment and contested the sum, claiming the amount outstanding was in fact 4s 4d. Agnes' deposition forms part of a far wider suit of testamentary following the death of Richard Wright's master, Roger Collinson the elder. Collinson resided in Norwich and dealt in cloth. He extended credit to his customers and Wright maintained the debt books, oversaw the delivery of the cloth in and around Norwich, and collected payments. Because Agnes bought her cloth on credit, it appears that the death of Roger Collinson sparked a desire to settle her account with Richard Wright.

The case highlights many of the facets of early modern commerce. The cloth sold by Richard Wright in his shop was sold on behalf of a merchant in Norwich who had extensive networks in the city. Agnes had gone to a shop, a permanent fixture of the local marketplace, and was accompanied by a relative. She was served by Richard Wright, who seems to have been

[1] NRO, DN/DEP/19/20, 214–24. It is probable that 'calyengs' were hose or stockings.

able to persuade her to purchase more than she had intended, and also in the shop was Elizabeth Wright, Richard's wife, who bore witness to the credit extended by her husband. The exchange was settled in both coin and a form of credit in a deferred payment which required ongoing management by Agnes when she requested her daughter to settle the account several months later.

Depositional evidence gives detailed insight into the work that went on behind acts of buying and selling. Transactions were rarely settled at the point of exchange and instead consumers built up a 'portfolio of contractual obligations', often solidifying social networks through credit and debt.[2] As in the testimony of Agnes More, deponents often described these protracted commercial exchanges and the methods of payment that were used. When Keith Wrightson described the structure of markets in early modern England, he envisaged four overlapping spheres that reflected increasingly complex markets moving from the local to the national. The evidence for buying and selling recorded in the database relates predominantly to the primary sphere of commerce, characterised by Wrightson as a 'kind of quasi-commercial extension of neighbourliness' in highly localised markets.[3] The work-task data offers a unique sample of this day-to-day commerce and the forms of credit that propped up local exchange. All households were, to some degree, enmeshed in networks of obligations in the early modern economy. Yet this normative credit that so often functioned as an alternative currency in the marketplace has left little evidence in the written records.[4]

The management of household debt was a crucial component of housewifery. Alexandra Shepard has shown married women demonstrated agency as 'asset managers' in a household, as they brokered credits and kept account of reciprocal obligations.[5] Focusing in this chapter on the objects bought, sold, pawned, exchanged, lent, and borrowed in the depositions shows the consumer good oscillating from an object of consumption to a store of value and means of exchange. It also reveals the amount of work this entailed. Depositions recount the central role played by married women as determinants of value and worth in household economies and broader networks of credit and pawn. Deponents recall these exchanges in detail and the data allows for some quantitative analysis of the borrowing and lending patterns of men and women in rural economies. The work-task method for recording work activities means that the work of both buyers and sellers is recorded as

[2] Shaw, 'Liquidation or certification?', p. 278.
[3] Wrightson, *Earthly* Necessities, p. 93.
[4] Muldrew, *Economy of Obligation*, p. 95.
[5] Shepard, 'Crediting women'.

well as the work tasks of individuals mediating sales, from the shepherds appraising a flock prior to a sale to the maid servant ferrying messages back and forth regarding the price of a litter of pigs to her master. Approaching commerce through the lens of work presents a new perspective on these quotidian transactions. Breaking down the act of acquiring goods into its constitutive tasks, the methodology ascribes a value to the hidden labour in economic work – mediating payments, appraising and pawning goods, and managing household finances – which has previously been unquantified in histories of everyday commerce.

The category of commerce is the second largest in the work-task dataset. In total there are 2,115 commercial work activities including the subcategories of buying, selling, exchange, going to market, and running a stall or shop. The analysis can also be expanded to include the work tasks related to financial management and pawning, both subcategories within the category of management, to capture a broader range of exchanges and the continued management of credit. A large proportion of the evidence for commerce in the work-task database comes from cases concerning theft. In the category of commerce, 63 per cent of work tasks come from cases of theft, a figure that is even higher when looking at incidences of buying, where 74 per cent of work tasks were marked as integral. The high proportion of integral work tasks arises from a repeated narrative on the part of deponents accused of theft: of having purchased goods rather than stolen them. This is particularly clear in instances of pawning where goods that were given in pawn were later claimed to have been stolen: 87 per cent of the incidences of pawning were integral to the case and derived almost exclusively from cases of theft. Though the goods themselves, usually clothing though also tools and cutlery, were contested, the pawning of the good after the theft usually was not. Moreover, and as explained in Section 1.1, the narratives behind buying, selling, and pawning commercial goods were intended to form plausible accounts of everyday commerce. They were meant to be believable, and in many cases were no doubt true. This chapter therefore includes all commercial and money management tasks, regardless of their information status. Removing integral cases from the analysis of everyday commerce would significantly diminish the amount of data available, much more so than for other categories of work recorded, and those integral cases still contain valuable and unrivalled evidence of the everyday operation of money matters. It is also the case that the main issue with integral tasks is that they inflate the size of certain categories and types of work, especially commerce, relative to others. With the focus here on patterns *within* commerce, the prevalence of buying, selling, and exchange in our sources is less of an issue, and arguably a strength.[6]

The chapter begins with an overview of buying and selling recorded in the category of commerce. It assesses the types and values of goods bought and sold and the gender differences between buyers and sellers. The chapter then focuses on those work activities associated with the management of household finances and credit, namely negotiating prices and reckoning accounts. The final part of the chapter analyses the spaces of commerce, bringing together the categories of commerce, financial management, and pawning. Exchanges at market were insufficient to meet the daily demands of household consumption, and the spatial analysis draws attention to the permeability of the home to commerce. Considering commercial work within and outside the household as well as ascribing secondary units of spatial analysis, the chapter finishes by considering the gendering of spaces of commerce.

8.1 Buying and Selling

The history of early modern retail has been plagued by a notion of latent development and an unchanging commercial environment from medieval markets and fairs until the arrival of the 'consumer revolution', epitomised in the expanding shops and department stores of eighteenth-century London.[7] Attempts to find a consumer society predating the avaricious consumption of the middling sort in the eighteenth century focus on the spaces of retail and practices of advertising. Shops operating from the front of a domestic dwelling in the early modern period have now been recast as sophisticated spaces of retail, carefully displaying wares on shutter doors to entice prospective customers.[8] The chains of indebtedness recorded in the debt books of shopkeepers have been considered in light of ongoing social and economic relationships that prefigure the socialisation of shopping in the late eighteenth century.[9] But these approaches to retail and consumption are, by their nature, urban centric. Although Beverley Lemire in her work on plebeian commercial circuits highlights the interconnectedness of commerce in fixed shops, itinerant markets, and an undercurrent of 'murkier quotidian traffic', producing a 'disorderly amalgam of commercial energy, custom

[6] Removing integral tasks was also found to make little difference to the gender division of labour within commerce subcategories.

[7] Benson and Ugolini (eds.), *Nation of Shopkeepers*; Blonde et al., 'Retail circuits'; McKendrick et al. (eds.), *Birth of a Consumer Society*.

[8] Cox, *Complete Tradesman*; Stobart, *Sugar and Spice*; Walsh, 'Social relations of shopping'.

[9] Walsh, 'Social relations of shopping'.

and opportunism', evidence for this everyday exchange is thin and where it exists, largely unquantifiable.[10] We know comparatively less about the daily buying and selling that occurred in rural economies in the sixteenth and seventeenth centuries.

As discussed in Section 3.2, commerce was more prevalent in the task repertoire of large towns than it was in countryside task repertoire, but within the category of commerce just 11 per cent of work tasks were located within large towns, with 45 per cent of work tasks located in market towns and the rest in smaller rural communities. The approach to depositional evidence used here shifts the focus from urban studies of commerce and retail, and instead presents a quantitative analysis of the daily commerce that sustained rural households. Including analysis of exchange and pawning too widens the definition of commerce to include alternative currencies. In instances of exchange, we find descriptions of payments in kind and the exchange of household goods to meet immediate consumption needs, as when the wife of Thomas Monsawyt visited her neighbour, the wife of William Wallys in Downham, Cambridgeshire, in 1565 to exchange an egg for a piece of bread or when Alice Buckley acquired wool through the exchange of 'starch and soap and such other commodities, of her neighbours' in Rochdale, Lancashire, in 1627.[11] These descriptions of how goods came to be acquired in the rural household go some way to quantifying the informal networks of reciprocity that supported early modern commerce and the continued dependence on systems of reckonings and payments in kind when access to coin was constrained. Probate inventories capture the objects accumulated by a household during its lifetime but can say little about the biography of those objects, who bought them, owned them, or used them.[12] As shown by Sara Pennell, the gendering of consumer goods appears not in their ownership but in their use.[13] The details of commerce in the work-task database provide a window into the goods bought and sold and consumed daily by households, as well as the gendered consumption patterns in rural economies at the point of purchase, placing consumables in focus alongside durable goods.

Despite contradictions in household manuals, women engaged with all forms of commerce, accounting for roughly half of all actors buying, selling, exchanging, going to market, and running a stall or shop. Women travelled to and from markets where they bought and sold

[10] Lemire, 'Plebian commercial circuits', p. 246.
[11] CUL, EDR/2/7, *William Wallis v. Thomas Monsawyt*; LaA, QSB/1/31, 53–4.
[12] Weatherill 'Meaning of consumer behaviour'.
[13] Pennell, 'Consumption and consumerism', p. 555.

produce. As sellers they are often described working alongside their husband, as when, in 1620, the wife of James Morgan sold shoes at her husband's stand in Tiverton market in Devon, but they also appear as independent sellers in market spaces.[14] Wilmot Horne sold pilchards at Modbury market in Devon in 1598 and Susan Darby was described selling oatmeal and salt at her stall outside the Black Swan Inn on market day in Norwich in 1694.[15] Three women, Mary Parker, Catherine Ford, and Agnes Durant, all held stalls adjacent to the Guild Hall in Exeter selling fish in 1674, which they described as their 'usual employment or trade'.[16] They described their stalls as being alongside that of Thomas Hockland who was also there selling fish at his own stall. The depositions also describe women accessing markets as consumers. Going to market could be sociable and women were more likely to attend market in groups; in 1695, Anne Greenwood, Claire Adams, and Sara Roberts travelled together to the market in the centre of Norwich at Christmas time.[17] Marital status appeared an important factor in determining access to commerce. Married women made up just over half of all female buyers and sellers in the database at 51 per cent, whilst never-married women made up 11 per cent and widowed women 12 per cent, with the marital status of 26 per cent of women doing these tasks unknown. It is a pattern mirrored across the database, though married women appear in buy and sell work activities at a slightly greater frequency than they do across the dataset as a whole, where married women performed 43 per cent of female work tasks. Work repertoires in Section 2.3 show a similar pattern with commerce accounting for a greater proportion of the work tasks of married and widowed women.[18] There are some slight variances within the buy and sell categories. Widowed women were more frequently recorded as sellers than buyers, and never-married women were more likely to appear as buyers than sellers.

The roles of buyer and seller were not clearly gendered. Women made up 51 per cent of all buyers and 43 per cent of all sellers recorded in the category of commerce. There was relatively little evidence of proxy shopping, where shopping was carried out for someone else. Of a total of 1,053 work activities that recorded buying goods, 44 were done 'for another', just 13 of which were explicitly carried out in service. The work-task data does not therefore reflect the trend for indirect shopping

[14] DHC, QS/4/Box 24, Baptist, Exam of Robert Gloyne.

[15] DHC, QS/4/Box 5, 56; NRO, DN/DEP/53/58A, *Darby v. Deverack*.

[16] DHC, Chanter 875, Ford v Durrant.

[17] NRO, DN/DEP/53/58A, *Greenwood v. Cosfer*. On Christmas as a key time of commerce, see Section 4.2.

[18] See Table 2.8.

amongst the wealthy and middling sorts who requested specific items be purchased on their behalf by others, or who delegated the task of daily shopping to household servants.[19] Instead, the daily commercial exchanges recorded were most commonly to meet the consumption needs of an individual's own household. The nature of these everyday exchanges, in particular the gendered disparity in objects handled in the marketplace, has eluded historians of early modern retail. McIntosh makes a broad assumption of a gender division in patterns of consumption suggesting that men purchased goods for their work and the physical maintenance of their home, while women purchased food, clothing, and household goods, objects that were of lower value and usually for immediate consumption.[20] Her concluding remarks reflecting on women in the market, that 'as producers and sellers of goods, they were clustered within activities related to their work at home (dealing with food, drink, and cloth/clothing), and they normally operated on a small scale', reinforce an idea of women's commercial work being limited to the domestic sphere.[21] Table 8.1 shows the objects purchased and sold by men and women.

Women do dominate as buyers in consumer goods, purchasing finished goods such as aprons, knives, stockings, pewter flagons, saucers, and salt cellars, but men also formed a significant proportion of buyers in this category, accounting for 35.4 per cent of buyers of food and drink and 34.0 per cent of buyers of housewares. Contrary to expectations, women account for a large proportion of buyers of raw materials. They were 49.0 per cent of buyers of wool and animal skins and 41.8 per cent of buyers of grain, grass, and crops; unfinished materials that required further processing. Women formed a significant proportion of sellers of these unfinished goods, most significantly making up 51.9 per cent of sellers of wool and skins. Evidence from the depositions suggests that some women worked alongside their husband in a joint enterprise. Nicholas Snell and his wife dyed and sold wool in Tiverton, Devon, in 1620, and in 1659 William Spurlocke sent his wife to Yeovil market in Somerset to sell the skins of four sheep he had killed earlier.[22]

The values of goods bought and sold, however, differed greatly between women and men. When buying livestock, women predominantly bought poultry and in small quantities, buying a single hen or a couple of geese, whereas men bought sheep and cows and did so in larger quantities, often whole flocks of 40 or 60 sheep in a single purchase. The average value of livestock bought by women was 4s, compared to

[19] Walsh, 'Social relations of shopping'. [20] McIntosh, *Working Women*, p. 239.
[21] Ibid., p. 250. [22] DHC, QS/4/Box24, Easter, 7; SHC, Q/SR/98, 65–7.

Table 8.1 *Types of goods bought and sold, by gender*

Types of goods		Buying				Selling			
		F tasks adj.	M tasks	Total tasks	% by F adj.	F tasks adj.	M tasks	Total tasks	% by F adj.
Raw materials	Livestock	73	239	312	23.3	62	207	269	23.1
	Horses	0	30	30	0.0	3	22	25	10.5
	Wool/skins	67	70	137	49.0	52	48	100	51.9
	Grain/grass	47	65	112	41.8	21	52	73	28.5
	Timber/wood	0	28	28	0.0	5	24	29	17.8
Manufactured products	Textiles	124	36	160	77.5	75	40	115	65.3
	Equipment/tools	13	30	43	30.2	8	21	29	27.0
	Iron	3	14	17	15.6	10	12	22	46.3
Consumer goods	Food/drink	246	135	381	64.6	142	113	255	55.8
	Clothing	106	45	151	70.2	54	40	94	57.6
	Housewares	39	20	59	66.0	13	13	26	49.9
	Light/fuel/cleaning	18	10	28	64.5	8	12	20	39.3
	Silverware	5	4	9	56.4	10	2	12	83.8
	Furniture	5	3	8	63.3	0	2	2	0.0
	Books/paper	3	2	5	56.4	0	4	4	0.0
Unclear	Unclear	31	21	52	59.7	13	23	36	36.0
Total		780	752	1,532	50.9	477	635	1,112	42.9

Notes: adj. = adjusted (x2.59).

livestock bought by men with an average value of £2 6s 10d, a figure inflated by some infrequent but high-value sales of large herds of livestock. Similar patterns are found when comparing the average values of purchased wool, skins, and grains: women purchased smaller quantities and handled smaller sums. Women account for 77.5 per cent of buyers of textiles, unfinished cloth, lace, linen, yarn, and ribbons to be made up into clothing. When buying textiles, the average value of goods bought by women, 5s 10d, was greater than that of men, 4s 10d. Yet as sellers of textiles the average value of goods sold by women was just 1s 7d. Women were not excluded from the buying and selling of raw materials, though the average value of the goods they dealt in was less than their male counterparts.[23]

Table 8.1 does show women to have made up a greater proportion of buyers of consumer goods. It shows men made up a greater proportion of buyers of tools and equipment, including nails, paint, ladders, knives, and a hatchet, whilst women made up a greater proportion of buyers of housewares. Women were the principal purchasers of pots, pans, and dining ware, and took responsibility for the furnishing of the kitchen. These goods, however, were also the tools of housewifery and the skillet, brass pan, or pewter tankard can also be regarded as tools and equipment much like the ladder or hatchet. The food and drink recorded in the broader category of consumer goods does not reflect prepared meals but rather staples of bread, cheese, ale, fruit, and raw ingredients. Just two deponents recalled purchasing a meal, whilst 47 per cent of food purchasers recalled buying raw meat that required further preparation and cooking. Pots, pans, and knives were essential tools in the kitchen to process these raw ingredients for consumption in the home or to be used in further trades preparing food and drink for sale. Kitchen wares were not only tools of housewifery but also important stores of wealth. Large pans were carefully selected, and a range of kitchen and dining goods were acquired over a lifetime.[24] As consumers, women were aware of the value of their goods with a constant view of the burgeoning second-hand market. Alexandra Shepard has shown a circulating knowledge of the value of household goods to be essential when individuals attested to their own worth before the court, or when neighbours judged the creditworthiness of one another.[25] Once considered auxiliary to activities of commerce, the trade of second-hand goods has been reassessed and

[23] For a comparison of these patterns of commerce in early modern England and Sweden, see Hailwood et al., 'Comparing the gender division'.

[24] Pennell, *Birth of the English Kitchen.*

[25] Shepard, *Accounting for Oneself.*

shown to be a valuable source of household income.[26] The consumer goods bought by women relate to other household work and were intended as stores of wealth.

The work-task approach offers a detailed and quantified view of everyday commerce. Both women and men were active as sellers and buyers. Gendered differences lay in the value of transactions and to a lesser extent in the types of goods exchanged. Women did not only deal in items related to housework and textiles, their buying and selling extended into raw materials and industrial goods. At the same time, it is helpful to see women's purchase of housewares as equivalent to men's purchases of tools: all were implements for use in future work activities. The chapter now turns to an analysis of the evidence for the borrowing and lending described in the database and the role assumed by women as 'asset managers' of credits, debts, and moveable household wares, governing the position of their household in a wider and interconnected nexus of credit obligations.

8.2 Credit and Debt

Buying and selling was rarely a straightforward exchange. Goods were often valued beforehand, and prices were mediated and relayed between interested parties. Ongoing credit needed to be recorded and managed, with debt books often consulted when accounts were reckoned. Accounts were routinely managed, and there was much work, often unrecorded, associated with the maintenance of household finances in a credit economy. Requesting, or in some instances demanding, the payments of debts often appears as the tangential justification by deponents for their movements or their presence within a household. In the case that opened this chapter, Agnes More sent her daughter to reckon her account with Richard Wright. Agnes was not managing her household finances in isolation but was doing so with the knowledge of wider chains of credit that came to contestation with the death of Roger Collinson, and sent her daughter on her behalf to carry the money.

Managing household finances and making payments in the early modern economy included hidden labour. For instance, in Tadcaster, Yorkshire, in 1662, a servant, Maria Blunt, was sent by her master Mr Foster to a neighbouring farmstead to request the price of newly birthed piglets. Upon arrival she was met by the housekeeper, Anne Tailor, who informed her each piglet was to be sold for 20d whereupon

[26] Lemire, *Dress, Culture, and Commerce* and 'Plebeian commercial circuits'; Shepard, 'Crediting women'.

Maria went back to her master who then gave her the coin and sent her back to Anne to purchase the piglet and to bring it home.[27] In Northallerton in the same county in 1692, Edward Rymer acted as a mediator to a sale, having been paid a shilling to find a buyer for two men selling a horse. He approached John Adam to 'help him to a good bargain' and settled a price between the two parties.[28] Professional opinions too were often sought to appraise goods, particularly in the sale of livestock. Two male shepherds, with the surnames Durington and Blackwell, were sought by Henry Bankes to value lambs in Settrington, Yorkshire, in 1611, that were proposed for sale. Both shepherds thought the price, 2s 10d for each lamb, was too dear and a new price of 2s 4d was agreed based on their expert appraisal.[29] This work negotiating deals and relaying information for sale was time-consuming work that rarely appears in other records of consumption. But using the work-task method mediating a sale or providing an appraisal of goods can be identified and included within the category 'exchange'.

There was also a large body of unseen work in managing credit obligations. Credit could generate large amounts of written documentation that needed to be maintained. Upon his deathbed in Norfolk in 1616, Robert Howling referred to a cupboard in which he had amassed bills and bonds that needed to be administered to settle his accounts.[30] Simply paying debts and moving money also required time and transport. In 1532 Arthur Bentley was desired by one Ranulf of Dynley to travel from Downham to Halifax, a distance of 27 miles, to carry money owed by Ranulf to Agnes Oitts.[31] Time could be wasted too when settling accounts. Stephen Jule made a visit to the home of Andrew Penrose in Holsworthy, Devon, in 1598 to ask for the repayment of 20d and was asked to 'bear with him until the fair at Holsworthy', delaying the repayment and prolonging the credit contract.[32] When a man known only as Magson entered the home of Alexander Tomlinson in the small village of Hawkshead, Lancashire, in 1623 tendering a debt he owed he refused to hand over the coin when Tomlinson admitted he did not have the bond ready, leaving the debt unpaid.[33] Individuals did not always manage their own finances: 17 per cent of financial management work tasks were performed 'for another'. Some of this work was explicitly paid or part of service: Richard Bruce was paid 10s in 1613 to deliver a sum of £4 10s to Mr Simpson in Cripplegate, London, and was

[27] BI, CP.H.4631, *Holt v. Taylor.* [28] NYCRO, QSB/1693, 223–4.
[29] BI, CP.H.754, *Henry Bankes v. John Colby.* [30] NRO, DN/DEP/37/40, 240.
[31] BI, CP.G.3483, *Oade v. Oade.* [32] DHC, QS/4/Box 5, 28–9.
[33] CALS, EDC/5/1624, 11.

promised a further 10s on his return; George Gullock was employed as an apprentice by Francis Squire in Okehampton, Devon, in 1675 to keep his accounts.[34]

More commonly the terms of 'for another' financial and commercial work were not explicit or specified. Many of these took the form of witnessing a transaction. In 1691, Isabella Richards asked John Hartnoll to accompany her to the home of Joanne Kerslake in Tiverton, Devon, to witness her repay a debt owed to Joanne. Anthony Taylor was requested by Thomas Postgate to accompany him to the house of William Wales in Chester-le-Street, Durham, to demand debts from William's wife in 1620.[35] Bearing witness to credit and commerce was a duty of neighbourliness, but it was also time-consuming work. However, such practices became the norm in an increasingly litigious society where 70 per cent of civil litigation at common law concerned debts.[36] Buying and selling in the early modern economy were underpinned by a swathe of hidden labour that regulated commerce outside the marketplace. Whilst some of this work is subsumed within the subcategories of commerce – such as exchange, buy, and sell – associated work, such as transporting money, demanding payments and rents, recording credits and debts, hiring tools and livestock, counting money, and managing accounts, falls within the subcategory of financial management within the broader management category. The subcategory of pawning within the management category also captures credit given against goods traded in pawn. Previously considered peripheral to commercial activities, pawning has since been reconsidered as central to early modern credit markets both as a survival mechanism for poorer households and as a legitimate means of utilising the wealth stored in consumer goods.[37] Combining the subcategories within commerce with the subcategories of pawning and financial management here captures the extensive work activities associated with the broader management of household finances.

Table 8.2 shows the marital status of women performing this broader range of tasks. Widows might be expected to account for a higher proportion of those undertaking financial management tasks. We know that wives were commonly named as sole or joint executor of their husband's will for instance, and both Susan Amussen and Amy Erickson have shown that female widows made up the majority of named

[34] HALS, HAT/SR/24, 5; DHC, Chanter 875, *Crocker als Coombe v. Coombe.*
[35] DHC, Chanter 8299, *Richards v. Kerslake*; DUIC, DDR/EJ/CCD/1/11, 68r–70r, 77v–8r.
[36] Muldrew, 'Culture of reconciliation'; Stretton, 'Written obligations', pp. 193–4.
[37] Shepard, 'Crediting women'; Fontaine, 'Women's economic spheres'.

Table 8.2 *Women's commercial and financial tasks by marital status*

	Commerce tasks (%)	Financial management tasks (%)	Pawning tasks (%)	Total tasks	% of total tasks by each marital status
Married	49.5	56.5	71.8	338	51.4
Widowed	12.2	12.9	5.1	78	11.9
Never married	11.9	6.5	7.7	73	11.1
Unknown	26.4	24.2	15.4	168	25.6
Total	100.0	100.1	100.0	–	100.0
Total tasks	556	62	39	657	–

executors across the seventeenth century.[38] Administering a will could be a costly and onerous task, taking months or years to complete, that utilised crucial skills in accounting and financial management, gained through running a household.[39] Women used bonds, bills, and acquittances pertaining to the debts of husbands who had entered credit agreements long before, knowing they would be settled as part of their probate. But work tasks associated with the legal administration of wills were not recorded in the work-task database, for reasons outlined in Section 1.2, meaning that this work of financial management described in testamentary suits in the church courts, peculiar to a female widow and bound to the administration of probate, was omitted from the database. Studies dedicated to the role of the female widow in the prolonged process of probate have already highlighted the administrative workload assigned to women at this stage of life. Filtering out those work tasks associated with executing a will allows a more direct focus on everyday commerce and the day-to-day management of household economies, rather than the special legal and economic status granted a widow during probate. It is this aspect of women's commercial work that is so often obscured in litigation due to coverture and which can only be quantified through a study of the scope and size adopted here. The proportion of commercial and financial work undertaken by widows in Table 8.2, at 11.9 per cent, is broadly in line with the proportion of women's tasks they performed across the dataset as a whole, of 10 per cent.

Table 8.2 shows that married women account for 51.4 per cent of the recorded female actors across the categories of commerce, financial management, and pawning. Qualitative evidence from the depositions

38 Erickson, *Women and Property*, p. 158; Amussen, *Ordered Society*, pp. 82–3.
39 Muldrew, 'Mutual assent', p. 52.

describes married women managing their household finances. In 1664 in Cheshire, Margaret Henshall was brought before the church court by her own husband in a plea for separation. Aside from her deriding the sexual prowess of her husband, claiming 'she would rather kiss her dog's tail than her husband's lips', she also boasted of her own financial success, claiming 'she had 60s in Mr Trevett's hands, 40s in old Mr Wilroxon's hands, 6s in Mr Wilroxon's hands, 15s in one Smalworod's hands and 5s in Mr Lockett's hands and that she had interest for it'.[40] Deponents in the case attested more widely to Margaret's management of her household finances, claiming she had 'the profit of three or four cows constantly to dispose of' and what 'corn or malt her husband had he never kept locked from her but she might dispose of it as she pleased'. John Lowe, reflecting on her management, claimed that her 'keeping and ordering of her husband's house was wary and thrifty enough' and that Margaret was of 'mild and sober character towards her neighbours'. Margaret herself mocked her husband's inability to maintain his household finances and his insatiable appetite, claiming that 'her husband had eaten or destroyed more than the whole family had done', tying his manhood to his financial inadequacy and insatiable greed. Clearly, Margaret Henshall had some control over her household finances and was able to use her household surplus to generate a profitable income. Her thriftiness was praised by her neighbours, though her husband took issue when she bragged of her financial independence and her rejection of him in the marital bed after publicly, and apparently haughtily, refusing to 'submit and yield' herself to him following a court order. Tensions in the household were fixed on Margaret's management of her husband's estate; whilst Margaret claimed to have lent money at interest her husband claimed she had, in fact, indebted the household. The Henshall case demonstrates the extension of housewifery to financial management within and beyond the household, as Margaret engaged in the credit market for interest, and the deeply ingrained language that associated financial management with gendered ideals around thrift, neighbourliness, appetite, and subservience.

Table 8.3 shows the gender division of creditors and debtors across the same categories used in Table 8.2. Credit has been defined broadly to include deferred payments, though it excludes the borrowing and lending of goods such as tools and household items. Creditors and debtors have been identified where named individuals recall a financial transaction involving a bond or bill, purchasing/selling goods on credit, or

[40] CALS, EDC/5/1664, 43.

Table 8.3 *Gender division of labour in commerce and finance comparing creditors and debtors*

	Creditor				Debtor			
	F tasks adj.	M tasks	Total tasks	% by F adjusted	F tasks adj.	M tasks	Total tasks	% by F adj.
Commerce	10	44	54	18.5	13	50	63	20.6
Financial management	54	76	130	41.2	13	73	86	14.9
Pawning	52	14	66	78.8	44	20	64	68.8
Totals	116	134	250	46.4	70	143	213	32.9

Notes: adj. = adjusted (x2.59).

borrowing and lending money. Where deponents simply recall reckoning their accounts without qualifying details, both actors have been listed as creditor and debtor, assuming the accounts were ongoing and reflected a longer chain of obligation back and forth. In the work-task database, women make up nearly half of all creditors, 46.4 per cent, but make up a smaller percentage of all debtors, at 32.9 per cent. This may in part be reflective of legal limitations on women's ability to contract credit. Laws of coverture not only limited women's legal ownership of property in their own right but could also diminish their credibility as potential borrowers if their assets were bound to their husband.[41] The majority of female debt recorded in the database was contracted via pawn, utilising household wares or personal affects over which women had greater claims of ownership. There is some evidence that married women did take on debt independently from their husband. As discussed above, in 1620 Thomas Postgate went to the house of William Wales in Durham to demand debts owed by William's wife, Elizabeth. Leonard Askell, bailiff of Chester-le-Street in Durham, was sent to execute an order against William Wales to recover the debts owed by his wife. Upon his arrival he was handed a defamatory letter written by William against his wife's creditor, Thomas Postgate, which Elizabeth defiantly attested she had seen her husband write. Elizabeth had contracted the debt herself, and it was from Elizabeth that Thomas had sought repayment. However, when the case was pursued in the civic courts under common law, it was William who was presented as debtor and his goods that were to be seized to satisfy the debts. We learn of the intricacies of the debt and Elizabeth's role in contracting it as the defamatory letter, passed between Wales, Postgate, and Askell, was presented in the church courts in a subsequent plea of defamation.[42]

The evidence for commerce conducted on credit is limited for both men and women. Deponents that recall buying and selling rarely recounted the methods of payment explicitly. When they did, these sales were more often associated with high-value transactions involving livestock. In 1620 Robert Croke was travelling back from the fair at Lydeard, Somerset, droving sheep he had just purchased, when he happened upon John Martyne to whom he owed money. He sold him two of the sheep for 7s or 8s, and John paid him part of the sum in coin and 'turned up the rest in the money which he owed him'. When Robert returned home, he sold five weathers and one ram to one Pyme of Lydeard for 43s or 44s, who paid 'the odd money presently' and owed the remaining 40s for

[41] Erickson, 'Coverture and capitalism'; Muldrew, 'Mutual assent'.
[42] DUIC, DDR/EJ/CCD/1/11, 68r–70r, 77v–8r.

which Robert 'did give him time'.[43] Large sums of credit were commonplace in the buying and selling of livestock and helped establish credit networks in marketplaces. That women do not appear frequently as creditors or debtors in the category of commerce is perhaps reflective of the lower value of their commercial transactions and exclusion from large-scale transactions in livestock. Commercial credits in the database refer to the purchase of consumables, as when Agnes Moore bought cloth on credit from Richard Wright in Pullen St Mary in 1580 for 3s 4d, as we saw at the outset of this chapter, or when Agnes Vigures settled her mother's accounts with Onesimus Penrose for linen in his shop whilst she bought 'some small commodities' herself in Holsworthy, Devon, in 1639.[44] Instances of buying and selling that explicitly referred to coin describe women handling coins of lower denominations, with a range of 1d to 8s when buying and selling ale, thread, and a penny's worth of milk. This mirrors trends in civic courts where female litigants sued less often and for smaller sums related to sales credit for household consumables.[45]

Women make up just 14.9 per cent of debtors in the category of financial management, where the credit described was larger and related to the extension of coin, yet they comprised 41.2 per cent of creditors in this category. Much of this credit was extended in coin and frequently described female creditors lending to male debtors. Anne Hodson lent £3 to Philip Wood in Mundford, Norfolk, in 1688. The debt was recalled upon her death by her executors in 1694.[46] Margaret Slater lent 12d to Henry Dewhurst at Preston fair in 1626, where she sold yarn and recalled purchasing stockings, a pewter flagon, malt, and flax herself for cash. Her detailed description of the fair and her transactions tells us about the flurry of buying and selling at the fair, and is explored in the introduction to Chapter 3.[47] The widow, Dorothy Rogers, lent 4s 6d to Richard Charrington when he came to her door in Coveney, Cambridgeshire, in 1661, under the guise of asking for tobacco, only to then request a loan.[48] There is some evidence that women acted in partnership when lending money. In 1699 in Newcastle upon Tyne, John Hudson accompanied Henry Mitford to witness a repayment to Alice Parkinson in her home. When Henry placed the money on the table, wrapped in a handkerchief, Alice questioned what she should do with the coin because she had given it to Henry in gold and wanted it returned in gold. John Hudson recalled that she claimed the gold was not

[43] DHC, QS/4/Box24, Baptist, 18. [44] DHC, QS/4/ Box 43–4, Epiphany, 36–7.
[45] Muldrew, 'Mutual assent', p. 11. [46] NRO, DN/DEP/53/58A, *Hull v. Fyrth*.
[47] LaA, QSB/1/17, 25–6. [48] CUL, EDR/E10/109, 30–1.

hers but was in fact her sister's, demanding of Henry that 'I gave it thee in gold and I will have it in gold'.[49]

B. A. Holderness' assertion that female widows were principal creditors in rural economies is not reflected in our data.[50] The majority of female creditors in the database were married, at 73 per cent, whilst just 7 per cent were widowed. We are familiar with the money-lending activities of single women and widows through studies of probate that show them to be savvy investors in their local economy. Amy Froide has challenged assumptions about 'spinsters' as economically redundant and has shown never-married women to be sources of credit in female kin networks and as significant investors in their communities.[51] Judith Spicksley too has shown through a study of wills that never-married women were a significant source of credit with an increasing tendency to put money out to 'use' in the later sixteenth century.[52] Single women also appear more frequently as creditors than they do debtors in Muldrew's study of borough courts, appearing as independent litigants suing for unpaid debt.[53] Yet for married women too, engaging in the credit economy was an important survival strategy in the management of the household finances. Credit, both for consumption and investment as a secondary income, was 'a mechanism that enabled many to get by and a few to flourish'.[54] The work-task data reflects this important economic work performed by married women in day-to-day commerce.

A striking feature of Table 8.3 is women's dominance of the pawn trade. They make up 78.8 per cent of creditors in pawn and 68.8 per cent of debtors. Early modern trade was propped up by auxiliary currencies. The mutability of goods to serve as credit and coin facilitated exchange where the coin supply was insufficient to meet the demands of daily commerce. Beverley Lemire has identified a professionalisation of the urban pawn trade from the seventeenth century onwards. Using the account books of John Pope in the early eighteenth century, she has shown women to have regularly pawned household goods, cloth, and clothing for credit.[55] Yet evidence for informal pawning dominated by plebian women is sparse despite the trade in second-hand goods being a crucial stream of income for poorer households. There were fewer licensed and insured female pawnbrokers, and they directed less wealth than their male counterparts.[56] The instances of pawning captured in the

[49] BI, CP.G.1699, *Mitford v. Parkinson*.
[50] Holderness, 'Widows in pre-industrial society'.
[51] Froide, *Never Married*; and? *Silent Partners*. [52] Spicksley, 'Never married women'.
[53] Muldrew, 'Mutual assent', p. 55. [54] Lemire, 'Introduction', p. 4.
[55] Lemire, 'Petty pawns'. [56] Lemire, *Business of Everyday Life*, p. 33.

work-task database are reflective of the informal exchange of goods, particularly between women, that facilitated commerce. The depositional evidence describes goods given in pawn for coin as well as goods given in pawn in lieu of payment where the debtor intended to retrieve their goods and settle their debt at a later date. It depicts an informal system of pawning in which married women were able to extend and receive credit; 72 per cent of women contracting credit on pawn were married. When Edmond Edgcomb went to see the tinker Degory Merrifield of Tavistock, Devon, to pawn pewter platters in 1651, Degory was accompanied by his wife.[57] In 1618 John Chappel of Ilminster, Somerset, went to pawn spoons with 'Cawcombe's wife'.[58] Even in instances where men sought to pawn an object with a male creditor, women are described as being witnesses. In 1668 John Buttal sought to pawn serge cloth with the servant Thomas Edwards in Fiddington, Somerset. The exchange was witnessed by the wife of Edwards' master and a female maid.[59] The one example in the database of a woman pawning goods for a loan from a male creditor comes from Chewton Mendip, Somerset, in 1638, where Joan Story sought to pawn a coif for 10d in her local alehouse from John Stanford and his wife.[60] In the instances described here married women were integral to the pawning industry as creditors, mediators, appraisers, and witnesses.

The biography of pawned objects suggests that women formed credit networks through family and kin. In a case of theft in Ashburton, Devon, in 1670, Welthian Tapper was found in possession of a smock which she claimed to have had from Jane Weiger who had pawned it to her for 2 groats. The same smock was received by Jane Weiger as pawn from Elizabeth Trust for 12d.[61] In 1630 Joan Nichols of Totnes in Devon had pawned various items she had received from her father. One blanket she had pawned to her mother-in-law for 5s 6d.[62] All but one of the women seeking to pawn goods for credit did so with another woman. The goods exchanged in pawn appear gendered. Women handled cloth, clothing, silverware, cooking pots, and ribbons, while men pawned clothing, cloth and silverware, tools, building materials, livestock, and animal skins. The objects of pawn mirror those most commonly bought and sold listed in Table 8.1, and those that were borrowed and lent. Women borrowed pails, spoons, blankets, clothing, shoes, linen, and the tools of spinning and needlework including flax, needles, and a wharrow-

[57] DHC, QS/4/Box55, Easter, 4. [58] SHC, QS/SR/29, 59.
[59] SHC, Q/SR/111, 87–8. [60] SHC, Q/SR/77, 28.
[61] DHC, QS/4/Box 84–5, Michaelmas, Info of Margery Soper.
[62] DHC, QS/4/Box 32, Baptist, 28–30.

spindle (used to twist thread on a spinning wheel). Though women did occasionally seek to borrow horses they did not do so as often as men. Men borrowed agricultural tools, such as cudgels, spades, knives, rope, and carts, and animals, such as greyhounds for hunting or ferrets for chasing out rabbits, but most commonly they borrowed and lent horses and oxen. The value of the goods given in pawn also differed. The value of women's pawned objects ranged from 3d to 5s 6d with an average value of 1s 11d. The value of men's pawned objects was significantly greater with a value ranging from 8d to 40s with an average value of 6s 9d. This may reflect both the value of goods which men and women had access to and ownership of, as well as the amount of credit that was required in order to conduct further commercial transactions.

Women's predominance in the pawning trade reflects their commercial knowledge and their ability to judge the worth of the moveable domestic objects they encountered in the home and in the market. Alewives were particularly well placed to act as creditors in the pawn trade. Deponents describe giving objects in pawn for coin, which they then went on to spend in the alehouse, as well as paying for food, ale, and bed and board, in kind. In Bishop's Nympton, Devon, Hugh Mortymer came to a reckoning with a married woman with the surname Sage after spending a night at her inn in 1629, where he exchanged three handkerchiefs and a falling band in lieu of 7d owed for his stay and meal. The same Hugh Mortymer went on to stay for a night at an alehouse in neighbouring South Molton, and gave the alewife a calico band, a ruff, and a handkerchief in lieu of his supper, bed, and breakfast.[63] In 1620 in Broadwoodwidger, Devon, Mary Delling took a smock she had bought from a 'tinker's wife' on credit to exchange for bread and drink to the value of 9d to the alewife Pearse.[64] Alewives were routinely handling second-hand goods as payment in kind, presumably with a view to its later use or resale.

Alexandra Shepard has cautioned against oversimplifying women's tendency to deal in apparel and household goods in the credit economy at a time where the 'consumption of goods represented investment strategies rather than simply "spending"'.[65] Women's specialist knowledge in cloth and stitchery acquired through work, as discussed in Sections 7.3 and 7.4, placed them in an advantageous position to determine the value of these goods as stores of wealth.[66] Their borrowing and lending against these objects in pawn 'became the sum and substance of plebeian budgeting, the source of liquidity for affluent and plebeian

63 DHC, QS/4/Box32, Epiphany, 33. 64 DHC, QS/4/Box24, Epiphany, 26–7.
65 Shepard, 'Minding', p. 56. 66 Lemire, *Dress, Culture, and Commerce.*

patrons throughout Europe.'[67] Capturing the trade in pawned goods outside the accounts of professional money lenders demonstrates the authority of married women as creditors within their local communities, with valued experience in determining the quality and worth of household goods and the creditworthiness of their neighbours. It was a tactile job that required experience acquired through touching and appraising consumer goods at the market and in the home.

Muldrew has shown how credit formed an undercurrent to all commercial exchange, acting both as a determinant of material wealth and as a social index to judge creditworthiness.[68] But the work behind the management of these obligations has not previously been quantified. Requesting outstanding payments, witnessing transactions, transporting money, writing accounts, and managing the paperwork generated from credit such as bonds and bills and acquittances were all work tasks that required time-use. The wider sample of data used here, combining the commerce subcategories with those of financial management and pawning, shows the breadth of work undertaken to sustain economic exchange. The depositional evidence reveals the role played by married women in the credit economy. Traditional sources used for studies of credit and debt, consumption, and property ownership exclude married women and as a consequence the understanding of women's credit has been skewed towards never-married women and widows. The work-task approach used here illuminates the commercial work undertaken by married women. Moreover, looking specifically at the objects bought as consumer goods and then used as payment in kind or as pawns, shows the ways in which a female-oriented knowledge of domestic wares enabled them to value goods for resale and as stores of wealth.

8.3 Spaces of Commerce

In 1661 Margaret Dayleigh, a single woman, stood atop a small lighting keel in the River Tyne at Newcastle dock, where she sold a groat's worth of coal to Christobell Lockering. Witness to the transaction at the dock was the married woman Isabella Sanderson and the blacksmith Arthur Shaft, who left his workshop to 'cool himself by the quay side' being hot with working at his trade.[69] Amidst the busy working docks surrounded by male-dominated industry, craft, and trade, Margaret operated a keel and sold her coal, and Christobell bought her wares. Women, though

[67] Lemire, *Business of Everyday Life*, p. 93. [68] Muldrew, *Economy of Obligation*.

[69] DUIC, DDR: Consistory court depositions (loose), 1662–3, *Christobelle Lockering v. Anna Atkinson*.

subjected to greater regulations in markets and trade, populated spaces of commerce. They navigated and traversed regulations in the pursuit of profit.[70] Buying and selling was recognised by conduct writers as a crucial form of women's work whereby a wife might support her husband by selling surplus produce from household production at market or buying goods for household consumption.[71] Provision for the household, buying and selling, was one such occasion where it was conceded by Dod and Cleaver in *A Godly Form of Household Government* that a wife may engage in work outside the household without her husband.[72] Indeed, over half, at 56 per cent, of all 'go to market' activities in the work-task database were performed by women. As exacting consumers and managers of their household economy, David Pennington has suggested that women were active and even forceful participants in shaping regulation in the market.[73] The final section of this chapter considers the spaces of commerce. As discussed in Section 3.5, the home was frequently a site of commerce that was open to the interruptions of neighbours and customers, blurring the boundaries of private and public. Qualitative accounts in the depositions draw out the constantly shifting function of the home as both a space for domestic living and a site of commerce.

The presence of permanent and enclosed shops opened from a single room in a domestic dwelling blurred boundaries between commerce, craft, and domestic life. Shops were often located within the front room of a residential house and selling through the open window of a home or workshop was commonplace. Wooden shutters opened wide with a shelf spanning the sill to form a counter through which cash and goods could pass. Semi-permanent wooden structures, propped outside a home, could also facilitate the selling of wares in the street.[74] Deponents refer to shops, stalls, homes, and workhouses with little distinction drawn between spaces of retail, manufacturing, and domestic living. Shoemakers Row in Cambridge was a hive of craftwork and commerce. Margaret Scoggin, giving testimony in a case of defamation, described walking along Shoemakers Row in December of 1593 towards the house of Thomas Coe, when she heard Lucy Fleming, who was working in her shop, chiding with Winifred Coe, who was standing in the doorway of her own shop. The dispute was overheard by Thomas Hailes, who had entered the shop of Thomas Coe to purchase needles and thread, where he was served by

[70] Pennington, *Going to Market*, p. 6.
[71] Flather, *Gender and Space*, pp. 32–4., Amussen, *Ordered Society*.
[72] Dod and Cleaver, *Godly Form*. [73] Pennington, *Going to Market*, p. 4.
[74] Cox, *Complete Tradesman*, pp. 77–9.

Thomas' wife Winifred.[75] Shoemakers Row epitomises the close interconnection between home and retail spaces. The shop of Thomas and Winifred Coe was described interchangeably as a home and a shop and was itself located in a street of crafting workshops and retail stalls . Sellers were also mobile and traversed the threshold between spaces of commerce and spaces of the home. The baker Robert Phillip sold bread from a horse-drawn cart to Margaret Butler at the window in her loom house in Leeds, Yorkshire, in 1625; and whilst her husband sold bread at the inn in Chipping Barnet in Hertfordshire in 1606, Bridget Ilsbury went door-to-door selling their bread to nearby households.[76] Travelling pedlars and itinerant workers are captured in the depositions but remain anonymous or are referred to with suspicion, like the 'four strange men' travelling along the highway towards Minehead, Somerset, in 1638, who offered to sell their wares to Thomas Burnell on his way to work; or the 'strange woman' selling second-hand clothes in a doorway on the periphery of Peter's fair in Holsworthy, Devon, in 1610.[77]

All the work tasks in the database were marked as having been performed either in the actor's own household, outside the household, or unknown where there is not enough evidence to confidently locate the task.[78] The household is taken to reflect the physical space of a familial dwelling, including the connected grounds and associated outbuildings. Those activities recorded as outside the household reflect commerce and trade that occurred outside the bounds of an individual's own home but could have taken place within another person's home. The majority of commercial work activities recorded in the database were performed outside the household, at 58 per cent, with those that were unknown accounting for 33 per cent, and those within the household just 10 per cent. Table 8.4 shows the number of commercial work tasks performed within the household and outside the household and the gender division of labour in each category.

Table 8.4 shows that men performed over half of all commercial work outside the household for which we know the location. Significantly, they account for 65.4 per cent of all selling activities outside the household, yet this relationship is reversed when looking at the selling activities performed inside the household where women account for 56.7 per cent of sellers. The same is true of exchange activities, with women taking on a greater proportion of these tasks when performed within their own household, at 85.2 per cent, yet accounting for just 26.5 per cent of tasks

[75] CUL, EDR/2/19, Winifred Coe v Lucretia Fleming.

[76] BI, CP.H.1704, *Pricilla Rawdon v. Robert Philip*; HALS, ASA8/8/103 and 106–8.

[77] SHC, Q/SR/77, 18; DHC, QS/4/Box 16, Michaelmas, 21.

[78] See Section 1.2.3.

Table 8.4 *Locations of commercial and financial tasks, by gender*

	Own household			Outside the household		
	M tasks	F tasks adj.	% by F adj.	M tasks	F tasks adj.	% by F adj.
Buy	37	47	56.0	470	513	52.2
Sell	65	85	56.7	308	163	34.6
Exchange	4	23	85.2	31	18	26.5
Go to market	0	0	0.0	88	111	55.8
Run stall/shop	10	10	50.0	16	10	38.5
Pawning	6	21	77.8	6	10	63.0
Financial management	32	41	56.2	174	85	32.8
Total	148	227	60.5	1,093	910	45.4

Notes: adj. = adjusted (x2.59). This is only based on the 2,378 tasks for which we know the location, which is 68 per cent of commerce and financial tasks. The categories of own household/outside the household are explained in Section 1.2.3.

when performed outside the household. A similar inverse relationship in the division of commercial labour can be seen in the category of financial management. When performed outside the household, men account for 67.2 per cent of the work activities performed and women just 32.8 per cent. When the same work is located within the household, women's proportion of financial management increases to 56.2 per cent and men's decreases to 43.8 per cent.

The distinction between work done in or around an actor's own household, as opposed to outside the household, is revealing, but it does not capture very precisely the full range of physical spaces of retail. Nor does the category of commerce done within the household reflect the blurred boundaries of domestic and retail spaces that characterised buying and selling in early modern England. Additional categories of space can be imposed on the data to allow for a more in-depth analysis, as in Table 8.5. A large proportion of the exchanges recalled in the depositions are not firmly located in a particular space but instead refer broadly to sales usually occurring some time prior to the deposition, and this is reflected in the 'Location not stated' column. Where a 'stall' is described as being in a market or on a market day, this has been included in the category 'market', to indicate that it was probable it was part of the temporary infrastructure of the marketplace. Where a stall is described as being part of a household or attached to a place of craftwork, such as a smith or shoemaker's shop, it has been included in the category of 'shop/stall' to reflect its more permanent nature. It should be noted, however,

Table 8.5 *Detailed locations of commercial and financial tasks*

	Market	Shop/ stall	Fair	House	Field/ ground	Road	Alehouse/ inn	Other	Location not stated	Total tasks
Buy tasks	229	121	107	204	30	41	34	33	727	1,526
Sell tasks	147	97	60	153	32	25	33	9	555	1,111
Exchange tasks	6	13	5	36	0	0	13	0	29	102
Go to market tasks	192	1	3	0	0	0	0	0	0	196
Run stall/shop tasks	6	27	3	11	0	0	0	0	5	52
Pawning tasks	0	0	0	37	0	0	25	0	76	138
Financial management tasks	6	27	5	149	11	18	35	10	165	426
% of all tasks	16.5	8.1	5.2	16.6	2	2.4	3.9	1.5	43.9	3,551
% of all tasks with known location	29.4	14.4	9.2	29.6	3.6	4.2	7	2.56	0.0	1,993
Total tasks	586	286	183	590	73	84	140	52	1557	3,551

Notes: F adjusted (x2.59).

that over the period the movement towards more permanent market infrastructure makes these distinctions harder to draw. The final category of note, 'other', includes those spaces that were clearly described but not large enough to warrant their own category, and includes churchyards, abbeys, mills, slaughterhouses, and bakehouses.

Though the 'unknown' category remains large, at 43.9 per cent, the data nonetheless shows that a significant proportion of commerce bypassed formal marketing structures. Combining the results for fairs and markets reveals that just 21.7 per cent of all commercial work took place in formal marketplaces. A significant proportion of commercial work, 16.6 per cent, is instead recorded as having been conducted in a home. In the database, shops appear more commonly in parishes categorised as large urban settlements, whilst homes were the most frequently cited spaces of commerce in rural parishes without markets. The results support Britnell's estimates for the late medieval rural economy, that less than half of all commercial transactions would have been conducted in formal marketplaces, and that private homes were important sites of trade.[79]

Shops, stalls, alehouses, and inns – 'intermediate zones' between 'private' and 'public' spaces – account for 12.0 per cent of commercial work. Alehouses and inns were important spaces in which commerce was conducted and accounts were reckoned.[80] In many cases the settling of debts is cited by deponents as the justification for their meeting at the alehouse. In 1691 in Tiverton, Devon, Juliana Keens was called upon to bear witness to the payment of a debt at the 'beerhouse' belonging to Joanne Kerslake.[81] Reckoning accounts was often accompanied by drinking as when Richard Sutton and William Hurstfield sat in the alehouse of Randolph in Middlewich, Cheshire, in 1662, where they drank and 'made bargains' settling their account with one another for three hours.[82] Alehouses were convenient sites to meet along well-travelled roads. Prior to setting off for London in 1684, Henry Webster met a Mr Jay to settle a debt at the White Lion Inn in Bungay, Suffolk; and in 1670 John Mundy awaited a carrier who owed him money, Thomas Barge from Yeovil, at the Sign of the Greyhound in Salisbury, Wiltshire.[83] Pawning activities were only recorded as conducted in a home or public alehouse or inn, indicating that in the rural economy access to licensed pawn shops was limited, though the pawning of goods appears commonplace. Despite the professionalisation of retail spaces in

[79] Britnell, 'Markets, shops, inns', p. 121.
[80] On alehouse work, see also Section 5.3.
[81] DHC, Chanter 8299, *Richard v. Kerslake*.
[82] CALS, QJF/90/1, 39–41.
[83] NRO, DN/DEP/51/55, 31–2; WSHC, D1/42/61, 20–4v.

the early modern period, buying, selling, pawning, exchanging, and negotiating in less regulated spaces formed a large sector of rural commerce.

Though shops might be situated as permanent sites of retail in and around a market, they could also be an extension of the home and double up as a domestic dwelling. In 1595 Agnes Hope came to the shop of Robert Wolley in St Albans, Hertfordshire, to buy cambric. Being a seamstress, she stayed in the shop to work on some sewing, taking advantage of the warmth thrown out by a pan of coals that had been warmed for Robert Wolley's wife who had just delivered a baby, 'because [she] the mother was then very cold'. Agnes Hope was not the only one to take advantage of the warmth. Gathered in the shop were James William and Hugo Summer, both of whom described themselves as being a familial relation to Robert Wolley, and William Towe, all of whom stood or sat around the coals with the new mother and baby. The stall was open, as the defamatory words spoken by William Towe were heard by Alexander Dame from the 'other side of the street'.[84] The space of commerce was functioning as a place of work for Agnes Hope, a space of warmth and refuge for a new mother, a place of congregation for friends and family, and a space of commercial activity for Robert Wolley. There is no sense of the shop or stall being a private space despite the intimate activities going on inside, as Agnes tended to her sewing and Robert Wolley's wife recovered from her birth. Wolley's shop provided a practical function of warmth that rendered it useful for multiple purposes and in doing so had drawn in a range of work and social activities. Flather has shown domestic spaces to be gendered by actors and their work.[85] But rather than transitioning from a female space to a male space dependent upon its intended use, the commercial space of the shop here is at once a private space of domestic living and a public one of commerce.

That is not to say that spaces of commercial work were not in any way gendered. Although qualitative evidence demonstrates the blurred boundaries of these spaces, there are some noticeable and important trends within the data. Few spaces were rigidly gendered, but shops, stalls, inns, and alehouses harboured a higher number of female actors performing commerce tasks, whilst the transitory spaces of commerce – fields and roads – were male dominated. Markets, fairs, and houses exhibited a near-even presence of men and women. This pattern shifts however when analysing just the activities of buying and selling. To explore this in greater detail, Figure 8.1 examines the location of

[84] HALS, AS8/8, 5. [85] Flather, *Gender and Space.*

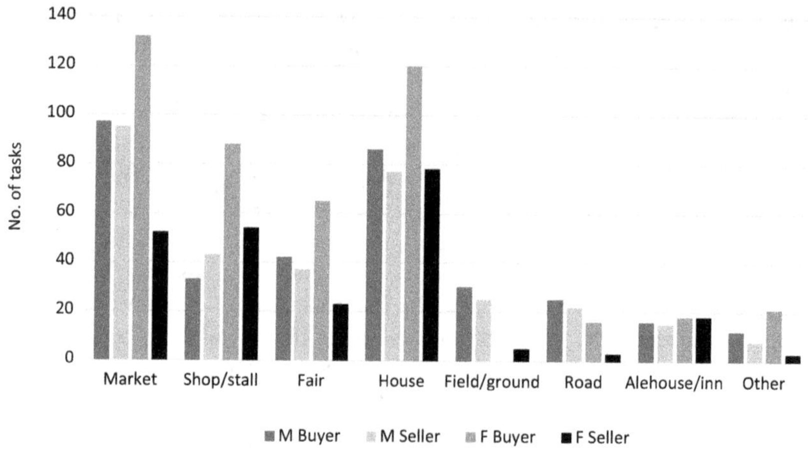

Figure 8.1 Buyers and sellers by location
Notes: F adjusted (x2.59).

buying and selling by gender. All of the buyers in fields were men, and they made up 83 per cent of sellers in fields. Though women account for 40 per cent of buyers along roads, they account for just 11 per cent of sellers. Roads and fields were outdoor and transitory places of commerce and were dominated by men. This may reflect the tendency of men to sell livestock either in fields or along the road whilst droving, a subcategory they dominated.[86]

Women form a greater proportion of workers in those spaces that were most likely to have also been domestic dwellings: shops, stalls, alehouses, and inns. In stalls and shops women make up 73 per cent of buyers but also 55 per cent of sellers. Qualitative evidence from the depositions suggests that women took an active role in selling produce at stalls. When in 1597 John Dawlyn approached the stall of the butcher Lodovicus Spratly in Southwark to settle a debt, Lodovicus only left his stall when his wife, Fortuna, came to take over and run the stall selling meat.[87] Fairs and markets show a near-even gender division of commercial work between men and women overall, but men appear more frequently as selling, accounting for 60 per cent of sellers. Markets were the most commonly recorded place for women buying goods, accounting for 29 per cent of women's buying activities. On the other hand, homes were the most frequently cited places of selling for women, accounting for

86 Men undertook 85 per cent of droving tasks, even using adjusted figures. See Appendix B.
87 HALS, ASA8/8, 26–8.

33 per cent of their selling activities. Despite buying and selling work tasks having a near-even gendered split when taking an adjusted figure, the role of buyer and seller does appear gendered according to the space of commerce. Women's selling activities were more frequently recorded in shops or were more closely bound to the domestic space of the home, whilst men's selling was more frequently recorded in the regulated spaces of commerce, markets and fairs, on the one hand, or in the unregulated spaces of fields and roads as they undertook the droving of livestock, often on their way to market, on the other.

8.4 Conclusion

Approaching early modern commerce through the lens of work recasts buying and selling as time-use work activities, and highlights the ongoing work associated with the arrangement of protracted sales and the management of the household economy. It goes some way to quantifying the back and forth of early modern rural commerce, such as the importance of valuations and appraisals, and the requesting and payment of debts. Depositional evidence also captures the range of currencies that underpinned early modern buying and selling, including coin, credit (both by written instrument and verbal agreement), deferred payments, pawning, the exchange of goods, and payments in kind. The range of commercial work recorded in the database and analysed in this chapter is therefore broad and provides a fuller picture of the operation of commerce and money management, especially for rural England, than has been possible before.

In the process, important but nuanced gender differences have been identified. The analysis of consumer goods shows women bought and sold goods for sums that averaged less than their male counterparts. Though they appeared more frequently purchasing consumer goods, including cooking instruments and kitchenware, these can be recast as tools of housewifery that were not so different from the tools used by men. Nor were women absent from buying and selling raw materials, and the data shows a near-even gendered division of sellers of wool and skins, whilst women made up over 40 per cent of buyers of grain and grass. A striking feature of the data is the prevalence of women in the credit economy. Pawning, in particular, was a female-dominated trade, and a real strength of the work-task approach is that it captures the trade in pawn and second-hand goods that frequently eludes the archive.

The work-task approach is also particularly effective at capturing and quantifying the commercial work of married women in day-to-day commerce. For instance, a key finding of the data here is the prevalence of married women as creditors, something unexpected, given the emphasis placed on widows and never-married women in credit networks up to now. This supports the findings of the Swedish Gender and Work project, as well as those of Chapter 2, which show that marriage enabled women to engage in a wider range of economically responsible activities.[88] Depositions routinely describe married women witnessing and managing the credit of their wider household. Married women described extending credit often did so as part of their role as alewives, accepting part payments in pawned goods and extending credit for consumption in their own alehouse. In the rural economy alewives thus appear as important nodes in localised credit networks.

There were key differences in men's and women's relationship to credit. Men's credit in the rural economy was often closely bound to the livestock trade, with larger value purchases occurring in markets far from home and conducted on credit. Women's credit mirrors the lower values recorded for the goods they bought and sold, and was linked to the buying and selling of goods for household consumption. Their economic authority over household finances and credit derived from their ability to judge the value of the moveable household goods in the market and home. The spatial descriptions in the depositions also capture the significant quantity of commerce that by-passed regulated spaces of trade, as well as enabling an analysis of the gendering of commercial spaces. These divisions were not rigid, with men and women appearing across all types of commercial space. But women appeared more frequently as consumers in markets and fairs and as sellers in more domestic spaces, whilst men appeared more frequently as sellers in both the most regulated spaces of commerce, fairs and markets, and the least, roads and fields. What emerges most clearly from the evidence of commerce and money management, however, is that these were forms of work that played a key part in the work repertoires of rural women and men and were central to the everyday experience of the early modern economy.

[88] Ling et al., 'Marriage and work'.

Conclusion

In July of 1637 Jane Whittell of Bedford in Leigh, Lancashire, was asked by her neighbour to look after two ducks and a drake to stop them straying into the ripening corn before harvest. Unfortunately, the ducks did stray, not into the corn but onto a neighbour's property. Jane accused the neighbour's servant, Anne, of tempting the ducks away by feeding them before shutting them inside. In her defence, Anne said that she had been told by her mistress to shut up any stray ducks and pointed out that she had returned the ducks when Jane challenged her. Jane wanted to know what had happened to the drake, but Anne claimed she had never seen it. The dispute went to the Lancashire quarter sessions held at Wigan in Michaelmas that year, with depositions from Jane and Anne taken by John Atherton, the local JP.[1] This is just one of a multitude of entirely unremarkable disputes that provided evidence for this book. When Jane agreed to care for the ducks, it is very unlikely she anticipated it would lead to a dispute in court. We can be certain, however, that she had no inkling that almost 400 years later, a historian who shared her name would be using the evidence of that legal dispute to write a history of work in early modern England.

Thousands of disputes, crimes, misadventures, and enquiries provide evidence for this study. Individually such cases are often trivial, but EN MASSE they provide a new way of looking at the early modern economy. The findings enable areas of the economy that were previously shrouded in obscurity to be illuminated with new clarity. They allow us to recover the crucial role women played in all areas of the economy. They cause us to think again about the relationship between work and the market in early modern England. They suggest that focusing on the experience of work offers a corrective to many existing approaches to preindustrial economic development. This conclusion explores all these implications, beginning with the types of work that the work-task approach reveals and

[1] LaA, QSB/1/190, 54.

conceals, before moving on to look at the relationship between work and the market, and what it was like to work in early modern England: the experience of work.

9.1 Hidden Work

The work-task approach reveals many aspects of work that historians had either failed to find adequate evidence of before, most prominently women's work, or have overlooked altogether. But there were also types of work that we did not collect or find evidence about, and types of work that remained underrepresented in the work-task data. The work-task approach is very effective at documenting women's work. Whereas previous studies provided examples of women working in a wide variety of activities, the work-task approach allows this to be quantified. We show that women worked in all the major areas of the economy. Of the 62 subcategories of work shown in Appendix B, women made up the majority of those carrying out work tasks in 27, and less than 10 per cent in only 12. Areas which women were largely excluded from were most common in crafts and construction, followed by agriculture and land, and transport. Yet even within these categories, we find women outnumbering men in textile and clothing production, in milking and gathering food, and in carrying goods and messages.

Our evidence suggests a flexible division of labour but one that varied in different parts of the economy.[2] Men and women participated roughly equally in commerce, although close analysis shows that men dominated higher-value transactions. Women did just over a third of agricultural work. They were most prominent in the core farming activities of livestock husbandry and arable agriculture but less involved in or absent from wood husbandry, hedging, and hunting and fishing. They dominated milking and dairying, almost to the exclusion of men. In contrast, the gender division of labour in crafts and construction was sharply defined. Women were almost or completely absent from apprenticed crafts. Sheilagh Ogilvie has credited guilds with excluding women from craft occupations in south-west Germany and more widely across early modern Europe.[3] Our evidence suggests something slightly different: that apprenticeship presented a barrier to women's entry into many specialist occupations whether or not guilds were present. England's labour laws required certain crafts to be entered only via apprenticeship, although they did not specify that apprentices should be male.

[2] Whittle and Hailwood, 'Gender division of labour'; Hailwood et al., 'Comparing the gender division'.

[3] Ogilvie, *Bitter Living*, pp. 329–31 and *European Guilds*, pp. 232–305.

Women dominated all categories of housework and all but one of carework. Yet the assumption that these types of work were predominantly unpaid work by married women done within the family is incorrect: housework made up a larger proportion of unmarried women's work than that of married women and much of it was work 'for another'. Using the proportion of 'for another' housework and carework, we can re-estimate women's labour force participation, the measurement of work that excludes unpaid housework and carework. Broadberry et al. based their calculations of GDP on an estimate that 43 per cent of women's work was labour force participation compared to 97 per cent of men's work.[4] Our evidence suggests that 76 per cent of women's work was labour force participation as a minimum estimate.[5]

Jan de Vries bemoaned the inability of historians to look within the 'black box' of the household economy.[6] While the work-task approach does not allow forensic analysis of the working patterns of particular households, it does enable us to look at the average work patterns or repertoires of particular types of workers, such as married women, or men and women of particular age groups.[7] This shows that it was young unmarried women who did most housework. Carework was mostly skilled healthcare and midwifery, and involvement in this increased throughout women's lifecycle. The largest work category in our data for both married and widowed women was commerce, rather than housework.[8] We can also compare the work patterns of wives of men with particular occupations. This shows that the wives of husbandmen, artisans, and labourers had more in common with each other than with their husbands' work patterns. All these wives were significantly involved in commerce. The wives of artisans and labourers did equal amounts of crafts and construction work, mostly in textile and clothing production. The wives of husbandmen did slightly more agriculture than the other wives, but the difference was not great.[9] Thus, it should not be assumed that married women's work was defined by their husband's occupation: women had their own patterns of productive and manufacturing work, as well as their distinct involvement in housework and carework.

4 Broadberry et al., *British Economic Growth*, p. 348.

5 The other 24 per cent of women's work was housework and carework that was either not paid, carried out for members of their own household, or for which there was no information. For a more detailed discussion, see Whittle, 'Putting women back in'.

6 de Vries, *Industrious Revolution*, p. 8.

7 On the working patterns of households, using nineteenth-century data, see Burnette, 'How not to measure'.

8 See Table 2.8. 9 See Table 2.18.

Rather than guessing the work of labourers and servants according to where they lived or their gender, the work-task data allows the types of work these women and men did to be explored. This shows that labourers had high involvement in agriculture and transport, both of which were likely to be related to their paid work, but they also engaged in commerce, which was more likely connected to their own household economy. Servants' engagement in commerce was significantly lower because they lived in the households of others. Male servants, like labourers, had work repertoires dominated by agriculture and transport.[10] For female servants, housework was their biggest category of work, but agriculture still accounted for more than 20 per cent of their work tasks.[11] It has been suggested that husbandmen were interchangeable with labourers.[12] Our data indicates this was not the case: while there were similarities in work patterns, husbandmen did more agriculture and commerce, while labourers did more food processing (mostly threshing), and transport.[13] This suggests the balance between wage labour and independent farming was different for these two groups, with labourers doing more of the former and husbandmen more of the latter.

Some types of work were more prominent than expected in the dataset: transport was one of these. As Section 3.3 made clear, the transport category only includes tasks that had moving something as their main purpose, and that involved movement between properties. In addition to this, nearly every subcategory of work involved some transport activities. These demonstrate the difficulties faced when working in the early modern economy: the distances that had to be covered, typically on foot, to engage in commerce, sell or return the yarn you had spun, arrange building work, or pay a debt, for instance. Every communication required someone to be sent in person carrying a message. Goods had to be loaded and unloaded, often transported in small quantities because of limited capacity to carry more. It is here that the inefficiencies of the early modern economy lay.

Other types of work were either under-recorded, or less prominent than expected. Regional specialisms were often barely visible: this is a consequence of the methodology but also reflects the reality of early modern work. Both specialist occupations and regionally specific activities such as sea-fishing or lacemaking were drowned out by the multitude of more generic tasks that nearly everyone carried out in every place: activities such as commerce, agriculture, housework, carework, and

[10] See Table 2.15. [11] See Table 2.20.
[12] Shaw-Taylor, 'Rise of agrarian capitalism', p. 54. [13] See Table 2.15.

transport.[14] For mariners, miners, and larger towns, more information about work could have been collected from the specialist courts that regulated their work, but this would have overrepresented them within the sample as a whole.

For two, or possibly three, types of work, the issue was the opposite: we know they were ubiquitous but are recorded less than expected. These were spinning, childcare, and cookery in the sense of meal preparation. The reasons are slightly different in each case. Independent estimates of the spinning needed to support the cloth industry demonstrate it is under-recorded in our dataset.[15] This is largely because people felt no need to mention something so common and when they did mention it, spinning was often referred to as 'working' without the details needed to record it as a specific work task, as when women were described 'working in the doorway' of their houses. For childcare the issue is twofold: childcare seems to have been combined with other work activities in most cases, and children themselves started working at a young age. This meant dedicated time spent caring for children was largely limited to very young infants and sick children. Childcare took up less time than might be expected in early modern England. The issue with cooking is similar. Early modern cookery books and historical reconstructions of dishes prepared for feasts have perhaps encouraged an overestimation of the time people spent cooking. If we separate out food processing and the collection of water and fuel, the actual preparation of meals seems to have taken relatively little time: a large pot often simmered on the hearth without a great deal of supervision. Ingredients were presumably quite quickly cleaned, chopped, and added to it. Bread was typically purchased.

There were types of work that we deliberately did not record. This includes the work of administering justice and the probate process, as well as the drawing up and witnessing of documents including wills and contracts, and also office-holding duties including those undertaken by the clergy. These were all important forms of work, not only undertaken by men with occupational titles such as lawyer, clerk, and clergyman but by others such as the widows who typically administered their husband's probate, or the neighbours who were called in to witness documents. However, if they had been included in the dataset, they would have been grossly overrepresented, and would have swamped the other forms of work we were keen to collect. We also excluded crime for the same reason, despite the fact it was an important way of making a living for

[14] On regional similarities and differences, see Section 3.1.
[15] Muldrew, '"Th'ancient distaff"'.

many English people. Poaching, for instance, was undoubtedly common but is either not mentioned because it was criminal or forms the central focus of cases taken to the quarter sessions and therefore was not recorded.

A final important form of work is absent from the dataset. We did not record sex or pregnancy as work unless it was explicitly paid – and we found no examples of explicit payment. Using Margaret Reid's third-party criterion to define work, it is unclear whether, in an early modern context, sex or pregnancy meets the definition of work unless it was paid.[16] The church courts were full of accusations that women were 'whores', and to a lesser extent, that establishments were 'bawdy houses' or brothels, but this is evidence of the insults commonly hurled around early modern communities rather than precise evidence of work tasks. Very occasionally paid sex work formed the central focus of a case, but for that reason we did not record it, in the same way that other crimes and disorders central to cases were not included in the database. We found no cases where paid sex was mentioned incidentally. Paid sex work was undoubtedly present but was not commonly documented in the courts we consulted: urban court records might contain more evidence.[17]

The work-task approach cannot claim to recover the entire range of work in early modern England; however, it is more effective than any other existing approach at providing a holistic view of the most common types of everyday work undertaken by women and men. Its particular strengths are providing evidence about women's work, unpaid work, and the details of what people actually did in their working lives, including the tasks undertaken by people with particular occupations.

9.2 Work and the Market

Economic change in early modern England was rooted in market relations. Structural change that involved a shift from agriculture to work in manufacturing and services was premised on households' increased dependence on the market to buy their daily necessities, and the increased marketing of agricultural goods to provide those necessities. Urbanisation relied on the same dynamics. Proletarianisation indicates that even within agriculture, workers became more likely to work for wages than to use their own land and resources. Evidence of economic change is therefore located in the relationship between work and the

[16] Reid, *Economics of Household Production*, p. 11.
[17] See Ingram, *Carnal Knowledge*, pp. 404–5.

market. This had two main dimensions: an increase in paid work, and an increase in work that connected to selling and buying goods. In the work-task approach such work is indicated by work 'for another' and work in the commerce and management categories.

The 'for another' category is not equivalent to paid work. To recap, work 'for another' fell into three main subcategories: work that was explicitly paid, work undertaken by servants, and work that was done for people outside the household but for which no further details were available.[18] While the first two subcategories were paid, the third subcategory most likely included a mixture of paid work, work done in exchange, and work carried out by kindness or charity. Work for which no details at all were available about the context was counted as 'not for another', meaning that work 'for another' must be an underestimate of work undertaken for pay or for others outside the household. Nonetheless, rates were high.

Women did slightly more 'for another' work than men, at 36 per cent compared to 35 per cent. Similarly, women did almost as much work in the commerce and management categories as men, 48 per cent and 49 per cent respectively. This indicates that we should not assume women were less engaged in market work than men. In part, this was because housework and carework were much more likely to be done 'for another' than many historians have anticipated. The proportion was particularly high for carework at 78 per cent, the highest of any of our work categories. Rather than capturing large quantities of childcare, the carework category is dominated by healthcare and midwifery. This was predominantly carried out by women 'for another', showing that women dominated the grassroots of healthcare provision – not by caring for their own families but by providing skilled medical advice and care *outside* the household. The proportion of housework 'for another' was also relatively high at 44 per cent, only two percentage points lower than agriculture at 46 per cent. Both carework and housework were frequently commercialised as sources of income, rather than being subsistence services provided within the family.[19] The commerce and management categories captured the petty commerce of everyday market exchanges, as well as the tasks of credit and the pawning of goods. Men were more likely to undertake high-value transactions, but women were prominent in the marketplace and in money management. Marjorie McIntosh emphasised the 'limited set of choices' available to women in the market economy.[20] We are more inclined to emphasise the ubiquity of women's market work

[18] See Section 2.2. [19] Whittle, 'Critique of approaches'.
[20] McIntosh, *Working Women*, p. 251.

and the prominent role played by married women. Women did face restrictions, imposed by their lack of property rights within marriage (coverture), and by exclusion from most apprenticeships and professions, but they were nonetheless active within the market economy.

As explained in Section 1.4, the work-task data is not effective at tracking change within the study period from 1500 to 1700, as it is influenced by the changing composition of courts and types of cases. It is most reliable when using incidental evidence only. If the incidental evidence is divided into two periods, 1500 to 1630 and 1631 to 1700, this shows no significant change over time. Counterintuitively, there was a slight increase in agricultural work and decrease in work in crafts and construction. The gender division of labour also changed little, with a slight decline in the proportion of agricultural work done by women, and a slight increase in women's commerce and management work.[21] However, the work-task data can be used to interrogate other theories and datasets that explore change in the early modern economy, particularly the growth of non-agricultural occupations and the lengthening of the working year.

Work-task data can be used to dissect the composition of occupations, that is, to explore the types of work people with particular occupational descriptors actually did.[22] This shows that artisans with craft occupations spent a relatively small amount of time engaged directly in their primary occupation, and the proportion was lower for less wealthy artisans such as weavers and shoemakers. As expected, yeomen, husbandmen, labourers, and male servants did the largest proportions of agricultural work, but men with other types of occupations such as artisans, professionals, and gentlemen, also did significant amounts of agricultural work. Combined with the evidence that incidental work tasks changed little over time, this suggests that the occupational data which underlies discussions of structural economic change in early modern England overstates the extent of change.[23] Occupational profiles undoubtedly did change over time, with more men being identified by secondary sector, craft occupations. But it seems that the work at the level of work tasks changed little: work tasks were reshuffled into a slightly different occupational profile rather than the nature of the economy being transformed.[24]

21 See Section 1.4. 22 See Section 2.5.

23 For example, Broadberry et al., 'When did Britain industrialise?'; Keibek, 'Male occupational structure'; Wallis et al., 'Structural change'.

24 See Aucoin et al., 'Structural change', for further comparison between occupations and work tasks.

Another important strand of recent theories of early modern economic change has been the argument of increased 'industriousness' or work intensity, to explain how a smaller proportion of workers in agriculture could provide food for the increasing proportion of people with non-agricultural occupations. Here discussion focuses primarily on an increase in the number of days worked each year.[25] The need to explain this change is largely removed if we accept that the proportion of agricultural work, at the level of work tasks, did not change significantly. However, the work-task approach also provides more direct evidence about time-use. This shows long working days in the early modern period, a steady working year, and significant quantities of work undertaken even on Sundays.[26] There is no evidence of the observance of St Monday. This undermines Hans-Joachim Voth's much-quoted conclusion that the working year lengthened because the observation of St Monday declined after 1750.[27] In so far as St Monday was ever observed, it was restricted to male craftsmen in London, a very small proportion of England's overall workforce. The work pattern we observe makes sense, given the demands of a rural, agricultural economy: the care of livestock, in particular, was a constant requirement, not something that could be skipped on Sunday or Monday or avoided in the evening.

Evidence of a lengthening working year is also provided by Jane Humphries and Jacob Weisdorf. They show that unskilled day labourers had to work an increasing number of days per year to equal the wages of annual servants, rising from c.150 days a year to 250 days during the seventeenth century.[28] Leaving aside issues of how many days servants worked annually, and whether day labourer and service were interchangeable in the way their model suggests, a more fundamental question can be asked. Does this indicate labourers were doing more work in total or just more paid work? It is possible that the whole debate, from Jan de Vries' 'industrious revolution' to Broadberry et al.'s increased work intensity, has been focused on the wrong issue.[29] Rather than preindustrial workers replacing leisure with work under stimulus from a more commercialised economy, what took place was the replacement of independent work in small farms and workshops with paid work, or proletarianisation. Agriculture was increasingly dominated by wage

[25] Broadberry et al., *British Economic Growth*, p. 405; Humphries and Weisdorf, 'Unreal wages', p. 2880.
[26] Hailwood, 'Time and work', and Chapter 4.
[27] Voth, *Time and Work*, pp. 268–9.
[28] Humphries and Weisdorf, 'Unreal wages', esp. pp. 2880–1.
[29] de Vries, *Industrious Revolution*; Broadberry et al., *British Economic Growth*, pp. 340–70.

labour rather than independent farmers.[30] It may also be the case that paid work was more productive, because it took control of work away from the worker and forced other forms of work to be squeezed in around the paid working day and week. It remains unclear how far this applied to women as well as men. There are some indications that women's paid work in agriculture declined when men's increased: our evidence suggests this was replaced with work in commerce. Craig Muldrew indicates that women's paid work in spinning also increased.[31]

The polemical literature generated by those supporting Parliamentary enclosures in the late eighteenth century offers an interesting perspective on this issue. Rural dwellers who made at least a partially independent living from small farms and common land were characterised as 'subsisting in idleness', being 'less inclined to work', and as involved in 'lazy industry' and 'beggarly independence'. They were an 'idle, useless and disorderly set of people'. Small farmers were mocked because they 'wasted their time at market, full of their own importance'.[32] These were the remnants of the early modern economy, seen through the eyes of wealthy employers and their supporters, who wished to use these people as cheap and subservient labour. Economic historians should be wary of echoing these prejudices.

9.3 The Experience of Work

Adam Smith began *The Wealth of Nations* by describing the efficiencies of production that could be achieved by the increased division of labour into more specialised occupations. The pin-maker or nail-maker could work faster at producing pins or nails than a smith who did a wider range of metalworking. Indeed, pin-making could be separated into 18 different processes, each undertaken by a specialist worker.[33] But if given a choice, would you rather be the worker who sharpens the point on 48,000 pins each day, or a blacksmith working a forge, shoeing horses, mending tools, chatting to customers, and perhaps making a few nails? E. P. Thompson records the persistent complaint of skilled workmen in the 1830s that '"they wish to make us tools" or "implements" or "machines"'.[34] But workers are not tools; they are people. Smith noted three ways in which labour could become more productive: first, through the dexterity and skill achieved by focusing on specialist processes; second, by avoiding 'the time which is commonly lost in passing from one species of

30 Shaw-Taylor, 'Rise of agrarian capitalism'. 31 Muldrew, '"Th'ancient distaff"'.
32 Neeson, *Commoners*, pp. 28–33. 33 Smith, *Wealth of Nations*, pp. 18–25.
34 Thompson, *Making of the English Working Class*, p. 898.

work to another'; and, third, by using machines which 'facilitate and abridge labour'.[35] By all these measures, work in the sixteenth and seventeenth centuries was inefficient. People worked long hours, weeks, and years, but their work was relatively unspecialised and involved a great deal of movement from one task to another. Very little was mechanised. The work-task data highlights both the multiple processes involved in particular occupations, and the varied work patterns that combined multiple occupations, much like Smith's country weaver 'who cultivates a small farm, must lose a good deal of time passing from his loom to the field, and from his field to the loom'.[36]

Yet, although the early modern economy was not as efficient as those of later centuries in its use of labour, it was self-sufficient at a national level, sustainable, and efficient in its use of resources: qualities which are absent from modern industrial economies. It relied on human and animal power, with a small amount of wind and waterpower used in mills. Fuel for heating and industry was largely obtained from wood, although London was already dependent on mineral coal by 1700.[37] The use of land and natural resources was maximised. Trees and hedges were carefully managed for renewable timber; women picked shreds of wool dropped from sheep on common land to spin at home; rough pastures were periodically cleared and ploughed; birds, fish, and rabbits were caught and eaten.[38] Households were not self-sufficient, but householders strove for independence, achieved by engaging in multiple forms of work and monetising almost every product and service in the market. Independence did not mean isolation. Most work took place outside and even inside spaces were open to the sight and hearing of servants and neighbours. The prevalence of work 'for another' suggests cooperation and neighbourliness as well as the pervasiveness of paid work. The gender division of labour suggests a 'two-supporter model' in which wife and husband both worked to support the household, assisted by children and servants. The gender division of labour was flexible and adaptable, and wives often had their own occupations as well as sometimes assisting with their husband's work.

Early modern work should not be romanticised. The work-task database contains evidence not only of families running their own farms and independent workshops but also of artisans and the homeless begging for food and drink, people who stole to feed their families, children who were neglected or died while carrying out dangerous work, and family members and servants who suffered violent assault from relatives or

[35] Smith, *Wealth of Nations*, pp. 21–2. [36] Ibid., p. 23. [37] Wrigley, 'Urban growth'.
[38] See also Warde, *Invention of Sustainability*.

employers. But we should consider what has been lost as well as gained over the centuries. Most importantly, we should remember that although work tasks were the constituent elements that created the economy, the workers of early modern England were not tools or instruments – they were people, and their experiences matter in their own right. This book has aimed to make the experiences of all types of workers in England more visible. It provides a more complete view of how people experienced and contributed to the economy, women as well as men, and illuminates the central place of work in early modern lives.

Appendices

Appendix A Relationship between Categories and Court Type

	Tasks	% of tasks from QS	% of tasks from CC	% of tasks from CR	Top 3 case types (% of tasks in that category)
Agriculture and land	2,635	36.8	45.2	18.0	Tithe (30.4), Theft (23.9), Accidental death (18.0)
Carework	564	57.6	39.7	2.7	Paternity (26.4), Testamentary (18.3), Miscellaneous (15.8)
Commerce	2,115	74.2	25.5	0.3	Theft (63.3), Tithe (7.0), Defamation (6.3)
Crafts and construction	942	49.5	35.4	15.2	Theft (37.3), Accidental death (15.2), Defamation (12.7)
Food processing	607	75.3	17.5	7.2	Theft (67.5), Accidental death (7.2), Defamation (5.6)
Housework	748	56.6	25.5	17.9	Theft (41.3), Accidental death (17.9), Defamation (10.2)
Management	645	64.7	34.7	0.6	Theft (45.6), Unclear (12.7), Miscellaneous (9.8)
Transport	1,237	58.2	21.3	20.5	Theft (39.9), Accidental death (20.5), Unclear (10.2)
Other	157	68.2	22.9	8.9	Theft (30.9), Unclear (16.6), Witchcraft (14.6)
Total	9,650	56.5	32.2	11.3	Theft (40.5), Tithe (11.6), Accidental death (11.3)

Notes: QS = quarter sessions; CC = church courts; CR = coroners' reports.

Appendix B Gender Division of Labour by Subcategory

	M tasks	F tasks	Total tasks	% by F	F tasks adj.	% by F adj.
Agriculture and land	2,162	473	2,635	18.0	1,225	36.2
Animal husbandry	629	126	755	16.7	326	34.2
Collecting fuel	74	20	94	21.3	52	41.2
Dig marl/earth/clay	51	5	56	8.9	13	20.3
Farm transport	313	27	340	7.9	70	18.3
Fieldwork	683	129	812	15.9	334	32.8
Gardening	12	3	15	20.0	8	39.3
Gathering food	51	66	117	56.4	171	77.0
Hedging	30	0	30	0.0	0	0.0
Hunting and fishing	166	2	168	1.2	5	3.0
Milking	8	89	97	91.8	231	96.6
Wood husbandry	145	6	151	4.0	16	9.7
Carework	196	368	564	65.2	953	82.9
Childcare	22	102	124	82.3	264	92.3
Education	20	5	25	20.0	13	39.3
Healthcare	98	113	211	53.6	293	74.9
Midwifery	7	117	124	94.4	303	97.7
Other care	49	31	80	38.8	80	62.1
Commerce	1,559	556	2,115	26.3	1,440	48.0
Buy	752	301	1,053	28.6	780	50.9
Sell	635	184	819	22.5	477	42.9
Exchange	56	19	75	25.3	49	46.8
Go to market	88	43	131	32.8	111	55.9
Run stall/shop	28	9	37	24.3	23	45.4
Crafts and construction	738	207	942	22.0	536	42.1
Buildings	168	2	170	1.2	5	3.0
Clothes and shoes	109	76	185	41.1	197	64.4
Groundworks	62	1	63	1.6	3	4.0
Metalwork	85	2	87	2.3	5	5.7
Mill maintenance	29	0	29	0.0	0	0.0
Mining/quarrying	35	1	36	2.8	3	6.9
Other maintenance/ manufacture	38	7	45	15.6	18	32.3
Textile production	137	117	254	46.1	303	68.9
Woodwork	73	0	73	0.0	0	0.0
Food processing	476	131	607	21.6	339	41.6

(*cont.*)

	M tasks	F tasks	Total tasks	% by F	F tasks adj.	% by F adj.
Butchery	260	38	298	12.8	98	27.5
Dairying	0	14	14	100.0	36	100.0
Malting and brewing	25	38	63	60.3	98	79.7
Milling	47	9	56	16.1	23	33.2
Storage and preservation	22	12	34	35.3	31	58.6
Threshing and winnowing	117	20	137	14.6	52	30.7
Tobacco	5	0	5	0.0	0	0.0
Housework	225	523	748	69.9	1,355	85.8
Attend guests	3	10	13	76.9	26	89.6
Cleaning	22	48	70	68.6	124	85.0
Collecting water	22	91	113	80.5	236	91.5
Food and drink provision	123	195	318	61.3	505	80.4
Laundry	5	112	117	95.7	290	98.3
Light and fire provision	25	43	68	63.2	111	81.7
Locking gates and doors	25	19	44	43.2	49	66.3
Misc housework	0	5	5	100.0	13	100.0
Management	473	172	645	26.7	445	48.5
Arranging work	95	28	123	22.8	73	43.3
Financial	269	62	331	18.7	161	37.4
Pawning	38	39	77	50.6	101	72.7
Lend/borrow	67	39	106	36.8	101	60.1
Other management	4	4	8	50.0	10	72.1
Transport	1,029	208	1,237	16.8	539	34.4
Boats	55	1	56	1.8	3	4.5
Carry goods	355	150	505	29.7	389	52.3
Carting	205	6	211	2.8	16	7.0
Droving	129	9	138	6.5	23	15.3
Horses	110	13	123	10.6	34	23.4
Loading	106	9	115	7.8	23	18.0
Messages	46	18	64	28.1	47	50.3
Passengers	23	2	25	8.0	5	18.4
Other	108	49	157	31.2	127	54.0
Begging	30	27	57	47.4	70	70.0
Burning	8	3	11	27.3	8	49.3
Misc	49	16	65	24.6	41	45.8
Reading and writing services	21	3	24	12.5	8	27.0

Notes: adj. = adjusted (x2.59).

Appendix C Seasonal Distribution of Dated Harvest Tasks per Region and Proportional Monthly Redistribution of Undated 'Harvest Time' Tasks

C.1. *Dated harvest tasks*

Harvest type per month	Corn harvest						Hay harvest				Combined	
All tasks	In 'harvest time'	In 'corn harvest time'	Harvest tasks	Reap and shear tasks	Total	%	In 'haytime'	Mow grass/ make hay tasks	Total	%	Combined Total	Total %
July	2	4	0	0	6	6	3	34	37	68.5	43	27.9
Aug	34	5	10	5	54	54	4	7	11	20.4	65	42.2
Sept	16	2	4	11	33	33	4	2	6	11.1	39	25.3
Oct	7	0	0	0	7	7	0	0	0	0.0	7	4.5
Total	59	11	14	16	100	100	11	43	54	100	154	100
South-west tasks												
July	0	4	0	0	4	12.9	3	18	21	70.0	25	41.0
Aug	8	5	2	2	17	54.8	0	5	5	16.7	22	36.1
Sept	0	0	2	8	10	32.3	2	2	4	13.3	14	23.0
Oct	0	0	0	0	0	0.0	0	0	0	0.0	0	0.0
Total	8	9	4	10	31	100	5	25	30	100	61	100
East tasks												
July	2	0	0	0	2	4.7	0	11	11	91.7	13	23.6
Aug	15	0	2	0	17	39.5	0	1	1	8.3	18	32.7
Sept	14	0	1	2	17	39.5	0	0	0	0.0	17	30.9
Oct	7	0	0	0	7	16.3	0	0	0	0.0	7	12.7
Total	38	0	3	2	43	100	0	12	12	100	55	100
North tasks												
July	0	0	0	0	0	0.0	0	5	5	41.7	5	13.2
Aug	11	0	6	3	20	76.9	4	1	5	41.7	25	65.8
Sept	2	2	1	1	6	23.1	2	0	2	16.7	8	21.1
Oct	0	0	0	0	0	0.0	0	0	0	0.0	0	0.0
Total	13	2	7	4	26	100	6	6	12	100	38	100

C.2. *Monthly redistribution of undated 'harvest time' tasks*

Harvest type per month	Corn harvest		Hay harvest		Combined
All tasks	Monthly proportions (%)[a]	Redistributed tasks done in 'harvest time'	Monthly proportions (%)[a]	Redistributed tasks done in 'haytime'	Total tasks
July	9.4	32	70.2	40	72
Aug	52.9	180	21.0	12	192
Sept	33.2	113	8.8	5	119
Oct	4.4	15	0.0	0	15
Total	100	340	100.1	57	397
South-west tasks					
July	12.9	27	70.0	15	43
Aug	54.8	116	16.7	4	120
Sept	32.3	68	13.3	3	71
Oct	0.0	0	0.0	0	0
Total	100	212	100	22	234
East tasks					
July	4.7	4	91.7	18	23
Aug	39.5	37	8.3	2	38
Sept	39.5	37	0.0	0	37
Oct	16.3	15	0.0	0	15
Total	100	93	100	20	113
North tasks					
July	0.0	0	41.7	6	6
Aug	76.9	27	41.7	6	33
Sept	23.1	8	16.7	3	11
Oct	0.0	0	0.0	0	0
Total	100	35	100	15	50

[a] Redistribution done on a regional basis according to harvest type, using the corresponding monthly proportions from Table C.1. Due to the different sizes of the regional samples, the monthly proportions for All Tasks do not align in C.1 and C.2.

Notes: As discussed in Section 4.1, tasks described as happening in a 'harvest time' but otherwise undated have been assigned to specific months (July–October) based on the monthly proportions of harvest tasks for which we do have date data (C.1). Because regional seasonality differed, the monthly redistribution of 'harvest time' tasks (C.2) was done separately for the grain harvest and the hay harvest for each region based on the respective proportions in C.1. Certain principles were followed: tasks from the same case were assigned to the same month, tasks like 'haymaking' would be more likely to be assigned to July than September, while a task occurring 'late in the corn harvest' would be assigned to September over July. Additional to these harvest tasks, 25 undated tasks happening 'in Lent' were assigned to February (9), March (12), and April (4) based on when Lent fell that year. Other seasonal designations (spring, summer, winter) were too broad or nebulous in early modern convention to justify similar monthly redistributions.

Appendix D Monthly Weights Applied to Quarter Sessions Tasks

Deposition month	Quarter sessions exams sampled	%	Deviation from 12-month average (8.3%)	One-to-one multiplier	Weighted multiplier[a]	South-west[a]	East[a]	North[a]
Jan	698	7.5	−0.8	1.11	1.22	1.54	1.18	0.99
Feb	536	5.8	−2.6	1.44	1.36	1.81	1.14	1.17
Mar	645	6.9	−1.4	1.20	1.12	1.16	1.08	1.10
Apr	812	8.7	0.4	0.95	0.91	0.85	1.00	0.94
May	944	10.2	1.8	0.82	0.83	0.74	1.04	0.84
Jun	919	9.9	1.6	0.84	0.92	0.88	1.08	0.90
Jul	716	7.7	−0.6	1.08	1.13	1.11	1.17	1.14
Aug	636	6.8	−1.5	1.22	1.12	1.03	1.13	1.29
Sep	829	8.9	0.6	0.93	0.98	1.00	0.84	1.09
Oct	723	7.8	−0.6	1.07	1.04	1.08	0.98	1.08
Nov	795	8.6	0.2	0.97	0.90	0.87	1.04	0.88
Dec	1,040	11.2	2.9	0.74	0.87	0.92	0.81	0.88
Total	9,293	100	N/A	N/A	N/A	N/A	N/A	N/A

[a.] = 2/3rd one-to-one multiplier + 1/3rd one-to-one multiplier of the following month. The three regional weights do not average out exactly to the overall weighted multiplier because the regional samples are different sizes.

Notes: Appendix D outlines the monthly weighting applied to seasonality analyses in this book, as discussed in Section 4.1. These weights were *applied only to tasks from quarter sessions cases for seasonality analysis*, to approximate an even sample of depositions across all 12 months of the year. As the table shows, the number of sampled quarter sessions depositions was not evenly distributed according to the months in which depositions were taken/recorded. This presents an issue because a clear relationship existed between when a quarter sessions deposition was taken, and the time observation reported. A sampling of quarter sessions cases from the work-task dataset shows that around 50 per cent of time observations (usually linked to time of the crime) dated to the same month as when the deposition was taken, with a further 25 per cent of the time observations dated to the month prior to month of deposition. The remaining 25 per cent of time observations were spread throughout the rest of the months of the year prior to deposition. Assuming this latter dispersed portion had a negligible effect (in any systematic way) on the distribution of monthly tasks, the number of quarter sessions tasks in any given month would be influenced most strongly by the number of depositions taken in that same month, and half as much by the number of depositions taken in the following month. The 'Weighted Multiplier', used in all seasonality analysis, reflects this relationship, so that adjusted figures more confidently reflect work patterns, rather than legal or sampling patterns. In calculating a month's multiplier, 2/3rd weight was given to that month's one-to-one multiplier (the multiplier that would be used to reweight if the relationship between month of deposition and month of time observation was one-to-one) and 1/3rd weight to the following month's one-to-one multiplier. For example, January's weighted multiplier is the average of 2 × 1.11 (January's one-to-one multiplier) + 1.44 (February's one-to-one multiplier) = 1.22. These same principles and processes were followed in calculating monthly weights for the three regional samples, used in the seasonality analysis for Figure 3.1.

Bibliography

Ågren, M. (ed.), *Making a Living, Making a Difference: Gender and Work in Early Modern European Society* (Oxford, 2017).

'Introduction: making a living, making a difference', in Ågren, M. (ed.), *Making a Living, Making a Difference: Gender and Work in Early Modern European Society* (Oxford, 2017), pp. 1–23.

'Conclusion', in Ågren, M. (ed.), *Making a Living, Making a Difference: Gender and Work in Early Modern European Society* (Oxford, 2017), pp. 204–20.

'Households' in Macleod, C., Shepard, A. and Ågren, M. (eds.), *The Whole Economy: Work and Gender in Early Modern Europe* (Cambridge, 2023), pp. 26–52.

Airs, M., *The Tudor and Jacobean Country House: A Building History* (Stroud, 1995).

Alesina, A., Giuliano, P. and Nunn, N., 'The origins of gender roles: women and the plough', *Quarterly Journal of Economics* 128 (2013), pp. 469–530.

Allen, R. C., 'The great divergence in European wages and prices from the Middle Ages to the First World War', *Explorations in Economic History* 38 (2001), pp. 411–47.

The British Industrial Revolution in Global Perspective (Cambridge, 2009).

Allen, R. C. and Weisdorf, J. L., 'Was there an "industrious revolution" before the industrial revolution? An empirical exercise for England, c. 1300–1830', *Economic History Review* 64 (2011), pp. 715–29.

Amussen, S. D., *An Ordered Society; Gender and Class in Early Modern England* (New York, 1993).

Anon., *A Godlie Forme of Household Government* (London, 1575).

Antonopoulos, R. and Hirway, I. (eds.), *Unpaid Work and the Economy: Gender, Time-Use, and Poverty in Developing Countries* (Basingstoke, 2010).

Ash, E. H., *The Draining of the Fens: Projectors, Popular Politics, and State Building in Early Modern England* (Baltimore, 2017).

Ashcroft, L. (ed.), *The Diary of a Kendal Midwife: Elizabeth Thompson* (Kendal, 2001).

Aucoin, T., Chilosi, D., Colson, J., Hailwood, M., Wallis, P. and Whittle, J., 'Structural change, work tasks, and urbanization in early modern England', unpublished article.

Becker, G. S., *A Treatise on the Family* (Cambridge, MA, 1991).

Beier, A. L., *Masterless Men: The Vagrancy Problem in England 1560–1640* (London, 1985).

Ben-Amos, I., *Adolescence and Youth in Early Modern England* (New Haven, 1994).

Bennett, J. M., *Ale, Beer, and Brewsters in England: Women's Work in a Changing World, 1300–1600* (Oxford, 1996).

History Matters: Patriarchy and the Challenge of Feminism (Manchester, 2006).

Benson, J. and Ugolini, L. (eds.), *A Nation of Shopkeepers: Five Centuries of British Retailing* (London, 2003).

Blonde, B., Stabel, P., Van Damme, I. and Stobart, J., 'Retail circuits and practices in medieval and early modern Europe: an introduction', in Blonde, B. (ed.), *Buyers and Sellers: Retail Circuits and Practices in Medieval and Early Modern Europe* (Turnhout, 2006), pp. 7–30.

Bowen J. P. and Brown, A. T. (eds.), *Custom and Commercialisation in English Rural Society: Revisiting Tawney and Postan* (Hatfield, 2016).

Brayshay, M., *Land Travel and Communications in Tudor and Stuart England: Achieving a Joined-up Realm* (Liverpool, 2014).

Britnell, R., 'Markets, shops, inns, taverns, and private houses in medieval English trade', in Blonde, B. (ed.), *Buyers and Sellers: Retail Circuits and Practices in Medieval and Early Modern Europe* (Turnhout, 2006), pp. 109–123.

Broadberry, S., Campbell, B. M. S. and van Leeuwen, B., 'When did Britain industrialise? The sectoral distribution of the labour force and labour productivity in Britain, 1381–1851', *Explorations in Economic History* 50 (2013), pp. 16–27.

Broadberry, S., Campbell, B. M. S., Klein, A., Overton, M. and van Leeuwen, B., *British Economic Growth, 1270–1870* (Cambridge, 2015).

Brunskill, R. W., *Illustrated Handbook of Vernacular Architecture* (London, 1971).

Bullinger, H., *The Golden Boke of Christen Matrimonye* (London, 1543).

Burnette, J., 'The wages and employment of female day labourers in English agriculture, 1740–1850', *Economic History Review* 57 (2004), pp. 664–90.

'How not to measure the standard of living: male wages, non-market production, and household income in nineteenth-century Europe', *Economic History Review* (online prepublication, March 2024).

Buxton, A., *Domestic Culture in Early Modern England* (Woodbridge, 2015).

Capp, B., *When Gossips Meet: Women, Family and Neighbourhood in Early Modern England* (Oxford, 2003).

Carew, R., *Survey of Cornwall* (London, 1602).

Carter, P., 'Work, gender, and witchcraft in early modern England', *Gender and History* (online prepublication, July 2023).

Carus, A. W. and Ogilvie, S., 'Turning qualitative into quantitative evidence: a well-used method made explicit', *Economic History Review* 62 (2009), pp. 893–925.

Clark, A., *Working Life of Women in the Seventeenth Century* (London, 1919).

Clark, G., 'Review of *Time and Work in England, 1750–1830.* By Hans-Joachim Voth. Oxford: Clarendon Press, 2001', *Journal of Economic History* 61 (2001), pp. 1123–4.

'The long march of history: farm wages, population, and economic growth, England 1209–1869', *Economic History Review* 60 (2007), pp. 97–135.

Clarkson, L. A., *Proto-Industrialisation: The First Phase of Industrialisation?* (Basingstoke, 1985).

Coleman, D. C., 'An innovation and its diffusion: The "New Draperies"', *Economic History Review* 22 (1969), pp. 417–29.

Cooper, I., 'The speed and efficiency of the Tudor south west's royal post-stage service', *History* 99 (2014), pp. 754–74.

Cowan, R. S., *More Work for Mother: The Ironies of Household Technologies from the Open Hearth to the Microwave* (London, 1989).

Cox, N., *The Complete Tradesman: A Study of Retailing, 1550–1820* (Oxford, 2000).

Crawford, P., *Parents of Poor Children, 1580–1800* (Oxford, 2010).

Cressy, D., *Bonfires and Bells: National Memory and the Protestant Calendar in Elizabethan and Stuart England* (Berkeley, CA, 1989).

Croot, P., *The World of the Small Farmer: Tenure, Profit and Politics in the Early Modern Somerset Levels* (Woodbridge, 2017).

Crowley, J. E., *The Invention of Comfort: Sensibilities and Design in Early Modern Britain and Early America* (Baltimore, MD, 2001).

Davies, M. G., *The Enforcement of English Apprenticeship 1563–1642: A Study of Applied Mercantilism* (Cambridge, MA, 1956).

Davis, N. Z., *Fiction in the Archives: Pardon Tales and Their Tellers in Sixteenth Century France* (Cambridge, 1987).

de Moor, T. and van Zanden, J. L., 'Girl power: the European marriage pattern and labour markets in the North Sea region in the late medieval and early modern period', *Economic History Review* 63 (2010), pp. 1–33.

de Vries, J., *The Industrious Revolution: Consumer Behaviour and the Household Economy, 1650 to the Present* (Cambridge, 2008).

Dod, J. and Cleaver, R., *A Godly Form of Household Government* (London, 1630).

Dolan, F. E., *True Relations: Reading, Literature, and Evidence in Seventeenth Century England* (Philadelphia, PA, 2013).

Duffy, E., *The Stripping of the Altars: Traditional Religion in England, c.1400–c.1580* (New Haven, CT, 1992).

Dunlop, J. and Denman, R. D., *English Apprenticeship and Child Labour: A History* (London, 1912).

Dyer, A., 'Small market towns 1540–1700', in Clark, P. (ed.), *The Cambridge Urban History of Britain, Vol. 2: 1540–1840* (Cambridge, 2008), pp. 425–50.

Dyer, C., *An Age of Transition? Economy and Society in England in the Later Middle Ages* (Oxford, 2005).

Earle, P., 'The female labour market in London in the late seventeenth and early eighteenth centuries', *Economic History Review* 44 (1989), pp. 328–53.

The Making of the English Middle Class: Business, Society and Family Life in London, 1660–1730 (London, 1989).

Edwards, J. and Ogilvie, S., 'Did the Black Death "cause" economic development by inventing fertility restriction?', *Oxford Economic Papers* 74 (2022), pp. 1228–46.

Eibach, J., 'Das offene haus: Kommunikative Praxis im sozialen Nahraum der europäischen Frühen Neuze', *Zeitschrift für Historische Forschung* 38 (2011), pp. 621–64.

Ellis, F., *Peasant Economics: Farm Households and Agrarian Development* (Cambridge, 1988).
Ellis, W., *The Country Housewife's Family Companion* (London, 1750).
Emmison, F. G., 'Tithes, perambulations, and sabbath-breach in Elizabethan Essex', in Emmison, F. G. and Stephens, R. (eds.), *Tribute to an Antiquary: Essays Presented to Marc Fitch by Some of His Friends* (London, 1976), pp. 177–215.
Erickson, A. L., *Women and Property in Early Modern England* (London, 1993).
'Coverture and capitalism', *History Workshop Journal* 59 (2005), pp. 1–16.
'Married women's occupations in eighteenth-century London', *Continuity and Change* 23 (2008), pp. 267–307.
Erickson, A. L. and Schmidt, A., 'Migration', in Macleod, C., Shepard, A. and Ågren, M. (eds.), *The Whole Economy: Work and Gender in Early Modern Europe* (Cambridge, 2023), pp. 164–99.
Esquivel, V., Budlender, D., Folbre, N. and Hirway, I., 'Explorations: time-use surveys in the south', *Feminist Economics* 14 (2008), pp. 107–52.
Estienne, C., *Maison Rustique, or The Countrey Farme* (London, 1616).
Evans, N., *The East Anglian Linen Industry: Rural Industry and Local Economy 1500–1850* (Aldershot, 1985).
Evenden, D., *The Midwives of Seventeenth Century London* (Cambridge, 2000).
Everitt, A., 'Farm labourers', in Thirsk, J. (ed.), *The Agrarian History of England and Wales, Vol. 4: 1500–1640* (Cambridge, 1967), pp. 396–465.
'The marketing of agricultural produce', in Thirsk, J. (ed.), *The Agrarian History of England and Wales, Vol. 4: 1500–1640* (Cambridge, 1967), pp. 466–592.
Falvey, H., 'Relating early modern depositions', in Griffin, C. J. and McDonagh, B. (eds.), *Remembering Protest in Britain since 1500: Memory, Materiality, and the Landscape* (Basingstoke, 2018), pp. 81–106.
Fiebranz, R., Lindberg, E., Lindström, J. and Ågren, M., 'Making verbs count: the research project "Gender and Work" and its methodology', *Scandinavian Economic History Review* 59 (2011), pp. 273–93.
Fildes, V., 'The English wet-nurse and her role in infant care 1538–1800', *Medical History* 32 (1988), pp. 142–73.
Fisher, J., 'Bound to the Soil (Part I): The origins of compulsory apprenticeship schemes in south-west rural England c.1670–1750', *Continuity and Change* (forthcoming).
'Bound to the Soil (Part II): The political economy of compulsory apprenticeship systems in eighteenth-century rural England', *Continuity and Change* (forthcoming).
Flather, A., *Gender and Space in Early Modern England* (Woodbridge, 2007).
'Space, place, and gender: the sexual and spatial division of labor in the early modern household', *History and Theory* 52 (2013), pp. 344–60.
'Women, work, and land: the spatial dynamics of gender relations in early modern England 1550–1750', in Capern, A. L., McDonagh, B. and Aston, J. (eds.), *Women and the Land, 1500–1900* (Woodbridge, 2019), pp. 29–50.
Fontaine, L., 'Women's economic spheres and credit in pre-industrial Europe', in Campbell, G., Lemire, B. and Pearson, R. (eds.), *Women and Credit; Researching the Past, Refiguring the Future* (London, 2002), pp. 13–31

Fox, H., *The Evolution of the Fishing Village: Landscape and Society along the South Devon Coast, 1086–1550* (Oxford, 2001).

Dartmoor's Alluring Upands: Transhumance and Pastoral Management in the Middle Ages (Exeter, 2012).

Fox, H. S. A., 'Farming practice and techniques: Devon and Cornwall' in Thirsk, J. (ed.), *The Agrarian History of England and Wales, Vol. 4: 1500–1640* (Cambridge, 1967), pp. 303–23.

French, H., 'Legal and judicial sources', in Sangha, L. and Willis, J. P. (eds.), *Understanding Early Modern Primary Sources* (London, 2016), pp. 35–57.

Froide, A. M., *Never Married: Singlewomen in Early Modern England* (Oxford, 2005).

Silent Partners: Women as Public Investors during Britain's Financial Revolution, 1690–1750 (Oxford, 2017).

Fumerton, P., *Unsettled: The Culture of Mobility and the Working Poor in Early Modern England* (Chicago, IL, 2006).

Gershuny, J. and Sullivan, O., *What We Really Do All Day: Insights from the Centre for Time Use Research* (London, 2019).

Glennie, P. and Whyte, I., 'Towns in an agrarian economy 1540–1700', in Clark P. (ed.), *The Cambridge Urban History of Britain, Vol. 2: 1540–1840* (Cambridge, 2008), pp. 165–94.

Goldberg, P. J. P., *Women, Work, and Life Cycle in a Medieval Economy: Women in York and Yorkshire c.1300–1520* (Oxford, 1992).

Women in England c.1275–1525: Documentary Sources (Manchester, 1995).

Gowing, L., *Domestic Dangers: Women, Words, and Sex in Early Modern London* (Oxford, 1996).

Common Bodies: Women, Touch, and Power in Seventeenth Century England (New Haven, CT, 2003).

Ingenious Trade: Women and Work in Seventeenth Century London (Cambridge, 2022).

Habermas, J., *The Structural Transformation of the Public Sphere: An Enquiry into a Category of Bourgeoise Society* (Oxford, 1992).

Hailwood, M., 'Sociability, work and labouring identity in seventeenth-century England', *Cultural and Social History* 8 (2011), pp. 9–29.

Alehouses and Good Fellowship in Early Modern England (Woodbridge, 2014).

'Time and work in rural England, 1500–1700', *Past and Present* 248 (2020), pp. 87–121.

Hailwood, M. and Waddell, B., 'Work and identity in early modern England', *Transactions of the Royal Historical Society* 1 (2023), pp. 145–58.

Hailwood, M., Whittle, J., Lindström, J., Ling, S. and Ågren, M., 'Comparing the gender division of labour in early modern Sweden and England', *Continuity and Change* (forthcoming).

Hamling, T. and Richardson, C., *A Day at Home in Early Modern England: Material Culture and Domestic Life, 1500–1700* (New Haven, CT, 2017).

Hanawalt, B. A., *The Ties that Bound: Peasant Families in Medieval England* (Oxford, 1986).

Handley, S., *Sleep in Early Modern England* (New Haven, CT, 2016).

Harley, D., 'Provincial midwives in England: Lancashire and Cheshire, 1660–1760', in Marland, H. (ed.), *The Art of Midwifery: Early Modern Midwives in Europe* (London, 1993), pp. 27–48.

Harms, T. and Gershuny, J., 'Housework now takes much less time: 85 years of US rural women's time use', *Social Forces* 95 (2016), pp. 503–24.

Harrison, W., *The Description of England: The Classic Contemporary Account of Tudor Social Life*' (ed.) G. Edelen (New York, 1994).

Harte, N. B., 'The economics of clothing in the late seventeenth century', *Textile History* 22 (1991), pp. 277–96.

Hatcher, J., *Rural Economy and Society in the Duchy of Cornwall 1300–1500* (Cambridge, 1970).

The History of the British Coal Industry, Vol. 1: Before 1700 (Oxford, 1993).

'Women's work reconsidered: gender and wage differentiation in late medieval England', *Past and Present* 173 (2001), pp. 191–8.

Hatcher, J. and Stephenson, J. (eds.), *Seven Centuries of Unreal Wages: The Unreliable Data, Sources and Methods That Have Been Used for Measuring Standards of Living in the Past* (Basingstoke, 2018).

Herrup, C. B., *The Common Peace: Participation and the Criminal Law in Seventeenth Century England* (Cambridge, 1987).

Hill, B., *Women, Work, and Sexual Politics in Eighteenth-Century England* (London, 1989)

Hindle, S., *On the Parish? The Micro-Politics of Poor Relief in Rural England c.1550–1750* (Oxford, 2004).

'Work, reward, and labour discipline in late seventeenth-century England', in Hindle, S., Shepard, A. and Walter, J. (eds.), *Remaking English Society: Social Relations and Social Change in Early Modern England* (Woodbridge, 2013), pp. 255–80.

Hobsbawm, E. J, and Scott, J. W., 'Political shoemakers', *Past and Present* 89 (1980), pp. 86–114.

Holderness, B. A., 'Widows in pre-industrial society: an essay upon their economic functions', in Smith, R. M. (ed.), *Land, Kinship, and Life-Cycle* (Cambridge, 1984), pp. 423–42.

Horrell, S., Humphries, J. and Weisdorf, J., 'Family standards of living over the long run, England 1280–1850', *Past and Present* 250 (2021), pp. 87–134.

'Beyond the male breadwinner: life-cycle living standards of intact and disrupted English working families, 1260–1850', *Economic History Review* 75 (2022), pp. 530–60.

Humphries, J., 'Enclosures, common rights, and women: the proletarianization of families in the late eighteenth and early nineteenth centuries', *Journal of Economic History* 50 (1990), pp. 17–42.

Humphries, J. and Weisdorf, J., 'The wages of women in England, 1260–1850', *Journal of Economic History* 75 (2015), pp. 405–47.

'Unreal wages? Real income and economic growth in England, 1260–1850', *Economic Journal* 129 (2019), pp. 2867–87.

Hutton, R., *The Rise and Fall of Merry England: The Ritual Year, 1400–1700* (Oxford, 1994).

The Stations of the Sun: A History of the Ritual Year in Britain (Oxford, 1996).

Ingold, T., 'The temporality of the landscape', *World Archaeology* 25 (1993), pp. 152–74.

Ingram, M., *Church Courts, Sex, and Marriage in England, 1570–1640* (Cambridge, 1987).

Carnal Knowledge: Regulating Sex in England 1470–1600 (Cambridge, 2017).

Jenner, M. and Wallis, P. (eds.), *Medicine and the Market in England and Its Colonies c.1450–c.1850* (Basingstoke, 2007).

Johnson, M., *Housing Culture: Traditional Architecture in an English Landscape* (Washington, 1993).

English Houses 1300–1800: Vernacular Architecture, Social Life (Harlow, 2010).

Johnson, T., 'The economics of shipwreck in late medieval Suffolk', in Bowen J. P. and Brown A. T. (eds.), *Custom and Commercialisation in English Rural Society: Revisiting Tawney and Postan* (Hatfield, 2016), pp. 121–38.

Jones, E. L., *Seasons and Prices: The Role of the Weather in English Agricultural History* (London, 1964).

Keibek, S. A. J. and Shaw-Taylor, L., 'Early modern rural by-employments: a re-examination of the probate inventory evidence', *Agricultural History Review* 61 (2013), pp. 244–81.

King, C., *Houses and Society in Norwich, 1350–1660: Urban Buildings in an Age of Transition* (Woodbridge, 2020).

King, P., 'Customary rights and women's earnings: the importance of gleaning to the rural labouring poor, 1750–1850', *Economic History Review* 44 (1991), pp. 461–76.

Kreidt, P., Medick, H. and Schlumbohm, J., *Industrialization before Industrialization: Rural Industry in the Genesis of Capitalism* (Cambridge, 1981).

Kussmaul, A., *Servants in Husbandry in Early Modern England* (Cambridge, 1981).

A General View of the Rural Economy of England, 1538–1840 (Cambridge, 1990).

Lane, J., *Apprenticeship in England 1600–1914* (London, 1996).

Langdon, J., *Mills in the Medieval Economy: England 1300–1540* (Oxford, 2004).

Le Goff, J., *Time, Work, and Culture in the Middle Ages*, trans. Arthur Goldhammer (Chicago, IL, 1980).

Lee, R. D. and Schofield, R. S., 'British population in the eighteenth century', in Floud, R. and McCloskey D. (eds.), *The Economic History of Britain since 1700, Vol. 1: 1700–1860* (Cambridge, 1981), pp. 17–35.

Lemire, B., *Dress, Culture and Commerce: The English Clothing Trade before the Factory, 1660–1800* (London, 1997).

'Petty pawns and informal lending: gender and the transformation of small-scale credit in England, circa 1600–1800', in Bruland, K. and O'Brien, P. (eds.), *From Family Firms to Corporate Capitalism: Essays in Business and Industrial History in Honour of Peter Mathias* (Oxford, 1998), pp. 112–38.

'Introduction: women, credit and the creation of opportunity: a historical overview', in Campbell, G., Lemire, B. and Pearson, R. (eds.), *Women and Credit; Researching the Past, Refiguring the Future* (London, 2002), pp. 1–12.

The Business of Everyday Life: Gender, Practice, and Social Politics in England, c.1600–1900 (Manchester, 2005).

'Plebian commercial circuits and everyday material exchange in England, c. 1600–1900', in Blonde, B. (ed.), *Buyers and Sellers: Retail Circuits and Practices in Medieval and Early Modern Europe* (Turnhout, 2006), pp. 245–66.

Leong, E., '"Herbs she persueth": reading medicine in early modern England', *Renaissance Studies* 28 (2004), pp. 556–78.

'Making medicines in the early modern household', *Bulletin of the History of Medicine* 82 (2008), pp. 145–68.

Ling, S., Hassan Jansson, K., Lennersand, M., Pihl, C. and Ågren, M., 'Marriage and work: intertwined sources of agency and authority', in Ågren, M. (ed.), *Making a Living, Making a Difference: Gender and Work in Early Modern European Society* (Oxford, 2017), pp. 80–102.

Lowe, N., *The Lancashire Textile Industry in the Sixteenth Century* (Manchester, 1972).

MacCaffrey, W. T., *Exeter 1540–1640: The Growth of an English County Town* (Cambridge, MA, 1958).

Macleod, C., Shepard, A. and Ågren, M. (eds.), *The Whole Economy: Work and Gender in Early Modern Europe* (Cambridge, 2023).

Mann, J. de L., *The Cloth Industry in the West of England from 1640 to 1880* (Oxford, 1971).

Mansell, C., 'The variety of women's experiences as servants in England (1548–1649): evidence from church court depositions', *Continuity and Change* 33 (2018), pp. 315–38.

'Reconstructing the labour of care in early modern England', *Historical Journal* 67 (2024), pp. 21–41.

Female Servants in Early Modern England (Oxford, 2024).

Markham, G., *The English Husbandman* (London, 1613).

The English Housewife (London, 1615).

McIntosh, M. K., *Controlling Misbehaviour in England, 1370–1600* (Cambridge, 1998).

Working Women in English Society 1300–1620 (Cambridge, 2005).

McKendrick, N., Brewer, J., Plumb and J. H.(eds.), *The Birth of a Consumer Society: The Commercialisation of Eighteenth Century England* (London, 1982).

McRae, A., *Literature and Domestic Travel in Early Modern England* (Cambridge, 2009).

Meldrum, T., *Domestic Service and Gender 1660–1750: Life and Work in the London Household* (Harlow, 2000).

Mendelson, S. and Crawford, P., *Women in Early Modern England 1550–1720* (Oxford, 1998).

Mileson, S., 'Openness and closure in the later medieval village', *Past and Present* 234 (2017), pp. 3–37.

Mokyr, J., 'The economics of apprenticeship' in Prak, M. and Wallis, P. (eds.), *Apprenticeship in Early Modern Europe* (Cambridge, 2019), pp. 20–43.

Moring, B. and Wall, R., *Widows in European Economy and Society, 1600–1920* (Woodbridge, 2017).

Mortimer, I., 'The triumph of the doctors: medical assistance to the dying, 1570–1720', *Transactions of the Royal Historical Society* 15 (2005), pp. 97–116.

'The rural medical marketplace in southern England c.1570–1720', in Jenner, M. S. R. and Wallis P. (eds.), *The Medicine and Its Market in England and its Colonies, c.1450–1850* (London, 2007), pp. 69–87.

The Dying and the Doctors: The Medical Revolution in Seventeenth Century England (Woodbridge, 2009).

Muldrew, C., 'Culture of reconciliation: community and the settlement of economic disputes in early modern England', *Historical Journal* 39 (1996), pp. 915–42.

The Economy of Obligation: The Culture of Credit and Social Relations in Early Modern England (Basingstoke, 1998).

'Mutual assent of her mind? Women, debt, litigation, and contract in early modern England', *History Workshop Journal* 55 (2003), pp. 47–71.

Food, Energy, and the Creation of Industriousness: Work and Material Culture in Agrarian England, 1550–1780 (Cambridge, 2011).

'"Th'ancient distaff and whirling spindle": measuring the contribution of spinning to household earnings and the national economy in England, 1550–1770', *Economic History Review* 65 (2012), pp. 498–526.

Nagy, D. G., *Popular Medicine in Seventeenth Century England* (Bowling Green, OH, 1988).

Neeson, J. M., *Commoners: Common Right, Enclosure and Social Change in England, 1700–1820* (Cambridge, 1993).

North, S., *Sweet and Clean?: Bodies and Clothes in Early Modern England* (Oxford, 2020).

Oakley, A., *The Sociology of Housework* (Bristol, 2018).

Ogilvie, S., *A Bitter Living: Women, Markets, and Social Capital in Early Modern Germany* (Oxford, 2003).

The European Guilds: An Economic Analysis (Princeton, NJ, 2019).

O'Hara, D., *Courtship and Constraint: Rethinking the Making of Marriage in Tudor England* (Manchester, 2000).

Oja, L., 'Childcare and gender in Sweden c. 1600–1800', *Gender and History* 27 (2015), pp. 77–111.

Orlin, L. C., *Locating Privacy in Tudor London* (Oxford, 2007).

Outhwaite, R. B., *The Rise and Fall of the English Ecclesiastical Courts, 1500–1860* (Cambridge, 2007).

Overton, M., *Agricultural Revolution in England: The Transformation of the Agrarian Economy 1500–1850* (Cambridge, 1996).

Overton, M., Whittle, J., Dean, D. and Hann, A., *Production and Consumption in English Households, 1600–1750* (Abingdon, 2004).

Parker, K. L., *The English Sabbath: A Study of Doctrine and Discipline from the Reformation to the Civil War* (Cambridge, 1988).

Paul, K. T., 'Accounting for men's work: multiple employments and occupational identities in early modern England', *History Workshop Journal* 85 (2018), pp. 26–46.

Pelling, M., 'Occupational diversity: barbersurgeons and the trades of Norwich, 1550–1640', *Bulletin of the History of Medicine* 56 (1982), pp. 484–511.

Penn, S., 'Female wage-earners in late fourteenth-century England', *Agricultural History Review* 35 (1987), pp. 1–14.

Pennell, S., 'Consumption and consumerism in early modern England', *Historical Journal* 42 (1999), pp. 549–64.

The Birth of the English Kitchen, 1600–1850 (London, 2016).

Penney, N. (ed.), *The Household Account Book of Sarah Fell of Swarthmoor Hall* (Cambridge, 1920).

Pennington, D., *Going to Market; Women, Trade and Social Relations in Early Modern English Towns, c.1550–1650* (London, 2015).

Phelps Brown, E. H. and Hopkins S., 'Seven centuries of building wages', *Economica* 22 (1955), pp. 195–206.

Pinchbeck, I., *Women Workers and the Industrial Revolution 1750–1850* (London, 1930).

Porter, G., 'Cobblers all: occupation as identity and cultural message', *Folk Music Journal* 7 (1995), pp. 43–61.

Porter, R. (ed.), *Patients and Practitioners: Lay Perceptions of Medicine in Preindustrial Society* (Cambridge, 1985).

Rackham, O., *Trees and Woodland in the British Landscape: The Complete History of Britain's Trees, Woods and Hedgerows* (London, 2001).

Ramsay, G. D., *The English Woollen Industry, 1500–1750* (London, 1982).

Rappaport, S., *Worlds within Worlds: Structures of Life in Sixteenth Century London* (Cambridge, 1989).

Reid, D. A., 'The decline of Saint Monday 1766–1876', *Past and Present* 71 (1976), pp. 76–101.

'Weddings, weekdays, work, and leisure in urban England 1791–1911: the decline of Saint Monday revisited', *Past and Present* 153 (1996), pp. 135–63.

Reid, M. G., *Economics of Household Production* (New York, 1934).

Reinke-Williams, T., *Women, Work, and Sociability in Early Modern London* (London, 2014).

Roberts, M., 'Sickles and scythes: women's work and men's work at harvest time', *History Workshop* 7 (1979), pp. 3–28.

'"Words they are women and deeds they are men": images of work and gender in early modern England', in Charles, L. and Duffin, L. (eds.), *Women and Work in Preindustrial England* (London, 1985), pp. 122–80.

'"To bridle the falsehood of unconscionable workmen, and for her own satisfaction": what the Jacobean housewife needed to know about men's work, and why', *Labour History Review* 63 (1998), pp. 4–30.

Rogers, J. E. T., *A History of Agriculture and Prices in England: 7 Vols* (Cambridge, 1866–1902).

Sarasúa, C., Erdozáin, P. and Hernández R., 'Nursing babies to fight poverty: wages of wet nurses in Spanish foundling hospitals in the eighteenth and nineteenth centuries', *Revista de Historia Económica* 41 (2023), pp. 243–71.

Sarti, R., *Europe at Home: Family and Material Culture 1500–1800* (London, 2002).

Shannon, W. D., 'Risks and rewards in wasteland enclosure: lowland Lancashire c.1500–1650', in Whittle J. (ed.), *Landlords and Tenants in Britain,*

1440–1660: Tawney's 'Agrarian Problem' Revisited (Woodbridge, 2013), pp. 150–65.

Sharpe, P., 'Time and wages of west country workfolks in the seventeenth and eighteenth centuries', *Local Population Studies* 55 (1995), pp. 66–8.

Adapting to Capitalism: Working Women in the English Economy, 1700–1850 (Basingstoke, 1996).

'The female labour market in English agriculture during the Industrial Revolution: expansion or contraction?' *Agricultural History Review* 47 (1999), pp. 161–81.

Shaw, J., 'Liquidation or certification? Small claims disputes and retail credit in seventeenth-century Venice', in Blonde, B. (ed.), *Buyers and Sellers: Retail Circuits and Practices in Medieval and Early Modern Europe* (Turnhout, 2006), pp. 277–95.

Shaw-Taylor, L., 'Labourers, cows, common rights, and Parliamentary enclosure: the evidence of contemporary comment c.1760–1810', *Past and Present* 171 (2001), pp. 95–126.

'The rise of agrarian capitalism and the decline in family farming in England', *Economic History Review* 65 (2012), pp. 26–60.

Shaw-Taylor, L. and Wrigley, E. A., 'Occupational structure and population change' in Floud, R., Humphries J. and Johnson, P. (eds.), *The Cambridge Economic History of Modern Britain, Vol. 1: 1700–1850* (Cambridge, 2014), pp. 53–88.

Shepard, A., 'Care' in Macleod, C., Shepard, A. and Ågren, M. (eds.), *The Whole Economy: Work and Gender in Early Modern Europe* (Cambridge, 2023), pp. 53–83.

Meanings of Manhood in Early Modern England (Oxford, 2003).

Accounting for Oneself: Worth, Status, and the Social Order in Early Modern England (Oxford, 2015).

'Crediting women in the early modern English economy', *History Workshop Journal* 79 (2015), pp. 1–24.

'Minding their own business: married women and credit in early eighteenth-century London', *Transactions of the Royal Historical Society* 25 (2015), pp. 53–74.

'Worthless witnesses? Marginal voices and women's legal agency in early modern England', *Journal of British Studies* 58 (2019), pp. 717–34.

Slack, P., 'Great and good towns 1540–1700', in Clark P. (ed.), *The Cambridge Urban History of Britain, Vol. 2: 1540–1840* (Cambridge, 2008), pp. 347–76.

Smith, A., *An Inquiry into the Nature and Causes of the Wealth of Nations* (London, 1776).

Smith, A. H., 'Labourers in late sixteenth-century England: a case study from north Norfolk [Part I]', *Continuity and Change* 4 (1989), pp. 11–52.

'Labourers in late sixteenth-century England: a case study from north Norfolk [Part II]', *Continuity and Change* 4 (1989), pp. 367–94.

Smith, C., 'Medieval coroners' rolls: legal fiction or historical fact', in Dunn, D. E. S. (ed.), *Courts, Counties and the Capital in the Later Middle Ages* (Stroud, 1986), pp. 93–115.

Snell, K. D. M., *Annals of the Labouring Poor: Social Change and Agrarian England 1660–1900* (Cambridge, 1985).

Souden, D., 'Migrants and the population structure of later seventeenth-century provincial cities and market towns' in Clark, P. (ed.), *The Transformation of English Provincial Towns* (Hutchinson, 1984), pp. 133–68.

Spenceley, G. F. R., 'The origins of the English pillow lace industry', *Agricultural History Review* 21 (1973), pp. 81–93.

Spicksley, J., 'Never married women and credit in early modern England', in Dermineur, E. M. (ed.), *Women and Credit in Pre-Industrial Europe* (Turnhout, 2018), pp. 227–52.

Stephens, W. B., *Seventeenth Century Exeter: A Study of Industrial and Commercial Development, 1625–88* (Exeter, 1958).

Stephenson, J., *Contracts and Pay: Work in London Construction 1660–1785* (Basingstoke, 2020).

'Working days in a London construction team in the eighteenth century: evidence from St Paul's Cathedral', *Economic History Review* 73 (2020), pp. 409–30.

Stobart, A., *Household Medicine in Seventeenth Century England* (London, 2016).

Stobart, J., *Sugar and Spice: Grocers and Groceries in Provincial England, 1650–1830* (Oxford, 2013).

Stretton, T., 'Written obligations, litigation, and neighbourliness, 1580–1680', in Hindle, S., Shepard, A. and Walter, J. (eds.), *Remaking English Society: Social Relations and Social Change in Early Modern England* (Woodbridge, 2013), pp. 189–210.

Strocchia, S. T., 'Introduction: women and healthcare in early modern Europe', *Renaissance Studies* 28 (2014), pp. 496–514.

Styles, J., *The Dress of the People: Everyday Fashion in Eighteenth-Century England* (London, 2007).

Swanson, H., *Building Craftsmen in Late Medieval York* (York, 1983).

Tadmor, N., 'The concept of the household-family in eighteenth-century England', *Past and Present* 151 (1996), pp. 111–40.

Tait, J. (ed.), *Lancashire Quarter Sessions Records, Vol. 1: Quarter Sessions Rolls, 1590–1606* (London, 1917).

Tankard, D., *Clothing in Seventeenth-Century Provincial England* (London, 2019).

Taylor, H., 'The price of the poor's words: social relations and the economics of deposing for one's 'betters' in early modern England', *Economic History Review* 72 (2019), pp. 828–47.

Thirsk, J. (ed.), *The Agrarian History of England and Wales, Vol. 4: 1500–1640* (Cambridge, 1967).

Agricultural Regions and Agrarian History in England, 1500–1750 (Basingstoke, 1987).

'Industries in the countryside', in Thirsk J. (ed.), *Rural Economy of England: Collected Essays* (London, 2016), pp. 217–33 [originally published 1961].

Thomas, K., 'Numeracy in early modern England. The Prothero Lecture', *Transactions of the Royal Historical Society* 37 (1987), pp. 103–32.

Thomas, S. S., 'Early modern midwifery: splitting the profession, connecting the history', *Journal of Social History* 43 (2009), pp. 115–38.

Thompson, E. P. 'Time, work-discipline, and industrial capitalism', *Past and Present* 38 (1967), pp. 56–97.

The Making of the English Working Class (London, 1968).
Customs in Common (London, 1991).
Thorner, D. B., Kerblay, B. and Smith, R. E. F. (eds.), *A.V. Chayanov on the Theory of Peasant Economy* (Homewood, IL, 1966).
Tilly, L. A. and Scott, J., *Women, Work, and Family* (London, 1987).
Tilney, E., *The Flower of Friendship: A Renaissance Dialogue Contesting Marriage*, (ed.) V. Wayne (Ithaca, NY, 1992).
Tiratelli, M., 'The working week in the long nineteenth century: evidence from the timings of political events in Britain', *Social Science History* 46 (2022), pp. 291–313.
Tusser, T., *Five Hundred Points of Good Husbandry* (London, 1580).
Unwin, T., 'Rural marketing in medieval Nottinghamshire', *Journal of Historical Geography* 7 (1981), pp. 231–51.
Valenze, D., 'The art of women and the business of men: women's work and the dairy industry c.1740–1840', *Past and Present* 130 (1991), pp. 142–69.
Verdon, N., *Rural Women Workers in Nineteenth Century England: Gender, Work, and Wages* (Woodbridge, 2002).
'"Subjects deserving of the highest praise": farmers' wives and the farm economy in England, c.1700–1850', *Agricultural History Review* 51 (2003), pp. 23–39.
Vickery, A., 'Golden age to separate spheres? A review of the categories and chronology of English women's history', *Historical Journal* 36 (1993), pp. 383–414.
Voigtländer, N. and Voth H.-J., 'How the west "invented" fertility restriction', *American Economic Review* 103 (2013), pp. 2227–64.
Voth, H-J., 'Time and work in eighteenth-century London', *Journal of Economic History* 58 (1998), pp. 29–58.
Time and Work in England 1750–1830 (Oxford, 2000).
Wallis, P., 'Apprenticeship and training in premodern England', *Journal of Economic History* 68 (2008), pp. 832–61.
'Apprenticeship in England', in Prak, M. and Wallis, P. (eds.), *Apprenticeship in Early Modern Europe* (Cambridge, 2019), pp. 247–81.
Wallis, P., Colson, J. and Chilosi, D., 'Structural change and economic growth in the British economy before the Industrial Revolution, 1500–1800', *Journal of Economic History* 78 (2018), pp. 862–903.
Walsh, C., 'The social relations of shopping in early modern England', in Blonde, B. (ed.), *Buyers and Sellers: Retail Circuits and Practices in Medieval and Early Modern Europe* (Turnhout, 2006), pp. 331–53.
Warde, P., *The Invention of Sustainability: Nature and Destiny, c.1500–1870* (Cambridge, 2018).
Waring, M., *Counting for Nothing: What Men Value and What Women Are Worth* (Toronto, 1999).
Weatherill, L., 'The meaning of consumer behaviour in late seventeenth- and early eighteenth-century England', in Brewer, J. and Porter, R. (eds.), *Consumption and the World of Goods* (London, 1993), pp. 206–27.
Webster, C. (ed.), *Health, Medicine and Mortality in the Sixteenth Century* (Cambridge, 1979).

Whittle, J., *The Development of Agrarian Capitalism: Land and Labour in Norfolk, 1440–1580* (Oxford, 2000).

'Servants in rural England c.1450–1650: hired work as a means of accumulating wealth and skills before marriage', in Ågren, M. and Erickson, A. L. (eds.), *The Marital Economy in Scandinavia and Britain 1400–1900* (Aldershot, 2005), pp. 89–107.

'Housewives and servants in rural England, 1440–1650: evidence of women's work from probate documents', *Transactions of the Royal Historical Society* 15 (2005), pp. 51–74.

'The house as a place of work in early modern rural England', *Home Cultures* 8 (2011) pp. 133–50.

'Enterprising widows and active wives: women's unpaid work in the household economy of early modern England', *History of the Family* 19 (2014), pp. 283–300.

(ed.), *Servants in Rural Europe 1400–1900* (Woodbridge, 2017).

'A different pattern of employment: servants in rural England c.1500–1660', in Whittle, J. (ed.), *Servants in Rural Europe 1400–1900* (Woodbridge, 2017), pp. 57–76.

'A critique of approaches to "domestic work": women, work and the preindustrial economy', *Past and Present* 243 (2019), pp. 35–70.

'Gender and consumption in the household economy', in Eibach, J. and Lanzinger, M. (eds.), *The Routledge History of the Domestic Sphere in Europe: Sixteenth to Nineteenth Century* (Abingdon, 2020), pp. 199–217.

'Home and work', in Flather A. (ed.), *A Cultural History of the Home in the Renaissance* (London, 2021), pp. 103–26.

'Attitudes to wage labour in English legislation, 1349–1601', in Whittle J. and Lambrecht, T. (eds.), *Labour Laws in Preindustrial Europe: The Coercion and Regulation of Wage Labour, c.1350–1850* (Woodbridge, 2023), pp. 33–54.

'Putting women back into the early modern economy: work, occupations, and economic development', *Economic History Review* (online prepublication, January 2024).

Whittle, J. and Griffiths, E., *Consumption and Gender in the Early Seventeenth-Century Household: The World of Alice Le Strange* (Oxford, 2012).

Whittle, J. and Hailwood, M., 'The gender division of labour in early modern England', *Economic History Review* 73 (2020) pp. 3–32.

Whittle, J. and Jiang, L., 'Gender, wages, and agricultural labour in England, c.1480–1680', *Agricultural History Review* 72 (2024), pp. 169–190.

Whyte, I., *Migration and Society in Britain 1550–1830* (Basingstoke, 1999).

Wiesner-Hanks, M., *Women and Gender in Early Modern Europe* (Cambridge, 2019).

Willan, T. S., *Inland Trade: Studies in English Internal Trade in the Sixteenth and Seventeenth Centuries* (Manchester, 1976).

'Manchester clothiers in the early seventeenth century', *Textile History* 10 (1979) pp. 175–83.

Williamson T., Barnes G. and Pillatt, T., *Trees in England: Management and Disease since 1600* (Hatfield, 2017).

Wilson, A., *The Making of Man-Midwifery: Childbirth in England 1660–1770* (London, 1995).

Ritual and Conflict: The Social Relations of Childbirth in Early Modern England (London, 2013).

Winchester, A., *Common Land in Britain: A History from the Middles Ages to the Present Day* (Woodbridge, 2022).

Wood, A., *The Memory of the People: Custom and Popular Senses of the Past in Early Modern England* (Cambridge, 2013).

The Politics of Social Conflict: The Peak Country, 1520–1770 (Cambridge, 1999).

Woodward, D. (ed.), *The Farming and Memorandum Books of Henry Best of Elmswell 1642* (London, 1984).

Men at Work: Labourers and Building Craftsmen in the Towns of Northern England, 1450–1750 (Cambridge, 1995).

'Straw, bracken and the Wicklow whale: the exploitation of natural resources in England since 1500', *Past and Present* 159 (1998), pp. 43–76.

'Early modern servants in husbandry revisited', *Agricultural History Review* 48 (2000), pp. 141–50.

Wrightson, K., 'Popular senses of past time: dating events in the north country, 1615–1631', in Braddick, M. J. and Withington, P. (eds.), *Popular Culture and Political Agency in Early Modern England and Ireland: Essays in Honour of John Walter* (Woodbridge, 2017), pp. 91–108.

Earthly Necessities Economic Lives in Early Modern Britain 1470–1750 (Yale, 2000).

Wrigley, E. A., *People, Cities, and Wealth: The Transformation of Traditional Society* (Oxford, 1987).

cWrigley, E. A., *The Early English Censuses* (Oxford, 2011).

'Urban growth in early modern history: food, fuel and transport', *Past and Present* 225 (2014), pp. 79–112.

Wrigley, E. A. and Schofield, R., *The Population History of England, 1541–1871: A Reconstruction* (London, 1981).

Xenophon, *Oeconomicus: A Social and Historical Commentary* (ed.) Pomeroy, S. B. (Oxford, 1994).

Yi, Y-A., 'Margaret G. Reid: Life and Achievements', *Feminist Economics* 2 (1996), pp. 17–36.

Zell, M., *Industry in the Countryside: Wealden Society in the Sixteenth Century* (Cambridge, 1994).

PhDs

Burnett, A., '"His wief the chiefe doer of it": female ale-sellers in south west England, 1550–1700', unpublished PhD thesis, University of Bristol (2024).

Collins, N., 'Time-use and gender in England, 1700–1850', unpublished PhD thesis, University of Exeter (2024).

Jiang, L., 'Wage labour and living standards in early modern England: a case study of the Shuttleworth accounts, Lancashire 1582–1621', unpublished PhD thesis, University of Exeter (2022).

Keibek, S. A. J., 'The male occupational structure of England and Wales, 1600–1850', unpublished PhD thesis, University of Cambridge (2016).

Yallop, H. J., 'The history of the Honiton lace industry', unpublished PhD thesis, University of Exeter (1987).

Working papers

Erickson, A. L., 'Marital status and economic activity: interpreting spinsters, wives, and widows in pre-census population listings', *Cambridge Working Papers in Economic and Social History* 7 (2012).

Gary, K., 'The distinct seasonality of early modern casual labor and the short durations of individual working years: Sweden 1500–1800', *Lund Papers in Economic History. Education and the Labour Market* (2019).

Goldin, C., 'U-shaped female labor force function in economic development and economic history', *Working Paper 4707, National Bureau of Economic Research, Cambridge, MA* (1994).

Schneider, B., 'Technological unemployment in the British Industrial Revolution: the rise and fall of hand spinning', *Oxford Economic and Social History Working Papers* (2023).

Shaw-Taylor, L., Sudgen, K. and You, X., 'A preliminary estimate of the female occupational structure of England and Wales 1700–1911', *CamPop, Reports and Papers* 33 (2019).

Stephenson, J., 'Looking for work? Or looking for workers? Days and hours of work in London construction in the eighteenth century', *Discussion Papers in Economic and Social History* 162 (Oxford, 2018).

Wrigley, E. A., 'The PST system of classifying occupations', *CamPop, Occupational Structure Project, Papers, Reports, and Conference Presentations, Paper 1* (undated).

Official publications

United Nations, *System of National Accounts* (1993).

United Nations, *Report on the Fourth World Conference on Women* (1995).

United Nations Development Programme, *Human Development Report* (1995).

United Nations, *System of National Accounts* (2008).

Online resources and websites

CamPop, Economies Past Website: https://www.economiespast.org

CamPop, The Occupational Structure of Britain 1379–1911: https://www.campop.geog.cam.ac.uk/research/occupations/

CamPop, PST Coding Scheme: https://www.campop.geog.cam.ac.uk/research/occupations/datasets/coding/

Court Depositions of South West England, 1500–1700: http://humanities-research.exeter.ac.uk/womenswork/courtdepositions/

English Dialect Dictionary Online: https://eddonline4-proj.uibk.ac.at/edd/

Oxford English Dictionary (OED) Online: www.oed.com

Index

For EU product safety concerns, contact us at Calle de José Abascal, 56–1°,
28003 Madrid, Spain or eugpsr@cambridge.org.

www.ingramcontent.com/pod-product-compliance
Lightning Source LLC
LaVergne TN
LVHW011703200926
848484LV00004B/1048

* 9 7 8 1 3 1 6 5 1 9 9 4 3 *